Sergei Dovlatov and His Narrative Masks

Northwestern University Press
Studies in Russian Literature and Theory

Series Editors
Robert Belknap
Caryl Emerson
Gary Saul Morson
William Mills Todd III
Andrew Wachtel

Sergei Dovlatov and His Narrative Masks

Jekaterina Young

NORTHWESTERN UNIVERSITY PRESS / EVANSTON, ILLINOIS

Northwestern University Press
www.nupress.northwestern.edu

Printed in the United States of America

10 9 8 7 6 5 4 3 2 1

ISBN 978-0-8101-2870-5

The Library of Congress has cataloged the original, hardcover edition as follows:
Young, Jekaterina.
Sergei Dovlatov and his narrative masks / Jekaterina Young.
p. cm. — (Northwestern University Press studies in Russian literature and theory)
Includes bibliographical references and index.
ISBN 978-0-8101-2597-1 (cloth text : alk. paper)
1. Dovlatov, Sergei—Criticism and interpretation. 2. Russian literature—Foreign countries—History and criticism. 3. Soviet Union—Intellectual life. I. Title. II. Series: Studies in Russian literature and theory.
PG3479.6.O85Z96 2009
891.7344—dc22

2009007888

∞The paper used in this publication meets the minimum requirements of the American National Standard for Information Sciences—Permanence of Paper for Printed Library Materials, ANSI Z39.48-1992.

Contents

Preface vii

Acknowledgments xi

Note on the Text xiii

Abbreviations of Works by Sergei Dovlatov xv

Chapter One Dovlatov in Leningrad 3

Chapter Two Dovlatov in Emigration 36

Chapter Three *The Zone* 56

Chapter Four *The Compromise:* Journalism and Fiction 87

Chapter Five Dovlatov's *Sanctuary* and Pushkin 110

Chapter Six *The Suitcase* and *The Fridge* 131

Chapter Seven *Ours* 162

Chapter Eight Tales of Émigré Life 179

Chapter Nine Dovlatov's Posthumous Reputation 202

Notes 213

Selected Bibliography 247

Index 263

Preface

This book is a study of the prose of Sergei Dovlatov (1941–90) in the context of the literary process in Russia. His literary career was both extraordinary and, in a perverse way, typical. He grew up in the city of Leningrad, to which he felt a deep affinity, and where he spent most of the first thirty-seven years of his life. He started writing just as the "thaw" period of the early 1960s, when the writers of "youth prose" were at the height of their popularity, was coming to an end. In the harsher atmosphere that followed he achieved no success or recognition as a writer of fiction and published hardly anything in the Soviet Union. He worked for much of the time as a journalist, but for considerable periods was virtually unemployed. However, even his unsuccessful attempts to publish aroused the hostility of the Soviet authorities, and in 1978, under great pressure to leave the country, he finally decided to emigrate.

His career during the next twelve years, which he spent in the United States, forms a total contrast to his earlier life. The stories he had already written were published to great acclaim and swiftly translated into English (and many other languages), enjoying unprecedented success in journals such as the *New Yorker.* He continued to revise and polish his earlier work, as well as writing new stories and editing a newspaper for the Russian émigré community. The last five years of his life coincided with the period of perestroika in the Soviet Union, and in these more liberal conditions his work began to filter back to his homeland. He did not live to see the collapse of the Soviet Union in 1991.

Since his death his work has returned to Russia a thousandfold. His popularity has reached almost cult status: his works have sold in editions of hundreds of thousands, a literary prize has been named after him, and his style is widely imitated. He is the subject of memoirs by nearly everyone who knew him and many who probably did not. Conferences have been devoted to him, many of his works have been dramatized, and films and television programs have been made about him.

What might explain this popularity? Dovlatov was not a political animal; there is nothing in his work of that high philosophical and political seriousness that most readers associate with the Russian literary tradition. It was not for any active political opposition to the regime that he was forced to leave the country. His opposition was of an aesthetic nature, expressed in a concern to escape the stylistic straitjacket imposed by the political arbiters of literary decorum. Dovlatov was acutely aware of his work's linguistic surface. Before writing his stories down, he often told impromptu versions to friends, and was renowned as a master storyteller. He would revise them on the basis of others' responses or his own further reflections. He cared intensely about the acoustic properties of his prose, going to great lengths to avoid unnecessary repetitions of the same sound. He simplified his syntax, excising subordinate clauses wherever possible, seeking immediate impact and maximum clarity. The resulting texts have a deceptive simplicity, which exercises an immense appeal on a public more familiar with a didactic solemnity on the one hand and the overelaborate experimentation of much post-Soviet writing on the other.

Generically Dovlatov's work can all be characterized as "short prose": stories of anything from a couple of pages to fifty or more, usually structured into cycles. It is mainly written in the first person, though at times a scantily disguised third-person surrogate takes over the narration. Its subject matter is largely based upon his own life experience, and is sometimes taken to be unvarnished autobiography. This, though, is as deceptive as his stories' linguistic surface. For it is also highly self-conscious writing, in the sense that it focuses no more sharply upon the characters and events it depicts than upon the process by which the writer turns this material into fiction. His volume *The Compromise* shows this process in its most naked form, as the author juxtaposes, as it were, two forms of fiction: a newspaper article written for the Soviet press, and a story about the circumstances in which it came to be written. He was a brilliant observer of social mores, both in the Soviet Union and later in the United States, and his acute awareness of absurdity enabled him to reveal unexpected similarities between the two. Dovlatov depicts this world with a detached and ironic eye, noting its absurdity, understating its cruelty, and asserting his humane values not through moral judgments but through the precision of his style.

This book consists of nine chapters. The first two describe the literary circumstances and outline the biographical facts of Dovlatov's life in its two discrete periods, before and after emigration. Chapters 3 to 8 are concerned with specific groups of stories. In principle these six chapters take his work in chronological order, but in the case of Dovlatov that is a somewhat unstable category. Some stories originally written in the early 1960s were not published until the 1980s, when he was in America. It is perfectly clear that he revised them for publication, so that, as texts, they cannot truly be said to belong to the 1960s. Nevertheless, it is equally impossible to establish with certainty what he revised when, or how many times his stories underwent revision, so there is no way of creating an alternative chronology. His unremitting concern for stylistic perfection meant that he was inclined to revise his work constantly. He also published stories at different times under different titles, and altered the composition of his story cycles. The expedient of treating his work in chronological order of original composition seems the only practicable way of solving this problem. At the same time, since his *published* work virtually all belongs in the last decade of his life, there is no real issue of development in his writing, and the chronological approach is not designed to illustrate processes of change. The final chapter of this book is concerned with his posthumous reputation.

Acknowledgments

In the course of preparing this book I made two visits to New York to consult Dovlatov's family archive. I experienced the utmost kindness from Elena Dovlatova and wish to record my deep gratitude for her help and generosity. I have also received invaluable assistance and advice from Ksana Mechik-Blank, Katia Dovlatova, Andrei Ar'ev, Mikhail Roginsky, Elena Skul'skaia, and Ivan Tolstoy.

I am extremely grateful to Arlen Blium, Viacheslav Dolinin, and Boris Ivanov for help in fathoming the unofficial Leningrad literary world of the 1960s and 1970s, as well as to Irina Vladimirovna Vakhtina and Nikolai Borisovich Vakhtin for their help on the Gorozhane group of prose writers.

I am grateful for permission to reproduce previously published material: "Dovlatov's *Sanctuary* and Pushkin," in J. Andrew and R. Reid, eds., *Two Hundred Years of Pushkin* (Amsterdam, 2003), 135–53; "The Aesthetics of the *Gorozhane* Group," *The Slavonic and East European Review* 81, no. 1 (2005): 14–37; "Dovlatov's *Compromise:* Journalism, Fiction, Documentary," *Slavonica* 6, no. 2 (2000): 44–68; and "Sergei Dovlatov," in *Dictionary of Literary Biography 285, Russian Literature Since 1980* (Bruccoli Clark, 2003), 48–60.

I am grateful for help received from the Hoover Institution in Stanford, from the Open Society Archive in Budapest, from the St. Petersburg branch of the Memorial Organization, and from the archivist of the Eastern Europe Institute of Bremen University, Gabriel Superfin.

I am indebted to the British Academy for the award of a research grant which allowed me to undertake research in Russia, Hungary, and the United States (New York and Stanford) and to the AHRC (Arts and Humanities Research Council), whose award under the Research Leave Scheme made time available for the writing up of my earlier research.

This book would not have happened without my husband, John Elsworth, whose insightful comments have greatly improved the text and whose help in the translation of Russian quotations is warmly appreciated. His encouragement and moral support throughout the project have been indispensable. I have great pleasure also in acknowledging the moral support of my daughters, Helen and Sophie, who encouraged me throughout the seemingly endless process of researching and writing this book.

Note on the Text

Bibliographical references follow a modified Library of Congress transliteration system. Elsewhere, to make the text more readable to a general audience, first and last names ending in –ii have been changed to –y, such as Dostoevsky or Merezhkovsky rather than Dostoevskii or Merezhkovskii. We have also, for the sake of readability, collapsed –iia endings to –ia. Names are given in their standard English form when one exists.

Frequently cited works by Sergei Dovlatov are cited parenthetically in running text according to the abbreviation list; citations to all other works appear in the notes. Except where a published translation is cited, Jekaterina Young has translated all works originally written in Russian.

Ellipses in square brackets indicate omitted material. Unbracketed ellipses appeared in the original text being quoted.

Abbreviations of Works by Sergei Dovlatov

C — *The Compromise,* translated by Anne Frydman (Chicago: Academy, 1990; first published by Alfred A. Knopf, 1983).

O — *Ours: A Russian Family Album,* translated by Anne Frydman (New York: Weidenfeld and Nicolson, 1989).

S — *The Suitcase,* translated by Antonina W. Bouis (New York: Grove Weidenfeld, 1990).

SS — *Sobranie sochinenii v chetyrekh tomakh,* 4 vols., ed. A. Iu. Ar'ev (St. Petersburg: Azbuka, 2000).

Z — *The Zone: A Prison Camp Guard's Story,* translated by Anne Frydman (New York: Alfred A. Knopf, 1984 and 1985).

Sergei Dovlatov and His Narrative Masks

Chapter One

Dovlatov in Leningrad

IT IS NO SECRET that in the mid-1950s, when Khrushchev came to power following the death of Stalin, the Soviet regime controlled every aspect of life in the Soviet Union. The extent of that control is well illustrated by the fact that special permission had to be sought by the minister for agriculture to transmit weather forecasts on radio for a period of five to seven days in advance instead of just three. The following extract is from a letter to N. S. Khrushchev on October 1, 1954, seeking ratification of this permission:

> Glavlit proposes as expedient to permit the chief directorate of the meteorological service of the Ministry of Agriculture of the USSR to conduct in open order weather forecasts on radio for a period of not more than 5–7 days in advance, giving details of the following elements that are of great importance for agriculture: temperature, frost, precipitation, strong winds (*without indication of their direction*).[1]

Maintaining secrecy about the wind direction seems to belong in the realm of fantasy, but apparently it was thought that this information might have strategic value for an enemy.

Even if the wind direction remained a problem for agriculture, in literature warmer winds were beginning to blow. Mikhail Zoshchenko, who had been subjected to a withering attack by Zhdanov in 1946, was reinstated in the Union of Writers. At the end of 1953 Il'ia Erenburg's "O rabote pisatelia"[2] ("On the Work of the Writer") and V. Pomerantsev's "Ob iskrennosti v literature"[3] ("On Sincerity in Literature") were published, articles which discussed the writer's right to show personal partiality and to adopt an individual stance in the description of reality. In the following year Erenburg's novel *The Thaw* appeared, and gave the decade the name by which it has since been known.

Although, as we shall see, the thaw was itself a short and ambiguous period, it ushered in fundamental changes in the cultural situation which could not all be reversed when the authorities thought better of it a few years later. Until this time, the doctrine of "socialist realism" had for a generation determined not only the content of literature but also the techniques that writers had to use if they wished to be published. V. M. Piskunov has summarized the stultifying effect that strict adherence to these principles had had:

> The disappearance from literature of the hero capable of independent thought—of the creation of his own world, even of the creation of other characters similar to himself, the hero who is the author's equal and bears full responsibility for his own actions, was one of the sorry consequences of the establishment of "socialist realism." [. . .] The canons of "socialist realism" placed upon the author full responsibility for the words and deeds of the hero, and attributed to him the role of rigorous *judge* of all his characters. With hindsight this same role was foisted on the classics: Pushkin mercilessly judges . . . Lermontov exposes . . . Gogol dethrones . . . Tolstoy unmasks . . . and so on.[4]

The relaxation of cultural shackles brought about by the thaw in general, and by the Twentieth Congress of the Communist Party in 1956 in particular, allowed literature to play a greatly increased social role during the 1960s. This was manifested in the publication of previously proscribed literature, in the appearance of new translations of Western writers, and in the assimilation of both by young writers making their debut in this period. In the years between 1956 and 1963 many writers whose work had previously been suppressed were partially returned to the reading public. The poetry of Tsvetaeva and Mandelstam began to be published in limited selections, while some works by prose writers such as Iury Olesha, Isaac Babel, Aleksandr Grin, and Andrei Platonov once again became available. This "thaw" period was at the same time specifically characterized by the publication of translated twentieth-century literature: Hemingway, Thomas Mann, Salinger, Saint-Exupéry, Faulkner, Remarque, and many others. The publication in 1964 in the journal *Inostrannaia literatura* (*Foreign Literature*) of several excerpts from French antinovels by Natalie Sarraute and Alain Robbe-Grillet, with their lack of plot, character, or metaphor, was also important in restoring to Russian literary life a sense of belonging to the world community. It was not many years later that Russian writers in the Soviet Union also became fully aware of the work of Vladimir Nabokov, some of which (although, of course, not published in the U.S.S.R.) was circulating among Leningrad intellectuals. Vladimir Maramzin describes its effect:

> The appearance of a new, fully formed writer cannot but occasion consternation among the writing fraternity. [. . .] But when an entire unknown island of

prose floats to the surface of a nation's literature (the case with Nabokov), assimilating it at one go is extremely difficult—particularly for writers.[5]

American literature in translation played a particularly important role in the literary process in Russia in the 1960s. Translated literature, as Boris Eikhenbaum pointed out in his article "O. Henry and the Theory of the Novella," has often occupied a special place in Russian fiction: "In the history of twentieth-century Russian literature, it seems, a special place will have to be assigned to translated fiction, in the way this was done with the study of Russian literature of the beginning of the nineteenth century, when works by Russian authors (at least in prose) were a rarity."[6] Eikhenbaum was discussing the situation in the 1920s, but the situation in the 1960s provides a parallel, as a further period when translated literature played a particularly important part in the development of Russian prose.[7] The increased vigor and immediacy of the language of prose in the 1960s and '70s, its easily recognizable contemporary intonation, owed much to the impact of translations. Debates raged in the pages of journals on the legitimate use in literary texts of colloquial expressions or dialects, so prevalent in translated literature. What had been important in the 1920s and before, however, and became so again in the literature of the Soviet Union in the 1960s, was that a real human personality, his circle of interests and passions as an individual, became the central focus of the art of storytelling.

The publication in 1959 of two volumes of Ernest Hemingway's short stories influenced a whole generation of Russian writers. Hemingway was, to be sure, one of the major prose writers of the twentieth century and was admired all over the world. However, his popularity in the Soviet Union in the 1960s, his role in public life, is explicable not just by the quality of his writing.[8] In the 1960s Hemingway was perceived not only as a famous writer and a colorful personality but as embodying a particular moral and aesthetic attitude. P. Vail' and A. Genis summed up his role as follows: "The most important American in Soviet history was the writer Ernest Hemingway. It was in his books that Soviet readers found the ideals that shaped the outlook of a whole generation. The style of his prose changed the style of our life."[9] In comparison with the 1950s, Hemingway's prose was felt as a rebellion against ideological constraints in the name of immediate physical experience.[10] Hemingway's heroes eat, drink, kill bulls, make love, and hunt. Hemingway's heroes' code of courageous behavior in desperate situations provided a certain encouragement for Soviet people. Although it did not stimulate actual rebellion on their part, it at least constituted a notional alternative approach to reality.

Within a year of the publication of the two volumes of Hemingway's selected fiction, Rita Rait-Kovaleva's translation of Salinger's *Catcher in the*

Rye was first published (1960) in *Inostrannaia literatura.* His short stories "For Esmé—with Love and Squalor" and "A Perfect Day for Bananafish" were translated in 1961. The emergence of the journal *Inostrannaia literatura* in 1955 was itself one of the crucial symptoms of the Soviet Union's newfound receptivity to foreign culture after the death of Stalin. It continued the traditions and format of the journal *Internatsional'naia literatura* (1933–43; *International Literature*) and, like its predecessor, carried critical and theoretical material, diaries, correspondence, and surveys of foreign literatures, as well as translations. Just as it had in the United States in the 1950s, *The Catcher in the Rye* created an immediate stir in the Soviet Union in the 1960s. Holden Caulfield became the idol of the younger generation. It has been said that Rait-Kovaleva did not so much translate the slang of American teenagers as invent the Russian equivalent single-handedly.

Rita Rait-Kovaleva's translation of *The Catcher in the Rye* was so much in tune with the time that it exercised a great influence upon the writing of the younger generation, and its language became part of ordinary usage. Writers such as Vera Panova, Vasily Aksenov, and Georgy Vladimov wrote reviews of the novel's translations.[11] There were theater productions of *The Catcher in the Rye.* Salinger's work struck a chord in the minds of Soviet citizens who felt an urgent need to expose and overcome what was expressed by Holden's favorite word, *phony* (*lipa*). "What did, in fact, take place—whether through the reception of Hemingway [. . .] or through a myriad of other receptions, such as Aksenov's reading of J. D. Salinger's *Catcher in the Rye* prior to writing his own *Oranges from Morocco*—was that Russia opened up to what had until then been its antagonistic 'other.' "[12] As Genis observed: "The search for 'truth' was the standard theme in all major works of this period. The word 'truth' itself was a key word in both the literary and political struggle of the 1960s."[13] Salinger was so well received in the Soviet Union that he quickly began to overshadow Hemingway himself, as happened in other countries, too: "For one thing, these critics seem much impressed with Salinger's increased popularity abroad as a spokesman—he begins to approach the universal acceptance of Hemingway, which in itself is awesome."[14]

Dovlatov read American fiction avidly both in Rait-Kovaleva's translations and in others, and besides Hemingway, he also admired Faulkner, Sherwood Anderson, Salinger, and others. His early prose was greatly influenced by American fiction and, as Andrei Ar'ev has noted, its traces can be found in later works as well, such as *Filial* (*A Branch Office*).[15] Genis has also commented on the importance of American fiction for Dovlatov: "Dovlatov learned from them something that was rare in our literature, to give priority, first and foremost, to the plasticity of the language over the expression of ideas. This is perhaps the reason why Dovlatov's love for American literature turned out to be reciprocal: they spoke different languages, but equally simply."[16]

The dual impact of the rediscovery of Russian literature of the 1920s and '30s and of foreign literature newly translated at the end of the '50s and in the early '60s gave birth to the phenomenon of "youth prose," which was the most distinctive development in prose during the thaw period. This was the name given to a group of writers who published largely in the journal *Iunost'* (*Youth*), founded in 1955. They typically depicted youthful protagonists grappling with personal problems and moral dilemmas, and in their style they developed a more natural language than was used by their immediate predecessors. This movement is usually associated with such names as Vasily Aksenov, Anatoly Gladilin, Iury Kazakov, Rid Grachev, and Andrei Bitov. It was the work of Aksenov and Gladilin that provoked the greatest polemics, while Aksenov was considered the indisputable leader of this avant-garde trend in Soviet prose.

If, as Katerina Clark argues in her book *The Soviet Novel*,[17] postwar socialist realism changed the focus of its attention from great heroes and their deeds to moralizing on smaller issues of the struggle between the good and the even better, or, as Benedikt Sarnov described it, "the conflict of the good and the excellent" (*konflikt khoroshego s otlichnym*),[18] then the focus of attention in the thaw period changes yet again. What was crucial in this period is summed up by the writer and critic Boris Ivanov:

> What was placed at the foundation of literary language was sincerity. Interests, moods, emotional states became the springboards of plot, and came to determine the perception of events and the material surroundings. Lyricism dominated all genres, all varieties of youthful art. This literature, almost entirely lacking themes of a political or industrial nature, discovered the *feeling man.*[19]

Even in this changed situation, however, it remained the case that an author was expected to make his moral sympathies clear. Authors were not supposed to adopt a posture of neutrality. Some of the topics singled out in the critical literature as worthy of positive depiction were admiration for scientific and industrial progress, man's conquest of nature, and the individual's courage and endurance in the service of these causes. Nevertheless, much of the literature of the thaw period and later is concerned precisely to escape even this implicit moralizing.

The retrieval of the literary experimentation of the immediate postrevolutionary period stimulated a general interest in the methods of constructing a literary text.[20] One of the issues at the forefront of the debates was the question of point of view. Piskunov considers that the return of the first-person narrative into mainstream literature in the 1960s gave authors the possibility of using honestly the subjectivity of the storyteller protagonist, who was, most commonly, the hero of what came to be called "confessional prose" (*ispovedal'naia proza*). This type of first-person narrative evoked indignation among some critics, as Piskunov records.

> It is hard to remember now what disgust was aroused among orthodox critics of the 1960s by this "confessional" prose, as it was christened for its creators' subjectivism, escapism, infantilism and other sins. It seems strange now that first-person narration, born in Spain in the sixteenth century and firmly established in European prose from the seventeenth century onwards, should need to be defended and its right to exist confirmed three centuries later.[21]

A few examples of authors whose experimentation with the short-story form typifies this period will help to clarify this argument. It was mentioned earlier that the acknowledged innovator of the early 1960s was Vasily Aksenov.[22] His *Kollegi* (*Colleagues*), published in 1960 in *Iunost'*, and then made into a film, is one of the classics. The protagonists, boys from the city, have a slightly ironic attitude to everything: love, jazz, sports, fashionable clothes. They try to live honestly. Aksenov introduces a new hero who is not restricted by ideological dogmas; he also experiments with forms of storytelling (and with different time planes), not so much in *Colleagues* as, for example, in *Apel'siny iz Marokko* (published in 1963; *Oranges from Morocco*), where each chapter is written from the point of view of a different storyteller. It was a weighty aesthetic decision to allow the protagonists to speak in their own voices. Although this allows the writer to show the surrounding world with more variation, and allows the reader to make up his or her own mind, nevertheless, the problem of the author's position and outlook (*mirovozzrenie*) is not entirely adequately solved, and as a result, in some of the first-person narratives in *Oranges from Morocco,* the authorial voice still makes an appearance. In terms of composition, Aksenov's story "Papa, slozhi!" ("Put It Together, Daddy") is in many ways a more interesting innovation. The action of the story takes place on a Sunday, when the protagonist is reluctantly looking after his little daughter instead of going to the football match with his friends, because his wife is ostensibly at a conference. The child is learning to read, and as they walk around the city she reads out the letters of shop signs and asks her father to put them together to make words (hence the title). This provides Aksenov with his main compositional device. The story is told partly by a third-person narrator and partly through the hero's internal dialogue with himself. Through a series of outwardly unconnected events he puts together in his own mind, like the words he composes for his daughter, a realization that his wife is unfaithful. But at the same time he understands how deeply he loves his daughter.

Vasily Shukshin made his debut with a short-story collection, *Sel'skie zhiteli* (1963; *Village People*). His charming, often feckless heroes were the opposite of what one imagined as the "positive hero." Shukshin's training as a film director is evident in his writing, both in the deftness of his dialogues and in the highly developed visual quality of his descriptions. He later turned a number of his own stories into successful films. He developed *skaz* technique, allowing his characters to tell their own stories in their own language and from their own point of view (*prostorechnoe skazovoe povestvovanie*). Arguments went on in the 1960s as to whether he belonged to the urban or the village tendency in prose, though it was soon understood that he belonged to neither.

Andrei Bitov's protagonist, as developed in his stories of the 1960s, is a person whose difficulty in coming to terms with reality has existential rather than ideological roots. This differentiates him from other writers of the '60s. One of the stories published in his short-story collection *Bol'shoi shar* (*A Big Balloon*) in 1963, "Zheny net doma" ("My Wife Isn't at Home"), aroused the wrath of Soviet critics because of the confusion and dismay experienced by the story's hero. Another important landmark of the 1960s was Bitov's *Uletaiushchii Monakhov* (*Monakhov in Flight*). Each chapter of this planned novel was published as a separate story, while the novel in its entirety appeared only in 1990. Bitov called this work a dotted-line novel (*roman-punktir*). As Deming Brown observes, "such writers as Bitov [. . .] seem to represent an extreme reaction against literary practices inherited from the Stalin period; the only trace of socialist realism in their works is clearly parodic."[23] Bitov's stories are antididactic. The author leaves the reader to make up his or her own mind in the maze of emotions.

Fazil' Iskander achieved fame with the publication in 1966 of the satirical story "Sozvezdie Kozlotura" ("The Goatibex Constellation"). The stories that eventually came to comprise the novel *Sandro iz Chegema* (*Sandro from Chegem*) were in many cases first published separately under such titles as "Diadia Sandro i pastukh Kunta" ("Uncle Sandro and Kunta the Shepherd"), "Chegemskie spletni" ("Chegem Gossip"), and "Umykanie" ("The Abduction of the Bride"). Sandro, though, is a typical picaresque hero: Iskander rejected the canons of socialist realism, continuing rather the traditions of Rabelais and Cervantes. He also experimented with narrative point of view, employing in a number of his stories about childhood the viewpoint of a naive childish consciousness.

Another author whose writing in this period broke new ground was Valery Popov. Some of his stories in the 1960s and '70s are constructed in the manner of travelogues. The routes traveled are not exotic; for example, he describes a visit to relatives on the Volga ("Poiski kornia"—"Quest for Roots"), or a business trip ("Iuzhnee, chem prezhde"—"Further South Than

Before"), or a holiday on the Black Sea ("Drugaia zhizn' "—"Another Life"). However, although the narrator sees new places, meets new people, and is involved in unexpected situations, these are not travelogues. The emphasis is upon the narrator's complex reactions and the construction of a world that is unusual and even absurd. The events narrated appear random; the author is not concerned to tell a story about a specific character. He is more interested in the intonation and rhythmic precision of his stories, almost all of which are first-person narratives.

Dovlatov himself later confessed to a fascination with youth prose: "Their heroes were our contemporaries. I was a bit of a Viktor Podgursky myself. With a tendency towards astral journeys."[24] In April 1963, however, he delivered a harsher judgment on it:

> I read attentively all the latest literary articles in the newspapers. I read all of Aksenov's and Gladilin's stories. And I read Balter's story "Good-bye, Boys," too. I didn't like any of it. They had all taken it upon themselves to describe city boys from good families, well-read and educated, who were seeking their place in life. I knew dozens like that, and even now I still meet them. All the general regime camps and light security camps are full of lads like that. In books they come out charming, witty, and smart. But it seems to me that if you're going to write about them then you need to write about how they suffer from VD as well, how they contract unsuitable marriages, smash up other people's cars when they're drunk, get involved in speculation, abandon their pregnant girlfriends, that is, to write about all the tragic outcomes to which idleness and the extended quest for one's place in life always lead. Thanks to all these Aksenovs our generation (I mean—mine) will enter history under the rubric "the generation of boys."[25]

Nevertheless Dovlatov fully embraced the innovative aspects that the "youth prose" writers introduced into their writing: their use of colloquial speech and the slang of the younger generation; their experiments in point of view; their exploration of the newly permissible theme of the personal.[26]

An extremely important role in the literary process in the late Soviet Union belonged to "literary associations" (LITOs). These were semiformal gatherings in which young and aspiring writers had an opportunity to read their work to others and hear informed and competent criticism. Like many others, Dovlatov attended such meetings. In Leningrad in the 1960s there were many different associations supervised by different writers. One such literary association which Dovlatov attended (along with Andrei Bitov, Genrikh Shef, Efimov, Maramzin, Voskoboinikov, and many others) met at the Sovetskii Pisatel' publishing house and was, for a time, led by Dovlatov's aunt Margarita (Mara) Dovlatova. He also attended others, led by such writers as David Dar, Gleb Semenov, Mikhail Slonimsky, and Vera Ketlinskaia. In his interview for *Novyi bereg* (*New Shores*) Efimov describes the importance of belonging to a literary association.[27] It provided a disciplined environment for discussion. Participants were compelled to discuss the literary works with greater responsibility and, because of the formality of the meeting, were less likely to wander off into irrelevance. Such associations also conferred a certain legality upon the meetings and spared their members from being accused of disseminating samizdat. They established a forum in which it was possible to hear an informed opinion on a manuscript from peers and the mentors who supervised the associations. To writers like Dovlatov, who were not published, it also gave encouragement to continue writing. In *Remeslo* (*The Craft*) Dovlatov tells how important kind words about his manuscripts from literary mentors were to him: "My work was praised in private by well-respected people. Gor, Panova, Bakinsky and Metter all liked my stories" (*SS* 3:35). According to Lev Losev, the Leningrad writers were more fortunate in their teachers than, for example, the Moscow writers, where the main patron of the young was Kataev, "whose thunderous style corresponded perfectly to the stylist's reptilian morality. In the Petrograd school people were not taught to write badly (Kataev's 'mauvism'), but to write well. Here we were not taught to link arms and set forth in gangs to conquer 'literary platforms.' "[28] Many Leningrad writers have expressed gratitude to their mentors, particularly to David Dar, Gleb Semenov, Viktor Bakinsky, Gennady Gor, and Aleksandr Volodin. Many years later, in his essay "My nachinali v epokhu zastoia" (*SS* 4:252–57; "We Started in the Era of Stagnation"), Dovlatov wrote with affection and gratitude that

> at the dawn of my now long-standing literary endeavors I had at my side "official writers of the period of stagnation," who believed in me, gave me of their time, encouraged me to believe in my own powers, and who now, at least such of them as are still alive, read my stories in Soviet journals and write me letters ending with the words: "I told you all this, you silly boy, thirty years ago." (*SS* 4:257)

A group of writers who were of particular importance to Dovlatov in the years immediately following his return from military service were known as the Gorozhane (Urbanists). They were one of a number of free literary associations operating in Leningrad in the mid-1960s, among the largest of which were VERPA[29] and the neo-avant-garde group Khelenukty.[30] The case of the Gorozhane group provides a vivid instance of opposition to officialdom that was not specifically political, but primarily aesthetic. The general cultural situation in Leningrad was different from Moscow, where there were many more opportunities for publication, and this is possibly one of the reasons why underground cultural life was more varied in Leningrad. There, according to Lev Lur'e, young writers of the 1960s had at their disposal "oases of permitted and controlled freethinking" such as the literary club Derzanie (Daring) that met at the Pioneers' Palace.[31] This was a short-lived phenomenon: by the 1970s Derzanie had been shut down, many literary associations at the Writers' Union were closed, and there remained absolutely no official outlets for young artists, so that practically all were forced underground. This was the time when Andrei Bitov, for example, moved to Moscow. As Bitov himself said in a recent interview, he wanted to publish *Pushkinskii dom* (*Pushkin House*) abroad and he knew that in Moscow he would be more protected.[32]

Igor' Efimov in an interview with John Glad summarizes why Leningrad writers concentrated more on their style and language:

> Leningrad writers, even at the best time in the mid-sixties, had about four times fewer opportunities to publish than Muscovites. And perhaps because of this situation of greater hopelessness, of greater restriction by the censorship, they developed a slightly more chamber style, with greater concentration on the inner world of the human being and with greater attention to the details of a person's psychological condition.[33]

One of the more popular meeting places for young intellectuals in Leningrad was the legendary café Saigon on Nevsky Prospekt. This café figures large in the memoirs of writers and artists who grew up in the city. They gathered there to read their stories and poems and to discuss literature. Particularly when literary organizations and clubs were closed down by the authorities, Saigon became a place where a young writer could hear an honest opinion about his or her work, or exchange manuscripts and publications from abroad. This in turn attracted the attention of the KGB. The then chairman of the KGB, Iury Andropov, summed up the "dangers" of samizdat publications: "On the basis of the preparation and dissemination of samizdat literature there takes place a certain consolidation of like-minded people, and attempts to establish something like an opposition can be clearly detected."[34] It was Leningrad that had the largest number of underground samizdat publications and associations. It is in Leningrad that Katerina Clark places the center of new experimentation in prose:

> There, in the early sixties, an entire mini-movement, the self-styled "urbanists" (*gorozhane*), sprang up. They were but a small part of the large movement toward more modernist and sophisticated writing, generally known as the "new prose" (Bitov and the later Aksenov were other writers in the "new prose" movement).[35]

Apart from a few such comments, very little has hitherto been written about the Gorozhane group. Access to a variety of public and private archives has made it possible to discover a quantity of fresh information about them. The Gorozhane group initially consisted of four members: Boris Vakhtin, Vladimir Maramzin, Vladimir Gubin, and Igor' Efimov. Later Sergei Dovlatov joined them:

> I was unanimously accepted as a member of the Gorozhane association. But a typical feature of my biography immediately made itself known—the ability to arrive as everyone else is leaving. [. . .] So, having invited me to join, the association immediately fell apart. [. . .] In sum, many people don't even know that I was the fifth "urbanist." (*SS* 3:26–27)

The group appears to have chosen its name as an act of opposition to the strengthening trend of village prose (*derevenskaia proza*). If there was village prose, why should there not also be urban prose? "It was not so much a question of opposition, as of the definition of 'spheres of influence.' [. . .] We perceived ourselves as urbanists without any challenge or any hostility towards other tendencies."[36] It was not a question of literature in which the plot is necessarily tied to some specific location, be it a factory workshop, a university, or a communal apartment, but rather of a literature that preserves the traditions of Russian urban writing with its tendency to the phantasmagorical and its depiction of psychological states specific to urban life. The urbanists were less concerned with the tragedy of Russian people's alienation from the land, and more with that of their alienation from their language.

Village prose was concentrated around the journal *Novyi mir* (*New World*), whose editor in chief was Aleksandr Tvardovsky. Tvardovsky himself, the son of a peasant who had been persecuted as a kulak, encouraged this trend. Vladimir Maksimov noted in his interview with John Glad that had Ivan Denisovich been a worker (*rabochii*), Solzhenitsyn's story would never have been published. But Ivan Denisovich was a peasant and in his psychological makeup retains the typical characteristics of a peasant. According to Maksimov, the Soviet authorities who decided what to publish and what not to publish felt a subconscious nostalgia for the peasantry.[37] This is not surprising in view of Russia's long peasant tradition. In public consciousness the village was often perceived as the keeper of the nation's spiritual values. However, after the revolution the emphasis on the leadership of the industrial proletariat and on industrialization, to say nothing of collectivization, entailed a consistent downgrading of rural life. To be a village person, to preserve loyalty to a village way of life, became more than unfashionable. By the 1970s the peasantry as a class was in danger of extinction: collectivization, world war, and the building of socialism had emptied the Russian villages and impoverished the peasants. Aleksandr Solzhenitsyn and Tvardovsky were not the first to consider the plight of the peasantry, or even to publish the first examples of village prose. In the 1950s the documentary prose of Valentin Ovechkin, for example, and the works of such writers as Efim Dorosh, Aleksandr Iashin, and others had brought to public attention the damage collectivization had done to the village and to the religious values and traditions of the peasantry.[38] A large percentage of the Soviet rulers were of peasant origin and—despite their own complicity in their destruction—sympathized with the cause of the peasantry, and this appears to be one of the reasons why village prose was able to flourish. As far as urban writers were concerned, Andrei Bitov, Iury Kazakov, and Fazil' Iskander, for example, were not published in *Novyi mir* under Tvardovsky. As Vladimir Maksimov sums it up: "No urban literature of any real distinction was published in Tvardovsky's journal. [. . .] Everything that was powerful in *Novyi mir* was the peasants."[39]

It was against this background that the Gorozhane group was formed. This is how Vladimir Maramzin recalls the event:

> In 1964 we all gathered at Vakhtin's, who then lived in the district of Chernaia Rechka, in order to publish an almanac, uniting us all in the literary association Gorozhane (Urbanists). This idea belonged to Vakhtin. Long before the notorious *Metropol'* (*Metropolis*) he wanted to demonstrate the readiness of young writers to take the first steps.[40]

All the writers who united in the Gorozhane group could well have become perfectly successful official writers. By forming a literary association and deciding to publish a joint almanac, they set themselves the task of publishing a volume that would reflect their own aesthetic choices and not the choice of officialdom.

In January 1965 the four authors submitted their collection of short stories under the title *Gorozhane* to the Leningrad branch of the Sovetskii Pisatel' publishing house.[41] In their application they gave the following reason why they wanted to publish their stories as a collection: "As far as we know, this almanac is the first to continue the traditions of the first years after the revolution, when authors appeared in print not only as individuals, but as groups, if such a group considered that that was what the interests of literature required."[42]

Such a statement on the part of the Gorozhane and their conscious emulation of the 1920s was entirely understandable amidst the general optimism of the mid-1960s. The atmosphere of the "thaw" years encouraged the hope that it would now be possible to build socialism with a human face.

For a Soviet person of the 1960s the nation's achievements, especially in space exploration, generated a kind of universal optimism. Many writers and artists now saw the Stalin period as one in which the natural development of the arts had been stifled, and such an invocation of the buoyant culture of the 1920s expressed their sense of a need to retrieve a lost tradition. For what most attracted the Gorozhane to the 1920s was that decade's freedom of artistic experimentation.

The anthology was not accepted for publication by Sovetskii Pisatel'.[43] The rejection letter from the editor in chief of the publishing house, M. Smirnov, is dated December 28, 1965, nearly a year after submission, and it was accompanied by a copy of the reader's report provided by a member of the Union of Soviet Writers, Nison Aleksandrovich Khodza, dated the previous day (December 27, 1965).[44] Smirnov wrote: "We do not consider it possible to accept the almanac for publication. However, we considered it appropriate to pass some of the stories to *Molodoi Leningrad* [*Young Leningrad*], where they are being published."[45]

Khodza's report contains both general criticism of the anthology and specific praise for individual stories. It is clearly no coincidence that those he praises are the ones that were passed on to *Molodoi Leningrad,* just as it is clear that the decision to pass them on was taken long before the authors received the formal reply.[46]

Of Boris Vakhtin, Khodza writes that he will not be surprised if in a few years' time Vakhtin's name becomes one of the most famous in the Soviet Union, but he can only recommend two of his "interesting, psychological" stories for publication: "Ee lichnoe delo" ("Her Private Business") and "Nozhnitsy v more" ("Scissors in the Sea"). On the critical side, he writes that in his opinion,

> in B. Vakhtin's stories the main ingredient is missing, without which there is no literature—there are no real people, the philosophy of our society is absent, there are no genuine conflicts. The protagonists' experiences seem to me to be made up, not observed, and their entire life is totally isolated from the surrounding world.[47]

The reports on the other authors are very much in the same vein; for example, about Vladimir Gubin, Khodza writes: "An interesting writer has appeared, a writer who is seeking his own style and who doesn't wish to trot along well-trodden paths."[48] He then discusses the stories from the cycle "U nas v mekhanicheskom tsekhe" ("In Our Mechanical Workshop"), which he dislikes: "The atmosphere of the stories does not convey the familiar atmosphere of our factories. Everything in it is somehow deliberate, people walk and think not in a 'straight' line, but invariably in 'zigzags.'"[49] Khodza criticizes Efimov for lapses in style, but does say: "The author, I repeat, is a real writer and in contrast to other young writers, he is keenly aware of the interdependence of form and content."[50] The only author not discussed in detail by Khodza is Vladimir Maramzin. In fact, he does not say anything positive about him, but as an afterthought, he adds a handwritten sentence: "The story 'Ia, s poshchechinoi v rukakh' ["Myself, Holding a Slap in the Face"] could take pride of place in any journal."[51]

The archive of Irina Vladimirovna Vakhtina, Boris Vakhtin's widow, also contains a typewritten report, "Zametki na poliakh sbornika 'Gorozhane'" ("Notes in the Margin of the Collection *Gorozhane*"), written by Vera Ketlinskaia, who subsequently became editor in chief of *Molodoi Leningrad.*[52] She saw the main deficiency of the Gorozhane in the following:

> Perhaps the most important thing is that by the end of the collection the people inhabiting the stories create a heavy and cheerless mood. Each on his own is perhaps possible, but when they are grouped together and when they go from story to novella, from one author to another, and at the same time they live in an environment where they don't have anything to do with intelligent people, with people who think and feel interestingly and on a large scale—then it turns out simply untruthful.[53]

Ketlinskaia also notes the influence of Zoshchenko and Platonov on Vakhtin in particular:

> The influence of Zoshchenko and to some extent Platonov is at times very noticeable. I like Zoshchenko and knew him well personally, but you can't after all consider Zoshchenko and his characters outside his historical context! Zoshchenko created the perfect image of a petty bourgeois, but is Vakhtin confident that such a character exists in our times? Zoshchenko himself often said that the petty bourgeois had changed, had become more educated, his speech more cultured, and that he had acquired a capacity for social and political mimicry. Vakhtin transposes into the sixties Zoshchenko's petty bourgeois of the thirties, but with one important difference. Zoshchenko's petty bourgeois was *militant,* with his own opinion on *everything* (there were plenty of such people in those days).[54] However, Vakhtin's petty bourgeois is characterized by a mindless passivity and an inability to think at all, which is found repeatedly in various places: "we did not have any view about what had happened."[55]

Just how much this generation of Leningrad writers was under Platonov's spell is described in an episode in Dovlatov's *Nevidimaia kniga* (*The Invisible Book*) that circulated in samizdat, but was edited out in the final published version. Dovlatov is eager to show his work to Sergei Vol'f, who was an authority among the Leningrad intellectuals for his short, laconic prose and poetry.[56] Vol'f asks the young author who his favorite writers are. Dovlatov lists Böll, Hemingway, and some Russian classics.

> "That's a shame," Vol'f uttered thoughtfully, "a shame."
>
> He made his farewells and left.
>
> I was somewhat upset. Later Zhenia Rein said to me:
>
> "You should have named Andrei Platonov, he'd have bought you a drink. At the moment they're all reading Platonov."
>
> "Have you read him?"
>
> "Yes," Rein replied, "I've been an admirer of Platonov since 1936."
>
> Then, stopping short, he added:
>
> "You can half believe me . . ."[57]

Igor' Efimov is represented in the almanac *Molodoi Leningrad* by the novella "Neskol'ko ogorchenii iz zhizni zavodskogo inzhenera" ("Some Disappointments in the Life of a Factory Engineer"); Boris Vakhtin by two stories, "Ee lichnoe delo" and "Nozhnitsy v more"; Vladimir Gubin by "Zhen'ka s inoi planety" ("Zhen'ka from Another Planet"); and Vladimir Maramzin by "Ia, s poshchechinoi v rukakh" ("Myself, Holding a Slap in the Face").

What was it that united the group? Why did they decide to act together? In many ways, the four "urbanists" (and indeed the fifth) were very different writers. There were other brilliant storytellers published in this particular issue of the almanac *Molodoi Leningrad:* Andrei Bitov, Maia Danini, Rid Grachev, and Valery Popov, to name just a few. Katerina Clark, for example, considers that they "were peripheral figures if we judge their importance by the volume of material they actually managed to get published. Their anthology, *The Urbanists,* for instance, was rejected for publication. But they are interesting because they have more of the attributes of a cohesive group, with its own ideology, than did any other 'new prose' writers."[58] The Gorozhane themselves considered that the strongest bond uniting them was hatred of indifferent, colorless language (*nenavist' k presnomu iazyku*), and that it was their dream to bring real irony back into literature.[59] They were united by their concern for literary style far more than by the urban thematics which appeared to provide their raison d'être:

> Any game, any tricks, the destruction of traditional sentence structure, the unexpected growth of subordinate clauses, the sharpest thought hidden somewhere in a participial phrase and leaping out from there to sting it, like an ambush—everything is useful in this struggle to win over our contemporary reader, who has read everything and seen everything.[60]

David Iakovlevich Dar, who was one of the mentors of young writers and poets in Leningrad, considered that the authors of *Gorozhane* were united by their sharpness of vision and by their linguistic solutions, which are unexpected and fresh, going against the canons of stable literary language.[61] They managed to create an impression of novelty in language, which in its turn produces an emotional effect on the reader.[62]

The four authors compiled and produced a few copies of a second and last collection of *Gorozhane* in 1966. D. Dar wrote the introduction to this volume too, and it too was designed by Boris Shvartsman, using the same evening cityscape photograph used for the first volume.[63] It contained Gubin's "Bezdozhd'e do sentiabria" ("Drought till September"), Efimov's "Mesiats v kolkhoze" ("A Month on a Collective Farm"), Maramzin's "Chelovek, kotoryi veril v svoe osoboe naznachenie" ("The Man Who Believed in His Special Destiny"), and what is perhaps Vakhtin's best story of all, "Odna absoliutno schastlivaia derevnia" ("One Utterly Happy Village").[64] Part 2 contained Gubin's "Vpechatlenia, poteri" ("Impressions, Losses"), Efimov's "Iz pisem, iz razgovorov, iz zapisnykh knizhek" ("From Letters, Discussions, and Notebooks"), Maramzin's "Sam, vse sam" ("Myself, All by Myself"), and Vakhtin's "Neskol'ko stranits iz 'Dnevnika bez imen i chisel' " ("A Few Pages from 'The Diary Without Names and Dates' "). In his introduction to the second collection, Dar emphasized the fact that the young authors had "faith in the party and in older colleagues who oversee literature" and understood the "inexhaustible possibilities of socialist realism, provided, of course, that it is not confused with bureaucratic realism, which has always existed in literature."[65] An explanation of what Dar meant by "bureaucratic realism" is found in his letter to the Fourth Congress of Soviet writers:

> It is high time to abandon the illusion that civil servants and party functionaries understand better than artists what serves the interests of the party and the people, and what harms them. How many of them there have been in Russia, those various Benckendorffs, Ilichevs, Polikarpovs, who have tried in vain to throttle and enslave Russian art! And how many of them even now dictate to us in the name of the party and the government how to write books, how to paint pictures, how to produce films, and determine which works of art are to become the property of the people, and which should be hidden from the people.[66]

Dar also notes that he read with interest the majority of the manuscripts included in the second collection: "Of course this is not like the way others write. But who said that everyone has to be like everyone else?"[67]

Dovlatov was proud of the fact that the Gorozhane had invited him to join the group. Considering the age gap and the fact that the individual members of the group were established in their own right as writers, this acceptance served as a kind of recognition for Dovlatov. The group planned a third volume, but times changed, and in the event this volume did not materialize. Nevertheless, once accepted as a member, Dovlatov participated in the meetings of Gorozhane, and their view on his work was always of importance to him, as his correspondence with Maramzin testifies:

> Since early years I have always held you in high esteem, both as a writer and as a person, and I am proud that you, Efimov, Volodia, and Boris approved of my works and suggested I become one of the "urbanists," which at that time was a far greater honor for me than it is now to become a "New Yorker" author. If my position were ever such that I had to speak of my literary teachers, I would name Igor', Lifshits, and yourself. There are, of course, writers whom I like more than I do you, but I would find it hard to name a writer with a greater imaginative range, or simply with a greater talent.[68]

There was evidence even before the fall of Khrushchev in 1964 that party policy toward the arts was beginning to recoil from the relative liberalism of the thaw period. During the thaw Khrushchev had encouraged the intelligentsia to support his criticism of Stalinism. The publication of Alexander Solzhenitsyn's novella *Odin den' Ivana Denisovicha* (*One Day in the Life of Ivan Denisovich*) in *Novyi mir* in 1962 was part of his attempt to legitimate his own power. However, the intelligentsia's criticism extended beyond Stalin himself to the entire Soviet system that had made him possible, and it is here, of course, that the dissident movement had its roots. Khrushchev's successors drew the conclusion that all such criticism had to be suppressed. Brodsky was exiled to the far north, and Siniavsky and Daniel were sentenced under Article 58 of the Penal Code for "anti-Soviet agitation and propaganda," their guilt being established by identifying the opinions expressed by fictional characters with those of the authors themselves.[69] Far from intimidating writers, however, the trials gave rise to a flood of protests, once a transcript of the proceedings was published abroad. Fearing the effect of such publicity on the Soviet Union's reputation abroad, especially among Communist sympathizers, the government adopted in 1970 the new tactic of committing dissidents to mental hospitals on grounds of alleged psychiatric illness.

The invasion of Czechoslovakia in 1968 and the subsequent repression of dissent initiated the years now known as the period of stagnation, and for Russian intellectuals the decade of the 1970s was markedly different from the 1960s. Hopes for an expansion of creative freedom were quickly disappointed. The 1960s had been a period in which the traditional devices

Russian writers have used to convey concealed messages—subtexts and "Aesopian" language—flourished. As Ol'ga Sedakova has written: "In the '60s the technique of subtexts and allusions blossomed extraordinarily. It did not seem so fruitless and ridiculous as it did later: it seemed that this was the first step, a little further—and everything would be said without recourse to parables."[70] Such an approach ceased to be either feasible or attractive in the following decade. In his paper "Blesk i nishcheta russkoi literatury" (*SS* 4:362; "The Brilliance and Poverty of Russian Literature") Dovlatov admits that the short "thaw" was a time of great illusions, which were subsequently dashed:

> If in Stalin's time talented writers were first of all published, then vilified in the press, and finally shot or destroyed in the camps (Babel, Pil'niak, Mandelstam), then now no one was shot, hardly anyone was sent to prison, but no one was published either. The best writers wrote, in the manner of conspirators, "for the desk drawer," as they say, while the less honest and resilient ones served the state with might and main, and received in return access to extremely attractive material benefits. (*SS* 4:363)

Most young authors in this period hoped to join official Soviet culture, but found themselves faced with unusually difficult choices. Some capitulated to the dictates of ideological censorship and internalized them, as Evgeny Dobrenko explains: "The Soviet writer has never had a sterner censor than he himself: the Soviet writer is himself a censor."[71] Others either abandoned literature completely, or joined the underground authors of samizdat. Among these young authors were some who understood that publication in the official press was incompatible with creative freedom and never even attempted to publish.[72] Many unofficial artists and authors lived in a sealed world and were unable, because of political, ideological, and aesthetic censorship, either to exhibit or to publish. In this almost "cosmic" isolation, such artists were completely thrown back on their own devices, and became for each other what other people should have been for them: viewers, critics, connoisseurs, historians, and even collectors, or as Dovlatov called it, a "second cultural reality" ("vtoraia kul'turnaia deistvitel'nost' "; *SS* 3:16). This "second cultural reality" became the only reality not only for Dovlatov but for many of his contemporaries. One of the explanations as to why this came about is given in Andrei Siniavsky's article "Dissidenstvo kak lichnyi opyt" ("Dissidence as Personal Experience"), in which he says that there was really no choice: "The experience of writers' fates in the Soviet Union makes it clear that literature is a risky, and indeed sometimes fatal path, and that the writer who tries to combine literature with material comfort very often ceases, in Soviet conditions, to be a genuine writer."[73] It was the poets of this generation, who should have entered literature in the later 1960s but were never able to do so, that Sedakova describes as the "lost generation." Dovlatov has a fictional treatment of this state of affairs in *The Invisible Book.* The protagonist is seeking advice from established writers. The fictional established writer Granin advises the protagonist:

> "A writer has to publish. Obviously not to the detriment of his talent. There is a loophole between conscience and baseness. And you have to find a way through that loophole."
>
> I summoned all my courage and said:
>
> "It seems to me that just beside that loophole there's a snare set up." (*SS* 3:28)

Like other writers Dovlatov sought publication of his work, but practically all his stories were rejected. It was inevitable that some of his stories began circulating in samizdat and living in the "second cultural reality" whether the author wanted this or not.

Throughout the period from the 1960s to the fall of the Soviet Union the institution of censorship, Glavlit, continued to operate with unremitting diligence. In the mid-1970s complaints were voiced against authors who were regarded as insufficiently militant in implementing the party's priorities, and those "who have sought to reduce the diversity of present-day Soviet reality to problems that have irreversibly receded into the past."[74] So the chief censor in Leningrad, B. Markov, kept an eagle eye on the periodicals in an attempt to make sure that no unacceptable material seeped through to their pages:[75]

> It is a matter for concern that in six issues for the current year Glavlit has been forced to make 20 interventions (for the whole of the previous year there were 16). It is sufficient to say that from the proofs of the March, May, and July issues material was removed concerning the security of the USSR's state frontiers (I. Dvorkin's[76] story "Eight Hours' Flight" ["Vosem' chasov poleta"], S. Dovlatov's "At His Own Request" ["Po sobstvennomu zhelaniiu"],[77] and E. Voevodin's[78] "A Pound of Salt" ["Pud soli"]).[79]

This letter was addressed to A. F. Popov, the editor in chief of the journal *Neva,* in 1973.[80] Markov was apparently losing patience with the journal. He quotes from the editor's publication handbook (*Edinye pravila pechataniia nesekretnykh izdanii*) on the kind of material that it was allowed to publish in "open publications." Dovlatov would later exclaim in *The Invisible Book:* "Why is it that my straightforward, honest, sole inclination is crushed by countless organs, persons, and institutions of a great state?!" (*SS* 3:8).

In a fictional letter ostensibly informing him of the rejection of one of his stories, he invents a quotation from the editor of *Iunost'*, telling him what to write: "Nothing tragic, nothing gloomy. We shall sing and laugh like children! . . ."[81]

Just how closely the contents of journals were followed is testified by a complaint, again written by B. Markov to his Communist Party boss P. K. Romanov, on the ideological and political content of the journal *Avrora.*[82] There are a number of stories Markov objects to. The first is by F. Iskander, "Nochnye tainy" ("Secrets of the Night"; published in *Avrora* no. 6, 1972), in which a young boy named Chik listens to a story about the murder of a man, told by the boy's distant relative Iason. It is known that Iason used to be a thief. According to Markov, Chik does not seem to be upset about the profession of his relative; in fact, he finds it quite normal.

> We have found it necessary to draw the attention of the CPSU Regional Committee to this story by F. Iskander. [. . .] The author has pretensions of depicting the Abkhazian national character. However, F. Iskander's story "Secrets of the Night" can only create a false conception of the life and manners of this fraternal Soviet people.[83]

In the same document A. Bitov is chided for the imprecision of his ideological position (*nechetkost' ideinykh pozitsii*) for a story published in *Avrora,* "Fenomen normy" ("The Phenomenon of the Norm"). This is a sketch (*ocherk*) about Georgia, dedicated to the fiftieth anniversary of the U.S.S.R. in 1972. The censor quotes extensively from this work, drawing the attention of the party bosses to this publication in which "the much-vaunted 'Georgia for the Georgians,' born under the excessively sprightly pen of the writer A. Bitov, is contrasted with the Georgia of new factories, plantations, scientific centers!"[84]

Nothing escapes the censor's attention: a note on the cover of *Avrora* no. 3 about the sculptor V. Petrov has an epigraph from the work of Anna Akhmatova: "Did you but know out of what rubbish / Verses may grow, knowing no shame . . ." ("Kogda b vy znali, iz kakogo sora, / Rastut stikhi, ne vedaia styda . . .").[85] A. Ageichik's sketch "Tri etazha moria" ("Three Floors of Sea"), also dedicated to the fiftieth anniversary of the U.S.S.R., has an epigraph from Boris Pasternak. "Anyone would think that the journal's authors were incessantly concerned lest the names of these poets be forgotten. At the same time the editors of *Avrora* pretend to know nothing of the huge errors with which their work was marked," comments B. Markov.[86] The censor blocked publication in *Avrora* of Valery Popov's story "Fanych": "The censor judges it to be a worthless attempt to exploit the form of the fantastic story for a lampoon of reality."[87]

These instances serve to exemplify the operation of party policy on cultural affairs. It appeared that the regime could not tolerate experimentation. Slander against "Soviet reality" was a crime punishable under existing Soviet law. Stern warnings were addressed to the editorial board of *Avrora*, who, according to Markov, had not drawn the correct conclusions from criticism offered earlier and continued with the publication of material "in which the revelation of the diverse aspects of the complex life of Soviet society, the examination of the urgent problems of the formation of the spiritual profile of Soviet man, are replaced by a mundane naturalism, a retreat into infantilism, a vulgar flirtation with the reader."[88]

The appearance of samizdat was an inevitable consequence of such a state of affairs, and one of the most significant events in the history of post-Stalin literature. The autonomy of the individual human being was such a serious matter to the post-thaw generation that it came into conflict with official literature. Of necessity many writers found samizdat the only outlet. Solzhenitsyn's appeal for greater creative freedom, made at the Fourth Congress of the Writers' Union, was supported by many other writers. One of these was Georgy Vladimov, whose short novel *Vernyi Ruslan* (*Faithful Ruslan*) had been banned by the censor and subsequently published in samizdat. He warned that literature could not exist without freedom and that obstacles placed in writers' way by the censorship merely provoked them to resort to samizdat. These writers, though, had already learned an important lesson in freedom from Boris Pasternak, as Piskunov describes: "It is the author of *Doctor Zhivago* who embodies for us fidelity to aesthetics itself and the philosophy of freedom, handed down to us by the great Russian culture of the past—from Pushkin to Blok, from Chaadaev to Berdiaev."[89] Pasternak's example in invoking the religious philosophy of the early twentieth century and offering an understanding of history entirely at variance with Marxism sent shock waves through Russian literary circles as people gradually became familiar with the novel. It was also of immense importance as one of the first examples of *tamizdat*.[90] Technological progress and a higher standard of living had now given many Soviet citizens access to shortwave radios, enabling them to follow events that the Soviet authorities did not wish to be known. As Yurchak writes:

> This allowed for the shortwave radio to emerge as one of the most important tools for cultural production in the late Soviet context. This tool was completely enabled by the state, but its meaning was not determined by the state in any predictable way. The forms of cultural production that this tool influenced included a huge explosion in the popularity of Western jazz, rock and roll, foreign languages, and general knowledge about the world.[91]

The inner freedom of the individual was constantly emphasized. Maramzin describes his fellow writers' reaction to their reading of Nabokov. Crucially, among the many lessons learned from Nabokov, he emphasizes the inalienability of freedom: "Life allows even that which is prohibited by human laws. The only thing it does not allow is an attack on another's freedom. You cannot take another person's freedom with impunity—I am speaking of Dolores Gaze. The result is always tragedy. In essence this is a book about freedom."[92] An even more uncompromising manifestation of inner freedom was offered by the poet Joseph Brodsky, with his total lack of involvement in everyday life, or, as Dovlatov wrote about him in *Remeslo* (*The Craft*): "He did not live in the proletarian state, but in the monastery of his own spirit. He did not fight the regime. He did not notice it" (*SS* 3:26) This became typical behavior, as Yurchak also notes: "In the following decade, Brodsky's way of being became increasingly widespread among urbanites a decade younger than him—the last Soviet generation."[93]

Samizdat by its nature lacked certain of the characteristics normally taken for granted in the literary process. In the first place the communal, uncontrolled samizdat process meant that the individual author could not determine the life of the text. Once the text entered samizdat, the system of editing, copying, and recopying for transmission acquired a life independent of the original author or the fixed content of the text. This particular aspect of samizdat must have been very difficult for Dovlatov, who ardently tried to preserve the precision and rhythm of his texts. Second, by the same token, there could be no normal process of criticism. All criteria for the quality of a work circulating in samizdat were often distorted.[94] What were these stories or pictures for the disinterested outside world? What were they not only for their creators, but for other people? This tormenting question hung over everyone who had to work for many years without objective criticism. At the same time samizdat publications enjoyed a special cachet. The expression "unpublishable work" (*veshch' nepechatnaia*) was used as a sign of special virtue, as Boris Ivanov explains: "The expression 'unpublishable work,' as a sign of its especial quality, was first heard in the Leningrad LITOs in the middle of the '60s. Evidently this designation spread among the wider public in this meaning significantly later—towards the end of the 60s."[95]

In the late 1960s the dissident movement established *Khronika tekushchikh sobytii* (*The Chronicle of Current Events*) as a regular bulletin listing the authorities' acts of repression. This marked a split between political samizdat on the one hand and its apolitical equivalent, embodied particularly in the 1970s by the Leningrad second culture, on the other. However, the authorities made no distinction between the two, and treated cultural nonconformism as simply another form of political dissidence. An instructive example was the attempt to publish the independent almanac *Metropol'* (*Metropolis*) in 1979 in Moscow. At the express wish of its editors the almanac did not include any inflammatory writing, but concentrated entirely on literary quality. However, its editors met the same fate as political dissidents: Aksenov was forced to emigrate and Evgeny Popov was barred from publication. However, *Metropol'* was circulated in samizdat and eventually published in *tamizdat*. In general during this period, samizdat was performing a valuable function not only in disseminating unpublishable literary works, but also in bringing to Russian readers their own literary and philosophical past. Samizdat works were often subsequently published abroad, where they circulated among the émigré community, and were ultimately smuggled back into the Soviet Union. In this way it became possible for writers who were unable to publish in the Soviet Union to gain recognition abroad.

Summarizing the essential features of the young writers of the 1960s, Boris Ivanov writes: "For the young writers of the '60s [. . .] the crucial struggle was for the status of 'SOVIET WRITER.' The acquisition of the status of Soviet writer implied the prospect of publication and a firm legal position."[96] If the literature of the 1960s had at its center the "feeling man," then for the writers of the 1970s psychological issues no longer made any sense. Writers in the 1970s stopped fighting for the official status of a writer; they valued above all their independence and preferred to work at the social periphery as lift operators, night watchmen, and boiler room attendants.

By the end of the 1970s the Soviet authorities' principal means of suppressing cultural nonconformism was to pressure writers into emigrating. It stripped its most vocal critics of their Soviet citizenship, thus making it impossible for them to return. Dovlatov was one who eventually fell into this category.

Dovlatov began writing while still at school. In *The Invisible Book* he gives a fictional description of his younger years:

> A plump, shy boy . . . Poverty . . . My mother gave up the theater in an attack of self-criticism and works as a proofreader . . .
>
> School . . . Friendship with Alesha Lavrent'ev, who is fetched from school in a Ford . . . [. . .][97]
>
> Dark yards . . . My incipient leaning to the plebs . . . [. . .] My funeral oration, which elicited tears from Zhanna, the electrician's daughter . . . I know how to talk, to tell stories . . .

> Endless bad marks . . . Indifference to exact sciences . . . [. . .]
>
> 1952. I send four poems to the newspaper *Lenin's Spark*. One, of course, is about Stalin. Three are about animals . . .
>
> Tolstyi, zastenchivyi mal'chik . . . Bednost' . . . Mat' samokritichno brosila teatr i rabotaet korrektorom . . .
>
> Shkola . . . Druzhba s Aleshei Lavrent'evym, za kotorym priezzhaet "ford" . . . [. . .]
>
> Chernye dvory . . . Zarozhdaiushchaiasia tiaga k plebsu . . . [. . .] Moia nadgrobnaia rech', vyzvavshaia slezy Zhanny, docheri elektromontera . . . Ia umeiu govorit', rasskazyvat' . . .
>
> Beskonechnye dvoiki . . . Ravnodushie k tochnym naukam. . . . [. . .]
>
> 1952 god. Ia otsylaiu v gazetu 'Leninskie iskry' chetyre stikhotvoreniia. Odno, konechno, pro Stalina. Tri—pro zhivotnykh . . . (*SS* 3:12–13)

Apart from this fictional "biography" by Dovlatov himself, where fiction and fact are so intertwined that it is difficult to ascertain what corresponds to reality, there is little to corroborate any of the biographical data. Dovlatov deliberately obscured his biography. One of the sources that can be used to confirm some of the events in Dovlatov's life is his extensive correspondence with and the very brief memoirs of his father, Donat Mechik. Dovlatov provided some information in response to a request for biographical material from the American Slavicist Donald Fiene.[98] He gave his date of birth as September 3, 1941, in Ufa, in the Bashkir Autonomous Socialist Republic. His father, Donat Mechik, was a theater director and his mother, Nora Dovlatova, an actress. In his memoirs Donat Mechik wrote that he and his wife did not doubt that their son was going to become an actor and it never occurred to them that he would be drawn to literature, although he did write poetry while still at school, and was occasionally published. In his childhood Dovlatov spent a lot of time in the theater, and his father noted: "Serezha was always drawn to the concrete objects in the theater. The variety of things and furniture."[99]

After the war the family returned to Leningrad, as Dovlatov described in his letter to Fiene:

> In 1945[100] we returned to Leningrad, where I attended high school from 1948 to 1958, without showing the slightest talent for literature, but becoming so absorbed in drawing that I completed the course at the Art School on Tavricheskaia Street in parallel, that same School where the famous Russian artist Mikhail Shemiakin studied.[101]

After school Dovlatov worked as a milling-machine operator at a printing house and then in 1959 enrolled in the philological faculty of Leningrad

State University to study Finnish, but he was expelled after the third year, officially for poor progress, but in fact for contacts with foreigners and for talking too much ("za dlinnyi iazyk" as he put it). While still a student, he married Asia Pekurovskaia at the beginning of 1960 and subsequently divorced her around summer 1962. "We didn't have any children. Asia's child was born much later, and who its father is is a mystery," writes Dovlatov to Fiene.[102] In 1963 Dovlatov married Elena Davidovna Ritman. (They had two children: Katia, born in the Soviet Union in 1966, and Kolia, born in the United States in 1981.)

Since Dovlatov had not completed his university course, he was called up into the army (from 1962 to 1965). He served in the troops of the Ministry of Internal Affairs as a GULAG guard. He was first stationed in Syktyvkar, the capital of the Komi Autonomous Republic and a port on the Sysola River, and then dispatched to Ust'vymlag. Dovlatov's first attempts at writing began before the army, but it was in the army that he concentrated on it in earnest, as letters to his father testify.[103] The bulk of the letters consist of poems he had written in the army, and in many of them he discusses the process of writing poetry. He seeks his father's opinion about his poems and also offers his own criticism of them. In these poems Dovlatov describes everyday life in the camp. In the summer of 1962 he sent his father a large number of poems, noting in a letter that the events described in the poems are "pure truth" (*chistaia pravda*) and that these poems are a great success with his fellow soldiers. He confesses that earlier when he attempted to write, the topics of his poems were arbitrary and made up. Now he can hardly keep up with the material that army service seems to supply. Dovlatov mentions that he writes about one poem every second day and he realizes that this is too much. His intention is to select them and polish them later, but he is not keen for people at home in Leningrad to learn about his literary attempts. He writes in his letters that the poems help him to keep his sanity. He realizes how important it is to express himself simply and clearly in poetry, but at the same time he dreams of writing a novella (*povest'*). He doesn't think he will become a poet: "It's just that at present poems help me out, and then the lads like them."[104] Later on, though, he doesn't doubt that "if I do ever write seriously, then it will be in prose."[105] He reports to his father that he has written a twenty-three-page-long story, "Stoit tol'ko zakhotet' " ("You Only Need to Want It"), but has torn it up. He also reports that some of his poems have been published in local papers and that, in order to earn some extra money, he is writing for *Molodezh' Severa* (*The Youth of the North*) and *Krasnoe znamia* (*Red Banner*). Already in these letters to his father he sometimes refers to himself as Boris in order to deflect the censor. He already feels confident that he can tell stories: "I can tell stories like Sheherezade, three years without a break."[106] What is important to him is the appreciation of the audience to whom he relates his stories orally.

By the autumn of 1963 Dovlatov writes to his father that he intends to show him some of his short stories.[107] It is clear from the correspondence that writing poems and stories meant far more to him than simply a distraction from the boredom and dangers of military service. He was thinking carefully about form and style and evidently already treating life as material for future texts. Andrei Ar'ev takes the view that service in the army changed Dovlatov's style radically and turned him into an accomplished, serious writer.[108]

In the army Dovlatov made friends with a certain Viktor Dodulat, a quite uneducated man, but who played the guitar and composed some funny and simple songs. Dodulat made up some melodies to Dovlatov's poems. Apart from tremendous success among fellow soldiers, this process would most probably have helped Dovlatov to hone his style, to get rid of redundant words. In the autumn of 1962 Dovlatov wrote that he was very glad to be in charge of the library of his army battalion. He had written four short stories. Significantly, the short stories are not discussed in the letters to his father, whereas he often comments that his poems, in which there are no images or comparisons and the facts are simply told, are more successful.[109] Dovlatov also read the literary journals, such as *Voprosy literatury* (*Problems of Literature*) and *Literaturnaia gazeta* (*Literary Gazette*), which Donat Mechik sent him, particularly articles reflecting some of the discussions about literature.[110] In some letters he commented upon articles he had read:

> Another thing I liked was Naumov's article about Voznesensky. I liked his supercilious tone and the way he mocked the critics' profound scientific reflections about Voznesensky's run-of-the-mill verses. And the quotations he introduced from little-known "young" writers provided very good illustration for his article.[111]

Dovlatov's dislike of Voznesensky's poetry has found a place in his fiction. In both his *Zapisnye knizhki* (*SS* 4:155; *The Notebooks*) and in *Nevidimaia kniga* (*SS* 3:44–45; *The Invisible Book*) there is a story with slight variations about Voznesensky. In these short anecdotes Voznesensky's presence provokes Andrei Bitov to hit him. Bitov's behavior was then to be discussed at a disciplinary meeting. Bitov explains to the meeting how it happened: "I go into the restaurant. Andrei Voznesensky is standing there. I ask you, what could I do but punch him on the nose?" (*SS* 3:45)

An avid reader of Dovlatov, Valery Khait, describes how in a recent television interview Andrei Voznesensky adamantly denied the truth of this humiliating story, and Khait comments: "No, it didn't happen. But it might have done. Because it corresponded to the human qualities of the future author of 'Izops,' which Dovlatov had intuited."[112]

At that point Dovlatov was still not quite decided what to do after the army, and did not contemplate becoming a writer.

> I often wonder what I am going to do after the army, which is a good sign in general, but I haven't thought of anything yet. Maybe I could write an amusing story, after all I do know the life of all the camps, from general regime to special, I know lots of tales and legends from the criminal world, that is to say, as the camp language has it, I dig the lingo [*po fene voloku v etom dele*].[113]

In May 1963, however, he wrote to his father that he had written a short story in which "one ghastly case in a camp for especially dangerous prisoners is just described in a calm manner."[114]

After about a year in Ust'vymlag, Dovlatov spent the remaining years of his military service not far from Leningrad. He returned from the army in 1965 with a number of short stories. Several of these were later included in the novel *Zona: Zapiski nadziratelia* (*The Zone: A Prison Camp Guard's Story*).

After army service Dovlatov worked for twelve years at a variety of newspapers, first local ones belonging to specific industrial enterprises, and later for such publications as the journal of the Central Committee of the Komsomol organization, *Koster* (*Campfire*), and *Sovetskaia Estonia* (*Soviet Estonia*). From 1965 to 1969 Dovlatov worked at the newspaper of the Marine Technology Institute, *Za kadry verfiam* (*Shipbuilders' Newsletter*), first in charge of the literary section and from 1967 as deputy editor.[115] Dovlatov was only twenty-four when he joined this paper, and he acquired much useful experience there, although he always remained very critical of the work he did in the 1960s. Tat'iana Vol'tskaia tells that he introduced into the newspaper a humor page, "Na polubake" ("On the Fo'c'sle"), which continues to this day. He continued to read his stories in public, and in *The Invisible Book* there is a semi-fictionalized account of an occasion in 1967, when a selection of his stories was discussed at the Union of Writers.

> I learned that my stories were going to be discussed in the Union of Writers. There was an announcement in the monthly program of the Maiakovsky House. Nine years have gone by and I am leafing through the thin blue book with excitement.
>
> December 13, 1967:
>
> Discussion of Dovlatov's stories. Begins at 1700. The 170th anniversary of the birth of Heine. Begins at 1700.
>
> The surnames were printed in the same size fonts. Admirers of Heine gathered on the second floor. Mine on the third. I swear—there were

> significantly more of mine. [. . .] Only one person harshly criticized my stories—the writer Boris Ivanov. (*SS* 3:29)

This story is corroborated in Liudmila Shtern's memoirs:

> In December of 1967 Dovlatov phoned me and invited my husband and me to his first reading at the Writer's Club. [. . .] The reading took place on December 13th in a small room on the first floor. In the formal rooms upstairs they were celebrating the anniversary of Heinrich Heine's birth. [. . .] I don't remember everything he read. What remained was the impression of strict, precise prose, without vulgar chic, without cheap metaphors, and without the then fashionable village turns of phrases *à la russe.* One story, though, "Chirkov and Berendeev," I remember almost by heart even today. [. . .] Certain phrases from this story became sayings in our circle. [. . .] The people who took the floor praised the young writer. Only Boris Ivanov to a background of general discontent mumbled something unfavorable.[116]

In the spring of 1969 Dovlatov resigned from his job at the newspaper and decided to acquire a new profession as a monumental mason. He also decided to make a cardinal break with his previous literary style; as he explained to L. Shtern: "I write very carefully and with great effort, and in this last year under great pressure, because I have decided to break my style and forego many devices which I have to some extent at my command, to destroy what I am familiar with."[117] He entered university once again to study journalism, but again did not finish the course. He had difficulty finding jobs, and for some time he worked as V. F. Panova's literary secretary. In 1971 Dovlatov separated from his wife Elena. In 1972 he moved to Tallinn, Estonia, where the regime was comparatively liberal. He had high hopes of persuading the publishing house Eesti Raamat to publish his collection of stories, entitled (as he wrote to Fiene) *Gorodskie rasskazy*[118] (*City Tales*), although in other correspondence the title[119] is given as *Piat' uglov: Zapiski gorozhanina*[120] (*Fiveways: Notes of a City-Dweller*). However, one of Dovlatov's acquaintances was arrested, and during the search some manuscripts of Dovlatov's were confiscated. He was sacked from *Soviet Estonia,* and the page proofs of his book were destroyed. This had a devastating effect on Dovlatov, and at the beginning of 1975 he returned to Leningrad.

During his Tallinn years he lived with Tamara Zibunova, with whom he had a daughter, Aleksandra, born in September 1975. In February 1976 they broke up. "A biblical discussion on the subject of guilt would lead to an excessive accumulation of argument, reproaches, and eloquence."[121] They continued to correspond, and Dovlatov cared about his daughter Aleksandra.

He helped them materially as far as he could, as many letters from Leningrad and New York testify.

Back in Leningrad, Dovlatov found himself in great difficulties since he did not have a job, and was not even able to apply for one until the review of his case was completed. He wrote to Zibunova on March 23, 1975: "My life is a nightmare. I don't know what is going to happen. I'll try to keep my spirits up, go on writing, and not lose hope."[122] Judging from his correspondence, many friends tried to help him: "I'm trying to write a play for the puppet theatre. Lesha (Losev, alias Lifshits) strongly recommends me to. He's also advising me on it. People around are kind. Everyone wants to help, but there's no way."[123]

The general situation in Leningrad was increasingly difficult. Vladimir Maramzin and Mikhail Kheifets were arrested for compiling a five-volume edition of Brodsky's collected works (since his emigration in 1972, Brodsky's name was not allowed to be mentioned), and Efim Etkind was harassed by the KGB for his consulting role on the project. Also in 1975 a group of unofficial poets put together an anthology entitled *Lepta* (*Offering*), and although Lenizdat declined to publish it, the compilers and contributors were nevertheless "invited for interviews" with the KGB.[124] Many of them, such as Viktor Krivulin, Evgeny Rein, Konstantin Kuz'minsky, Oleg Okhapkin, and Elena Shvarts, were acquaintances of Dovlatov's and some were his close friends. Then a group of poets and artists celebrated the anniversary of the Decembrist uprising beside the *Bronze Horseman,* the equestrian statue of Peter the Great on Senate Square in Leningrad. The ambiguity of this unofficial reenactment of an officially celebrated act of protest was not lost on the authorities, who "invited" the participants "for interviews." After the death of Ol'ga Berggol'ts the KGB confiscated all her diaries and manuscripts, including poems written in prison in 1938–39.[125] All these events naturally had an impact on the small Leningrad intellectual community.

In July 1975 Dovlatov wrote to Zibunova that his attempts to find work had come to nothing: "I applied for two jobs—as director of a cemetery—or, to be more precise, of the 'Literary Avenue' (part of the Alexander Nevsky Lavra [Monastery])—and was turned down. And I also wanted to become an engraver—but it didn't work out."[126] He reported in his letters that he had sent some stories to *Avrora,* but had not heard yet, and that he was hoping to complete a story about journalists, "Vysokie muzhchiny" ("Lofty Men"), based on his experiences at *Soviet Estonia,* by September. He also sent a children's story to *Koster.* In the summer of 1975 Dovlatov completed a play for the puppet theater, *Ne khochu byt' znamenitym* (*I Don't Want to Be Famous*). He was particularly pleased with a song he had written for the finale of the play:

Everybody fights the fight
For the right to be himself,
Everybody battles bravely, face uncovered;
No one else's name will fit
A blacksmith or a sailorman,
Everybody has his own—and that's how it is.

Za pravo byt' samim soboi,
Otvazhno boretsia liuboi,
Idet na chestnyi boi, litsa ne priacha,
Chuzhoe imia ne k litsu,
Ni moriaku, ni kuznetsu,
U kazhdogo svoe. I ne inache![127]

Nevertheless, this play was returned by two theaters with a request for changes. He sent nine stories to *Avrora,* "all the most peaceful ones" (*vse naibolee mirnye*), as he put it, and half a novel. It was not accepted for publication, in spite of the fact that the relevant editors liked his work. In fiction Dovlatov summed up all the rejection letters he had received, attributing the story to Maramzin, who allegedly says: "If the manuscript was given to Brezhnev, he'd read it and say: 'Personally I like it. But what will the people upstairs think?!' " (*SS* 3:72)

Dovlatov's works circulated in samizdat, and in 1976 some of his stories found their way to the West. Dovlatov's first publication in the West was the story "Po priamoi" ("Straight Ahead"), which appeared in *Kontinent* no. 11, 1977. Two further stories were published in *Vremia i my* (*Our Times*) in the same year: "Golos" ("The Voice") and "Na chto zhaluetes', serzhant?" ("What's Your Complaint, Sergeant?"). They were also broadcast on Radio Liberty. He also sent his book *Nevidimaia kniga* (1977; *The Invisible Book*) abroad for publication in the United States.[128] All in all his position became increasingly precarious. In 1976 Dovlatov's friend Lev Losev emigrated to the United States, taking practically all of Dovlatov's work with him on microfilm, although Dovlatov himself was still not certain that he would emigrate too. In *The Invisible Book* there is a fictional story about Losev's emigration. Losev had a stable job, was a famous playwright, and had generally reached the peak of Soviet prosperity, which Dovlatov summarizes as: "A four-room flat, Finnish furniture, suede, and trips to the south" ("Chetyrekh-komnatnaia kvartira, finskaia mebel', zamsha, poezdki na iug"; *SS* 3:86). Everybody in the story makes a show of being shocked at his wish to leave the country and repeats a single phrase: he earns a good salary. No one dares to suggest that anyone could have other motives than material ones, because, as Dovlatov writes, that would involve admitting that such a person was running away from the Soviet Union.

During 1976–77 the confrontation between unofficial writers and artists and the KGB became even more acute and the likelihood of journalistic work or publication of his prose became negligible, so Dovlatov found work as a guide in Pushkinskie Gory, the Pushkin family estate near Pskov that had been turned into a museum. He returned to Leningrad in the autumn of 1977. On November 27, 1977, he wrote to Zibunova:

> Lena is leaving in a month. Various circumstances are keeping me here. Including my fatherhood. According to current laws it isn't enough to have a paper confirming the absence of claims. So this is what I ask of you. Don't breathe a word about Sasha being on my passport. I'll sort something out here. [. . .] Although I'm sure it will come to the surface. Since they have a file on me.[129]

Still without employment, Dovlatov continued to write. In March 1978 he announced: "I'm writing a novel about the Pushkin museum. About Pushkin, literature, the village. I hope to God it comes out as I've planned. For the first time I have a plot from the outset, ideas, complex structure. Only I mustn't rush it, mustn't surrender to habit. I'm setting great store by this project."[130] In the course of 1978 Zibunova was also summoned to the KGB and interrogated about Dovlatov. On April 2, 1978, he sent her a letter via Mikhail Roginsky (Dovlatov's friend and fellow journalist from *Soviet Estonia*) telling her that he had made up his mind to emigrate: "I've decided finally: I do not wish to go to prison for some fabricated crime. So I have to go. If they don't let me out I'll suffocate. So much is clear."[131]

The authorities also kept up the pressure on him. The KGB called in many of his acquaintances, particularly those he did not get along with, hoping to find some incriminatory material. *The Invisible Book* was broadcast by Radio Liberty, and there were also other radio broadcasts about him organized by the Gertsen fund and by the French PEN club, of which he was a member. Dovlatov was beaten up in broad daylight by some ostensible "hooligans" and actual plainclothes policemen and then forced to sign a paper admitting that he "put up malicious resistance" (*okazyval zlostnoe soprotivlenie*). For this "malicious resistance" he could be sentenced under article 191 of the Penal Code to five years' imprisonment. He was arrested and imprisoned for ten days in Kaliaevskii Prison in Leningrad. After this Dovlatov was summoned to the KGB and in a fatherly tone asked why he was not leaving the country. He said he did not have an invitation. An invitation was an essential document, without which one could not apply for an exit visa. He was told to apply all the same and advised to say that he wanted to be reunited with his wife Elena and their daughter, who had left the Soviet Union the previous year, 1977. When Dovlatov pointed out that they had been formally divorced in 1971, the KGB replied: "Your divorce is a formality. But we aren't formalists."[132]

And so in 1978 Dovlatov left the Soviet Union, joining the ranks of numerous friends and colleagues who had found themselves compelled to do the same. He spent some six months in Vienna, during which time he contributed to various periodicals and revised for publication a number of his stories, the manuscripts of which had been looked after and brought out by Lev Losev. Then he emigrated to the United States, where he was destined to spend the rest of his life.

One of the manuscripts Losev smuggled out for Dovlatov was a novel entitled *Piat' uglov* (*Fiveways*). There are many references to this work in Dovlatov's correspondence. In the family archive in New York there are several versions of a novel by this title, dating from 1973, 1974, and 1976. But there are also references to such a work in a letter to Liudmila Shtern as early as 1968. It was by this title that Dovlatov hoped to publish a collection of "urban tales" in Estonia. In a letter to Efimov in 1982 he still refers to a novel by this title:

> My novel is now called *Fiveways*. I've recently rewritten it, by the way. Or rather, I have edited it while copying it from the microfilm. It's about 500 pages. [. . .] I absolutely have to finish one more part, where the action will take place in the West. The plot, if you recall, consists in the way the author and the hero gradually merge into a single documentary person, and this person—is the writer. Now, in *The Invisible Book*, which at present is the last, fourth part of the novel, the hero does not yet become the writer. Previously I wanted to bring it all to an end with a piece about the museum, and in that museum kill the hero off. [. . .] There will be a separate story about the museum, but I must finish the novel.[133]

It is in fact only in *Inostranka* (*A Foreign Woman*) and in a group of stories written in the summer of 1988, "Rasskazy o minuvshem lete" ("Stories of Last Summer"), that Dovlatov finally achieved that fusion of author and hero of which he had spoken in this letter. And there is no published work of his by the title *Fiveways* (although it is not impossible that one of the versions extant in manuscript will eventually see the light of day), nor any work even approaching the length he attributes to it. Nevertheless, it appears that this uncompleted novel represented for him something like a magnum opus, of which most of his stories were notionally part. It is very clearly the case that *Fiveways* was extensively cannibalized in the composition of many of his published stories and collections. At the same time it needs to be borne in mind that, given his passion for the revision of his texts, and his horror at the idea that superseded versions of his works might be published by other people, it seems very unlikely that any extant manuscript is in a form that he would willingly have published.

The title *Fiveways* is itself full of significance. It refers to a particular intersection in the center of Petersburg, Vladimirskaia Ploshchad' (Vladimir Square), near which Dovlatov and many of his literary friends lived. Many writers of the past, such as Dostoevsky, had also lived in this region of the city. Dovlatov's retention of this title is clear evidence of his conscious allegiance to the Petersburg tradition in Russian literature. This is a tradition going back to the foundation of the city itself in the early eighteenth century, but associated particularly with Pushkin, Gogol, Dostoevsky, and Bely in the prerevolutionary period, and with poets such as Akhmatova, Mandelstam, and Brodsky since. This is surely in part what Dovlatov's colleagues must have had in mind in calling themselves "urbanists"; their concern is not with the city as such, or with any city, but with the literary tradition associated specifically with Petersburg. This is how one of the quintessential contemporary Petersburg writers, Andrei Bitov, explains his relationship with the city:

> Petersburg is a very strange place. It was a planned system, in the same way that socialism was a planned system. [. . .] It's both the most awful city and the nicest city—Europe combined with this imperial thing. Very strange. But what we received, what helped us—as Brodsky has often emphasized—is that we shared the same physical space as its past inhabitants; Soviet power has not destroyed that space, so that we led a "socialist life" in socialist times, and we were cut off from our own culture, we had no way of reading even our own literature, still we lived in the same space as our cultural ancestors, in the very same buildings.[134]

Chapter Two

Dovlatov in Emigration

"LEFT THE COUNTRY, leaving and about to leave . . . You can't help wondering why. Why clever, talented, serious people are leaving the country? Why people who love their country and for whom such a decision was not easy are leaving nevertheless, in spite of the fact that they will miss this country terribly." "Why is this happening?" (*Komu eto nuzhno?*)[1] asked Viktor Nekrasov in a statement to the Western press in 1974. Why was the mass emigration of the 1970s and '80s necessary? Soon after this statement Nekrasov himself, a winner of the Stalin Prize in 1947 for his book *V okopakh Stalingrada* (*In the Trenches of Stalingrad*) and one of the most popular Soviet authors, was forced to emigrate.

Exile has historically been used as a form of punishment, particularly for political opponents of those in power (not just in Russia). Perhaps the best-known precedent in Soviet times was in the autumn of 1922, when a large number of intellectuals, particularly religious philosophers such as Sergei Bulgakov, Semen Frank, Nikolai Berdiaev, and Nikolai Lossky (to list just a few of the better-known names), were forced to leave Russia on what came to be called "Filosofskii parokhod" ("The Philosophers' Ship"), although in reality there were two steamers and the majority left simply by train. Given the logic of the new Soviet order, this was consistent: the exile of these intellectuals coincided with the trials of the Left Social Revolutionaries. The Bolshevik Party could not tolerate different opinions and was consolidating total power; this was the beginning of totalitarianism.

Large-scale emigration from the Soviet Union began in the 1970s. The official Soviet position was that the only reason why a Soviet citizen would want to leave the country was to reunite with his or her family abroad, since everything else one might want, such as freedom of speech, employment, religious freedom, and so on, was guaranteed under the constitution. In the 1970s, owing mainly to pressure from the United States, it was made possible for Jews and Armenians to reunite with families abroad. Thus the bulk of the Third Wave of emigration was Jewish, although among writers in particular there were many non-Jews.

The Soviet authorities, as is well known, used this pretext of family reunification to oust many writers and dissident intellectuals who were "inconvenient" to the regime. Others simply defected. Just how anxiously the Soviet authorities observed the behavior of the new émigrés is testified by a note, marked "secret," written by Iury Andropov, then chairman of the KGB, "on the behavior of the writer Iur'enen abroad": "Since the moment Iur'enen announced his decision not to return to the U.S.S.R., he has been systematically publishing harsh, defamatory articles about the Soviet State and Society in the reactionary bourgeois and anti-Soviet émigré press, including NTS[2] publications."[3] The names of such writers were eliminated from the Soviet press. They were usually deprived of Soviet citizenship, so that just like the First Wave of Russian émigrés, they could not return. In their case, however, perestroika and the fall of the Soviet Union did make eventual return possible.

"When the Third Wave began to arrive in the West, its predominant mood was one of considerable optimism," writes John Glad. "An impressive number of writers had already enjoyed prominence in the USSR while others were trying their hand at writing for the first time. Both groups felt that whole new worlds of artistic opportunity were opening to them."[4] There was also a widespread anticipation that the older émigrés would welcome the new arrivals. These expectations were not quite fulfilled and, as Glad describes, the tension between various strands of emigration and within the Third Wave itself were considerable.[5] This is well documented; however, one crucial point needs to be emphasized: the First Wave generation had seen their mission as the preservation of Russian culture and language against the barbarian Communist influence. They deliberately cut themselves off from any contact with the U.S.S.R. (with notable exceptions) and some went as far as supporting the Nazis as a way of combating Bolshevism. L. D. Rzhevsky, an émigré of the Second Wave, writing in 1951, noted that even some émigré critics took the view that Soviet literature, music, and visual arts served only to confirm the death of art in the U.S.S.R.:[6]

> There is a well-established tendency of such negation. For example, N. Berberova, who is an intelligent critic and a talented writer, in her article "Vladimir Khodasevich, Russian Poet," published in the latest issue of *Grani,* writes: "It is time to acknowledge that irrespective of any political issues and contemporary political polemics, Russian poetry has come to an end." The light has gone out.[7]

He expressed regret that émigré Russian literature was so much focused on the past: "On the whole the profile of our émigré literature sometimes seems to me in a certain sense Egyptian: a huge eye inserted *en face*, gazing predominantly into the past."[8]

In his final summary Rzhevsky called for efforts to overcome the provincialism of émigré literature and to include the study of the literary process in the Soviet Union: "Representing our national culture doesn't mean mourning its past or standing aloof from its present, but fighting for its future."[9] Regrettably, there were few among the First or Second Wave who agreed with his position. Those First or Second Wave Russian émigrés who were still active as writers or editors firmly believed that their task was to preserve Russian culture. In the 1970s this attitude was by and large shared by the major émigré periodicals, *Novyi zhurnal* (*The New Journal*), *Russkaia mysl'* (*Russian Thought*), and *Grani* (*Facets*). Above all they were concerned to preserve Russian literature in its familiar forms. When the Third Wave arrived in the West, the differences were not easy to resolve. There were misgivings on both sides and many reasons for misunderstandings.

Most members of the Third Wave had grown up in the U.S.S.R., and the vast majority of them had never had the opportunity to travel abroad or even to visit other socialist countries. Practically all of the Third Wave writers were connected to a greater or lesser extent with the underground culture, particularly that of Moscow and Leningrad. A number of studies have appeared since the fall of the Soviet Union describing the multitude of underground cultural activities, particularly in Leningrad, where oppression by the authorities was more severe. In the 1970s and '80s, for example, there was a group of highly qualified translators who attempted to fill the gaps left by the officially translated literature and translated philosophical works, criticism, and literary theory, not only of western European thinkers (German philosophers of the 1930s and '40s such as Heidegger and Jaspers were particularly popular), but also of forbidden Eastern European authors (Bruno Schulze, Mrożek), as well as many Eastern mystics and occult writers. In the area of émigré literature, a conference dedicated to Khodasevich's ninety-fifth birthday anniversary was held in Leningrad in 1981.[10] During the thaw such émigré personalities as Ivan Bunin, Stravinsky, and others had been partially rehabilitated, although the ideological barriers to the study of émigré literature were still in place, so that the study of this became the domain of samizdat.[11] In many ways this generation of Russian writers was well informed about the First Wave; however, the First Wave's information about cultural life in the U.S.S.R. was inevitably patchy. For this reason the rift between the First and Third Waves of writers gradually became wider, and soon the Third Wave found that they could not have access to the journals and newspapers edited by members of the First Wave. As a consequence, they founded their own publications and even publishing houses. It was paradoxical that although the First and Third Waves of Russian emigration were united in their hostility to official Soviet ideology, the rift between the generations became insurmountable. However, the Third Wave, with their roots in Russian underground culture, did not limit their scope to mere ideological opposition, but concentrated on what Mikhail Berg calls "other repressed cultural values."[12]

In the course of the 1970s and '80s some of the most enterprising and famous representatives of unofficial culture settled in France, West Germany, Israel, and the United States (perhaps the largest group). These writers, poets, painters, and musicians knew how important publications abroad were to friends and colleagues they had left behind. A number of new newspapers (for example, *Al'manakh Panorama—Almanac Panorama, Sem' dnei—Seven Days, Novyi Amerikanets—The New American*) and journals were founded: Vladimir Maksimov founded *Kontinent* (*Continent*), Perel'man founded *Vremia i my* (*Our Times*), and the journal *Dvadtsat' dva* (*Twenty-two*) was published in Tel Aviv. In Paris Rozanova and Siniavsky founded *Sintaksis* (*Syntax;* previously this had been the title of a samizdat journal in Moscow), and Maramzin and Khvostenko founded *Ekho* (*Echo*). Apart from the publishing house Ardis founded by the American Slavicists Carl and Ellendea Proffer, Efimov founded Ermitazh (Hermitage) and Poliak founded Serebrianyi vek (Silver Age). This gave a new character to *tamizdat.* Where in the preceding decades the works of writers such as Pasternak or Solzhenitsyn, which could not be published in the Soviet Union, had appeared in the West under the imprint of Western or First Wave émigré publishing houses, the publications of the Third Wave, though excluded from the official literary process in the Soviet Union, were nevertheless an inalienable part of the independent underground culture there. So the Third Wave of Russian writers, who managed to maintain a dialogue with the Soviet Union, did not feel such cultural isolation as the First Wave had felt. Indeed, many Third Wave émigrés did not feel very different from those left behind. This gave Andrei Siniavsky reason to assert, in his interview with John Glad, that émigré literature had no autonomous status, but largely fed on Soviet culture:

> You see, I am convinced that you cannot create a culture in emigration. I am convinced of this now. Previously I could still have illusions, imagining that the culture of the First Wave of emigration represented some kind of culmination of the Silver Age. When I arrived here I saw what this Silver Age had turned into. Nothing was left of it. And I think nothing will be left here either. You see, emigration is not a place where an independent culture can be created. It is a place where the creativity of individual authors can be preserved. For this reason I do not perceive the culture of the First Wave of emigration as a unified culture. It was the place where Tsvetaeva and Remizov

> worked, where Nabokov worked and so on. However, this is not a unified cultural edifice.[13]

As John Glad observes, this was not the typical view of the emigration as a whole; it was commoner to deny that anything worthwhile could have been written in conditions of censorship in the Soviet Union. This very much echoes the views of the First Wave as quoted by Rzhevsky. And even as late as 1998, Boris Khazanov wrote in *Literaturnaia gazeta:* "Émigré prose, like Lot's wife, cannot take her eyes off the past."[14] The attitude of the Soviet literary establishment to émigré literature was one of contempt, and any attempt to ignore the dividing line between the two literatures met with outrage. Until perestroika the "revolutionary supremacy" of Soviet literature could not be questioned. However, it seems that during the 1970s and '80s there was no perceived difference between underground literature (or "second literature"—*vtoraia literatura*) and works published abroad, and many intellectuals in the Soviet Union read samizdat, *Kontinent,* and Russian books smuggled in from Third Wave publishing houses. What mattered more to recent émigré writers, in fact, was recognition, and this was particularly the case for those who were not established writers at the point of emigration. The arrival in the West of a number of Soviet writers (Solzhenitsyn, Voinovich, Aksenov, Brodsky, Zinov'ev, and Maksimov, to name just a few) was greeted with immense publicity. They were interviewed, their works were translated, lecture tours were arranged for them, and so on. From the perspective of American culture, the public image of a writer in exile was anchored in the concept of dissidence. Exile was the price of dissidence, and the exiled author was welcomed as an anti-Communist. For this reason it was necessary that the texts be originally written within the dissident tradition, regardless of the actual position of the writer vis-à-vis the political power in the home country. This was a crucial factor in the treatment of well-established writers. Assimilation was harder both physically and psychologically for writers who were not known in the West. For the last two centuries in Russia, it had been literature rather than religion or anything else that fundamentally determined popular consciousness. In the Soviet Union, for well-known reasons, officially approved writers enjoyed immense prestige, but being a nonconformist writer carried its own social prestige and recognition, too. In the West there was no recognition for these latter except among fellow émigré writers, and even that was not always forthcoming. To establish any sort of reputation was difficult. The available readership was very limited, even if their work circulated back in the Soviet Union. And as new arrivals became preoccupied with jobs and material acquisitions, interest in literature did not take priority and thus the readership failed to grow. This was bound to take a psychological toll on the writer, who now found that he had the freedom to write whatever he liked, but nobody wanted to read it. In this respect, the award of the Nobel Prize for literature to Brodsky was as important for the Third Wave as Bunin's Nobel Prize had been for the First Wave emigration: it was public recognition not only of the existence of Russian literature in exile, but also of the moral justification of political emigration. The prize was also perceived as condemnation of the repression to which literature was subjected in Soviet Russia.

There was another side to the coin. As S. Karlinsky observed:

> By the nineteen-thirties, the Western intellectual community, which had no objection to the numerous successful Russian painters, composers and dancers who were active in the West, came to regard the existence of an exile Russian literature in its midst with a mixture of hostility and studied indifference. It was during that decade of Stalinist purges and proliferating forced labor camps that large numbers of American, British, and French intellectuals (including such men as George Bernard Shaw, Theodore Dreiser, André Gide, and Thomas Mann) came to regard the U.S.S.R. as the finest example of a free and just social organization that humanity had so far been able to devise. A Russian writer who preferred to live abroad rather than contribute to the glorious experiment that was unfolding in his native country was automatically seen as a reactionary exploiter from the past and an obstacle to human progress in the present.[15]

The same accusation against Western intellectuals was also voiced by Nabokov in the final part of his novel *Pnin.* Writing in the 1970s, Karlinsky admitted that such attitudes have become more rare in recent decades. And yet, it was in the realm of literature that the Russian diaspora made its most significant contributions to Western and world culture.

As noted in chapter 1, many of the nonconformist writers who were forced into emigration in the 1970s and '80s were far less concerned with political opposition to the Soviet regime than with forms of aesthetic innovation (which the regime found equally unacceptable). Even if émigré literature in general was still dominated by anti-Soviet politics, many younger writers, such as S. Sokolov, A. Tsvetkov, J. Brodsky, and V. Maramzin, were characterized by apolitical literary concerns. Dovlatov was one of these.

Sergei Dovlatov emigrated in 1978. First he lived for six months in Vienna and then he was reunited with his wife and daughter in New York. In 1974 he had published two stories in the Soviet Union, and prior to his emigration he had also begun to publish in the West (see chapter 1). He had taken advantage of Carl and Ellendea Proffer's visit to Leningrad in 1977 to give them the manuscript of *The Invisible Book,* which was published by their publishing house, Ardis, the same year, while the English translation followed in 1979. Despite his difficulties, Dovlatov was reluctant to emigrate. In one of the episodes in his story *Zapovednik* (*The Sanctuary*), the protagonist is discussing emigration with his wife. In a foreign language, he says, we lose eighty percent of our individuality. We lose our ability to joke, to use irony. This prospect fills the protagonist with horror: "I was terrified of such a serious and irreversible step. It's like being born all over again. Moreover, of your own free will" (*SS* 2:237). Dovlatov did not speak English.[16] The fictional narrator in *The Sanctuary* remarks how unreal America was to him: "For me America was fiction. Something like a mirage. A half-forgotten movie with Akbar the tiger and Charlie Chaplin in it . . ." (*SS* 2:237). In reality, Dovlatov was much better versed in American fiction. In one of his letters to Raisa Orlova, he confesses:

> What I regret most is that you and I never got round to talking about American prose. I was and still am a great admirer of American fiction. Did you know that I know by heart passages from Stephen Crane and Faulkner and that I remember the names of all the characters in *Tobacco Road* and *Cannery Row* and I am able to list all the outfits of Harry Morgan's wife in *To Have and Have Not*? When I met Vonnegut I quoted to him about 20 lines from his *Slaughterhouse* [*Five*] and Vonnegut got scared stiff, thinking he had a dangerous madman in front of him.[17]

However, no amount of reading can really prepare one for life in a different country. "It is not possible to prepare for emigration. It is not possible to prepare for one's birth. It is not possible to prepare for the afterlife. One can only resign oneself to it" (*SS* 3:101), writes Dovlatov in *Remeslo* (*The Craft*). Since hardly anybody was able to travel or experience real life abroad, for most Soviet citizens the United States was imagined as something like paradise: not only freedom, independence, and fantastic technology, but an abundance of jeans, jazz, and other consumer products. "Everything that one can learn about America without actually having been there, I know," writes Dovlatov to L. Shtern.[18] However, for Dovlatov's generation most of the information about the West came from translated American literature and from the negative propaganda in Soviet newspapers. They assumed that social evils such as unemployment or slums were all invented by Soviet propaganda, and did not exist in reality. This somewhat naive understanding of America among Dovlatov's generation became something of an ideological, moral, and even artistic stance. On arrival their admiration for America was boundless: "It was only at the beginning that we were completely enthralled by America. As Joseph Brodsky used to say: For a whole year I could not believe that it was possible to say anything stupid in English."[19] Very soon, though, the realization came "that America was not a branch of paradise on earth."[20]

At the beginning, on September 18, 1978, writing from Vienna, Dovlatov's main emotion was that he was alive and free: "I am alive and free, that is the main thing. Such is man. After momentary adaptation one's negative emotions are immediately restored to previous levels. Comparisons acquire a purely creative character. I still have a feeling of freedom, well-being [. . .] and so on."[21] While waiting in Vienna for his U.S. visa, Dovlatov approached various Russian periodicals abroad and sent a number of his stories to them for publication. During this period two lengthy articles about Dovlatov appeared in the Paris émigré periodical *Russkaia mysl'*.[22] Dovlatov's letters to friends and relatives are full of anxiety and indecision. His eventual decision to leave the Soviet Union had been made in the hope of establishing his literary career; however, he was also anxious about how he would manage to live together with his wife and daughter and how he would be able to provide for them. A number of options were suggested to him by friends: enrolling as a Ph.D. student, with a view to finding some teaching job at a university, or journalism. All of these had a major stumbling block: his lack of English.[23] Dovlatov's own inclination was to try to find some menial job and learn English. At the same time, he wanted to find ways of placing in American periodicals translations of his old stories written in the U.S.S.R. Although Dovlatov realized that it was practically impossible to live on a writer's earnings, his ambition at this stage was publication, and he was editing the work he had managed to smuggle out: "*All* my manuscripts are here. I am slowly rereading and editing them. I am preparing a book for *Posev*. About journalism."[24] Dovlatov kept up correspondence with friends in the U.S.S.R. and those who had already emigrated. The six months he spent in Vienna were an eye-opener for him, not only as a glimpse of life in the West, but also for what he learned about his fellow countrymen, and the lengths they would go to get noticed. The more horrific the story one told, the greater publicity one received. Creating interest in the press helped these people to earn a living, at least in the first few months after their arrival. Dovlatov was unpleasantly surprised at the unscrupulousness of some: "X told a radio correspondent that there had been seven attempts on his life."[25] For this reason the officials in Vienna conducted lengthy and unpleasant interviews: "They are fed up to the teeth with dissidents."[26] At the same time, Dovlatov became acquainted with some of the right-wing émigré organizations such as the NTS (Narodno-Trudovoi Soiuz; People's Labor Union) and some of the press who were particularly keen to promote any story that discredited life in the Soviet Union. Already in his letter from Vienna to Efimov on December 16, 1978, Dovlatov expressed horror at the attitudes and naivete of the NTS: he had met Vladimir Poremsky, a Second Wave émigré and representative of the NTS and the émigré journal *Posev:* "His world outlook has not changed since the time of the Entente. He cherishes some wild ideas about a coup in the USSR."[27]

On February 22, 1979, Dovlatov, his mother Nora Sergeevna, and his dog Glasha set off for New York. On March 9, 1979, Dovlatov wrote to Efimov that in all probability Radio Liberty would give him temporary work, but that he was feeling desperate about obtaining any real position. Even enrolling in technical courses appeared to be a distant dream because of his lack of English. Much later, in an interview with Jane Bobko of the popular Californian weekly *Threepenny Review,* he remarked sadly: "I would like to quote what one old émigré woman said: I knew they spoke English in America, but hadn't imagined they did it to such an extent. . . ."[28]

Nevertheless, there were many positive developments. By March 1979 the English translation of *The Invisible Book* had been published. Three Russian-language publishing houses—Russica, Almanac, and Tret'ia volna (The Third Wave)—offered to publish Dovlatov's next book. He made appearances on the radio journal *Bereg* (*Shores*) and his popularity grew. He was still full of doubts, however, and on March 21, 1979, he wrote to Liudmila Shtern:

> My disorientation is much more comprehensive than the average émigré feelings. What do I have to complain about in that respect? They write about me in the papers. They talk about me on the radio. I've made two appearances, practically unpaid, but successful. My books are appearing and will go on appearing. I've got four publication offers. [. . .] In Leningrad, in spite of all the horrors, there was a feeling of purpose. Or rather, of prospects. [. . .] Now I have the feeling of a physical end, a limit.[29]

In his letter of March 22 to Efimov, he noted more optimistically that he might be able to risk not becoming a docker or a doorman. In spite of misgivings and lack of financial backing, Dovlatov, along with a number of fellow writers and journalists, also intended to found and edit a new Russian-language newspaper. He had in mind to create a paper addressed mainly to the Third Wave of Russian émigrés, who intended to make the United States their permanent residence and needed to find their place in American life. His idea was that the newspaper should concentrate mainly on practical matters, including legal and social advice, description of American structures, advice on how to find a job, a place to live, and so on, but that it should also include culture, politics, and sport. The need for such a paper was evident. The only other Russian-language publication in New York was *Novoe Russkoe Slovo* (*New Russian Word*), edited by Bunin's former literary secretary, Andrei Sedykh. The main readership of *Novoe Russkoe Slovo* was the older generations of émigrés, who were already well established in their everyday life in America and had different concerns from new arrivals. Dovlatov tried to mobilize his friends and fellow writers to submit stories and reviews. The new venture was due to be launched around June or July 1979. Dovlatov had no illusions about it: "There are a lot of complications with the paper. But it will be published. And it will be a miracle if it does not go bankrupt immediately."[30] The first issue of *Novyi Amerikanets* (*The New American*) was eventually published in February 1980. It caused a sensation, and an additional two thousand copies were printed (the first run was forty-five hundred copies). In the event the paper became so popular that in spite of financial and other difficulties, subscriptions reached eleven thousand within a year. The first anniversary of the paper was celebrated and widely reported in the English-language media. Dovlatov edited this weekly paper for two years, and during this period he wrote the editorials himself. Selected editorials were published separately under the title *Marsh odinokikh* (*March of the Lonely*); they vividly illustrate Dovlatov's journalistic skills.[31] *Novyi Amerikanets* in the form envisaged by Dovlatov had in the end to close down. However, the title itself continued without Dovlatov's editorship for some time afterward, and he continued to make occasional contributions. He was disappointed at its closure. In his last editorial he summed up why the attempt to publish a democratic paper for the broad émigré readership was premature and doomed to failure: lack of business experience on his part and on the part of his colleagues on the paper, and the preoccupation of the émigré population with material issues and their indifference to social structures.[32] Nevertheless, the paper was successful for a time thanks to its lively language and style, and to its breadth of coverage (from politics, literature, and microorganisms found in northwest Australia to advertisments by Jewish funeral services and car sales firms). All Dovlatov's editorials, which also span a wide range of topics, are marked by a witty style and sharp observations, which must have been a contributing factor to the paper's success. He was also an accomplished draughtsman, and many issues contain his drawings and illustrations. Here is an example of an editorial, which invites readers to consider the forthcoming presidential elections in the United States in comparison with the level of information available in the U.S.S.R.:

> At home the state was governed by mystical beings. What did we know about Stalin? That he smoked a pipe and was the best person in the world. What did we know about Lenin? That he wore a cap and was also the best person in the world. About Brezhnev we don't even know that much. All that is known is that he has some eyebrows.
>
> I remember how astonished I was to discover that Lenin liked cold beer. In this insignificant fact something human peeped through.[33]

There were many serious editorials about the political direction of the paper, about views on the future of Russia and religion. This is how one of the editorials characterized the paper's outlook: "In politics we subscribe to liberal democratic values. In aesthetics to the breadth and eloquence of the Renaissance. In philosophy to an elemental humanism."[34]

Novyi Amerikanets also published readers' letters, stories by Third Wave writers, announcements, reviews of cultural events, and many reports on life in the Soviet Union. Eventually the weekly became so popular that the rival *Novoe Russkoe Slovo* resorted to intimidating authors who wrote for *Novyi Amerikanets* and advertisers who patronized it, and generally tried to discredit the new paper. This came as a surprise and shock to *Novyi Amerikanets*'s board of editors, who were hoping for at least moral support from such a well-established paper. *Novoe Russkoe Slovo* even adopted disreputable tactics, spreading rumors that *Novyi Amerikanets* was in the pay of the KGB. Such intolerance to different opinions, coupled with other disagreements within the editorial board, led to the eventual demise of *Novyi Amerikanets.* Like much else, Dovlatov turned this incident into successful fiction.

The second part of Dovlatov's *Remeslo* (*The Craft*), entitled "Nevidimaia gazeta" (written in 1984–85; "The Invisible Newspaper"), describes in fiction the creation and eventual demise of *Novyi Amerikanets.* The tension between the First and Third Waves of emigration is illustrated by the relationship between *Novoe Russkoe Slovo* and *Novyi Amerikanets.* In particular, in an "open letter" to the editor of *Novoe Russkoe Slovo,* which in Dovlatov's fiction figures under the offensive title *Slovo i delo,* Dovlatov sums up the feelings of the recent émigrés:[35]

> We hate useless table-turning. We find infantile projects for the reorganization of totalitarian society ridiculous. We are amused by illusions of religious renaissance. We have understood one crucial thing. The Soviet leaders do not come from other planets. They are not extraterrestrial beings. Soviet rule is not the Tatar-Mongol yoke. Soviet rule is inherent in each of us. It is in our habits and inclinations. It is in our sympathies and antipathies. In our consciousness and in our soul. Soviet rule—is us.

This fictional "open letter" is a summary of a paper Dovlatov gave at a symposium, "Intellektual'naia zhizn' v SSSR" ("Intellectual Life in the USSR"), in Minnesota. The text of this paper, entitled "Ispytanie svobodoi" ("Trial by Freedom"), was published in *Novaia gazeta* (*New Paper*).[36] The article takes a broader view of emigration than merely a response to A. Sedykh and *Novoe Russkoe Slovo,* and is set in the context of Dovlatov's fiction. It appears as an expression of the émigré condition generally and the way it affects personal relations. Dovlatov makes the observation that as long as there was a common enemy in the Soviet Union, the differences between émigrés were not noticeable. Once this enemy was removed, the infighting began. John Glad remarked that "while the Third Wave was originally very cohesive and émigrés tended to socialise largely with each other in the 1970s and early 1980s, as time passed this cohesiveness naturally began to erode."[37] The greater the success Dovlatov had in American literary circles, the more vicious the personal attacks on him became:

> The paradox of my personal fate is that in the course of my four years in America, my relations with my fellow émigrés have become worse and worse, while contacts with American journals, publishers and private individuals (in spite of my monstrous English)—have become closer and more fruitful.
>
> There is also a paradox in the fact that I find it far easier to convince an average well-intentioned American of something, than a fellow countryman, who has gone through the same terrible totalitarian experience as myself.[38]

Since not many of the exiled writers were able to enter into a direct dialogue with the receiving culture through their work, the paper *Novyi Amerikanets* was an attempt at least to keep Russian readers informed and to establish a dialogue with them, however insignificant their number. The Third Wave contingent in the United States was on average highly educated, and the newspaper provided authors with at least a minimum of communication with a Russian-language readership. In trying to communicate with an American audience, most Third Wave writers had to resort to the help of translators and editors and thereby to relinquish some control over the representation of themselves, which added further to their sense of insecurity. In a letter to Iulia Gubareva, Dovlatov remarks: "I was not published at home, and here there is no audience. The Americans don't count. They aren't concerned with you, but with the translations. That is quite a strange feeling."[39] Nevertheless, Dovlatov perhaps understood the importance of good translation more clearly than others, as will be illustrated below.

"Only the Americans understand how great a measure of literary success it is to be published in the *New Yorker*," writes Lev Losev.[40] In February 1980 Dovlatov signed his first contract with the *New Yorker* and received a one-thousand-dollar advance, and in March of the same year he was paid another advance of three thousand dollars. On September 25, 1981, he was still negotiating with Efimov (who had by then founded his own publishing house) for the publication of *Zona* (*The Zone*) in Russian, but the *New Yorker* was interested in translations of some of the stories from the book: "A piece from *The Zone* is going to be published in *The New Yorker* as a short story (which it is) and two more excerpts are being read by the editor. They are well-disposed towards me and they even wrote a thank-you letter to Brodsky for recommending me to them." Kurt Vonnegut wrote to Dovlatov on the occasion of his stories' appearance in the *New Yorker* to tell him he had broken his heart: "I was born in this country and fearlessly served my country during the war, but I haven't managed to get published in *The New Yorker.*"[41]

Among Dovlatov's contemporaries were a number of writers whom Brodsky had recommended to the *New Yorker;* however, it was Dovlatov's laconic style that appealed to the journal most. Dovlatov himself also worked hard on the translations, carefully explaining to the translator the expressions and phrases that it was not possible to find in any dictionary, changed meanings, and various other nuances. This must have contributed to the success of his translations in the United States, for which he was awarded a prize for the best short story of 1986 from the PEN American Center. Apart from publications in the *New Yorker,* Dovlatov's stories were included in *Sixty Short-Stories,* a collection of the best short stories published in 1986, along with such writers as Kawabata, Mrożek, Böll, Borges, García Márquez, Calvino, Babel, and Malamud. Some well-established American writers like Kurt Vonnegut, Joseph Heller, and Irving Howe all wrote positive reviews of Dovlatov's work. Many of his stories also appeared in *Harpers, Partisan Review,* and *Grand Street.*

Dovlatov realized early on how much his success would depend on the translator, and instead of economizing on translators' fees, as many others did, he offered Anne Frydman and later Antonina Bouis coauthorship of the English versions. This is what he wrote to Anne Frydman on July 9 (ca. 1983–84):

> All my clever friends say that a good translator is my main achievement in America. And it really is very important. Mark Popovsky (he is a scientific journalist and is a friend of academician Sakharov) used to phone me every week and say: "I've found a translator who charges 8 dollars a page!" Then: "I've found a translator who charges 7 dollars a page!!" And in the end: "I've found a translator who charges 6 dollars!!!" The result was that the publishing house, Doubleday, returned his thick book about Vavilov (he is the founder of Russian genetics). The same happened to Aleshkovsky. And it is said that the translator [. . .] ruined Erofeev's brilliant book "Moscow to the End of the Line." And so on. But I turned out to be prudent and clever . . .[42]

So when Anne Frydman was unable for family reasons to complete as many translations for Dovlatov as there was a demand for, he tried to persuade another translator to take on the work and wrote to Donald Fiene on May 29 (ca. 1983), hoping to encourage him:

I am enclosing a copy of a note that I received from Linda Usher from *The New Yorker.* Let this note be an incentive for you to translate the story "Superfluous" (Lishnii).

Dear Sergei,

[. . .]

I'd like to have news of you, and to know whether you have found a translator for stories. We do miss seeing your work; I hope we will soon.[43]

Just how much effort Dovlatov put into the translations of his work is best illustrated by his correspondence with the translators. For example, on September 4 (ca. 1981–82) Dovlatov wrote to Anne Frydman (she was translating his book *Kompromiss* [*The Compromise*] at the time, which was published by Alfred Knopf in 1983):

"To comb" (*Prichesyvat'*) in this instance means to defeat, to overtake, leave behind. *Prichesyvat'*—is a slang word and can be used in many different instances. It can even be used like this: if a man has met a woman and achieved success with her, he can say: "I combed her" (*Ia ee prichesal'*). *Prichesat'* can also mean to defeat at cards or chess. "To comb solid"—means to be victorious without taking any risk, for certain.

Dovlatov's explanations are patient and meticulous:

"It is his cadre." Cadre is a bureaucratic name for a white or blue-collar worker. Hence—"cadre" [personnel] department. Lenin said: "Cadres armed with knowledge are decisive." A nice girl is also a "cadre." There is an expression to "cadrc a bird," that is, to get acquainted. If some young people are planning to go to dance, they say: Let's go to the Palace of Culture, there are some excellent "cadres" there. Or one can say: "What a cadre this Hinckley is, he almost killed the president . . ."[44]

The value of these explanations to the translator was enormous, but Dovlatov himself realized, more than many of his contemporaries, how important such translations were for his own future. Here is another example from his correspondence with Anne Frydman (July 27, ca. 1981–82):

Koordinatnye ATS . . . "ATS coordinates . . ." ATS stands for automatic telephone exchange. What "coordinates" are I don't know, but I recall that they were made at the factory where I worked as a sort of journalist. (In the Soviet Union every factory has its own paper.) The expression "ATS coordinates" is

> of no significance in the story and I used it because it is technical and sounds incomprehensible. You can use any type of technical product. The more incomprehensible it sounds, the better. But it has to be INCOMPREHENSIBLE IN AMERICAN.[45]

This is how Anne Frydman translated it: "In Porkhov we have a branch of the Red Dawn Factory. We construct sized coordinates for pay telephones" (*C,* 63).

He not only explains, but often gives a visual explanation of what a word means, or of differences between words. The above letter to Anne Frydman contains a drawing illustrating the difference between the words "trotting races" (*bega*) and "horse race" (*skachki*) and an illustration of the word "blockhouse" (*blokpost*). On March 4 (ca. 1985) Dovlatov explains one of the episodes in *The Compromise:* "The driver tells the protagonist, 'duck,' so that from the street he can't be seen drinking, but since he is drinking without a glass, straight from the bottle, it is very difficult to do it while ducking, because the vodka won't pour out."[46] There follows a drawing to show what is meant. Dovlatov explained to the translators not only the particular word in context, but often explained its origins and gave other helpful definitions. In the same letter to Anne Frydman:

> The word "to stop up" (*zatknut'*) and its derivatives are used, of course, outside the realm of propaganda. [. . .] But the expression "to shut the mouth of bourgeois propaganda" is a constant propaganda cliché, a stock phrase, something like an idiom. In the Soviet Union many things are done "to shut the mouth of bourgeois propaganda." Shcharansky was released not because Gorbachev felt sorry for him, but in order "to shut the mouth of bourgeois propaganda." [. . .] "To shut someone's mouth"—means to silence someone.[47]

Looking through various Russian-Russian dictionaries the translator could have made an informed guess at what "*pritonoderzhatel'stvo*" might mean, but would not have found its real meaning. This might have led to a failure in translation, as is explained in the same letter by the author: " 'Keeping a den of vice' (*pritonoderzhatel'stvo*) is an official expression, which corresponds to an article of the Criminal Code. Usually this article is applied to people who are inconvenient to the authorities, people who receive many visitors, foreigners, and so on."[48] With similar patience Dovlatov explains (in a letter dated March 21, probably 1983) difficult expressions to Donald Fiene, who at the time was translating Dovlatov's early story "Soldaty na Nevskom" ("Soldiers on the Nevsky Prospekt"). What is important for the translator is that Dovlatov contextualizes the various notions as well:

> "To be free with your hands" (*davat' voliu rukam*) means either to fight or to harass or pester women. There is no specific implication of sex here. Generally speaking, in Russian slang sexual expressions are rarely used. Russian is fairly prim in matters sexual. The reverse is more often the case. Expressions with a sexual connotation imply actions of a non-sexual nature. For example, if in the prison camp a prisoner shouts: "I'll fuck you up the arse," this does not express the prisoner's sexual intentions, it merely means "I will smash your mug, beat you up, cripple you . . ."[49]

And in the same letter: "The joke is that the old woman asks him to say his initials, that is, the first letters of his name and patronymic, but the simple man Vas'ka confuses the difficult word 'initials' (*initsialy*) with the word 'nationality' (*natsional'nost'*)."[50]

Dovlatov encouraged his translator not to hurry but to ask him as many questions as he liked. He not only acknowledged the translator's hard work, but was also fully aware that the attitude to translated literature in the United States was somewhat problematic; not even serious American writers could make a living from literature alone, to say nothing of translators. The position of even an excellent American prose writer (not to mention poets) was by no means as prestigious as that of his opposite number in the Soviet Union. In his interview with the journal *Slovo(Word)* Dovlatov explained that the Americans, as distinct from the Russians, preferred their own (not imported) literature. In the United States there was, according to Dovlatov, a respectful but somewhat ironic American expression, "European style." This meant deep, elegant, but obviously noncommercial literature. In the Soviet Union, on the other hand: "A membership card of the Writers' Union opens any doors. Marshals and film actors, hockey players and pop stars, Central Committee members and financial black market geniuses—all like to show off their friendship with writers."[51] In the United States business, medicine, or law are far more prestigious occupations. A writer is appreciated by a very limited circle of readers. If in the Soviet Union, for example, Bulat Okudzhava could attract audiences of ten or fifteen thousand, then in the United States Allen Ginsberg's readings were attended by thirty people at most. "In order to impress a young lady at home one could pretend to be a friend of Evtushenko's. Here such a trick has little effect."[52]

This was difficult for the émigré writer to comprehend and absorb, not only because literature in the Soviet Union was so dominant, but because a representative selection of Western novels was regularly published in the Soviet Union in translation, receiving considerable attention. Not surprisingly, many émigré writers began to consider that they had traded state censorship for censorship by the marketplace. This gave many Russian writers a reason to argue that writers have to write for their own people, because they are not needed elsewhere. Dovlatov considered that the Third Wave was making a mistake in trying to create a literature that would tell the truth about the totalitarian system in every detail and at any cost. He believed the task of literature to be higher and at the same time more modest, while also constant: "A true artist reconstructs in depth, without fear and without prejudice, the history of human heart . . ."[53]

During the perestroika period Soviet journals began to take an interest in Dovlatov's stories, and it fell to Andrei Ar'ev, Dovlatov's trusted friend, to prepare them for publication. Dovlatov was excited about the possibility but did not want journals to lay hands on old copies of his stories. On December 2, 1988, he wrote to Ar'ev: "There are old, outdated manuscripts of mine lying around everywhere. They aren't worth looking at. The most awful thing that could happen would be if something from this trash were to find its way into print. This would be much worse than not being recognized."[54]

It was in fact *Filial: Zapiski vedushchego* (*A Branch Office: Notes of an Anchorman*), a story written in the United States, which became Dovlatov's first postemigration publication in the Soviet Union. Dovlatov did not consider this to be his best story and very much hoped that either "Lishnii" ("Superfluous") or "Predstavlenie" ("The Performance") would be published first, but times were still politically sensitive, and it was felt that *A Branch Office* was more neutral. Ar'ev conscientiously fulfilled Dovlatov's wishes. On July 1, 1989, Ar'ev was making corrections to the page proofs of *A Branch Office* and wrote to Dovlatov: "In the lyrical passage in Pavlovsk I also decided in two cases to change the word tram to bus (don't worry, nothing in these sentences begins with letter 'b' and the rhythm of the sentence remains the same.)"[55]

Many of the Third Wave émigrés, including Dovlatov, were fascinated by the fact that there were communists in the United States. In the Soviet Union it was Angela Davis who embodied American communists. Her portrait was familiar to all Soviet citizens, but not a single Soviet person had ever seen or talked to a real live American communist. For this reason meeting the left-wing Slavicist and translator Donald Fiene was of great interest to Dovlatov, as his correspondence with him testifies:

> You should not be surprised by the lively reaction of my friends to the fact that you are a communist. You have to understand. We have never in our lives met idealistic party members. They were all exterminated, wiped out by Stalin a few years before we were born. For us the word "communism" is associated not with social and economic ideas, but with propagandistic clichés. The type of communist that is familiar and customary for us is a gloomy bureaucrat, a hypocrite and a dimwit.[56]

In his fiction he attributes left-wing attitudes to his literary agent Charlie. Dovlatov gets on well with his agent, but cannot hide his surprise at his ideals and asks the usual naive questions: "You hate capitalism. Why are you so rich then?" (*SS* 3:161). In one of his letters Dovlatov tries to find out from Fiene why Americans become communists voluntarily despite the fact that this was sometimes detrimental to their careers.[57]

Dovlatov had gradually come to realize that America was quite a different country from what he had at first supposed, that it was neither better nor worse, but that America was very varied and, as in other places, everything could be found there. As he writes in *Posledniaia kniga* (*The Last Book*): "the bad and the good, greatness and mediocrity, aggression and equability, carefreeness and pragmatism." He considered America to be a giant refugee camp for refugees from the whole world. A third of these refugees did not speak English any better than Dovlatov himself. He felt that America was so varied that everybody could fit in, and in an interview with Jane Bobko he said he felt at home there.[58] He explained that in some ways he had loved America even before he arrived there: he loved American films, jazz, and literature for their democratism: "for the absence of class barriers, for the great power of understatement, for the astonishing fusion of chastity and sensuality, for the humor and for the intelligible and attainable moral reference points."[59]

At the same time Dovlatov clearly saw the deficiencies of his adopted country. It is difficult to have freedom, he concluded in one of his newspaper articles, because "freedom is equally well disposed to evil and to good" (*SS* 2:423). The restrictions faced by writers in the Soviet Union turned out to have a positive as well as a negative aspect, so that emigrating and becoming free was not such an unambiguous blessing as many thought it would be. Describing the literary trends in emigration, Georgy Vladimov noted that when he was working on his story *Faithful Ruslan,* he all of a sudden realized that for the first time in his life he would not have either a censor or an editor, and would be free of all restrictions. However, there would be no support from friends either, nor would there be any critical advice on his text. Vladimov comments that not many writers were able to cope with this freedom, and he singles out Dovlatov as someone who against all the odds became in emigration such a master short-story writer:

> It seems to me that [. . .] only a few of the young writers who have [established themselves here] have learned to bear the burden of freedom. Of them I would single out Dovlatov. He has come into existence [entirely] in emigration; I believe he had never published a single line of prose in the Soviet Union. And [. . .] he somehow [. . .] understood his task [at once], he understood that freedom must not be squandered but [must be] conserved.

> And thanks to this understanding, Dovlatov has achieved the greatest success of [the] pleiad of writers who have sprung up in the West . . . [He is quite] simply [. . .] a master born in emigration.[60]

What did exile mean for Dovlatov? He accepted America and the American way of life to a large degree, but considered that he and his family, even his daughter Katia, who had arrived in the United States at the age of eleven and learned to speak perfect English, would never fully fit in, although he thought that his son Kolia would feel completely American. In one of his letters to a friend in the Soviet Union he writes that he does not live in America, but in Forest Hills, surrounded by seven thousand compatriots:

> The milieu is not a refined one, but it is the only one that is acceptable. The Americans are kind, open-hearted, cheerful people, helpful and optimistic, but completely alien. Friendship in the Russian sense with all its violent expressions of emotion, last shirts, quarrels, embraces, and tears is unimaginable here. Everything is based on different rules, on independence, on keeping yourself to yourself, on reserve and self-absorption. The word and the notion "privacy"—that is, in a loose translation, "the private sphere," is for the Americans sacred. It is a coat of armor with which they protect themselves from negative emotions.[61]

During the Gorbachev era, when open dialogue became possible and some writers even considered returning to the Soviet Union, Dovlatov, whose success and recognition in the United States was by then considerable, wrote to Donald Fiene (November 14, ca. 1987): "With the years I have become less and less interested in publication at home. Firstly, my books circulate there as it is, secondly, they cannot pay real money, thirdly, a new non-reading generation has grown up and fourthly, I am less and less connected with Russian reality."[62] He did want to go back to the U.S.S.R., but, as he explained in his correspondence with Donald Fiene (November 14, ca. 1987) and Andrei Ar'ev (January 6, 1988), he wanted to arrive with an official invitation: "I would like to come not just as a New York Jew, but as a writer. I am used to this status and I don't want to give it up even for a short period."[63]

In an interview with John Glad, who told Dovlatov that he considered him to be the chronicler of emigration and asked him how he thought Soviet people would react to his writing, Dovlatov replied:

> For some unknown reasons emigration in Russia has always been something substantive, that is, something indispensable. And indeed, there are historical

facts to support this: Kurbsky lectured the monarch, Herzen stirred up the whole of Russia for thirty years and almost brought it to revolution. Then there was the famous émigré Vladimir Il'ich Lenin and he did carry out a revolution. The first Soviet government consisted wholly of émigrés. As long as there remains a single émigré writer, his books are going to cost more on the black market than the most renowned Soviet book.[64]

Chapter Three

The Zone

DATES OF ORIGINAL COMPOSITION have not been established for all the stories comprising *Zona: Zapiski nadziratelia* (*The Zone: A Prison Camp Guard's Story*), but many of them were evidently written between 1965 and 1967 and belong among Dovlatov's very earliest works.[1] One of Dovlatov's first readers of these stories in the late 1960s was the writer Israel Metter, who was an unofficial mentor of young writers. In the introduction to his published correspondence, he recalls his first impressions of reading Dovlatov's early stories:

> When I read the stories what struck me was not merely and not particularly the extraordinary ugliness depicted in them, the nightmare of human existence, although that certainly gave me quite a shock—I was astounded by Dovlatov's literary skill, his mature talent, and the originality of his authorial position.[2]

It was evidently these stories or a selection of them under the title *Piat' uglov: Gorodskie rasskazy* (*Fiveways: City Tales*) that were accepted for publication by Eesti Raamat in Tallinn and reached the page-proof stage before being banned.[3] These stories of life in the prison camp were not published in the U.S.S.R. Nor did it prove possible to publish them in the early days of Dovlatov's emigration, although a number of other works were very quickly accepted. Igor' Efimov, who in the early 1980s founded his own émigré publishing house, Hermitage, was at first reluctant to publish them on the grounds that readers were tired of camp literature and would be unwilling to buy such a book. He nevertheless discussed with Dovlatov how best to tie the stories together into a single coherent cycle. Dovlatov felt they would have a greater impact in that form than simply as separate stories. He proposed to establish their coherence through the device of a connecting text:

> *The Zone* can be joined up by a simple device like this—invent a letter from a soldier a dozen pages long and present it in fragments between the stories,

> stretching it out over the whole book. The way Hemingway does it in the book *In Our Time* with his italics. It will come out rather like *The Compromise,* that is to say—unity of place and characters that migrate between one fragment and another. Plus the fragments of the soldier's letter that cement this whole dubious edifice.[4]

Efimov suggested the alternative of uniting the stories by the device of a "comrades' court" (*tovarishcheskii sud*), an idea to which Dovlatov responded positively.[5] "The letter is artificial and excessively literary. And you'd need to extend it into 12 or 13 parts—that's too conventional. But the court is a great idea."[6]

In the event, Dovlatov ultimately adopted neither of these solutions. The individual stories, though retaining their independent status, lost their separate titles and were linked by the device of letters to the editor, ostensibly letters from Dovlatov to Efimov, which describe the (fictional) process by which they were smuggled out of the Soviet Union and which discuss, in a conversational tone and a very free structure, many issues pertaining to their composition and to literature in general. The final work thus consists of an alternation between the commentary contained in the letters, which is printed in italics, and the stories themselves, which are untitled and printed in roman. Evidently Dovlatov had from the outset intended the commentary to have such a meta-narrative character. While still thinking in terms of the "comrades' court" device, and at a point when he was planning to open with the story "Po priamoi" ("Straight Ahead")—which is the last story in the final version—he had written to Efimov:

> After that I can write the court episodes and other intermediate sections, something in a pseudo-documentary vein, with the course of the "literary process" laid bare, that is to say—with the laboratory open to view and the devices unconcealed. So that the stories, even when they have become fragments of the book—remain as fiction, while the links, printed, let's say, in italics, should be documentary, in a free manner, straightforward and frank. Many people write like that these days, so that it won't be felt as mannered, the author takes part in the narration, as it were, and so on. Like Vonnegut in "Slaughterhouse."[7]

There was another reason for Efimov's misgivings. He was deeply suspicious of a new principle Dovlatov had introduced into his writing: an insistence that no two words in a sentence should begin with the same letter. Dovlatov explained this in detail in a letter to Naum Sagalovsky a few years later:

> I have to tell you a terrible secret. Or more precisely, share a literary secret with you. Only please do not think that I have gone mad.
>
> The point is that I have a sort of theory. I think that every prose writer has to put on some creative fetters, to introduce some discipline into his writing. In poetry rhyme and meter fulfill the role of such fetters. This discipline protects poets from verbosity and vacuity. Prose does not have such formal frames and I think one has to introduce them artificially. This is particularly true for those who do not possess by nature the kind of infallible selection mechanism that Zoshchenko had. It is well known that for ten years the famous French writer Georges Perec did not use in his prose the letter "*e*," which is the most popular letter in the French alphabet. As far as I am concerned, for the past six years I have written in such a way that all the words in a sentence begin with different letters. This even applies to prepositions. Even in quotations I avoid using two words in a sentence starting with the same letter. For example, in *The Sanctuary* I quote Pushkin: "And common folk shall keep the (people's) path well-trodden."[8] I could not use the original lines by Pushkin because there were two words in that line beginning with the letter "*n*" in Russian, so I had to change the word to "sacred" path: "And common folk shall keep the sacred path well-trodden . . ." I then made a footnote: "A distorted quotation. Pushkin has 'people's path.' " I had to reconcile myself to the particle "*ne*," as I could not think of anything. In short, this has become a psychosis for me.[9]

In June 1982 Dovlatov completed work on the manuscript of *The Zone* and sent it to Efimov, who wrote on June 18 that he had opened the manuscript with some trepidation on account of his anxiety about this new principle. However, when Efimov read the text, he was persuaded that it did work. He considered it a great improvement on the texts he had read fifteen years before.

> When the material all existed in the form of stories there was a heavy burden laid upon each story; it had to have a plot, and a deeper meaning, and a sub-text shmub-text. And many of them couldn't bear that weight and started cracking and drowning. Now, though, it has all acquired a much more natural form. And all the stories bind together into a single picture, into a natural recreation of the world that astonished you—the world of the Zone.[10]

Efimov wrote that he now found the book excellent and was delighted he had agreed to publish it. The first edition of *The Zone* was published in 1982.

Efimov, of course, was correct in saying that there was an abundance of prison camp literature. Prisons and torture chambers were always inherent in Russian life. But it was only in the twentieth century that they became such a commonplace feature in the life of the average citizen. Russian prison literature goes back to the seventeenth century, to Avvakum, who in the first autobiography in Russian literature, *Zhitie protopopa Avvakuma, im samim napisannoe, i drugie ego sochineniia* (1672–75; *The Life of Archpriest Avvakum*), describes the ordeals he suffered. This first example of prison camp literature was published in 1861, almost two hundred years after it was written, the same year as Dostoevsky's *Notes from the House of the Dead.* Shalamov, Solzhenitsyn, Siniavsky, Dombrovsky, Ginzburg, Aleshkovsky, and many others following in the footsteps of Dostoevsky and Chekhov write of unimaginable hardships: cold, pain, terror, hunger, weariness, exclusion from humanity, exile in marshes and forests. But they also write of exhilaration, commitment, hope, the longing for a home. It was Solzhenitsyn's *Odin den' Ivana Denisovicha* (*One Day in the Life of Ivan Denisovich*) which signaled in 1962 the rebirth of this genre in Soviet literature, and he became one of the main exponents of prison camp literature. His talent and courage brought him worldwide recognition. Many memoirs, novels, stories, poems, and songs have been written on this theme. Practically all of the aforementioned writers experienced prison life firsthand, and prison literature is written almost exclusively from the viewpoint of the victim. Dovlatov, however, was a camp guard and thus literally on the other side of the fence, and he utilized this experience in his narrative standpoint. *The Zone* thus embodied a novel approach to prison camp literature. If world prison literature operates within two basic moral reference points—the convict is a victim and correspondingly the regime is the negative force, or the convict is evil and the punitive forces are positive—then according to Dovlatov there is a third stance: the victims and the oppressors are extremely similar. "The high-security prisoners and the camp guards are incredibly similar. Such is the effect of reciprocal influence. On the two sides of the barbed wire is a single cruel world" (*SS* 3:17). Dovlatov's *Zone* deliberately surmounts the barbed wire that divides Russia and makes the prison experience everybody's property: everyone is an accomplice in history.

Discussing his use of the letters as a framing device, Dovlatov pointed to the example of American literature; however, there are classical examples from Boccaccio's *Decameron* to E. T. A. Hoffmann's *Serapion Brothers,* which have a freely framed text with a commentary that establishes the connection between the stories. As Dovlatov noted in his letter to Efimov, such devices were not unusual in the prose of the time. Contemporary examples from the 1960 and '70s include Vasily Belov's *Plotnitskie rasskazy* (*A Carpenter's Tales*) and Maia Danini's *Den' rozhdenia* (*Birthday*). In Dovlatov's case, the letters enable the author to put into the perspective of the time of publication stories that were written in the 1960s. This "playing at genre" (*igra v zhanr*), as Miroslav Drozda defines it, is part of the narrative structure:

> A constituent part of the narrative mask is this "playing at genre substitution," i.e., signaling that the text belongs to a different type (genre) of communication from that to which it belongs in fact. [. . .] The author, as he "plays at genre," can either attempt to create its complete illusion (for example, Babel in the story "A Letter" from the *Red Cavalry* cycle), or can employ the appropriate signals with the purpose of producing an ironical effect.[11]

In using the letters Dovlatov aims to create and succeeds in creating the complete illusion of a document, establishing a double time frame and telling the story of his life in exile in parallel with his earlier experiences. The brutal experience of service as a camp guard clearly affected Dovlatov's narrative style in *The Zone.* The work is like fragments of a frieze, which the reader has to assemble for himself. Some of the component stories were initially published separately, and, when collected in their final form, were printed in a sequence different from that of initial publication. Moreover, in none of the collected editions does the sequence of the parts correspond to any perceptible chronological sequence in the fictional world. The individual parts explore particular facets of experience, without presenting the totality of that experience as specifically cumulative. *The Zone* is held together by narrative voice. In spite of the seemingly unstructured nature of *The Zone,* there is an overall plot to be discerned, concerning the moral and intellectual development of the narrator. The linking of the stories into an integral whole is established principally by the commentary provided by the letters, but also by analogies in structure, and by the use of a single narrator. The relative independence of the stories is achieved through the "autonomy" of the related event.

Dovlatov also uses the letters to account for the fragmentation of the narrative. He establishes a distance between himself as author and the narrator in the fictional part of the book, who is given the name Boris Alikhanov. Alikhanov is presented in the third person at the beginning of the book, but he later appears only as a first-person narrator, and by the last chapter he is virtually indistinguishable from the author. The letters contain comments, explanations (of camp slang, for instance), biographical notes, and so on. They are dated approximately fifteen to seventeen years later than the action of the stories and shed light on the author's feelings and the transformation that he has experienced in the meantime:

> I was shaken by the depth and variety of life. I saw how low a man could fall, and how high he was able to rise.

> For the first time, I understood what freedom is, and cruelty, and violence. I saw freedom behind window bars, cruelty as senseless as poetry, violence as common as dampness.
>
> I saw a man who had been completely reduced to an animal state. I saw what he could be gladdened by. And it seemed to me that my eyes opened. (*Z*, 13; *SS* 2:16)

In Karen Ryan-Hayes's view, "[the letters] establish the dual, almost schizophrenic spatio-temporal situation of the text; the 'here and now' of America contrasts radically with the 'then and there' of the Komi prison camp."[12] Dovlatov responded in his writing to crucial, perhaps traumatic, life experiences. The GULAG brought him impressions that conflicted sharply with his previous life experience and cultural assumptions. "His tolerance and self-deprecation derive from seeing human nature at its most extreme—cruelty and utter disregard for life juxtaposed with deep compassion and sensitivity."[13]

Dovlatov also uses the letters to introduce his sociopolitical and philosophical thoughts, some of which were taking shape while he was still in the army. For example, discussing human nature, Dovlatov writes to his father: "I understood that the foundations of society rest on self-interest, terror, and venality. Or to express it in poetic language: 'On three great whales the earth is set: venality, self-interest, and fear [*Zemlia stoit na trekh bol'shikh kitakh: / Prodazhnost', sebialiubie i strakh*]' "[14] In *The Zone* this takes the form of a fictional letter to Efimov dated March 11, 1982:

> The foundations of society rest on self-interest, terror, and venality. The conflict between dream and reality has persisted through the millennia. Instead of the harmony desired on earth, chaos and disorder reign.
>
> What is more, we discover something similar within ourselves. We thirst for perfection, while vulgarity triumphs throughout. (*Z*, 38; *SS* 2:39)

As was mentioned in chapter 1, Dovlatov wrote a considerable number of poems while in the army and subsequently used the ideas expressed in them in later stories. For example, his poem "Pogonia" ("Chase"), which is subtitled "Veselaia pesenka" ("A Merry Song"), has nothing merry in it. It is an attempt to express horrific killings in a calm and dispassionate tone, such as he later used in many of his stories:

> The trail trickles over the snow
> Like a line across the page
> And death dangles like a drop
> On the tip of a bayonet

The forest waves beneath the wind
And the forest understands
That where the trail gives out
A wooden cross will stand
The snow glints like a tile
The road is long
And death dangles like a drop
On the tip of a bayonet.

A sled po snegu katitsia
Kak po listu stroka
I smert' visit, kak kapel'ka
Na konchike shtyka
Pod vetrom les kachaetsia
I ponimaet les,
Chto tam, gde sled konchaetsia
Sosnovyi budet krest
A sneg sverkaet kafelem
Doroga daleka
I smert' visit, kak kapel'ka
Na konchike shtyka.[15]

Dovlatov experienced in his duties as a guard an estrangement from his environment and an incompatibility with familiar modes of behavior. This feeling is transferred to his fictional narrator. Dovlatov's narrator Alikhanov feels isolated and lonely: "A smile both absentminded and anxious played constantly over his face. An intellectual can always be recognized by that smile, even on the taiga" (*Z*, 24; *SS* 2:25). In a letter to his father Dovlatov expresses the relation he perceived between the experience he had undergone and the narrative manner in which it can be expressed: "I also know that a person who even once in his life has experienced serious danger or has known great fear will never be a poser or a windbag."[16]

As mentioned, the distance between the protagonist Alikhanov and the author fluctuates as the narration moves from third person to first. One story describes events on New Year's Eve when the whole team of armed and drunken camp guards, including Alikhanov ("We have been drunk since Constitution Day"), rape a woman.[17] Alikhanov is not quite sure how he could have fallen so low. The author-figure, using the third-person narrative, distances himself from Alikhanov completely and refers to him simply as a "guard," "the guard looked round" (*nadziratel' ogliadelsia*). In later stories, however, where Alikhanov becomes the first-person narrator, the confessional intonation inherent in first-person utterances emphasizes the illusion of an intimate relationship with the reader, and this intimacy helps to identify the narrator with the author. It can thus be seen that Dovlatov used the alternation of narrative viewpoint as a means of expressing an unstable emotional state.

Dovlatov aimed to express the atrocities he had experienced in neutral tones, making the impact even more powerful. He wrote to his father: "You noticed that we talk calmly and even merrily about various horrendous things. I am glad that you noticed this. It is very typical for us."[18] The most Dovlatov's narrator says after going through a horrendous experience when a gang of prisoners attacked him with a knife is: "For a moment I felt a sickening chill in my stomach" (Z, 111; *SS* 2:105–6). Attacks (particularly knife attacks) on armed camp guards and military personnel are depicted as commonplace. This is reflected in one of the poems Dovlatov wrote in the army:

Let me just come out alive
Let me just survive
Let me not betray myself
When threatened with a knife.

Mne b tol'ko vybrat'sia zhivym
Mne b tol'ko vyzhit'
Mne b pod udarom nozhevym
Sebia ne vydat'.[19]

One of the camp guards tells the story of how some prisoners set about sawing his head off with a chain saw:

"Once in the logging sector they wanted to saw off my head with a Friendship brand power-saw."

"So what happened?" I asked.

"Well, what do you think happened? I took away the power-saw and smashed a guy's face in."

"That explains that."

"Then there was the business with an ax in a transit station."

"So? How did it end?"

"I took away the ax, gave this fellow one in the jaw . . ."

"I see."

"Once a zek high on *chifir* came at me with a knife."

"So you took the knife and punched him in the face?"

Bortashevich looked at me closely, then unbuttoned his fatigue shirt. I saw a small, white, soul-chilling scar. (Z, 125; *SS* 2:117–18)

There is a moving poem written by Dovlatov in 1962 about the killing of one of the soldiers on sentry post, while the other soldiers were on military maneuvers:

We stood in silence by the grave
Our grey coats gave us no warmth
The women prayed for us as in the war
As in the war, they took pity on the soldiers.

My stoiali molcha u mogily
Nas ne greli serye shineli
Baby, kak v voinu za nas molilis'
Kak v voinu, soldat oni zhaleli.[20]

There remains beneath Dovlatov's narrative much that is left unsaid about the tragedy of the camps and of the hardships which innocent people are caught up in and have to endure. He does not make any overt attempt to elicit compassion, but the effect on the reader is all the stronger for such reticence. This quality is particularly noticeable when suffering is described. Dovlatov was not concerned to evoke the horrors of the prison camps in the way that was prevalent at the time.[21] For Dovlatov/Alikhanov, there is a distinct therapeutic element in his writing, as testified in a letter to his father. "And, of course, poetry helps me out, too."[22] In *The Zone* Dovlatov formulates this in one of the "letters to the publisher": "My writing became an addition to life. An addition without which life would have been completely obscene" (*Z*, 22; *SS* 2:24).

While Dovlatov was working on the first edition of *The Zone* he wrote an article, "SSSR—Bol'shaia zona" ("The USSR—One Big Camp"), for *Novyi Amerikanets,* which he was then editing.[23] In this article Dovlatov describes some of the more horrific events he omitted from his fiction:

> I remember a night. The camp searchlights. Four lorries with their headlights directed at the Zone.
>
> Under the lights I see snow, black with blood. A nineteen-year-old lad with his stomach shot to pieces. He isn't screaming any more. He's just twitching his legs very rapidly. As though he's still running somewhere . . .
>
> There's a crowd of guards all round. The dog-handlers are restraining the eager dogs. Lieutenant Tvauri gives an order:
>
> "Finish him off!"
>
> "What about socialist legality?" I say.
>
> "I'll show you socialist legality," shouts Tvauri, "our law is the taiga!"[24]

In spite of all the horror and hardship, Dovlatov also expresses gratitude to his fate for those years. He is grateful that he survived, where many did not. He names some of his friends who died: Grigory Dermenzhi got lost in the taiga. Barkovets was forcibly drowned in an ice-hole. Oleg Sukhanov was knifed. Kondrashin met the most terrible death. The criminals put a plank on his chest and proceeded to jump up and down on him. Dovlatov admits that among the many books written by the victims of the regime there are many deservedly bitter words about the guards. While giving his due to the victims, he also asks for consideration toward the guards, whose life in the army is difficult and humiliating. Who are the guards? Mostly young, nineteen- or twenty-year-old conscripts. "Who taught them this savage job—guarding living people with automatic weapons?" asks Dovlatov. "Is it the corrupt komsomol? Or is it their parents, stupefied by work and alcohol? The life and death of a prisoner depends on these brutalized youngsters."

In the article "The USSR—One Big Camp" Dovlatov also explains the somewhat paradoxical fact that around the camps there are many settlements in which 90 percent of the inhabitants are former prisoners, who go on living there according to the unwritten laws of camp life: "Don't humiliate yourself by asking for things! Don't be afraid of death! Trust only yourself! And above all—always get your blow in first!"[25] It is puzzling that after finishing their sentences, the prisoners settle in these inhospitable places and do not try to return home and forget it all. One possible explanation is given by a doctor, who has spent thirty years imprisoned in the camps. His family has forgotten him, he would not be able to get used to life in Moscow again, to the wheeling and dealing it required. He also considered that here he was free, he did not have to pretend and lie, he could say to people whatever he thought. It is not surprising, Dovlatov concludes, because "this state of many millions of people lives by the laws of criminals . . ."[26] This is what makes life identical on both sides of the barbed wire.

A characteristic feature of Dovlatov's stories is the final twist in the plot. For Dovlatov, as for Chekhov, plot is secondary, and Viktor Shklovsky's description of Chekhov's endings can equally be applied to Dovlatov: "Chekhov created a kind of plotless prose. In the last lines everything is turned round, given new meaning and sound, experienced afresh. Test this on 'Rothschild's Violin' and 'Gooseberries,' on stories that resemble biographies; they contain a road upwards and a backward glance."[27] It is usually a slight detail that provokes the shift, but such an ending transforms the whole story, and the last line makes the reader rethink and reevaluate the text. Eikhenbaum considered this to be one of the typical features of the American short story: "Thus, the novella built on the principle of structural unity, centralization of the main effect, and a strong emphasis on the ending is typical for American literature. [. . .] The surprise of the ending takes on the nature of a game with the plot and with the expectations of the reader."[28] One of the stories in *The Zone* is about the tough, uncompromising, and thoroughly brutalized camp doctor Iavshits. He appears inured to others' suffering, and even if someone came to him with their head torn off, he would not bat an eyelid. In a dispassionate tone, Dovlatov/Alikhanov tells his story about how the prisoners (all criminals, sentenced for murder, robbery, violence) decide to kill an informer, Onuchin (also a violent criminal). Alikhanov is on duty; he knows the prisoners are planning to kill Onuchin, but he doesn't need to bother, as nobody is going to blame him. Needless to say, human life costs nothing, and the prisoners would not think twice before killing the guard as well. After all, they have nothing to lose. In the end both Onuchin and Alikhanov survive. The story is told in a simple, indifferent, even slightly monotonous tone. The author introduces several irrelevant interruptions into the narrative: the drilling of new recruits, descriptions of the quarters where the dog instructors live, how southerners suffer from cold in the army, and so on. There is only one remark that gives away his feelings: "For a moment I felt a sickening chill in my stomach" (*Z*, 111; *SS* 2:105–6). On the face of it, everything is well. Nothing in the narrative betrays the real emotional state of the narrator, which is revealed suddenly by an exceptional and unanticipated remark by the doctor: "Well, why are you crying? Wait, at least let me shut the door" (*Z*, 112; *SS* 2:107).

Perhaps the most vivid example of an unexpected ending is the story in which the narrator, attempting to force the recidivist Kuptsov to do some work, thrusts an ax into his hand. The reader, knowing something of the past history of their relations, half expects the ax to be used on the narrator, but Kuptsov asserts his freedom in a completely unexpected way—by chopping off his own hand. This story underwent various revisions. Initially it bore the title "Marsh odinokikh" ("March of the Lonely") and was also at one stage entitled "Kuptsov i drugie" ("Kuptsov and Others").[29] Later Dovlatov incorporated this story into the cycle *The Zone,* where it lost its title and was placed as the penultimate story after the letter of March 19. He had previously submitted the story "March of the Lonely" to various journals in the Soviet Union. The unpublished 1976 variant of *The Invisible Book* contains some fictional reviews of it, allegedly from editors, internal reviewers, or readers of various Soviet journals.[30] Dovlatov uses these "reviews" to offer comments upon the ending of this story. Is it a victory for Kuptsov? To a certain extent it is, although, as is also noted, this does not mean it is a defeat for the protagonist. In the course of the story the protagonist overcomes fear, and that is his triumph.

> The only real force in opposition to the hero is the Zone, the criminal world. And the hero enters the Zone, asserts himself in the struggle with that force,

> gets a knife in his back, and triumphs. He achieves what he wanted, he is a god, worthy of worship.
>
> And then Kuptsov appears. Another god, his antithesis, the last preserver of the thieves' "law."
>
> And Kuptsov wins. He has a different, harsh scale of values, and hopelessness is the pledge of his victory. He triumphs by throwing his wife to the executioners. He triumphs by performing in the name of the "law" a feat on a scale close to antiquity.
>
> How does the struggle for spiritual power, for the assertion of one's own personality in the world, end? Yes, it is possible to win, but only at the price of one's own blood.[31]

Kuptsov's act of chopping his hand off is the culminating symbol of an insistence on freedom and personality. Dovlatov's narrator is traumatized by this event, and is unable to return to his old values. Lipovetsky, is, of course, correct in considering that "Kuptsov professes a profoundly existential principle: the lone man is always right . . ."[32] Dovlatov comes to see this other Boris (significantly, Kuptsov's first name is also Boris, as is Alikhanov's) as his twin. The idea of Kuptsov being Alikhanov's double is introduced first in a letter to the publisher dated March 19, 1982, in which the authorial voice says the following about the similarity between prisoners and guards: "We were very similar to each other, and even interchangeable" (Z, 47) ("My byli pokhozhi i dazhe—vzaimozameniamy"; *SS* 2:47). This similarity is developed in a number of elements in the story. Kuptsov is described thus: "There seemed to be a steering wheel in front of him, and his ship seemed to be moving straight into the wind" (Z, 54; *SS* 2:54). The image of the wind is constantly associated with Kuptsov throughout the cycle: "He made me think of a man walking against the wind, as if the wind had chosen him as a permanent adversary, wherever he walked, whatever he did" (Z, 52; *SS* 2:51). And of the camp guards and Alikhanov in particular, Dovlatov writes: "Our weather-beaten faces were colored with purple blotches" (Z, 47; *SS* 2:46). In a poem dedicated to Dovlatov by V. Belanenko, the author of many prison songs, the motif of wind is also present:

> Sergei, you see, the wind's against us,
> It beats in our faces, the way men beat others for their baseness.
> We do not care. We plant our feet in the mud,
> We play at being important and severe.
>
> Sergei, ty vidish', veter protiv nas,
> On b'et v litso, kak chasto b'iut za podlost'

Nam vse ravno. My stavim nogi v griaz',
V znachitel'nost' igraem i v surovost'.[33]

Kuptsov and Alikhanov meet at a point in the story when the psychologically unstable guard Petrov, nicknamed Fidel, is keeping a group of prisoners in an icy river at gunpoint. The situation is rescued by Kuptsov, who fearlessly and calmly confronts Fidel (according to the regulations he could have been shot): "I'll put you out" (Z, 52), says Kuptsov. To Alikhanov, the narrator, who witnesses this scene, Kuptsov appears as someone battling against the wind. He admires Kuptsov's courage and would like to be similarly fearless. He deliberately walks across the dangerous parts of the zone in order to get used to the feeling of terror. The idea that Kuptsov and Alikhanov are doubles and are interchangeable has a parallel in the final story of the cycle (which formerly had the title "Straight Ahead"), in which Alikhanov as narrator becomes a prisoner and is taken by Fidel to the detention cell. His friend Fidel has a loaded gun pointing at his back. The protagonist feels anger, blaming Fidel as if he were the sole cause of all his misfortunes. But when the protagonist turns round, he winces on seeing Fidel's face. He walks toward him: "Fidel threw down the submachine gun and started to cry, and for some reason pulled off his sheepskin jacket and tore open his fatigue shirt, all the buttons flying off. I walked up and stood beside him. 'All right,' I said, 'let's go' " (Z, 176; *SS* 2:167).

What causes this breakdown in Fidel? In one of the stories (formerly entitled "Golos" ["The Voice"]), Fidel confesses to Alikhanov that, although he is not a believer, he was praying, because guarding criminals is simply unbearable:

> Dear Lord! What do You hate me for? Even though I'm a no-good shit, I am clean before the law. After all, I've never stolen anything. I just drink. And even that not every day. [. . .] Dear Lord! Do You see this brothel, I hope? Can You understand what guard duty means? [. . .] See to it that I don't drink myself to death. (Z, 28; *SS* 2:29)

In his article "The USSR—One Big Camp," Dovlatov concludes that the life of the prisoners in the camp and that of the guards in the barracks is the same: "The people leaving the Zone and those leaving the barracks are cruel, sullen, broken. And if this is a school, then it's a school of violence and evil . . ."[34]

Another example of their interchangeability comes in the repetition of an almost identical dialogue. When Alikhanov confronts Kuptsov and tries to make him work, Kuptsov protests: "How about feeding yourself? Does the Law allow that? There's no law that says I have to starve" (Z, 55; *SS*

2:54). Mirroring this, when the narrator himself becomes a prisoner, he says to Captain Tokar': "I should have something to eat. You don't have the right to starve me to death" (Z, 168; *SS* 2:157). Although it was probably Kuptsov who knifed him in an earlier episode, Alikhanov cannot stop thinking about Kuptsov and cannot stop admiring him. He gradually understands that "this last upholder of the Law in the Ust Vym complex was my double. [. . .] We were one. Because the only person you could hate that much was yourself" ("etot poslednii zakonnik ust'-vymskogo lagpunkta—moi dvoinik. [. . .] Chto my—odno. Potomu chto tak nenavidet' mozhno tol'ko odnogo sebia") (Z, 61; *SS* 2:61).

The theme of human loneliness, the loss of the feeling of unity with the world, is one of the main topics of twentieth-century literature. The process of the transformation of the hero into an "antihero" who fully realizes his own alienation from the world is often attributed to the influence of existentialist philosophy in the literature of the postwar period. However, it has been shown that the roots of this existentialist philosophy go back to Dostoevsky.[35] Dovlatov's reading of Dostoevsky is woven into the whole cycle of *The Zone*. In one scene Kuptsov is trying to make sense of a book he has read in which a man kills an old woman for money and is so tormented by his conscience that he voluntarily goes to the camp. To this Kuptsov then juxtaposes a story about a man who killed many people but was never caught and went on enjoying life into old age, teaching music, surrounded by grandchildren. Dostoevsky conflates the suffering that is inflicted on the innocent and the suffering that is experienced by those who inflict it. Dovlatov's succinct "Hell is in us ourselves [*Ad—eto my sami*]" (Z, 3) has to be read in a similar way.

In one of the ostensible letters to the editor Dovlatov emphasizes that his manuscript is not a complete work, but a kind of diary: "chaotic notes, a set of unorganized material" (Z, 4). He also adds, however, that there is a "general artistic plot" ("obshchii khudozhestvennyi siuzhet"; *SS* 2:8) to be discovered. Elsewhere he spoke of the style of New Orleans jazz as "entrancing chaos" (*voskhititel'nyi khaos*),[36] explaining that to an inexperienced and unsophisticated listener to this jazz, it seems at the beginning that the musicians are playing quite independently of each other, creating a chaotic accumulation of sounds, and only after a while is the listener able to grasp its form: "One gradually begins to grasp the harmonious pulse of the whole organism and is finally overwhelmed by the sense of a subtle and complex colorful harmony."[37] Much the same might be said about the composition of Dovlatov's own stories. Il'ia Serman draws attention to the care that Dovlatov lavished on the structure of his work: "Compositional precision is essential to him in order to come to terms with the material, which often carries in his case an element of the absurd."[38] Dovlatov himself often said that his stories were written "like Rozanov's dotted-line narrative" (*rozanovskim punktirom*). I. A. Mart'ianova has likened his writing to "montage," arguing that this "dotted-line" quality is a consciously adopted stylistic method based upon cinematic devices.[39] It has been noted by many critics (Ar'ev, Sukhikh, Genis) that Dovlatov's stories are punctuated by micro-novellas or anecdotes.[40] He had a tremendous sense of drama and used the interspersed micro-novellas to postpone the climax of the story. It might be argued that these micro-novellas in the case of Dovlatov have the same function as the "lyrical digressions" in *Eugene Onegin,* as defined by Vygotsky: "Precisely these digressions are the most important devices for the development and revelation of the plot. [. . .] The so-called digressions in *Eugene Onegin* comprise, of course, the very essence and the fundamental stylistic device in the structure of the entire novel, this is the melody of its plot."[41]

The story "Kuptsov and Others" provides a striking example of the way in which these techniques are employed. It is composed of various background episodes, giving a general flavor of camp life, and linked by brief flashbacks that have the character of a refrain. Interspersed among them are a series of episodes specifically concerned with the relations between the narrator and the recidivist thief, Kuptsov. It is these episodes that constitute the real plot of the story, as the narrator, in his role as guard, does everything in his power to force the thief to work. In the course of this he is stabbed in the back, presumably by Kuptsov, and comes to realize that his loathing of this man has come to be an indispensable part of his own life. The story culminates in Kuptsov severing his own left hand, thus making it impossible to work and winning, in a certain sense, the battle with the guard.

The epigraph to *The Zone* is a deliberate parody of those many novels where the claim is made that any resemblance to real people is accidental:

> The names, events, and dates given here are real. I invented only those details that were not essential.
>
> Therefore, any resemblance between the characters in this book and living people is intentional and malicious. And all the fictionalizing was unexpected and accidental. (Z, 1)

> Imena, sobytiia, daty—vse zdes' podlinnoe. Vydumal ia lish' te detali, kotorye nesushchestvenny.
>
> Poetomu vsiakoe skhodstvo mezhu geroiami knigi i zhivymi liud'mi iavliaetsia zlonamerennym. A vsiakii khudozhestvennyi domysel—nepredvidennym i sluchainym. (*SS* 2:7)

The initial impression is that the writer intends to give priority to "truth," to real life. The resemblance to real people is far from accidental, it is malicious, while it is the "artistic transformation," the "fiction," that is "accidental." But the parody, of course, is only a surface feature. It is instructive to compare this with Nabokov's *Real Life of Sebastian Knight*, where the narrator similarly insists that his priority is a truthful biography, while in reality it is aesthetic considerations that predominate. Despite the similarity to real-life events and the wealth of biographical material in his stories, Dovlatov is not in the first place concerned to depict real life in the camps. This is "pseudo-documentalism." Nabokov emphasizes that he is depicting the "real life" of Sebastian Knight and does not have at his disposal the techniques of a writer of fiction. Dovlatov's statement in the epigraph is almost indistinguishable from this, but as the novel develops it is completely subverted, to show that the "reality" the writer creates is the only one he is able to inhabit. Many crucial elements of *The Zone* come together in the story following the letter of February 23, which in earlier versions bore the title "The Voice." This can be construed as the voice both of the author and of the characters that are introduced into the narrative. The protagonist of "The Voice" is Alikhanov and the narrative is in the third person. The author clearly identifies himself with his alter ego Alikhanov: he is thinking about himself in the third person; his life has turned into the material of fiction: "Life has become malleable. It could be changed with the movement of a pencil with cold, hard facets and relief inscription 'Orion' " (Z, 36; *SS* 2:37).

Viktor Kulle sees this epigraph as revealing the principal aim of Dovlatov's prose:

> the priority of "artistic texture" over "artistic invention." This is a kind of relationship between the artist and the word which is relatively rare in our literature, when writing is not a means for the assertion or comprehension of a truth, for the improvement of society, or for moral self-perfection. The sole aim and meaning of writing is writing itself, "belles lettres" as such.[42]

Even before the Russian publication of *The Zone*, Dovlatov's translator Anne Frydman was simultaneously working on its translation.[43] Some of the stories appeared separately in English; the story "Po priamoi" ("Straight Ahead"), for example, was published in the *New Yorker* in January 1982.[44] On its appearance Dovlatov received a letter from Kurt Vonnegut congratulating him on such a brilliant story. Although Dovlatov was very pleased, he remarked sadly: "However much I might publish in English, nobody will ever write about my language, so to speak, and that is the only thing, as I am brash enough to believe, that is of any interest."[45]

Some of the stories in *The Zone* Dovlatov considered somewhat outdated and possibly still not quite satisfactory. In a letter to Anne Frydman he told her that he was writing a long story about the camps. The story is about high-security prisoners who rehearse and then perform a revolutionary play in which thieves and murderers, crooks and bandits play the roles of Lenin, Dzerzhinsky, and others.

> Maybe it would be worth replacing two or three short, bad stories in the English edition of *The Zone* with one better one. *The Zone* was written a very long time ago and there's a lot of rubbish in it. [. . .] It would be very easy to insert a new piece. It just needs to be successful, but at present Lena says it's quite funny.[46]

Dovlatov probably completed "The Performance" in the summer of 1983. On August 8 he sent the story to Anne Frydman, saying that he considered it much better than many in *The Zone.*[47] In November 1983 Dovlatov informed Efimov that in order to improve and enlarge the English edition of *The Zone,* he had added a story, a comedy from life in the camps. He was keen to publish the Russian text and submitted this story for publication in Maksimov's *Kontinent.*[48] Maksimov, who was not on good terms with Dovlatov, said he would nevertheless publish it, because although Dovlatov was a scoundrel, the story was very funny.[49]

The story in question (like practically all the stories in *The Zone*) initially had a title: "Predstavlenie" ("The Performance"), and this title is used in a number of publications.[50] This is one of his stories that has most frequently been discussed. Dovlatov himself considered it one of his most successful. It echoes Dostoevsky's *Notes from the House of the Dead,* chapter 11 of which is similarly entitled "Predstavlenie" ("The Performance"). Il'ia Serman in "Teatr Sergeia Dovlatova" considers that this was quite deliberate: "The play creates with its theme a temporal distance of half a century, the title of the story extends it even further, to the middle of the nineteenth century. The reader inevitably follows the path of historical juxtapositions and the analogies suggested to him by the story."[51] There are a number of analogies between Dovlatov's story and Dostoevsky's. The most crucial of them is that Dostoevsky challenges the nineteenth-century view of man's essential goodness, demonstrating that there is evil in every human being. Dovlatov similarly considers that evil is within us: "Hell is in us ourselves" (Z, 3). Dovlatov showed, however, that suffering does not ennoble people (as Dostoevsky thought), but makes people indifferent, and the difference between victims and torturers fades away.

In describing the convicts' play "Kedril-Obzhora," Dostoevsky uses the term "people's theater" (*narodnyi teatr*) to denote a tradition maintained by generations of prisoners:

> Just imagine prison, shackles, imprisonment, long sad years ahead, life as monotonous as drops of water on a grey autumn day. And all of a sudden all these downtrodden and imprisoned men were allowed to enjoy themselves for an hour, to forget the bad dream and give themselves completely to the theater.[52]

Dostoevsky's *Notes from the House of the Dead* claims to be the memoir of a murderer, described by the narrator. His attitude to the prisoners is quite different from Dovlatov's; he is surprised by their hostility. Dovlatov's "The Performance" is a first-person narrative: the author and narrator in this story are indistinguishable. In this story some prisoners are forced to take part and the rest of the prisoners are forced to watch. The play they perform, "Kremlevskie zvezdy" ("Kremlin Stars"), is by a fictional playwright, Iakov Chichel'nitsky.[53] It is dedicated to the sixtieth anniversary of the October Revolution. There are four participants in Chichel'nitsky's play: Lenin, Dzerzhinsky, Timofei—a Cheka agent—and his fiancée Polina. The young security officer is under the influence of Polina, a member of the bourgeoisie. Lenin is preoccupied with the health of Dzerzhinsky, whose work for the good of the revolution is doing him harm. He is trying to make Dzerzhinsky take a break from work in order to recuperate and restore his health. The fact that Dzerzhinsky is prepared to carry on working, sacrificing himself to the cause of the revolution, impresses Timofei very much, and he becomes more selfless. Polina reluctantly follows suit. In the story, it is hardened criminals who play all the roles, except that of Polina, who is played by a "free" woman from the nearby village. This is how the camp director, a general, addresses the prisoners before the play:

> Revolutionary holidays touch every Soviet citizen. Even those who have temporarily stumbled . . . killed someone, stolen, raped, in general made some kind of stir . . . The Party gives to these people the opportunity to reform, leads them through unrelenting physical labor toward socialism. In short, all hail the jubilee of our Soviet government. But as for drunkards and smokers, we will, as they say, call them to account . . . not to mention sodomists. As it is, half the she-goats in the area have been messed with, you no-good—. (Z, 149)

> Revoliutsionnye prazdniki kasaiutsia vsekh sovetskikh grazhdan . . . Dazhe liudei, kotorye vremenno otstupilis' . . . Kogo-to ubili, ograbili, iznasilovali, v obshchem, nadelali shorokhu . . . Partiia daet etim liudiam vozmozhnost' ispravit'sia . . . Vedet ikh cherez upornyi fizicheskii trud k sotsializmu . . . Koroche, da zdravstvuet iubilei nashego Sovetskogo gosudarstva! . . . A s p'ianykh i nakurennykh, kak govoritsia, budem vzyskivat' . . . Ne govoria o

skotolozhstve. A to polovinu sosedskikh koz oguliali, mat' vashu za nogu! . . . (*SS* 2:139–40)

There is no doubt that in the 1960s and '70s the prison, the camp, the "zone" was perceived as part of the social structure. S. Borisov, in "Motivy nepriiatia sotsial'no politicheskogo ustroistva SSSR v fol'klore zakliuchennykh 1970–kh godov" ("Motifs of the Nonacceptance of the Social and Political Organization of the USSR in the Folklore of Convicts in the 1970s") in *Fol'klor GULAGa* (*GULAG Folklore*), comes to the conclusion that "it is possible to speak of a peculiar 'dissidence' of the lower social groups passing through the GULAG, which is distinct from, but in part consistent with, the nonconformism of the intelligentsia."[54] In Dovlatov's eyes the boundaries of prison are extended to encompass the whole of the Soviet Union. On both sides of the barbed wire is a callous world. *The Zone* is the grotesque world of the Soviet Union of that time. The prisoners and guards that are gathered in *The Zone* condense reality *ad absurdum.* In their worlds the model of the country is reflected with only minor exaggeration. The people that Dovlatov gathered here are ideas, representing particular tendencies which exist beyond the boundaries of the camp. However insane these models might look, we have to bear in mind that any model of society only makes sense to those who share it. This idea is nowhere more clearly expressed than in "The Performance," particularly in its grotesquely moving ending:

> The multitude of faces joined into one trembling spot. The actors onstage froze. Lebedyeva pressed her hands to her temples. Khuriev waved his cleaning rod. A strange, dreamy smile set on the lips of the leader of the Revolution.
>
> "No more shall chains of violence bind us,
> Arise you slaves, no more in thrall,
> The earth shall rise on new foundations . . ."
>
> Suddenly, my throat contracted painfully. For the first time, I was part of my unique, unprecedented country. I was entirely made of cruelty, hunger, memory, malice . . . Because of my tears, I couldn't see for a moment. (*Z*, 157)

> Mnozhestvo lits slilos' v odno drozhashchee piatno. Artisty na sstene zamerli. Lebedeva szhimala rukami viski. Khuriev razmakhival shompolom. Na gubakh vozhdia revoliutsii zastyla strannaia mechtatel'naia ulybka. . . .
>
> . . . Ves' mir nasil'ia my razrushim
> Do osnovan'ia, a zatem . . .
>
> Vdrug u menia boleznenno szhalos' gorlo. Vpervye ia byl chast'iu moei osobennoi, nebyvaloi strany. Ia tselikom sostoial iz zhestokosti, goloda, pamiati, zloby . . . Ot slez ia na minutu poterial zrenie. (*SS* 2:147)

The protagonist, who up to this point was alienated from everybody, realizes that he, too, is made of "cruelty, hunger, memory, malice." "In the finale of 'The Performance' a manifest 'laying bare of the device' takes place. The juxtaposition of theater and life, of the world of socialist illusions and the zone is only possible on the basis of the absurd—it is precisely the absurd that unites them."[55] This becomes obvious not only to the narrator, but also to all of the characters in the story, write Lipovetsky and Leiderman, at the moment when Gurin in the role of Lenin addresses the audience:

> "Who is this?" Gurin exclaimed. "Who is this?"
>
> Out of the darkness, thin pale faces focused on the leader.
>
> "Who is this? Whose are these happy, young faces? Whose are these cheerful, sparkling eyes? Can this really be the youth of the seventies?"
>
> Romantic notes sounded in the voice of the actor. His speech was colored with unfeigned excitement. He gesticulated. His powerful palm, covered with tattoos, swept upward. ["Can these really be the ones we mounted the barricades for?] Can [these] really be the splendid grandchildren of the Revolution?"
>
> At first, there were a few uncertain laughs from the front row. After a few seconds, everyone was laughing hard. (Z, 156)

> — Kto eto?!—voskliknul Gurin.—Kto eto?!
>
> Iz temnoty gliadeli na vozhdia khudye, blednye fizionomii.
>
> — Kto eto?! Ch'i eto schastlivye iunye litsa? Ch'i eto veselye blestiashchie glaza? Neuzheli eto molodezh' semidesiatykh? . . .
>
> V golose artista zazveneli romanticheskie notki. Rech' ego byla okrashena nepoddel'nym volneniem. On zhestikuliroval. Ego sil'naia, pokrytaia tatuirovkoi kist' ukazyvala v nebo.
>
> — Neuzheli eto te, radi kogo my vozvodili barrikady? Neuzheli eto slavnye vnuki revoliutsii? . . .
>
> Snachala neuverenno zasmeialis' v pervom riadu. Cherez sekundu khokhotali vse. (*SS* 2:146)

Lipovetsky sums up Dovlatov's intentions succinctly: "[Dovlatov] used the facts of his own life as material for his 'absurd quest,' proving the paradoxical role of absurdity and chaos as the foundations of human existence, as the only valid sources of personal freedom, and as the forces uniting a person with other people and history."[56]

In the English translation of *The Zone,* Dovlatov confesses that this story is not part of the original version but "a later stratification," yet in the following early poem from the 1960s, this ending is already somehow anticipated:

I who used to read Hegel and Kant
Become more of an animal day by day.
Four times I have been lost at cards.
Then why do I hide my eyes in embarrassment
When I listen to your songs and weep.

Chitavshii ran'she Gegelia i Kanta
Ia zverem stanovlius' den' oto dnia
Ne zria intelligentnogo menia
Chetyrezhdy proigryvali v karty.
No pochemu togda glaza smushchenno priachu
Kogda ia pesni vashi slushaiu i plachu.[57]

In the translation Dovlatov also gives a more detailed explanation of why life on both sides of the wire was just the same. In the letter of June 11[58] (which is completely different in the Russian version; it is about the person who brought this extract to the West), he raises the issue of crimes Soviet people don't even notice:

> Blatant rudeness—isn't that a kind of crime? [. . .] Soviet rudeness takes a legitimate form of injunction. I have read many announcements in my life that startled me, but I especially remember three. The first one I saw on the wall of a Leningrad food store. It read: "THE GUILTY WILL BE PUNISHED!" After that, not a word. A threat ominously addressed into space. (*Z*, 129)

The other two announcements that Dovlatov discusses are "DON'T ASK ANY QUESTIONS!" which "gave off fumes of hopelessness" (and which he saw in the office of the chief of police in Zelenogorsk) and "NOT ALLOWED!!!" (which was on display at a village hospital). In one of his essays on literary topics, "Eto neperevodimoe slovo—*khamstvo*" (*SS* 4:323; "That Untranslatable Word—*Khamstvo*"), Dovlatov expands on this specifically Russian type of rudeness. He attempts the following definition of this untranslatable word:

> *Khamstvo* is nothing other than rudeness, impertinence, churlishness, and all this—multiplied by impunity. The whole point lies precisely in this impunity, in the certainty that these actions cannot be punished and are subject to no law, in the sense of utter helplessness that overcomes the victim. It is by its impunity above all that *khamstvo* lays you low. (*SS* 4:324)

It is the thief Gurin (playing the role of Lenin) who points to the "impunity" of the famous revolutionaries Lenin and Dzerzhinsky, who he claims killed millions of people: "While those two flooded Russia with blood, but that's all right" ("A eti—Rossiiu v krovi potopili, i nichego"); "Those people were the bloodiest no-termers ever" (Z, 146) ("Oni-to i est' samaia krovavaia bespredel'shchina"; *SS* 2:135).

In the Russian version of *The Zone* the letter to the publisher that precedes the "Performance" is the shortest of all the letters. The fictional author expresses his uncertainty: "Everything is crazily mixed up in this world" ("Vse diko zaputalos' na etom svete"; *SS* 2:121). In the previous chapter Alikhanov was ready to believe that the prisoners are basically good and that it is their surroundings that have turned them into criminals: their harrowing lives, the uselessness and the cruelty of the punishments inflicted on them. The narrator comes up with the standard excuses: "But they've been crippled by their lives, wrecked by society" ("No ved' zhizn' iskalechila, sreda zaela"; *SS* 2:119). He is thinking this because he has accepted an invitation to share dinner with the prisoners, only to be told that the rissoles he has eaten were made from Captain Tokar's only friend—his favorite dog Broshka. The nightmarish quality of camp life can be illustrated from almost every page of this work. Nevertheless, Dovlatov expressed disagreement with Shalamov's view that camp experience was unremittingly negative, arguing that there was beauty to be found in it as well. The point is made in a number of the letters in *The Zone,* where the prisoners' deep feelings and the importance of various camp myths (for instance, concerning successful mass escape) are described. Most of all, however, he finds this beauty in language: "And if you only use dark colors, you won't get it right. In my opinion, one of its delicious adornments is language" (Z, 91; *SS* 2:88).

In March 1963 Dovlatov wrote a detective story, "Zavtra budet obychnyi den' " ("Tomorrow Will Be an Ordinary Day").[59] In a letter to his father, he wrote that it was a story about a professional army officer who served all his life in corrective labor camps. The novel (*povest'*—"novella," as he called it) would have to be shortened and turned into a short story (*rasskaz*). Neither the original detective story nor the shortened version is extant, but reworked traces of this old story can be found in "Kapitany na sushe" ("Captains on Land"), which was incorporated into *The Zone* in three parts: part one after the letter of April 17, part two after May 3, and part three after May 17. In this story Dovlatov investigates the problems of fear and cowardice. The story has a plot: Captain Pavel Egorov, a professional officer with a degree in law, serves in the corrective labor camps in Siberia. Egorov gets a long-awaited break and travels to the Black Sea, hoping to relax, buy himself a shirt with parrots on it, and find a woman with not too many prejudices. Instead he meets a romantic postgraduate student, Katia Lugina. Their differences are characterized by the author in the following dialogue:

"Let's talk," she said
"About what, for example?" the captain asked flatly.
"Do you like Heine?"
"More or less."
"And Schiller?"
"And how." . . . (*Z,* 79; *SS* 2:75–76)

In spite of this they get married: he promises to polish up his reading. Katia is impressed with his courage and energy, which distinguishes him from the romantics of the 1960s who surround her. However, even on holiday, Egorov cannot get away from the realities of his life. In Sochi he meets a former prisoner: "sensing, with all his experience and also his skin, trouble ahead. He felt an unpleasant cold twinge in his stomach" (*Z,* 80; *SS* 2:76). He recognizes the man immediately as one of the prisoners he guarded and nearly killed, and it is clear this is not his first confrontation with him. Miraculously Egorov is not knifed; however, during this confrontation his whole life passes before his eyes: first, he imagines his own death, then the roles are reversed and he shoots the former prisoner: "None of this happened. The man sat motionless. It was the motionlessness of an antitank mine" (*Z,* 81; *SS* 2:78). Egorov is aware of how vulnerable he is; his life is not worth anything. Army officers are hated both by the guards and by the prisoners. He is lonely and he is brutalized by his experiences.

In the letter of May 3, Dovlatov writes that Egorov is a brainless and malicious animal, but that in the stories he had made him look quite likeable: "Here we witness the transforming power of art" (*Z,* 85) ("Nalitso metamorfozy tvorcheskogo protsessa"; *SS* 2:82). The prototype of Egorov must have been a collective image described in an article written for *Novyi Amerikanets,* "Kirpich s lampasami" ("Blockhead with Trouser Stripes").[60] In this article Dovlatov bemoans the fact that while in the nineteenth century the officer class was the pride of the whole nation, one cannot say the same about the large majority of Soviet officers. He describes the officers he came across as men of limited intelligence and considerable cruelty. One of the examples of an officer's needless cruelty still haunts the author in his worst nightmares: "Snow black with blood. A man on the snow. And Lieutenant Tvauri orders: finish him off! And they did finish him off. It was Vania Lymar', our former Komsomol organizer, who finished him off, and now he's an officer in the Soviet Army!"[61] The officer Khuriev, who appears as a fictional character in *The Zone,* is also described in this article as a lawyer and university graduate in real life, whose task was to instill in the conscripts hatred for the prisoners: "You have to hate the convicts. Every single one of them. That is your duty as citizens!"[62]

Egorov and Katia marry and she moves to live with him in the camps, escaping from various Mariks, Shuriks, Toliks, and other city boys in orange socks. She considers that he is strong and brave, unlike her other friends, and she is possibly under the illusion that he is like officers she has read about in Pushkin, Lermontov, and Tolstoy. In one of his letters to his father from the army, Dovlatov sends a poem dedicated to an officer's wife, Ekaterina Vladimirovna Olina. He comments that young women often got married to officers in order to "improve the material side of their lives." "And her girlfriends whispered: 'What's the matter with you? / Marry him, he'll protect you like a brick wall' " ("I podrugi sheptali: 'Chego zhe, chego zhe ty? / Vykhodi za nego, kak za kamennoi budesh' stenoi' ").[63] In the first part of "Captains on Land," Egorov does mention to Katia that if he is killed, she will be well provided for. But her life in the camps is unbearable: the cold, the darkness, the constant barking of dogs and the noise of the power saw. She recalls her other life, the life when poems were dedicated to her by Lenia Mak:[64]

> It's plain I've come at an awkward moment,
> The phonograph has long since stopped, it whispers,
> Better let's wait for a waltz, Katya,
> It's easier for me not to dance this one . . . (Z, 89)
>
> Vidno, ia tut ne sovsem kstati . . .
> Patefon davno zatikh, shepchet . . .
> Luchshe val'sa podozhdem, Katia,
> Mne ego ne tantsevat' legche . . . (*SS* 2:85)

These are in fact the last four lines of a poem written by Dovlatov himself, "Damskoe tango" ("Ladies' Tango"), with the name Tania in the original poem changed to Katia.[65]

Igor' Sukhikh regards this story as a tribute to the idol of the 1960s, Hemingway.[66] He finds similarities between the disintegration of an American couple's relationship in Hemingway's story "Cat in the Rain" and the relationship between Egorov and Katia. He writes that the only difference is that the lonely pair in Hemingway's story find a cat, whereas Egorov kills a dog. Undoubtedly, Dovlatov is indebted to Hemingway, although the relationship between Egorov and Katia cannot be described simply as disintegration. Katia's relationship to Egorov has become one of fear and complete alienation.

In the last story in *The Zone,* "Straight Ahead," there is a short digression, bearing a title almost identical with that of the lost story, "Zavtra—obychnyi den' " (*SS* 2:163; "Tomorrow Is an Ordinary Day"). It throws some light on the story "Captains on Land." The protagonist Alikhanov/Dovlatov finds himself in a library. The guard asks the librarian, a young woman, to get some of Bunin's stories for him to read. The protagonist accidentally touches her hands and is overwhelmed by emotions: "I thought with fear of how unaccustomed I had grown to the things which made life worth living, of how much happiness had swept by me on those nights full of hatred and fear [. . .] and the miserable, frozen, unchanging days drag on outside the window, delaying the mail" (Z, 174). ("Prosto zabyl o veshchakh, radi kotorykh stoit zhit' . . . [. . .] Chego lishilsia v eti dni, polnye nenavisti i strakha?! [. . .] A dni, kholodnye, nelepye, bredut za steklami, operezhaia pochtu"; *SS* 2:164.) The narrator wonders how and why this young woman of thirty can have come voluntarily to such a godforsaken place. It is obvious to him that she is not comfortable: her fear of the guard who wants to read Bunin is palpable.

In the third part of "Captains on Land" Katia is in critical condition in the hospital. The reader is not told how this has come about. In the letter of May 17 Dovlatov writes that the middle part of this story was lost, but that it contained a story about a horse and about a revolt in which Egorov was wounded. Dovlatov does not tell the story, but what he says is even more unsettling: "As he left the hospital, Egorov turned to the wall and burst into tears. He thought of Katya's face, childlike and angry, remembered her fingers with their chewed nails, recalled everything that had come before" (Z, 95). ("Vyidia iz bol'nitsy, Egorov zaplakal, otvernuvshis' k stene. On vspomnil Katino litso, detskoe i zloe. Vspomnil pal'tsy s obkusannymi nogtiami. Pripomnil vse, chto bylo"; *SS* 2:90.) Sukhikh[67] interprets this third story as a "variation" on the last pages of *A Farewell to Arms,* with the difference that in *A Farewell to Arms* the heroine Cat dies, whereas the Russian Katia is miraculously saved.[68]

The influence of Hemingway is indeed apparent in these stories, but more in their style than in their plot. What is perhaps most important is the similarity in the use of short, concise sentences, scenes consisting entirely of dialogue, and the immediate accessibility of both writers' prose. Each word in Dovlatov's work performs a function in the narrative. Possibly what Dovlatov most successfully emulated in Hemingway was his choice of language that serves to characterize each person, and the directness of his prose. In one of the letters to the publisher (April 4), the fictional author informs the publisher that he is going to bring him a prison story, but that its beginning is missing and he only remembers the first two sentences: "In the North, it generally gets dark early. And in the zone especially" (Z, 69). ("Na Severe voobshche temneet rano. A v zone—osobenno"; *SS* 2:68.) The main function of this passage seems to be an echo of the opening paragraph of Hemingway's story "In Another Country" (1927): "In the fall the war was always there, but we did not go to it any more. It was cold in the fall in Milan and the dark came very early."

In the Soviet Union political and revolutionary understanding was supposed to replace fantasy. Heroes were called upon to live real life and the proletariat was encouraged to build its kingdom on earth and not in heaven. It is perhaps because real life was so absurd and fantastic that its description is perceived as natural. This was exploited by such writers as Iuz Aleshkovsky (in *Maskirovka—Camouflage*), Abram Tertz (in *Pkhents, Liubimov*), and others. Nobody is surprised when in the second story of *The Zone* a helicopter lands in the middle of a wasteland where the prisoners, supervised by VOKHRA (armed guard), are working. This story in earlier collections had the title "Chudo—Mi-6" ("The Miracle of MI-6").[69]

The plot of the story, such as it is, is not only absurd, it is surreal. The helicopter pilot Dima Marconi "drops in" on his imprisoned friend, the former pilot Mishchuk, who has been sentenced for embezzlement. In the U.S.S.R. embezzlement of state property reached immense proportions. It was natural and understandable for people to steal. Dovlatov returns to this topic in later works as well. It was just unfortunate to get caught. In the short, prosaic epilogue to this story the reader is told that Mishchuk served his three years, but was not allowed to fly again. He worked as a mechanic and forgot about his years in the camp. Marconi was killed in a flying accident, and among the wreckage of his plane a large canister of caviar was found. He was just one of the lucky ones who was not caught.[70]

To the amazement of the prisoners, the helicopter lands inside the barbed wire of the logging area. Marconi gets out of the helicopter and the two friends have a conversation (reminiscent of Gogol in its surrealism) as if they had bumped into each other on the streets of Moscow:

> "How come you're so thin?" Marconi said.
> Then for some time they pretended to slug each other.
> "And how's Vadya doing?" Mishchuk asked. "How's Zhora over there?"
> [. . .]
> "Well, and you, old dog?"
> "Got married," Marconi said in a tragic tone, and hung his head.
> "Do I know her?"
> "No. I hardly know her myself. You're not missing much."
> [. . .]
> "And will we go drinking together when I get back? In one year, five months, and sixteen days?"
> "And how, will we go drinking together! It'll be stronger than Goethe's *Faust*." (Z, 18–19)

> — Do chego ty khudoi,—skazal Markoni.
> Zatem oni chas khlopali drug druga po zhivotu.

— Kak tam Vadia?—sprashival Mishchuk.—Kak tam Zhora?
[. . .]
— Nu, a ty, staryi pes?
— Zhenilsia,—tragicheski proiznes Markoni, opustiv golovu.
— Ia ee znaiu?
— Net. Ia sam ee pochti ne znaiu. Ty ne mnogo poterial . . .
[. . .]
— A my nap"emsia, kogda ia vernus'? Cherez god, piat' mesiatsev i shestnadtsat' dnei?
— Okh i nap"emsia . . . Eto budet posil'nee, chem "Faust" Gete. . . . (*SS* 2:21)[71]

The other prisoners who witness this arrival and this exchange are stunned, and each evaluates it in his own language: the speculator Adam says "Incredible!" ("Chudesa!"); the embezzler Leibovich exclaims "May I live so long!" ("Chtob ia tak zhil!"); the pickpocket Chalyi vows "I'd give a tooth" ("Zub daiu!"); the thief Murashka remarks approvingly "What a séance" ("Seans"), and even the speculator Beluga is impressed: "Phenomenal" ("Fenomenal'no"). One of them sums it all up philosophically: "Life continues, even when in essence it doesn't exist" (*Z*, 20) ("Zhizn' prodolzhaetsia, dazhe kogda ee, v sushchnosti, net"; *SS* 2:22). This quite improbable and grotesque exchange is perceived by the reader as completely natural. Igor' Sukhikh comments that this fragment of *The Zone* "is elegantly executed in the spirit of older comrades of the sixties, the authors of such works as *Oranges from Morocco* and *Chronicle of the Times of Viktor Podgursky*. And of course of A. Grin, who is peeping over their shoulders."[72] There is, however, a sense in which it points forward, rather than back, anticipating the younger generation of writers like Vladimir Sorokin (in particular *Ochered'—The Queue*). The assimilation of such banal, contentless language bears a strong resemblance to the way in which the alternative and conceptualist writers of the 1980s, such as Sorokin or Prigov, reproduce the exhausted and discredited language of the totalitarian regime. Here the banal chain of thought is interrupted by an absolutely precise question. Dovlatov employed this method extensively in his writing, showing a life deprived of logic. This gives his writing a light, ironic touch. The issues discussed are serious, yet on the surface of it the treatment is flippant. Discussing the nature of Soviet language, E. Markstein concludes:

> An important step in the assimilation of Soviet language can be seen in its understanding as *another's* word (in the Bakhtinian sense), which gives the writer the chance to incorporate it into authorial discourse, thereby creating intertextuality. The context (the authorial discourse) enters into a dialogue

> with the quotation and/or the other's word, which becomes subject to irony and through that irony is revealed as unviable, false.[73]

When writing *The Zone,* Dovlatov deliberately did not dwell on the cruelties of prison life: "Although the most monstrous, shocking details of camp life I omitted. I did not want to reproduce them. Because it would have looked like speculation. The effect would have been not in the artistic texture of the work, but in the material itself" (*SS* 2:17). Dovlatov was most passionately preoccupied with this "artistic texture" of his work and particularly with the role of the narrator. It can be said that Dovlatov's work is autobiographical, that the author is the protagonist and narrator and practically all the characters are real people and the author describes real biographical events, but this would be a simplification and only part of the truth. The collision between "real material" and "artistic texture" in Dovlatov's work is of great importance to him. P. Vail' and A. Genis in "Iskusstvo avtoportreta" ("The Art of the Self-Portrait") observe that "in Dovlatov the self-portrait is a complex genre."[74] Sukhikh in "Golos: O remesle pisatelia D" ("A Voice: About the Craft of the Writer D") writes: "So is it a confessional self-portrait or the mask of a cynic? Let's settle for the middle. Simply an image in which there is both autobiography and invention, and confession, and a spot of play, and a smidgen of cynicism, and lots else as well."[75] The result is not a single portrait, but rather a number of varying portraits, each revealing different facets of the real person, rather in the way that a painter's self-portraits will express different aspects of what is recognizably a single individual. The most subtle definition of this has been given by Mark Lipovetsky in his article "Razbitoe zerkalo" ("The Broken Mirror"):

> Dovlatov's whole output reminds one of a broken mirror, shattered into tiny fragments. Bent over this is the man, the author, who broke it. In each of even the tiniest fragments we see his face again and again. To be more precise, his faces, which are similar and at the same time not so similar to each other. [. . .] In the end, Dovlatov's absurdism is the basis for order: in human fate, in relationships with people, in the universe. Dovlatov's absurdism does not make the world intelligible; it makes understanding it possible. And this, perhaps, is the most amazing paradox of Dovlatov's poetics.[76]

Dovlatov discussed the autobiographical nature of his writing in his interview with John Glad. This is how Dovlatov defines the nature of his writing, attempting to blur the boundaries between himself and his imagined alter ego: "I write pseudo-documentary stories in the hope that now and again they produce the impression of reality, the impression that that's how it all was, although in fact a hundred percent of it wasn't, it's all invented."[77]

In practically all the stories Dovlatov is the storyteller, choosing this role for himself quite consciously. He thought of himself not so much as a writer, but rather as a storyteller:

> Everybody who writes knows what immense work and what skill is required to turn an event into a literary work, into a story. It seemed that he never invented plots, simply the whole of his life, the lives of his relatives and friends, even his distant acquaintances, as told in his words turned out, as though on purpose, to be rich in both plot and content, touching and funny.[78]

The tone of Dovlatov's stories is ironic and intimate, and the reader perceives them as though they were related orally. Concentration on oral rather than written language was typical for the "post-thaw" writers, who very soon after the end of the thaw realized that literature as a public act had suffered the same fate as political action and who therefore devoted their attention to discussions within a close circle of friends instead. Many authors first read their stories, poems, songs, and so on in such a circle. In the 1960s and '70s there was no chance of Dovlatov's camp stories being published, so he too read them first to a small circle of intimate friends. The tone of such stories inevitably has to be different. Consequently, the tone of the narrative in Dovlatov's stories is oral with the corresponding intonation, syntax, and colloquial vocabulary. In his interview with John Glad, Dovlatov explained that he mostly told his stories orally and only later started writing them down: "All my life I have told stories which I have either heard somewhere, or invented, or transformed."[79] Telling the stories to his friends and to fellow soldiers gave Dovlatov an opportunity to polish and perfect his stories, to reconsider some of the episodes, depending on the reaction of his listeners. This informal and intimate tone also created natural conditions for the author to take the reader into his confidence about the secrets of his literary craft. This is not simply an example of self-conscious fiction, of which so many could be cited from the twentieth century and earlier, but a deliberate experiment in genre, creating a form which straddles the boundaries between oral narrative and traditional fiction.[80] Eikhenbaum had already noted that the inclusion of such discussion of literary devices in a fictional text was a typical feature of American literature. This is an example of how Dovlatov shares the creative process with his reader: "When I was beginning to freeze, my consciousness registered the fact. What's more, in artistic form: 'Birds froze in flight . . .' " (Z, 22). ("Kogda ia zamerzal, soznanie registrirovalo etot fakt. Prichem v khdozhestvennoi forme: 'Ptitsy zamerzali na letu . . .' "; *SS* 2:24.)[81]

Against the background of the literary heroes of the 1950s, who are fighters and reformers, the image of Ivan Denisovich Shukhov (in

Solzhenitsyn's *One Day in the Life of Ivan Denisovich*) was the image of a simple and perhaps even primitive man. He was marked by the absence of any social resistance or open rejection of the system. By showing an ordinary day in the life of one prisoner, Solzhenitsyn draws a parallel with the everyday life of the whole nation. While Solzhenitsyn chose an ordinary man as representative, a born Russian peasant, Varlam Shalamov chose a member of the intelligentsia. Shalamov's choice allowed him to look at the events he describes from a different angle. A thinking hero allows him to be more analytic and to see the reasons for events. It is possibly because of this stance and in spite of the deep emotional resonance of Shalamov's prose, that it was Solzhenitsyn's work that had the greater impact on the development of contemporary prose. The influence of Shalamov's prose has been less not only because of the censorship that precluded the publication of *Kolymskie rasskazy* (*Kolyma Stories*), but also because Shalamov's hero, although participating in the fate of his fellow countrymen, was observing the events from the height of his rational thought.

Georgy Vladimov's short novel *Faithful Ruslan, the Story of a Guard Dog* is in some senses a precursor of Dovlatov's *Zone*. However, as in Solzhenitsyn and Shalamov, the main emphasis of the narrative rests on personality and society. The personality here takes the form of a guard dog, whose life becomes a parable of the life of Soviet man in the 1930s and '50s, his ideals and moral stance. This angle was obviously chosen by Vladimov quite consciously. Vladimov emphasizes that originally by nature the guards, whether people or dogs, were not evil, but they became evil through their employment. They were trained, schooled, forged, created by the years of the Soviet regime. Vladimov does not hold Ruslan responsible for the atrocities he commits, but instead blames the regime. At the same time, Ruslan has a quality that puts him closer to Solzhenitsyn in his optimism: Ruslan is faithful not only to his masters as he was trained to be, but he also has an inborn fidelity to his own nature. In his dreams he sees times when things used to be different, before he became a guard dog, and he is proud of his past. This was a feeling that became prevalent in the mid-1970s and found its expression in what is known as "village prose."

For a number of reasons, as discussed above, Dovlatov's *Zone*, originally written for the most part in the 1960s, only appeared in the 1980s. According to the author, it took him seventeen years to prepare the manuscript for publication. Putting the finishing touches to *The Zone* in the 1980s during the heyday of "new," "other," or "alternative" prose with its deviations into chaos, illogicality, and the absurd, Dovlatov brought into the text of the 1960s a new outlook: he showed that life within the camp and outside the camp were indistinguishable, that the real and the fantastic are the same, that chaos and absurdity triumph. The scale of human tragedy is certainly present, but it is made to appear on the surface quite bearable. Although it is acutely felt throughout the work, it nevertheless acquires some of the flippancy which is so typical of the "alternative" literature of the 1980s.

There was a continuation of the prison camp theme in Russian literature, notably Mikhail Kuraev's *Nochnoi dozor* (*Night Patrol,* published in 1988), also written from the point of view of a former prison guard. Kuraev's hero, Polubolotov, is not by nature a torturer or a sadist. Kuraev asks the reader to contemplate what it was that made his hero exchange freedom for loyalty; after all, like Ruslan, he could have lived a different life. Like Vladimov, Kuraev also takes the responsibility away from Polubolotov as an individual. Dovlatov believes that one can gain inner freedom even in unfavorable circumstances. He illustrates this in his story about the thief Kuptsov, who cuts off his hand rather than agree to breach the thief's code of behavior.

So prison camp literature of the 1960s and '80s has the documentary value of recording the harsh conditions of the prison camp, because in this sense it is no different from its predecessors: Avvakum, Dostoevsky, Chekhov. On the one hand (in the figure of Ivan Denisovich), it becomes the impulse for the aesthetics of village prose, and on the other hand it becomes the origin of the absurdist trend of the literature of the 1980s. In *The Zone* Dovlatov succeeded in overcoming the narrow thematic boundaries of prison camp prose and combining the camp theme with other tendencies in contemporary literature. In particular, he was one of the first to express that sense of the absurd which later became so typical for the attitudes of the 1980s. The significance of Dovlatov's camp theme lies not in the fact that it considered issues that were previously forbidden, but that it served as an impulse to the absurdism of the 1980s.

Chapter Four

The Compromise: Journalism and Fiction

ARRIVING IN TALLINN in late September 1972, Dovlatov was unable to find a permanent position and worked as a freelance journalist for *Molodezh' Estonii* (*Youth of Estonia*) and *Vechernii Tallin* (*Tallinn Evening News*).[1] During his first few months in Tallinn he even worked in a boiler room, which was not an unusual situation for members of the artistic intelligentsia. He was then taken on as a freelance contributor to the weekly paper *Moriak Estonii* (*Sailor of Estonia*), which belonged to the Estonian Marine Steam Navigation Company (Estonskoe Morskoe Parokhodstvo). He moved in with Tamara Zibunova, whom he had briefly met in Leningrad. By 1973 Dovlatov was working for the daily *Sovetskaia Estonia* (*Soviet Estonia*).

Sergei Dovlatov's novel *Kompromiss*[2] (*The Compromise*) is a collection of stories that reflect his experiences as a journalist for *Soviet Estonia* in the 1970s.[3] The intellectual atmosphere in the Baltic republics was more relaxed than in the rest of the Soviet Union. For the majority of young writers, any possibility of self-realization within the framework of official culture was out of the question. In this stifling atmosphere many intellectuals left Leningrad. Two of their favorite destinations were Tallinn and Tartu. In their book *60-e: Mir sovetskogo cheloveka* (*The Sixties: The World of the Soviet Man*), Vail' and Genis describe the more liberal atmosphere of the Baltic republics:

> At the beginning of the sixties the Baltic republics were perceived by many as the gateway to Europe: Gothic art, jazz, and street cafés. Siberians frequently wondered what currency was in use in Tallinn. The metropolitan intelligentsia preferred the cool Riga Bay to the all-Union sanatoriums of the Crimea. Writers sent their young heroes there in search of the meaning of life (V. Aksenov's *Ticket to the Stars*). Poets for some reason switched to English ("Friends and enemies, farewell, goodbye"—A.Voznesensky's *Autumn in Siguld*).[4]

Dovlatov gives varying (but not necessarily mutually exclusive) accounts of his own motivation for moving there: "There were no rational motives. I was able to get a lift" (*SS* 3:55). And in *The Compromise:*

> How could I answer? By explaining that I had no home, no country or refuge? That I've always been searching for a quiet harbor? Or that I only ask one thing out of life—to sit like this, quiet and without thinking?
>
> "The food supply," I said, "is good here. Night bars . . ." (*C*, 132)

> Chto ia mog otvetit'? Ob"iasnit', chto net u menia doma, rodiny, pristanishcha, zhil'ia? . . . Chto ia vsegda iskal etu tikhuiu pristan'? . . . Chto ia proshu u zhizni odnogo—sidet' vot tak, molchat', ne dumat'? . . .
>
> Snabzhenie, govoriu, u vas khoroshee. Nochnye bary . . . (*SS* 1:316)

It was also the case that for the real-life Dovlatov the chances of being published in Estonia were much greater because the censorship was not so strict. Almost any topic except issues of nationalism could be discussed in literature (particularly if it was written in Estonian). Problems of nationalism were an exception. For the small circle of Russian intellectuals living in Estonia, life there provided opportunities that were not available elsewhere. As mentioned in chapter 1, Dovlatov's *Fiveways* was accepted for publication there and even reached the page-proof stage. However, the KGB had a last-minute change of mind and the book was banned. Evidently it fell foul of directives from Moscow which had instructed that more attention be paid to the education of the masses.

The stories Dovlatov selected for this collection were the ones he thought were uncontroversial. The internal reviews by such specialists as Valery Ivanovich Bezzubov from Tartu University were excellent, and Dovlatov felt encouraged by them. In the unpublished edition of *The Invisible Book* he "quotes" Bezzubov's conclusion: "S. Dovlatov is a mature writer. His stories have undoubted literary qualities."[5] The director of the publishing house Eesti Raamat, Aksel Tamm, is said to have called Dovlatov's book *Fiveways* "the best Russian book in the last few years."[6] Other stories, less suitable for publication, circulated only among friends. One of those to whom Dovlatov gave some of these other stories to read was Vladimir Kotel'nikov. A number of them were then found and confiscated during a KGB search of Kotel'nikov's flat. In the published version of *The Invisible Book* Dovlatov devotes a few lines to "The Mysterious Kotel'nikov": "One thing made me a little wary: for a writer and a proletarian, he lived extremely comfortably. He bought fashionable clothes. He was interested in furniture . . . It isn't possible for a déclassé poet to take an interest in Finnish wallpaper. Or maybe I'm just a snob . . ." (*SS* 3:64). According to Zibunova, rumors circulated in

Tallinn to the effect that Kotel'nikov was set up by the KGB. One indication of this possibility was that although he was arrested in connection with Estonian nationalism, he was not charged or even called as a witness when the matter came to trial. In the unpublished version of *The Invisible Book,* Dovlatov recounts a conversation with a certain Captain Zverev. He is trying to find out whether the confiscated stories are going to be attached to his dossier. As a parting shot the captain asks Dovlatov: "Ever had occasion to go to Canada?—No, why?—No reason."[7] Initially puzzled, Dovlatov then recalls that in *The Zone* there is a story about an elderly Estonian nationalist who utters the senseless phrase: "A real Estonian should live in Canada!"[8] Dovlatov notes that when he wrote this story, which was originally called "Inostranets" ("The Foreigner"), he had not only never been to Canada, but had not even been to Estonia. His experience was limited to two grim characters from Estonia he had met in the army. "The bit about Canada I invented. An ironic dig at Estonian chauvinism, as it were."[9] However, the fact that Dovlatov had written stories that were deemed "anti-Soviet" had grave consequences for him. Apart from the banning of his book, there was a real threat of imprisonment. Such anti-Soviet activities were naturally judged incompatible with being a Soviet journalist. In February 1975 Dovlatov was called to a meeting of the editorial board of *Soviet Estonia.* He understood that he was to be dismissed "for actions incompatible with the prestige of the newspaper" and submitted his resignation. What shocked Dovlatov was his betrayal by colleagues he had trusted. Some of those with whom he used to have a drink or two now spoke out against him: "Dovlatov has slipped into the mire . . . He's harnessed himself to the chariot . . . He's brought shame on everything that's most dear . . ." ("Dovlatov skatilsia v boloto . . . Vpriagsia v kolesnitsu . . . Oporochil vse samoe dorogoe . . .").[10] Mikhail Roginsky, shocked at their behavior, apparently left the meeting with the words: "Lads! What's going on? What are you doing this to Sergei for?"[11] It is said that Roginsky was immediately called in by the editor, Turonok, and reminded that he was first in the queue for an apartment. Realizing the hopelessness of his situation, Dovlatov left Tallinn on March 8, 1975.

All this has to be put into a broader context. In 1974 and 1975 there was a wave of searches and arrests of suspected Estonian nationalists in Tallinn by members of the Estonian KGB, with reinforcements from Latvian operational units. There were similar campaigns carried out in Moscow, Leningrad, Ukraine, Armenia, and other places. One of the participants in the Estonian democratic movement was Sergei Soldatov, who, on December 19, 1974, in anticipation of arrest and possible death, wrote an open letter to friends and an address to "world public opinion": "The Torch of Freedom and Love should never be extinguished, for only its fire will kindle hearts. May God preserve our efforts on behalf of Light, Freedom, and Love in this world and be merciful to its enemies!"[12] Many others were arrested and imprisoned along with Soldatov. The atmosphere in Tallinn ceased to be congenial.

These years in Tallinn were the first time Dovlatov had worked regularly on a mainstream daily newspaper, and in many ways they represent the high point of his journalistic activity in the Soviet Union.[13] He never regarded journalism as his real profession, but both now and later, in the United States, he was glad of it as a source of employment and income. He considered his journalistic work to be *khaltura*, and he gives a definition of this specifically Soviet word, which has two meanings: "In the first case *khaltura* is supplementary, irregular, profitable work undertaken for additional income. In the second case *khaltura* is a piece of work, a product, a work outcome that is performed hastily, carelessly, any old how" (*SS* 4:319–20). Nevertheless, his work as a journalist for *Soviet Estonia* is not without importance. His articles in that paper have not been collected, and a number of them were written under forgotten pseudonyms and are in danger of being lost. These pieces are not *khaltura* in the second sense, but are journalism of high quality, and do not deserve to disappear into oblivion.

The most important "qualities" that Soviet journalists had to have were the standard trinity of "ideological correctness, party commitment, and accessibility to ordinary people" (*ideinost', partiinost', narodnost'*). In the course of Soviet history, many writers have satirized the totalitarian language of Soviet newspapers and official writings.[14] By the 1970s, though, Soviet people were quite immune to totalitarian slogans and largely ignored them.[15] Some "ideological vigilance" was necessary for working as a journalist, and when Dovlatov came to the editorial office of the newspaper in quest of a job, the first question he was asked sounded like a rebuke: "You're not a Party member, of course? I shook my head guiltily" (*C*, 3; *SS* 1:230). Nevertheless, Dovlatov was employed by *Soviet Estonia* thanks to the efforts of his friend, Mikhail Roginsky, who was the scientific and economic commentator for the paper and the prototype of Shablinsky in *The Compromise.*[16]

As a non–party-member, Dovlatov was employed to write columns such as Chelovek i professia (People and Professions), Gosti Tallina (Tallinn's Guests), Iumoreska (Humoresque), Reportazh (Reportage), Replika (Talk-Back), and Na temy morali (Morality Issues). He also wrote theater, concert, and book reviews. This type of material usually appeared on pages 3 and 4. He often signed his contributions to the paper, apart from his real name, as S. Ader and occasionally R. Must.[17] Reading through Dovlatov's contributions to *Soviet Estonia,* one is struck by their restraint and their distinctive style in comparison with other articles in the paper. One of his articles in the People and Professions category, "Na svoem meste" ("In Its Rightful Place"), is about technical specializations at an experimental factory producing shirts, and at a theater workshop that designs costumes.[18] The article is about the combination of imagination and technical expertise that is required to make items of clothing for ordinary wear and for the theater. "Ishchu cheloveka" ("Looking for a Man") is about the work of an address bureau that not only helps families to be reunited, but also helps the police to find criminals and fathers who refuse to pay child support.[19] "Dlia odnoi loshadinoi sily" ("For One Horsepower") is about the number-one specialist in Estonia at making horses' collars.[20] Although the main workforce in the fields are tractors, horses are also used and require good harness-makers. "Proektiruiutsia . . . noski" ("Socks . . . Are Being Designed") is about the collaboration between art, technology, and fashion that is needed for the successful design of socks.[21] "Vysokoe polozhenie" ("A High Position") is about a female crane operator who started as an ancillary worker but then, through study, advanced to a top position and became a representative on the Tallinn City Council.[22] The article "Chisto, svetlo . . ." ("Clean and Light . . .") is about the work of a factory that produces radios.[23] There is a technical explanation of how the sound engineer works and how the equipment is tuned, but Dovlatov expands the topic and gives an explanation that will be more familiar to the readers, comparing this work with that of a piano tuner.

The style of these articles is simple and the explanations accessible. Dovlatov is clearly aware of his readership's expectations. At the same time, however, he cheerfully indulges his passion for exotic vocabulary and precision in the use of words. In one article in *Soviet Estonia,* "Polchasa v srednevekov'e" ("Half an Hour in the Middle Ages"), he lovingly lists the most interesting relics:[24]

> Swords and chain mail, helmets and breastplates, battle-axes and poleaxes, spears and halberds, maces and pikes, berdiches and partisans, quarterstaffs and sophisticated tongs for pulling horsemen off their mounts, cannons and arquebuses, mortars and ships' tromblons, matchlock guns, flintlock guns and wheel lock guns, powder pouches and hunting knives.

> Mechi i kol'chugi, shlemy i laty, topory i sekiry, kop'ia i alebardy, bulavy i piki, berdyshi i protazany, boevye dubiny i khitroumnye kleshchi, kotorymi staskivali vsadnikov s konei, pushki i arkebuzy, mortiry i korabel'nye trombl-ony, ruzh'ia s fitil'nymi, kremnievymi i kolestsovymi zamkami, porokhovnitsy i okhotnich'i nozhi.[25]

His pleasure at using all these rare specialist words is palpable. A more contemporary vocabulary is used in an article entitled "K zvezdam!" ("To the Stars!"), about a powerful new telescope for the Estonian observatory.

Dovlatov remarks that the profession of an astronomer must dispose one to contemplation: "The very sight of the starry sky is a triumph of harmony and order."[26]

He also wrote articles for *Soviet Estonia* on literary themes. "Ia khochu vam rasskazat' . . ." ("I Would Like to Tell You . . .") is a review of a novella and four stories by Georgy Vasil'ev, *V storone ot asfal'ta* (*Away from the Road*). Vasil'ev wrote stories from the life of long-distance truck drivers. Dovlatov's evaluation of these short stories is of interest. Here is one example:

> The story "Someone Else's Route." It is about that which Saint-Exupéry called "the luxury of human contact," that is, to express it in archaic language, "about love for one's neighbor." The story is written with humor, with a smile. It turns out that the writer uses these devices skillfully, creating delicate contrasts with the dramatic aspects of the narration . . . . Georgy Vasil'ev does not try to captivate us with clever formal games, or to puzzle us with a sudden paradox, or to lead us off into uncharted labyrinths of the soul.[27]

In "Ia znaiu silu slov . . ." ("I Know the Power of Words") Dovlatov talks about the philologist, poet, prose writer, and critic S. V. Petrov, whose book *Kak pol'zovat'sia slovom* (*How to Use Words*) Dovlatov appreciated.[28]

In the category of "humoresques," Dovlatov published a number of pieces concerned with the problem of drink and drunkenness in Russia and the whole Soviet Union. This was a topic on which he continued to write in *Novyi Amerikanets* (see, for instance, "Tak pit' ili ne pit'?" ["To Drink or Not to Drink?"], no. 6, March 21–27, 1980).[29] He used the title "Kak ia brosil pit' " ("How I Stopped Drinking") on two occasions, once in *Soviet Estonia* (February 11, 1973) and once in *Novyi Amerikanets,* and in *Soviet Estonia* (January 6, 1973) there is a further article on the same theme, "Sila ubezhdeniia" ("The Power of Persuasion"). All these humoresques end in the victory of alcohol over the human being. The plot of these little stories entails either the wife nagging the alcoholic to stop drinking and the alcoholic agreeing to read books on the harmfulness of alcohol, or to cure his alcoholism through hypnosis, or (in the Soviet paper) a friend undertaking to stop the alcoholic drinking by his powers of persuasion. Many of these short humoresques are exercises that are later used as material in short stories. The humoresque "The Power of Persuasion" ends with the sentence: "The friends woke up in neighboring beds in the sobering-up station." It is a precursor to the ending of the "Fifth Compromise":

> Is it worth going into what happened next? How my companion climbed onto the stage and yelled, "They've sold out Russia"? And hit the doorman so hard that his cap rolled into the closet? And how we were taken to the po-

> lice station? And how they let us go, thanks to my press pass? And how I lost my notepad with all my notes? And how I then lost Kuzin himself? (*C*, 46; *SS* 1:266–67)

The brief ending of "How I Stopped Drinking": "My wife keeps on at me. Brings books about the harmfulness of alcohol. Tells me to read them. I've read them, I've read them. I've read a couple of hundred. And in the end I have decided once and for all to stop . . . reading!" is used in *The Sanctuary:* "You know, I've read so much about the harmfulness of alcohol! I've decided to pack it in for ever—reading" (*SS* 2:173).

In one of the humoresques in *Soviet Estonia* (September 30, 1973), "Obyknovennoe chudo" ("An Ordinary Miracle"), Dovlatov describes the miraculous transformation of a hotel receptionist: "They say that miracles don't happen. I don't agree. Because I witnessed a strange and miraculous transformation." Mr. Sidorov, who is on a business trip, needs a room, but the receptionist stubbornly repeats one phrase: "There aren't any vacancies" ("Mest net"). Then the following takes place:

> I inserted a ruble into my passport and held it out to the receptionist. He skillfully dropped it into the drawer of the desk and suddenly . . . smiled. He rose to his feet and gave such a shout:
>
> "Who is this who has come to see us? None other that comrade Sidorov from the State Flooring Company. His very own self! We have a deluxe suite for you."

Endemic Russian bribery and corruption is a topic Dovlatov discusses in many of his stories, newspaper articles, and even letters to friends. In a number of the stories he wrote in the United States, he tries to unravel the reason why bribery and corruption are rife among his fellow émigrés.

Dovlatov also wrote a number of witty and interesting humoresques on other topics for *Soviet Estonia,* such as "Pobeda nad Gennadiem Shatkovym" (July 7, 1973; "Victory over Gennady Shatkov"), "Isporchennyi telefon" (January 13, 1973; "Faulty Telephone"), "S Ivanovym shutki plokhi" (April 1, 1973; "It Is Not Worth Joking with Ivanov"), "Nichego strashnogo" (November 25, 1973; "Nothing Terrible"), and many more. Ultimately, however, the most important aspect of Dovlatov's journalistic work in Estonia is to be found in the way he exploited it to create his own brand of fiction.

The Compromise consists of twelve chapters, entitled "First Compromise," "Second Compromise," and so on.[30] Each story can stand on its own, and, as is the case with a number of Dovlatov's works, many were published separately in émigré journals. For example, the "Tenth Compromise" was published in the journal *Grani* (*Facets*) under the title "Lishnii"[31] ("Superfluous"), the "Eighth Compromise" was published in *Vremia i my* (*Our Times*) as "V goru" ("On the Way Up"), the "Eleventh Compromise" as "Ch'ia-to smert' i drugie zaboty" ("Somebody's Death and Other Concerns") in *Chast' rechi*, and the "Fifth Compromise" as "Iubileinyi mal'chik" ("The Jubilee Boy") in *Kontinent* (*Continent*).[32] As is the case in Dovlatov's earlier work, it is the first-person storyteller who unifies the novel. Unlike *The Zone,* where Dovlatov uses a fictitious name for the author-narrator, in this instance the real name Dovlatov is used. Each story is in two parts: a "quotation" from a newspaper, which is differentiated from the rest of the text by italics, and then the story behind the writing of that particular article, which is told by the first-person narrator, Dovlatov. However, it would be a mistake to see the relationship between the two parts of the stories as a simple contrast between the "fiction" of the newspaper article and the "truth" of the account of its writing. The "quotations" from the newspapers in *The Compromise* are dated between 1973 and 1976, and the majority (seven out of twelve) carry the date 1976. In fact, as mentioned above, the real Dovlatov returned to Leningrad in 1975. Most of the newspaper "quotations" purport to be from *Soviet Estonia,* but some are attributed to *Vechernii Tallin* (*Tallinn Evening News*) and *Molodezh' Estonii* (*Youth of Estonia*).[33] Only two real articles from *Soviet Estonia,* "Nariad dlia Marsianina" ("Clothing for a Martian") and "Samaia trudnaia distantsiia" ("The Most Difficult Distance"), are reproduced virtually word for word. *The Compromise* has an introduction in which the author reminisces about his journalistic activity. "Yellowed pages. Ten years of lies and dissembling. And yet, some people stood behind them: conversations, feelings, things that actually happened. Not on the pages themselves, but beyond them" (*C*, 4). ("Pozheltevshie listy. Desiat' let vran'ia i pritvorstva. I vse zhe kakie-to liudi stoiat za etim, kakie-to razgovory, chuvstva, deistvitel'nost' . . . Ne v samikh listakh, a tam, na gorizonte . . ."; *SS* 1:230.)[34]

In his interview with John Glad, Dovlatov discusses the significance of the "true story element" in fiction:

> It is most often not novels that become best sellers, but books built on some factual basis—local interest books or an account of some political event that forms the basis of the book, and so on. I take advantage of this and try to give my stories a documentary feel, but in essence, it's fiction, made-up stories, disguised as real events.[35]

This is precisely the technique Dovlatov employs in *The Compromise.* The work consists of stories about the writing of newspaper articles. In order to give the story "true documentary" flavor, he quotes newspaper articles within the body of the text. It is appropriate therefore to draw comparisons between the quoted passages and the original newspaper articles. The two genuine newspaper articles, "Nariad dlia Marsianina"[36] ("Clothing for a Martian") and "Samaia trudnaia distantsiia"[37] ("The Most Difficult Distance"), which are almost entirely reproduced in the fiction, are used by Dovlatov to discuss two taboo subjects: nationalism and sex. The rest of the chapters contain recognizable reworkings of stories from genuine newspaper articles without actually quoting a whole article. In these Dovlatov uses ostensible quotations, which are largely made up. The sources of many such "quotations" are traced in this chapter. The stories that were published separately in journals are not preceded in those versions by the newspaper "quotations" they acquire in *The Compromise.* In some of his articles, both real and fictitious, Dovlatov reworks phrases from his *Notebooks* to different effect. He said that he did not consider journalism to be a harmful occupation for a writer as many thought it to be. He claimed to use a different part of his brain when he was writing for newspapers. This chapter will compare the fictional material in *The Compromise* with the journalistic material published in *Soviet Estonia* and other papers and will also draw examples from elsewhere in Dovlatov's oeuvre to illustrate his reuse of material in different contexts.

Together with other mass media (to say nothing of literature), the press in the Soviet Union in the 1970s was viewed as being of major importance in the ideological struggle: it was there not merely to provide "news," but also served to guide and educate the population in the spirit of socialism and mobilize it for the task of "building communism." Apart from "central" or all-Union papers, published in Moscow, each of the fifteen republics published its own newspaper in Russian and in the language of the republic. *Soviet Estonia* was such a "republican" Russian-language publication. Newspapers in the Soviet Union were standardized: they were four to eight pages long (with some exceptions), and most of them carried their leading articles, commenting mostly on domestic issues, on the front page; good and evil were clearly defined (mainly as socialist and capitalist), and news from the capitalist world was never allowed to appear on the front page. In fact, even in the socialist world there was a strict hierarchy to be observed, as Dovlatov describes in *The Compromise.* Even the names of countries had to be listed in correct "ideological" order. First on the list should come the U.S.S.R., if applicable, then the socialist countries, but Hungary, for example, could not come before the German Democratic Republic. As the editor says: "You're a worker on a Party newspaper. Hungary goes to third! They had an uprising there" (*C,* 6; *SS* 1:231). An exemplary ordering of countries was given in this brief news item in *Soviet Estonia* on October 18, 1973: "Cuba, Mongolia, France, West Germany—to these and other countries go products with the trademark of the Tartu sports equipment factory . . ." Soviet journalists were urged to foster Soviet patriotism, loyalty, and confidence in ultimate victory.[38] Without specifically referring to the Soviet press, Roger Fowler has demonstrated that the press in general has the task of presenting "reality from specific angles."[39] His definition of the news as a construction of social reality is particularly applicable to the Soviet press: "Thus news is a *practice:* a discourse which, far from neutrally reflecting social reality and empirical facts, intervenes in what Berger and Luckmann call 'the social construction of reality.' "[40] Dovlatov's novel *The Compromise* shows how meticulously this reality was constructed in *Soviet Estonia.*[41]

On October 18, 1973, *Soviet Estonia* published in the column Chelovek i professiia (People and Professions) Dovlatov's article "Nariad dlia Marsianina" ("Clothing for a Martian"), together with M. Zhbankov's photograph of Voldemar Sild, a tailor by profession who worked for the Russian State Drama Theater in Tallinn.[42] As a village boy long ago Sild had dreamed of becoming a painter or a musician, but as the seventh child in the family, he had had to choose a more prosaic profession and became a tailor. By chance he met a painter, who invited him to make a few costumes for the theater, and he liked it so much that he stayed there the rest of his life. It was a difficult job, because, for example, in order to create the costume for the slave Aesop, Sild had to study ancient Greek history and painting as well as Greek drama. And in order to learn how to make Kutuzov's uniform, he traveled to the Hermitage in Leningrad. "Clothing for a Martian" is an article about a man totally dedicated to his profession. This is one of the articles Dovlatov looks back on when writing *The Compromise.* It is the "Seventh Compromise" in the novel and is dated April 1976. Most of the article is reproduced from *Soviet Estonia* of 1973 with few changes: Voldemar's background is not given and the name of the painter Karin Luts, who first introduced Sild to the theater, is omitted. Only one example of his costume research is given (on Aesop), and the fact that Sild collected books on costumes and fashions through the ages is also missing in the fiction. Apart from that, Griboedov's characters Chatsky and Skalozub give way to Pushkin's Onegin and Gogol's Sobakevich in the transition from the newspaper article to the text of *The Compromise.*

> Imagine Chatsky in baggy trousers or Skalozub in an elegant tailcoat. (Predstav'te sebe Chatskogo v meshkovatykh briukakh, ili Skalozuba v elegantnom frake. [*Soviet Estonia,* October 18, 1973, p. 4.])

> Imagine Onegin dressed in baggy trousers, or Sobakevich in an elegant tailcoat . . . (*C,* 69) (Predstav'te sebe Onegina v meshkovatykh briukakh, ili Sobakevicha v elegantnom frake . . . [*SS* 1:286].)

There are also small stylistic discrepancies between the original article and the text of *The Compromise.* An almost imperceptible change is made in the list of clothing: *kazakin* (a man's knee-length coat) is left out, and *mentik* (a hussar's pelisse) is added (presumably because of Dovlatov's avoidance of words beginning with the same letter); the two-syllable *armiak* (a peasant's coat of heavy cloth) is replaced by the three-syllable *arkhaluk* (a short caftan); and the comma is deleted after the word "clothes." "The frock coat, caftan, knee-length coat, military coat, peasant's coat—these are all absolutely distinct types of clothing, each with its own specific features and accessories" ("Siurtuk, kaftan, kazakin, bekesha, armiak—vse eto strogo opredelennye vidy odezhdy so svoimi spetsificheskimi chertami i aksessuarami"; *Soviet Estonia,* October 18, 1973, p. 4). "The frockcoat, caftan, military cloak, pelisse, smock frock—these are all absolutely distinct types of clothing, each with its own specific features and accessories" (*C,* 69) ("Siurtuk, kaftan, bekesha, mentik, arkhaluk—vse eto strogo opredelennye vidy odezhdy so svoimi spetsificheskimi chertami i aksessuarami"; *SS* 1:286).

Besides the stylistic differences between the newspaper articles and the language of the "fictional" stories, important contrasts are drawn between the picture of Soviet reality purveyed in the press and the experienced reality recounted in the stories. This is well illustrated in the "fictional" part of this story when the narrator, Dovlatov, is rebuked by the editor of the paper, Turonok (the real name of the editor of *Soviet Estonia*). Turonok tells him that the column People and Professions should be about people of rare professions containing some unexpected aspects. According to Turonok, it had transpired that Sild was a Nazi collaborator and had spent twelve years in prison for "murdering Soviet patriots" (unexpected indeed, but not in the sense intended). This was a serious mistake for a journalist to make. However, Soviet journalists did not have license to print an interview with anybody: permission had to be obtained from the appropriate authority. When the narrator points out that permission had been obtained from the theater director, Sild's employer, the editor tells him that the director was himself a former SS chief lieutenant and, to make matters worse, a homosexual.

Questions of wartime collaboration and the related issue of Estonian nationalism were a particularly sensitive matter and a taboo subject in the Soviet press. Besides the story of Sild, Dovlatov addresses this problem in the "Fourth Compromise" and even more fully in *The Zone.* In the latter work Dovlatov tells the story of a father, Kalju Pahapill, and his son, Gustav. After the Soviet occupation of Estonia in 1939 Kalju lives quietly with the motto, "Only Estonians should live in these parts," but when the Germans invade the country in 1941 he goes off to live in the forest. When the Soviet army then liberates Estonia in 1944, he is at first taken for a freedom fighter and given a decoration, but when he is called up to serve in the Soviet Army he runs away into the forest again, observing: "Estonians ought to live here, and as for Vankas, Fritzes, and various Greenlanders, there's no place for them here!" (Z, 6; *SS* 2:10). Caught by the Russians, he is beaten up, tried for desertion, and exiled to Kazakhstan, where he dies. Kalju's son, Gustav, qualifies as a telegraphist in Tallinn. In the fashionable Mundi-bar in Tallinn he modifies his father's motto: "A true Estonian ought to live in Canada!" (Z, 6; *SS* 2:10).

Recognizable traits of Kalju Pahapill can be found in one of the articles Dovlatov wrote for *Soviet Estonia,* dated August 1, 1974, "Frontoviki, naden'te ordena . . ." ("Front-Line Soldiers—Put on Your Medals . . ."), about Grigory Vasilievich Katuntsevsky, a retired captain who was decorated for bravery five times with the medal of the Red Banner. He was living in Tallinn. Kalju Pahapill was also decorated for bravery: "What does an Estonian need a medal for?" (Z, 5), Pahapill will exclaim in *The Zone.* "So he lived and worked as a glazier" (Z, 5; *SS* 1:10), writes Dovlatov about Pahapill, and about Katuntsevsky he writes: "From the age of twelve he had worked in the glass factory in Balakhna." Pahapill's close friendship with his dog Garun is described in *The Zone:* "The instructor spoke little in general. If he did speak, it was in Estonian, and not, for the most part, with his countrymen, but with Harun. The dog always accompanied him" (Z, 50; *SS* 1:10). The prehistory of this can perhaps be traced to Dovlatov's newspaper article "Esli podruzhilis' dvoe . . ." ("When Two Become Friends . . .") in *Soviet Estonia,* April 14, 1973: "Meelis Piarna had reared and trained the beautiful Alsatian Karri. Soon he would be called up into the Soviet Army. Meelis would not part with his friend: they would serve on the frontier together . . ." Mention of camps, of course, was not permitted in Soviet newspapers.

Dovlatov uses and reuses the same phrase with different effects in newspaper material and in fiction. In his *Notebooks* he writes: "My cousin's father used to say: I only stop worrying about Boria when he's in prison!" ("Otets moego dvoiurodnogo brata govoril:—za Boriu ia otnositel'no spokoen, lish' kogda ego derzhat v tiur'me!" [*SS* 4:134]). Writing Morality Issues for *Soviet Estonia* in a piece titled "Moi beglyi papa" ("My Runaway Dad"), Dovlatov describes case no. 4807, concerning a man who refused to pay child support and did everything possible to run away from his responsibilities as a parent, so that most of the time nobody knew his whereabouts.[43] In the Soviet Union refusal to pay maintenance was punishable by law: "It was then that Ostapenko's former wife, Alevtina Erikhovna, uttered this harsh, but just phrase: 'I am only at ease when he's in prison.' " ("Imenno togda byvshaia zhena Ostapenko—Alevtina Erikhovna proiznesla zhestkuiu, no spravedlivuiu frazu: 'Ia spokoina, lish' kogda on sidit v tuir'me.' ") In *The Compromise*

Dovlatov uses this same phrase again, this time to comic effect. The narrator (who is covering the story of the birth of Tallinn's four hundred thousandth citizen) introduces himself to the head of the maternity hospital, an Estonian called Dr. Teppe. The narrator asks whether Teppe himself has any children. He confesses that he does have a son, but that he will probably soon be jailed. The narrator lowers his voice and inquires whether it was because his son was a member of the Estonian underground independence movement: " 'My son,' Teppe said distinctly, 'is a black marketeer and a drunk. And I can only stop worrying about him when he's locked up' " (*C*, 33). ("Moi syn,—otchekanil Teppe,—fartsovshchik i p'ianitsa. I ia mogu byt' za nego otnositel'no spokoen, lish' kogda ego derzhat v tiur'me . . ."; *SS* 1:255.)

On October 25, 1973, *Soviet Estonia* carried a full-page dedication to Tallinn's four hundred thousandth citizen, a son born to Lijna and Uiri Simsalu. The birth was assisted by doctor Helgi Kaze and midwife Lorejda Ryuk. The article, "Zdravstvui, chetyrekhsottysiachnyi!" ("Welcome to the Four Hundred Thousandth!"), contains the text of a congratulatory message from the city Communist Party and the local council as well as a poem by A. Kivi[44] ("Welcome, little one, welcome, clever one, You're what we've been waiting for, Now it's our turn to celebrate, There are four hundred thousand of us" ["Zdravstvui, malen'kii, zdravstvui, umnitsa! Nam tebia ved' nedostavalo. Nynche prazdnik na nashei ulitse—Nas chetyresta tysiach stalo"]) and photographs of the hospital, the mother, the baby, and the doctors. On the same page there is an interview with the leader of the Tallinn City Council on the significance of the fact that the population of Tallinn had reached four hundred thousand. Dovlatov makes use of this material in the "Fifth Compromise," although he did not contribute to the actual newspaper article. The "newspaper article" reproduced here is Dovlatov's invention. In *The Compromise* the fictional newspaper report is dated two years after the real event, as November 1975. As in the factual event, the birth of the four hundred thousandth citizen coincides with the annual celebration of Liberation Day. In the fictional part of the "Fifth Compromise," the narrator is sent to report on the arrival of the four hundred thousandth citizen. He is briefed by the editor:

> "And remember"—Turonok stood up, closing our conversation—"the infant has to be publicizable. [. . .] Which means meeting all requirements. No damaged goods, nothing gloomy. No caesarean sections. No unwed mothers. A complete set of parents. A healthy boy meeting all the social requirements." (*C*, 27)

I zapomnite—mladenets dolzhen byt' publikabel'nym . . . To est' polnotsennym. Nichego ushcherbnogo. Nikakikh kesarevykh sechenii. Nikakikh

> materei-odinochek. Polnyi komplekt roditelei. Zdorovyi, sotsial'no polnotsennyi mal'chik.' (*SS* 1:249)

The list does not end there: many other categories, such as Jews, black people, and, in this instance, girls are excluded. The narrator dismantles one by one some of the "guiding" principles of Soviet ideology: friendship between the peoples, equality of people of all races and equality between the sexes, and the much-acclaimed "classless Soviet society." The journalist narrator requests the head of the maternity hospital, Dr. Teppe, to make arrangements for staff to report each new birth to him. Each "candidate" has to be vetted by the editor in advance, thus ruling out chance or the "real" four hundred thousandth birth.

The first to give birth to a boy is an Estonian woman with an Ethiopian husband: "The father is Ethiopian . . . on our side" ("Ego otets—druzhestvennyi nam efiop"; *SS* 1:256), reports Dovlatov to the editor Turonok. The child does not correspond to the editor's criteria, and just what the editor thinks of "friendship between the peoples" becomes apparent as he yells down the phone: "Wait for a normal—do you hear me?—*normal* human baby!" (*C*, 35) ("Dozhdites' normal'nogo—vy slyshite menia?—normal'nogo chelovecheskogo rebenka!"; *SS* 1:257). There is a huge gap between the official outlook ("An Ethiopian, on our side" ["druzhestvennyi nam efiop"]) and the blatant racism of the editor. A similar instance occurs in *The Craft*, where Dovlatov wants to write a review of the jazz pianist Oscar Peterson, but the editor has never heard of him, so Dovlatov resorts to using newspaper clichés to persuade the editor to print his review: "He is a Negro. Downtrodden national minority." ("On—negr. Ugnetennoe natsional'noe men'shinstvo"; *SS* 3:59.) The "downtrodden minority" is the official line, and the editor agrees to publish the review of the concert. However (according to Skul'skaia), this review was never published in *Soviet Estonia.*[45] Its text and comments are "reproduced" in *The Craft* as "Sem' not v tishine . . ." ("Seven Notes in Silence"). Commenting on the actual events "behind the story" (similarly to the *Compromise* stories), the narrator records that the great Canadian jazz pianist burst out laughing when he saw the article, telling the narrator that this was the first time a review of a concert of his had been published in such small print. On occasions when news about black people was printed and official newspaper commentators wanted to appear fair-minded, the language became absurd. Dovlatov refers to this in his *Notebooks,* quoting a report on a boxing match between a black boxer and a white blond-haired Pole: "The Negro boxer can be distinguished by the light blue edging on his shorts" ("Negritianskogo boksera vy mozhete otlichit' po svetlo-goluboi kaemke na trusakh"; *SS* 3:98).[46]

The next to give birth is the wife of a famous Tallinn poet, Boris

Shtein.[47] Both husband and wife are party members, and Shtein is overjoyed and writes a poem. In the "factual" part of the "Fifth Compromise," Dovlatov includes a poem attributed to Shtein in celebration of this event:

In factories, in the deepest mines,
On planets strange and far,
I see four hundred thousand heroes,
And my firstborn, too, is there! (*C*, 38)

Na fabrikakh, v zherlakh zaboev,
Na dal'nikh planetakh inykh—
Chetyresta tysiach geroev,
I pervenets moi sredi nikh . . . (*SS* 1:260)[48]

However, Shtein is a Jew, "and every Jew has to be submitted for approval" (*C*, 37; *SS* 1:259), and their baby is, of course, rejected.

Eventually, an Estonian woman with a Russian husband called Kuzin, a member of the Communist Party, both working class, gives birth to a boy. When the narrator interviews the husband (who is an alcoholic and far from certain how his wife became pregnant), he answers in clichéd phrases: "We work, like everyone else. We broaden our horizons. [People look up to us.] We use our leadership abilities" (*C*, 40). ("Trudimsia, kak polozheno . . . Rasshiriaem svoi krugozor . . . Pol'zuemsia avtoritetom . . ."; *SS* 1:261.) Not only is there no chance of simply waiting for the real four hundred thousandth citizen, but the Communist Party interferes further. The narrator has to persuade the father to call his son Lembit, after an Estonian folk hero. The editor is prepared to give a "bribe" of twenty-five rubles (and a symbolic "key" to the city, the price of which is deducted from the twenty-five rubles) to the father if he will register his son as Lembit (the article in the paper on October 25, 1973, notes that the name of the newborn has not been decided: "We don't yet know his name"). Anticipating a long and unpleasant discussion over the child's name (the narrator points out to the editor that calling him Lembit is the equivalent of asking a Russian parent to call his child "Bova" or "Mikula"), the narrator suggests going somewhere to talk things over: " 'You mean—have a drink?' Kuzin brightened" (*C*, 40) ("V smysle—poddat'?—ozhivilsia Kuzin"; *SS* 1:261). This is the first natural, nonclichéd sentence Kuzin utters. The story ends with the arrest of the narrator and the father of the newborn four hundred thousandth inhabitant of Tallinn for drunkenness.

The article in *Soviet Estonia* of June 4, 1973 (signed S. Ader), "Samaia trudnaia distantsiia" ("The Most Difficult Distance"), is about a young female scholar, Tijna Karu, who works in the field of cancer research. She also has another passion: Tijna has won the republic's athletics championship at 400 meters. The article describes what an effort it required to not only become a champion runner but to graduate in chemistry, complete a Ph.D., and at the same time live in a student hostel. Tijna Karu is also married and has a daughter. The article mentions that her husband has started on a postgraduate degree at Moscow State University and they have to live apart. The main points of this article are reproduced in the "Ninth Compromise." In the fictional part Tijna tells the narrator that she and her husband have become estranged. She wants to put things right and learn more about sex. Sex was another taboo subject in the Soviet Union, and in this respect too Estonia was freer, or at least the attitude was more matter-of-fact. A book in Russian, "The Technology of Sex," is found for Tijna.[49] Having read it, she decides to practice the recommendations in the book before trying them out on her husband, and the narrator fixes her up with a colleague: "I have to emphasize that all this was said without a trace of flirtatiousness, and in the Estonian manner—down-to-earth and businesslike" (*C,* 99; *SS* 1:325). The narrator goes through a list of possible candidates for Tijna to practice sex with. Several friends are listed in the story and rejected for one reason or another. One of them is a certain Klensky, who is rejected on the grounds that he has gonorrhea. The real Klensky, now a deputy in the Tallinn City Council, but formerly Dovlatov's colleague on *Soviet Estonia,* in an interview with the Internet magazine *Chas* expresses puzzlement, but does admit to recalling how the story could have arisen.[50] The story almost corresponds to reality. Dovlatov has managed to pick out of a real story the most characteristic trait and retell it in a fictional story that almost happened but not quite.

In the "Eighth Compromise," a young Estonian journalist named Evi is infatuated with the narrator. She works for a youth newspaper and writes articles about sex. Evi considers sex to be an important topic about which people are poorly informed. She is articulate and knowledgeable about matters sexual. The narrator has to concentrate in order to behave rationally. "Evi soon appeared, all pink, in a wet bathing suit. [. . .] Try staying reasonable yourself if there's a seventeen-year-old girl next to you who's just emerged from the sea. Or, to be more exact, from the river . . ." (*C,*123; *SS* 1:308). The image of the "wet swimsuit" in which a young girl appears illustrates Dovlatov's own coyness in the treatment of sexual topics. He also uses it in *The Zone:* "Boris draws Galya Vodianitskaya close. The girl is wearing a wet bathing suit" (*Z,* 35; *SS* 2:36). In the article "Bednyi Eros: Nepod'emnaia tema sovremennoi slovesnosti" ("Poor Eros: The Theme That Cannot Be Raised in Contemporary Literature"), Vladimir Novikov writes that the love theme in Russian literature for the past one and a half centuries has been constructed under the dominant influence of *Eugene Onegin:*

> The question of the hero's and heroine's feelings towards each other inevitably acquires a philosophical and symbolic dimension and turns, in principle, into a question of the possibility of harmony in this world. All the meetings and non-meetings of Turgenev's, Dostoevsky's, and Leo Tolstoy's characters took place under this sign. This is the trademark of Russia in world literature.[51]

Although Bunin's *Temnye allei* (*Dark Avenues*) springs to mind as an obvious exception, Novikov is right in concluding that there is a vacuum in contemporary Russian erotic literature: "And in general our erotic literature will take years to overcome the gap between the 'physics' and the metaphysics of love relationships and to grasp what connects the 'higher' and the 'lower'—the realm of the 'psyche' (I don't want to use the utilitarian word 'psychology')."[52] Dovlatov is no exception; on the whole he avoids scenes of intimacy, and the nearest he comes to eroticism is: "Evi kept stroking my hand and whispering in a tone of disturbing indecency" (*C*, 125; *SS* 1:310), which strikingly resembles Alikhanov's erotic reminiscences in *The Zone:* "She whispered to Alikhanov incomprehensible Indonesian words" (*SS* 2:36).

This was a feature of his own writing of which Dovlatov was by no means unaware. At a roundtable discussion organized by Radio Liberty in 1988, he recalled being asked by Wolfgang Kasack why he wrote so little about sex and God, the two themes most dear to émigré writers. His answer to the question was: "Because it is precisely in these themes that a writer's lack of talent reveals itself particularly easily and obviously."[53] He went on to list a large number of writers, both Russian and American, who had revealed their failings in this area, concluding that only Dostoevsky and Faulkner had succeeded in writing about the theme of sex in a direct manner that was at once chaste and sensual.

In another narrative strand of the "Eighth Compromise," Dovlatov tells the story behind one of the numerous "reports" printed every day in the papers about some economic achievement or other. Linda Peips, an Estonian milkmaid, "reports" to Brezhnev on the record amount of milk she has managed to get per cow: "I got a record sum* of milk off one cow" ("Ia nadoila s odnoi korovy rekordnoe chislo* moloka"; *SS* 1:288) quotes the narrator, indicating by the asterisk that he has left "the stylistic mistakes intact." In the fictional part of the story he explains that he had intentionally written the incorrect phrase ". . . off one cow" (". . . s odnoi korovy") because in it "resounded a truth to life and the touching simple-heartedness of a peasant" ("zvuchala zhiznennaia dostovernost' i trogatel'noe krest'ianskoe prostodushie"; *SS* 1:321). However, Comrade Brezhnev is so "efficient" that the telegram from him arrives before Linda Peips has managed to inform him about her great achievements.

The story about Linda Peips is also based on a true story reported in *Soviet Estonia* on February 6, 1975. Although Dovlatov was still working on the paper, he did not contribute to this article or the subsequent articles on the Peips story (for example on February 7 and 16). The real name of the milkmaid in the report is Leida Peips. In the article on the meeting of the collective of "the show farm Vil'iandi" ("oporno-pokazatel'nyi sovkhoz 'Vil'iandi"), the fact of the telegram from Brezhnev is reported thus: "The warm words in the letter of the First Secretary of the Central Committee of the CPSU Comrade L. I. Brezhnev in reply to the letter of the leading milkmaid Leida Peips excited everyone." However, far from the "touching simple-heartedness of a peasant," Leida Peips's speech as reported in the newspaper is full of the appropriate clichés expected of a famous milkmaid: "I am profoundly grateful to comrade L. I. Brezhnev for his warm words. His appreciation of my modest labor and of the achievements of the entire collective of the farm obliges us to seek and exploit reserves with even greater insistence in all areas of farm production." Similarly, in her "real" letter to Brezhnev she uses correct grammar: "Dear Leonid Il'ich! I wish to share with you a great joy. Today my dearest dream has been realized: I have become a candidate member of the many-million-strong party of Lenin." In Dovlatov's fictional words she expresses herself less formally and with an unintended ambiguity: "The communists of our farm have unanimously elected me their member!" ("Kommunisty nashei fermy druzhno izbrali menia svoim chlenom!"; *SS* 1:288).

The "nonfictional" part of the "Tenth Compromise" (which had appeared separately with the title "Lishnii") is from the Tallinn evening paper *Vechernii Tallin,* dated July 1976.[54] It is a brief "news" item about the arrest of a certain Ernst Leopol'dovich Bush, who had tried to pass himself off as a journalist. Evgeny Rein, in his article "Neskol'ko slov vdogonku" ("A Few Words as an Afterthought"), recalls a story Dovlatov told him about an unlucky and eccentric journalist friend in Tallinn. When Rein visited Tallinn, Dovlatov introduced him to this person, and he concludes that this was the prototype for the hero of "Lishnii." The journal text of this story had a dedication, which was omitted in later editions: "To Aleksandr Gross, irrepressible Russian reprobate, superfluous man, and disturber of the peace. How I long to immortalize your name!" ("Aleksandru Grossu, neuderzhimomu russkomu degradantu, lishnemu cheloveku i vozmutiteliu spokoistviia. Do chego zhe ia khochu obessmertit' tvoe imia!") Rein himself was struck by this eccentric and enigmatic person, quite recognizable in the story, although while reading the story he had difficulty in separating the factual and fictitious parts of it. Rein considers this blurring of the boundary between fact and fiction to be one of the mechanisms Dovlatov uses in the construction of many of his stories:

> Long before writing the story he created an image which artistically complemented reality. Prior to being put down on paper, this story was realized twice. At first in an oral form which was aesthetically expressive, almost grotesque, but connected with reality by hundreds of threads. Subsequent events that happened to the protagonist made the outline of the story. Reality itself, so to speak, wrote the story, leaning on what had been created by Dovlatov in advance.[55]

The story "Lishnii" ("Superfluous"), as published in *Grani* and later in *The Compromise,* is preceded by a preliminary version called "Kapitan, ulybnites'!" ("Captain, Smile!"), which was published in 1982.[56] This story is about a journalist called Mikhail Bush, who is originally from Archangel but works in Leningrad. There is a brief description of his parents, his weakness for older women, and his excellent dress sense, as well as the rebelliousness of his character. The main narrative of this story is the same as in the "Tenth Compromise": Bush wants to become a full-time journalist, but each time he is near his aim, he himself ruins his own chances. In the "Tenth Compromise" and in "Captain, Smile!" Bush is given the task of interviewing the captain of a capitalist vessel. His brief from the editor is as follows:

> You go to the commercial port. Have a chat with a few Western captains. Choose one of them who is the most sympathetic to socialist ideas. Ask him a few questions. Try and get the right kind of answers from him. In a word, do an interview with him. It's desirable that he should congratulate us on the sixty-third anniversary of the October Revolution. That doesn't mean he has to be shouting political slogans. Not at all. Restrained, respectful congratulations are quite sufficient. That's all we need. Got it? (*SS* 1:337–38)

Bush arrives in the port and finds out which of the ships is due to sail the soonest: a West German merchant ship with a captain called Paul Rudi. Bush makes arrangements with him for an interview, during which they discuss preferences in brandy, women, and money. The next day Bush writes an ideologically correct article, which is a complete fabrication from beginning to end and concludes on a high note, quoting Captain Rudi: "You just remember, my lad! Freedom is like air. You breathe freedom without noticing it . . . Soviet people can't understand that. They were born free, like the birds" (*SS* 1:341). The editor is pleased and the story is published. However, the next day Bush is summoned by the KGB. It transpires that Captain Rudi has been arrested because he was a former Estonian who had escaped to West Germany, and that the KGB has been hunting him for a while. It is Bush's ideological mistake that matters to the authorities rather than the fact that not a single word in his article was true.

Dovlatov made only a few changes to this story for its 1985 publication in *Grani,* and there are just minor discrepancies between this version and the final version in Dovlatov's collected works. The protagonist is renamed Ernst Leopol'dovich Bush and the story is set in Tallinn. This 1985 version was added to the Russian version of *The Compromise* with further minor changes: the dedication to Aleksandr Gross was removed, and instead a brief newspaper report was added from the section of the *Evening Tallinn* called "Oni meshaiut nam zhit' " ("They Spoil Our Lives"). This newspaper article describes an incident involving a certain citizen named E. L. Bush who was brought to medical sobering-up station no. 4. All the major elements in the 1982 version of the story are preserved, but expanded considerably.

The "Tenth Compromise" is the longest story in the novel. It has a frame, which begins with Dovlatov's arrival in Tallinn and ends with his departure. There is a brief epilogue which summarizes the "real-life events" of the characters that are depicted in the story: Grishania, who drove Dovlatov to Tallinn and was due to be arrested, turns up in the United States; the story of Shablinsky is told, a journalist on *Soviet Estonia,* with whom Dovlatov decides on the spur of the moment to go to Tallinn; and it is learned from newspapers that Captain Rudi spent four years in Mordovian prison camps. In this epilogue, a backward glance from the United States, the narrator relates various probable and improbable versions he has heard about the fate of Bush, the only person whose fate escapes him. He casts a last nostalgic look at this character, which echoes the original dedication: "Where is he now? That dissident and dandy, schizophrenic, poet and hero, disturber of the peace—Ernst Leopoldovich Bush?" ("Gde on teper', dissident i krasavets, shizofrenik, poet i geroi, vozmutitel' spokoistviia—Ernst Leopol'dovich Bush!") There is no doubt that the principal protagonist of the story is Bush, but, as often happens in Dovlatov's work, there is an implicit comparison with the narrator himself. In many ways their stories run in parallel and here too, just as in the story of Kuptsov in *The Zone,* narrator and hero, Dovlatov and Bush, are interchangeable.

In his account of language in newspapers, Roger Fowler gives the following definition:

> News is a representation of the world in language; because language is a semiotic code, it imposes a structure of values, social and economic in origin, on whatever is represented; and so inevitably news, like every discourse, constructively patterns that of which it speaks. News is a representation in this sense of construction; it is not a value-free reflection of "facts."[57]

The Soviet press did not even pretend to be a "value-free" presentation of facts. The first impression of Soviet newspapers, particularly to a Western reader, may be of uniformity, drabness, and tedium. Certainly, Soviet papers did not set out to entertain the reader. Nevertheless, the language of the newspapers consisted of material that was varied in its stylistic orientation, and it has been shown that Soviet newspaper language was by no means uniform. In the Soviet Union, too, there were many different types of newspapers and they carried a large variety of material: official announcements, reports on conferences, speeches of politicians, editorials, factual information, commentaries, and so on. The language and style do vary considerably from item to item.[58] This point is fully discussed in B. M. Boguslavsky's work, in which he also makes the distinction between "lighter" styles (such as reportage, humoresques, feuilletons) and more "traditional means of expression" (such as editorials, official announcements, analysis of foreign news).[59] In the "lighter" styles, according to Boguslavsky, the author's attitude can be expressed fully, whereas in the traditional newspaper category the author's voice is hidden away. The type of article Dovlatov wrote for *Soviet Estonia* as described above was such as to allow him to express his "authorial attitude," and these articles bear his distinctive imprint. For example, the article published in *Soviet Estonia* on October 18, 1974, "Byvaiu zdes' vse chashche . . ." ("I Come Here More and More Often . . ."), is about a young architect, Leonid Kopylovsky, winner of an All-Union competition. The news story is practically a textbook example of newspaper narratives in this more "personal" style. Analyzing the nature of news stories, Allan Bell divides the structure of such narratives into six elements: abstract, orientation, evaluation, complicating action, resolution, and coda. "A news text will normally consist of an abstract, attribution and the story proper."[60] In his article Dovlatov sets the scene and describes the initial situation. He then tells what happened: the architect came to learn about architectural design in Tallinn. Dovlatov proceeds to evaluate the story and concludes with a quotation from the architect on the strong impact the city landscape had on him. Under a similar heading, "Tallinn's Guests," the "Third Compromise" tells the story of Alla Meleshko, a ballet student. This "nonfictional" story has all the elements of Dovlatov's news story about the arhictect in *Soviet Estonia.* The structure of the narrative follows the same pattern; however, the language of the fictional narrative is different: the sentences are shorter and the language is considerably livelier. There is one point in the description of Tallinn at which the fictional and nonfictional stories overlap. The following passage from the story illustrates the difference eloquently: "It is a wonderful city, cosy and severe. It strikes you with the harmonic contrast between things old and modern. In its quiet and calm you feel a proud strength." ("Eto zamechatel'nyi gorod, uiutnyi i strogii. Porazhaet garmonicheskim kontrastom stariny i moderna. V ego tishine i spokoistvii oshchushchaetsia gordaia moshch' "; *SS* 1:235.) The corresponding quotation from the *Soviet Estonia* article "Byvaiu zdes' vse chashche . . ." illustrates the stilted character of newspaper language: "The ultramodern vertical outline of the hotel does not dominate over the Gothic outlines of old Tallinn, but echoes it in a contrasting way. A unique fusion of things ancient and modern arises, of two equal and aesthetically valid principles." ("Ul'trasovremennyi vertikal'nyi kontur otelia ne dovleet nad goticheskimi ochertaniiami starogo Tallina, a kontrastno pereklikaetsia s nim. Voznikaet unikala'nyi splav moderna i drevnosti, dvukh ravnopravnykh i esteticheski tsennykh nachal.")

The story of the article's composition subverts the original content of the article itself. Although the real and the fictional articles do not differ in the evaluation they reach, the stylistic changes between the real article and its fictional counterpart constitute a primary stage of subversion, which is completed by the story in its final form. Dovlatov deliberately eroded the boundary between his fictional and journalistic material in order to create a novel with documentary characteristics. As was shown above, he utilized his journalistic activity to this purpose in the following way: first he published the stories separately without a newspaper "quotation." Later he strengthened the stories, first by unifying them through a first-person narrator, and second by adding an introductory "newspaper article" which, as discussed, was either genuine, previously published and faithfully reproduced, or invented. In some cases a genuine source of this newspaper article has been traced; in others the source remains undiscovered.

In a letter to L. Shtern from Vienna, where he was waiting for his U.S. entry visa, Dovlatov wrote: "I have a semi-documentary manuscript about journalism."[61] In her book *O psikhologicheskoi proze* (*On Psychological Prose*), Lidia Ginzburg writes that often in practice the dividing line between documentary and fiction cannot be clearly established. There are large numbers of documentary works which do not lay claim to aesthetic significance. What Dovlatov utilized in *The Compromise* was the fusion between real-life experience and its aesthetic interpretation, creating, as Ginzburg indicated and Evgeny Rein noted, a "second reality":

> Fiction, as it departs from experience, creates a "second reality"; documentary literature provides the reader with a dual cognition and a twofold emotion. This is because his experience of the authenticity of the real-life event remains unmediated by any art at all. A few lines of newsprint affect us differently than does the greatest novel.[62]

What Dovlatov succeeded in achieving in *The Compromise* is a double impact on the reader by incorporating the news stories into his fiction, thereby creating an aesthetically structured second reality. In Dovlatov's case it becomes clear that the Soviet newspaper articles in fact possess less of the "reality of the life event" of which Ginzburg speaks and are closer to fiction than the documentary "fiction" that Dovlatov devised to reveal the true-life event.

Chapter Five

Dovlatov's *Sanctuary* and Pushkin

DOVLATOV'S NOVEL *ZAPOVEDNIK* (*THE SANCTUARY*) is loosely based upon the author's own experiences during a period spent working in the "Pushkin Hills" (Pushkinskie Gory) Museum at Mikhailovskoe. It was not unusual for members of the Moscow and Leningrad intelligentsia to work as guides at the museum, and when Dovlatov's life in Estonia became unbearable and he could neither find employment in Leningrad nor persuade publishers there to accept his work, he took a job in Mikhailovskoe as a way of earning a living. It is clear from his correspondence that he actually worked there in 1975–77; the action of the novel, however, is attributed to a slightly later time, around 1978. He evidently had the first idea about writing a story about Pushkin and literature while still in the army. It is common knowledge that all textbooks in the U.S.S.R. depict Pushkin's killer d'Anthès in the blackest of terms. Dovlatov admits it is a silly idea, but he decided to stand up for d'Anthès, arguing that there is a rational idea behind it. One of Dovlatov's letters contains a jocular poem about d'Anthès: "In all textbooks d'Anthès is depicted as a terrible man. I decided to defend him. It's a stupid song, but everybody likes it." Some of the ideas of *The Sanctuary* can be traced to this:

D'Anthès von Haekkern
Was of course a bastard
So why in heaven's name
Is he so famous later?
[. . .]
That fellow didn't even read
Pushkin's poetry
He didn't have a clue
About Pushkin being a genius.
[. . .]
So how was he to know
That idiots of both sexes

Would later come to call him
An enemy of culture.

Dantes fon Gekkern
Konechno byl podonkom
Togda na koi zhe khren
Izvesten on potomkam.
[. . .]
A tot i ne chital
Ego stikhotvorenii
Ne znal on ni cherta
Pro to, chto Pushkin—genii.
[. . .]
Otkuda mog on znat'
Chto duraki i dury
Kogda-to budut zvat'
Ego vragom kul'tury.[1]

Dovlatov spent several summer seasons, from 1974 onward, working in the Pushkin Hills Museum, known more widely as the Sanctuary. As noted in chapter 1, he told Zibunova in March 1978 about his plans for the new novel. The first draft of *The Sanctuary* was completed in Leningrad. Ar'ev explains in his interview "Sergei Dovlatov po obe storony okeana" ("Dovlatov on Both Sides of the Ocean") that *The Sanctuary* was simply rewritten in the West according to Dovlatov's new, absolutely strict rules, which "allowed him to work on every sentence, on every word individually."[2] Ar'ev explains that this allowed Dovlatov to achieve the strictest control over every line, even over every sound, in his writing.

In the issue of *Novyi Amerikanets* for September 27, 1980, Dovlatov published an excerpt from his book *Fiveways* entitled "Pskovskie otkrytki" ("Postcards from Pskov"), which later formed part of *The Sanctuary.* In the May 16, 1980, issue of *Novyi Amerikanets* he had already published the story "Schastlivaia derevnia" ("A Happy Village"), which also forms part of the final version of *The Sanctuary.* "Postcards from Pskov" also has a brief introduction explaining the story behind it and outlining the real state of affairs in the Pushkin Museum: "About the false exhibits, prepared by one Samorodsky. About the notorious textbook veneer. About the neglect of real historical materials. About the profound ignorance of the guides and the tourists. About the grandiloquent obscurantism of the director, S. S. Geichenko."[3] In the same brief introduction, Dovlatov writes that he had in mind to dedicate this piece to Abram Tertz and call it "Progulki s Dantesom" ("Walks with d'Anthès"): "After all, Pushkin's murderer, d'Anthès, and the falsifier of [Pushkin's] biography, Geichenko, can be regarded as intellectual allies."[4]

The family archive contains a 1978 draft version of *The Sanctuary*, which had the working title *Naslednik* (*The Heir*). This also has an epigraph, which throws some light on the completed work:

> I know it is immodest, but I would still like to address my story to Pushkin. If only because he is the only real person here. The rest of the characters are invented . . .
>
> Pushkin has long been silent, but his is the silence of the root, that listens to the sound of the leaves without anger, without partiality, without condescension.
>
> And one final thing. I don't regard enmity as the antithesis of love. And not indifference either. But the lie. Correspondingly, the antithesis of hatred is truth. I've been wanting to speak out about this for a long time.[5]

Dovlatov was working on this draft in April 1978 when life was particularly difficult for him and he was under pressure to leave the country. Evidently he took the decision to emigrate at about the time he was at work on this version.[6] *The Sanctuary* can in general be clearly felt as Dovlatov's goodbye to Russia. The early version brings this feeling to the fore even more acutely. On page 53 of the manuscript he cites the following poem, attributed to an anonymous writer ("Someone wrote"):

Is it rusty fetters,
Is it just a snare—
My unfinished books
Hold me here.
I feel within myself
no lightness and no strength—
To fly off into the Empyrean,
To a place I have never lived,
Where I have not sown and have not reaped,
Where by dint of that
Russia, mother and stepmother,
Will haunt my dreams . . .

To li rzhavye verigi,
to li zapadnia —
Nedopisannye knigi
Derzhat zdes' menia.
I ne chuvstvuiu v sebe ia

legkosti i sil —
Uletet' kak v empirei,
V krai, gde ia ne zhil,
Gde ne zhal ia i ne seial,
Gde po toi vine,
Mat' i machekha Raseia,
Budet snit'sia mne . . .

The comparison of this draft version with the completed final version of *The Sanctuary* gives us a glimpse of the effort Dovlatov put into the language and style of this work. Many scenes were cut down to a minimum. For example, the love scene when the narrator's wife visits him in the Sanctuary is greatly reduced. The poverty of the village is merely hinted at with a few sentences in the final version, whereas the draft specifically recalls the villagers' dislike of Stalin, because they remembered the famine. In the final version the protagonist is quite vague about his feelings: "Strange as it may seem, I felt something akin to love" ("Kak ni stranno, ia oshchushchal chto-to vrode liubvi"; *SS* 2:224), whereas the draft is more descriptive: "I took a step towards my wife, and we kissed. I mumbled something incoherent.—'I love you too,' said Olia.' " ("Ia shagnul k zhene, i my potselovalis'. Ia probormotal chto-to nevniatnoe.—I ia tebia liubliu,—skazala Olia.")[7] The protagonist's wife here is called by the name of Pushkin's secondary heroine Olia, while in the final version she is Tania. The draft is also structured differently from the final version. The first part of the draft ends with the departure of the protagonist's wife. The concluding paragraph is telling: "I looked in on Misha, but he wasn't there. Over his dirty bed a gun was glinting, a ponderous double-barreled shotgun of Tula manufacture with a reddish stock. I took it down and wondered: 'Maybe it's time I shot myself?' " ("Ia zaglianul k Mishe, ego ne bylo. Nad griaznoi postel'iu mertsalo ruzh'e, uvesistaia tul'skaia dvustvolka s krasnovatym lozhem. Snial ego i dumaiu: 'A ne pora li mne zastrelit'sia?' ")[8]

It has been mentioned that Dovlatov used his observations as a journalist in many works of fiction. The reverse is also true. This draft version of *The Sanctuary* contains a sketch which shows that Dovlatov reused some of his literary material in his journalism. The protagonist has the following conversation with Mikhail Ivanych, who has a hangover and complains: " 'I'm shaking all over' . . . I gave him a ruble. At lunch I asked him: 'Well, then, feeling better?'—'You what?'—'Cleared your head?'—'Aha. Like water on a hot frying pan, fizzed right through me!' " ("— Kolotit vsego . . . Ia dal emu rubl'. V obed sprashivaiu:—Nu kak, polegche?—Kogo?—Opokhmelilsia?—Aga. Kak na skovorodu plesnul, azh zashipelo!")[9] This dialogue is abbreviated and used in the humoresque "To Drink or Not to Drink?" published in

Novyi Amerikanets: " 'Well, then Liosha, feeling better?'—'You bet,' he says. 'Like water on the hot stone in the baths, fizzed right through me! . . .' " ("—Nu kak, Lesha, popravilsia?—Popravilsia,—govorit. Slovno na kamenku v bane plesnul, azh zashipelo! . . .")[10]

The Sanctuary was still not finished in 1981, but at this time Dovlatov confirmed his original idea of publishing it as a separate novel. Writing to Efimov in June, he expressed some uncertainty about how to continue, suggesting that his hero might well finish up being murdered on Pushkin's birthday.[11] In February 1982 he wrote to Efimov that at one time he had wanted to include the story about the Sanctuary as the final part of his novel *Fiveways,* but had changed his mind: "Previously I wanted to bring it all to an end with a piece about the Sanctuary, and have the hero killed there. [. . .] But there will be a separate story about the Sanctuary, and the novel still has to be finished."[12]

In January 1983 Dovlatov was still working on *The Sanctuary.* It was to be published by Efimov, and Dovlatov wrote to him to explain what he had in mind to depict and what he still needed to do with the story:

> I wanted to depict a literary person in the Sanctuary, whose problems lie in the same aspects as Pushkin's: money, wife, creative work, and the state. And it isn't at all a question of the hero's ability, that doesn't matter; what matters is the Sanctuary itself, which is understood in the manner of a mausoleum, and the indifference and blindness of the people around, "they only know how to love the dead" and so on. [. . .] The wife (one of the aspects) is completely lifeless, I have to think of something.[13]

Finally Dovlatov sent the completed work to Efimov on June 21, 1983. He wrote about his own work, as usual, in deprecating tones, saying he was quite unsure about its quality: "No plot, no idea, ordinary language. So what do I think it does have? I think it has voices, images, and people, something like a panorama of village life; and finally it has some kind of love story."[14]

The museum is known as "Pushkinskii Zapovednik," a name which has connotations of "nature reserve" or "bird sanctuary," a place for the preservation of rare and exotic species, but which also has reverberations akin to the modern English "theme park." It is a kind of Pushkinland. That is to say, Dovlatov presents it not merely as a museum, a legitimate preservation in the present of something valuable from the past, but as a fictionalized past, a willfully manipulated version of the past designed to fulfill a specific function in the present.

Paul Debreczeny has discussed in his book *Social Functions of Literature: Alexander Pushkin and Russian Culture* how the cult of Pushkin has evolved through the last two centuries: "There have been other poets in history whose cult was engendered as much by personal myth as by poetic works. What makes Pushkin unique is an unprecedented reinforcement of literary achievement by social circumstance and the need for a national myth."[15] Through the centuries there were different reasons for Pushkin's elevation to sainthood; one of the compelling reasons for this in postrevolutionary Russia, when the myth of Lenin was a more logical choice, is explained by Debreczeny:

> If the official version of Lenin's personality presented to the public for adoration lacked the complexities of a human being, Pushkin's image was not flattened out and thus provided an opportunity for vicarious enjoyment of vivid images in the midst of grey Soviet reality. Needless to say, his colorful literary texts continually reinforced the text of his life.[16]

It also needs to be added that the reading and studying of Pushkin mainly in hagiographic terms was encouraged by the Soviet authorities with a particular aim in mind. He was used to manipulate society, to deflect interest from real issues, but at the same time to allow some safe topics for public discussion. No diversion from ready-made clichés about Pushkin was allowed. This is one aspect of Dovlatov's novel *The Sanctuary*.

Dovlatov was not alone at this time in reevaluating his attitude to Pushkin. From the late 1960s onward the Soviet intelligentsia began to approach Pushkin with light-hearted irreverence—Andrei Siniavsky's *Progulki s Pushkinym* (*Walks with Pushkin*) written around the mid-1970s is perhaps the most famous example—and to establish distance from official writing on Pushkin. This state of affairs is illustrated in *The Sanctuary*, when the narrator is examined on Pushkin and tries to express his own opinion of the poet's achievement, saying that Pushkin's writing goes beyond Russian tradition, that Pushkin is not such a typical Russian writer, and concluding that "Pushkin is our belated Renaissance" (*SS* 2:187). The reaction to such a nonstandard answer (however banal it may seem) is complete bafflement and hostility: "What has Goethe to do with it? [. . .] Not to mention the Renaissance!" (*SS* 2:187). Dovlatov shows that this culture of false enlightenment has become the dominant culture of the Sanctuary and of the entire Soviet Union.

Siniavsky's *Walks with Pushkin* evoked outrage and fierce polemics in the émigré press and when it eventually reached the Soviet Union during perestroika. Irina Rodnianskaia, in "Osvobozhdennyi plennik . . ." ("The Liberated Captive . . ."), points out that the polemics about Pushkin go back a long way, and cites an earlier exchange between V. Rozanov and V. Soloviev. What is the key to Tertz-Siniavsky's book? Why did writers, Dovlatov included, in the 1970s turn to a reevaluation of Pushkin? Rodnianskaia convincingly shows how Pushkin was manipulated to serve the totalitarian state.

Just as Schiller in Nazi Germany was proclaimed "Hitler's comrade in arms," so Stalin exploited Pushkin, particularly in the ambitious 1937 celebrations of the centenary of the poet's death. However, what Siniavsky and others saw in Pushkin was freedom, and they rebelled against this political usurpation of a writer's personality: "Broadly speaking the point is the freedom, the island of freedom, which the author of the book seeks to secure for himself amidst the ocean of miscellaneous restrictions. [. . .] I will say straightaway—it is the freedom of art."[17] This island of freedom was also important for Dovlatov and his contemporaries. As Siniavsky wrote in response to the hostile émigré community: "I wrote *Walks with Pushkin* [. . .] as a continuation of my concluding speech at the trial—in defense of free art."[18]

Writing about Andrei Bitov's *Pushkinskii dom* (1978; *Pushkin House*), Susanne Fusso describes the position of the Soviet postmodernist writer as "alienated from the history of culture, which has been preserved and petrified by hegemonic forces. Culture is a museum, not a living presence."[19] This is exactly the situation that Dovlatov depicts in Pushkinland.

The Sanctuary is a microcosm of Soviet reality (as, indeed, could be said of Dovlatov's earlier work, *The Zone*). At the forefront of the author's attention is the double life of the Sanctuary (the Soviet Union), which reveals the prevalent underlying hypocrisy. Pushkin is the great national treasure. He is in the hands of the authorities and becomes an instrument of propaganda. Crowds of tourists flock to this national park. Some come here because they have received travel vouchers from the trade union, some because they are compelled to take part in cultural and educational programs. Some come here seeking adventure:

> "Tatusia, can you hear? Stay at home . . . The weather is lousy . . . But the main thing is—there aren't any fellers there at all . . . Hello! Can you hear? Lots of girls come away without getting a proper holiday . . ."
>
> — Tatusia, slyshish'?! Ekhat' ne sovetuiu . . . Pogoda na chetyre s minusom . . . A glavnoe, tut absoliutno netu muzhikov . . . Ale! Ty slyshish'?! Mnogie devushki uezzhaiut, tak i ne otdokhnuv . . . (*SS* 2:264)

On the whole the tourists (the term preferred by the staff of the Sanctuary is "pilgrims") are indifferent to poetry, and if instead of Pushkin a few lines of Esenin are read to them, nobody even notices. "Now and then the poet addressed his nurse in verse. Everyone knows, for example, the touching lines . . . 'Are you still alive, old woman? I am too, I send my love to you! Let the wondrous light of evening . . .' " ("Poet to i delo obrashchalsia k niane v stikhakh. Vsem izvestny takie, naprimer, zadushevnye stroki . . . [. . .] Ty eshche zhiva, moia starushka, / Zhiv i ia, privet tebe, privet! Pust' struitsia nad tvoei izbushkoi . . ."; *SS* 2:202.)[20] For most tourists who come the mere fact that they are there is important, because they know that Pushkin is the symbol of culture. However, the visitors' level of ignorance about Pushkin is illustrated in Dovlatov's letter to Liudmila Shtern:

> The tourists ask fantastic questions:
> 1. Was Anna Karenina Esenin's mistress?
> 2. Who was Boris Godunov?
> 3. Why did Pushkin and Lermontov fight a duel?[21]

This ignorance on the part of the tourists is matched by the willful falsity of much of the information purveyed. When the narrator indicates that he wants to become a guide in the Sanctuary, he is told that he needs to train: "Study the instructions. In Pushkin's life there is so much that is still not researched. One or two things have changed since last year . . . 'In Pushkin's life?' I exclaimed." ("Proshtudirovat' metodichku. V zhizni Pushkina eshche tak mnogo neissledovannogo . . . Koe-chto izmenilos' s proshlogo goda . . .—V zhizni Pushkina?—udivilsia ia"; *SS* 2:177.) There is no portrait of Pushkin's ancestors available, so a substitute is found: a white general, sunburned from campaigns in Asia:

> "Well, what's the difference, Hannibal or Zakomelsky . . . The tourists want to see Hannibal. That's what they pay the money for. They don't give a toss about Zakomelsky?! So, our director put Hannibal up . . . To be precise, he put Zakomelsky up to stand for Hannibal."
>
> — Da kakaia raznitsa—Gannibal, Zakomel'skii . . . Turisty zhelaiut videt' Gannibala. Oni za eto den'gi platiat. Na figa im Zakomel'skii?! Vot nash direktor i povesil Gannibala . . . Tochnee, Zakomel'skogo pod vidom Gannibala. (*SS* 2:177)

Dovlatov is not concerned to set against this falsehood and ignorance some notional "truth" about Pushkin. Nevertheless, it can be seen that in *The Sanctuary* he is pursuing the process of recuperating the cultural legacy of the Pushkin period in his own way. Dovlatov's account of his semi-fictitious narrator's experience in Pushkinland is at the same time an exploration of parallels between the literary scene in Pushkin's time and his own, raising questions of style and narration, and of parallels in the relationship between the artist and the state in those two periods.

The Sanctuary is framed by the journeys of the narrator (called Boris Alikhanov, the same name Dovlatov used for the narrator of *The Zone*) from Leningrad to Pushkinskie Gory at the beginning, and back again at the end, some two or three months later. Arrival and departure are marked by bouts of heavy drinking. On his journey to the Sanctuary, the narrator hints at his inebriated (post-*zapoi*) state: "My hands were trembling horribly" ("Bezobrazno drozhali ruki"; *SS* 2:172). "I was hesitating whether to have another drink or not" ("Ia kolebalsia—dobavliat' ili ne dobavliat'?"; *SS* 2:174). At the end of the story the narrator is alone in his Leningrad flat: "On the eleventh day hallucinations began" ("Na odinnadtsatye sutki u menia poiavilis' galliutsinatsii"; *SS* 2:275). The climax of the story is the visit to the Sanctuary by the narrator's wife, their last meeting before her impending emigration with their child. Their dialogue on this occasion picks up themes from earlier conversations between them that have been given in flashback. The story's closed structure emphasizes the sense of a dead end experienced by the narrator, which is intimated on the journey out—"I tried to dispel the feeling of catastrophe and dead end" ("Popytat'sia rasseiat' oshchushchenie katastrofy, tupika"; *SS* 2:181)—and fully realized at the end, as he returns to his empty Leningrad apartment. His wife and child are far away, he is not sure he will ever see them again, he has no money, and he has run out of alcohol and finds it difficult to move his limbs (because he is too drunk); he is also on the verge of psychological breakdown. His apartment is under siege by the KGB and the police. There is a last telephone conversation with his wife, who is calling from Austria. There is no escape. "Now I had to get to sleep in an empty, stifling room . . ." ("Teper' nado bylo usnut' v pustoi i dushnoi komnate . . ."; *SS* 2:276). The narrator's last "optimistic mirage" is the sentence that emerges from his hallucinations: "Only death is irreparable!" ("Nepopravima tol'ko smert'!"; *SS* 2:275).

Apart from these arrivals and departures, there is little in *The Sanctuary* that can be called action. The story is essentially plotless, since, as Iury Lotman argues, the movement of the protagonist within defined boundaries cannot be seen as event or action.[22] The story's focus of interest lies in the development, largely through dialogue, of various themes, all of which are concerned in one way or another with literature. Foremost among these is the exploitation of Pushkin's biography, as revealed in conversations with various guides and administrators. The problem of literary recognition and the difficulty of being published, besides being the primary motivation of the journey, is the subject of discussions between the narrator and his wife, as well as with officers of the KGB. The narrator's situation is contrasted with that of Stasik Pototsky, who, having read a dozen contemporary books, had decided to become a writer. His trivial, anodyne stories, produced at the rate of one a day, are published with success. "The most vivid features of his stories were the stylistic flaws and the misprints" ("Naibolee iarkimi v nikh byli stilisticheskie pogreshnosti i opechatki"), writes Dovlatov. Of his approach to writing, Pototsky says: "I am a writer like Chekhov, sod it. Chekhov was quite right. Stories can be written about anything." ("Ia—pisatel', blia, tipa Chekhova. Chekhov byl absoliutno prav. Rasskaz mozhno napisat' o chem ugodno"; *SS* 2:207.)

Dovlatov introduces into the text a direct polemic with Viktor Likhonosov, as a representative of the *derevenshchiki* (village prose writers). The main trends and characteristics of village prose have been extensively studied. Deming Brown describes the main preoccupation of the genre thus:

> Village literature is oriented on peasant *families*—their antecedents and traditions, their formation and ferment, and often their alienation and break-up. Village writers like to dwell on memories of rural childhood and youth—sometimes idyllically happy, sometimes confused, deprived, and impoverished. The contrast, and frequently the conflict, of generations is emphasised. Particular prominence is given to elderly persons, especially women, who are shown to embody the best elements of peasant culture and serve as the last repositories of ancient Russian spiritual values.
>
> The village writers lovingly describe their own birthplaces and the fields, forests, meadows, rivers, lakes, and living creatures around them. Their characters speak in local dialects; the characters' folk beliefs and their arts and crafts display regional peculiarities. In paying such close attention to ethnic detail, writers are not only attempting to preserve a cultural heritage but also pleading against the obliteration of the culture itself.[23]

Having spent some time in the countryside around Pskov, Dovlatov was shocked at the state of the Russian village. His reaction is reflected both in his journalism and in *The Sanctuary.* He wrote two newspaper articles on the fate of the Russian village, one for *Russkaia mysl',* "Derevnia v 'chernom spiske' "[24] ("The Village on 'the Blacklist' "), and one for *Almanac Panorama,* "Esli b garmoshka umela"[25] ("If the Accordion Knew How to . . ."). In "The Village on 'the Blacklist' " Dovlatov responds to an article in *Literaturnaia gazeta* with the optimistic title "I malomu poseleniiu—zhit'" ("Even a Little Village Is to Live"), about the large number of villages that are dying out. In sharply polemical tones he discusses the depiction of the Russian village in literature, the exotic charm of Shukshin's eccentrics and dreamers, Rasputin's strong characters, Astaf'ev's descriptions of lively and vivid peasant speech—all this, says Dovlatov, reconciled one to the painful reality of peasant life. Nevertheless their prose was tragic: "The motifs of their prose rang bitterly and tragically. The material impoverishment of the village economy, the loss of traditional spiritual and moral values, the loss of agricultural skills, flight to the industrial regions."[26] Dovlatov writes that as an urban dweller he had been willing to consider this prose absolutely truthful, until he himself lived in a variety of villages while working as a guide in the Sanctuary and found that the reality was much more painful than literature. The peasantry as a class has almost died out, and all the basic peasant skills are lost. This is not surprising in Dovlatov's view, since the peasants themselves say: "I can't tell the difference between corn and millet."[27] The question "Would the peasants like to have the ownership of the land back in their own hands?" receives a stunning reply: " 'Whoever would want that,' replied Timokha, 'it's too late . . . Any of us would swap that land straight away for a quarter bottle of vodka. To say nothing of a half-liter. We've forgotten how to plow, that's the trouble.' "[28] In the second article Dovlatov also responds to a reader's letter in *Literaturnaia gazeta,* bemoaning the fact of the disappearance of the accordion from Russian life. Dovlatov asks why it was the disappearance of the accordion in particular which upset the writer. Why is he not upset by the disappearance of everything else, such as horses, cows, and sheep? This is what Dovlatov suggests the accordion could really have told:

> The accordion would tell how the village hooligans, put up to it by activists, laid waste to the churches and insulted the priests, how layabouts and good-for-nothings burned and robbed the farms of their better-off, hard-working neighbors, who didn't drink, how the country people were denied passports and returned to a state of serfdom, how the peasants were forbidden to own horses, which meant that they could not gather and transport hay for the cows and sheep, how our land was exhausted as a result of crazy experiments with maize, and how the uneducated Lysenko and his obscurantists, with the help of comrade Stalin himself, destroyed the country's leading agronomist, Nikolai Vavilov, thereby putting a brake on the development of agricultural science for years to come![29]

Viktor Likhonosov describes in his novels the contradictions between town and country, and the description of bygone life in the village is most nostalgic. In his comments on village prose, Dovlatov's narrator warns against false patriotism, anticipating, perhaps, the movement's later swing to right-wing chauvinism: "I think that the love of birch trees triumphs at the expense of love for human beings. It develops as a surrogate patriotism" (*SS* 2:176). The narrator's response to Likhonosov's work subtly indicates a parallel between the official "culture-as-museum," embodied in Pushkinland, and the village prose writers' attitude to the preservation of the past:

> Of course, he is a good writer. Talented, vivid, supple. He's marvellous at reproducing living speech. (Tolstoy would have loved to hear such a compliment!) And all the same, at bottom—a hopeless, miserable feeling that you can't shake off. A fleshless, tedious theme: "Where are you, Russia?! Where

has everything disappeared?! Where are the songs, the embroidered towels, the headdresses? Where is the hospitality, the devil-may-care attitudes and the grand scale? Where are the samovars, the icons, the feats of heroism and the holy fools? Where is the sterlet, the carp, the honey, the unpressed caviar? Where are the ordinary horses, for God's sake?! Where is the chaste bashfulness of feelings?!" They rack their brains over it: "Where are you Russia? Where did you disappear? Who disfigured you?!" Who! It's obvious who! There's nothing to rack your brains over . . .

Konechno, khoroshii pisatel'. Talantlivyi, iarkii, plastichnyi. Zhivuiu rech' vosproizvodit zamechatel'no. (Uslyshal by Tolstoi podobnyi kompliment!) I tem ne menee, v osnove—beznadezhnoe, unyloe, nazoilivoe chuvstvo. Khudosochnyi i nudnyi motiv: 'Gde ty Rus'?! Kuda vse podevalos'?! Gde chastushki, rushniki, kokoshniki?! Gde khlebosol'stvo, udal' i razmakh?! Gde samovary, ikony, podvizhniki, iurodivye?! Gde sterliad', karpy, med, zernistaia ikra?! Gde obyknovennye loshadi, chert poberi?! Gde tselomudrennaia stydlivost' chuvstv?!' Golovu lomaiut: 'Gde ty Rus'?! Kuda devalos'?! Kto tebia obezobrazil?!' Kto, kto . . . Izvestno, kto . . . I nechego tut golovu lomat'. . . . (*SS* 2:213)

Dovlatov's description of the village of Sosnovo provides a sharp contrast to the loving descriptions found in village prose:

I walked through the village hoping to meet someone. The grey unpainted houses looked impoverished. The stakes of the ramshackle fences were crowned with earthenware pots. Chicks were fussing around in pens covered with sheets of plastic. Chickens strutted out with a nervy, cartoon-like step. Squat, shaggy-haired dogs were yapping loudly.

Ia shel po derevne, nadeias' kogo-to vstretit'. Nekrashenye serye doma vygliadeli ubogo. Kol'ia pokosivshikhsia izgorodei byli uvenchany glinianymi sosudami. V nakrytykh polietilenom zagonakh suetilis' tsypliata. Nervnoi mul'tiplikatsionnoi pokhodkoi vystupali kury. Zvonko tiavkali lokhmatye prizemistye sobaki. (*SS* 2:190)

Dovlatov's depiction of everyday village life is in a grotesque and even mocking tone; nevertheless, one can feel the author's sympathy for and even closeness to his dissipated, drunken characters and his bitterness over their fate.

Dovlatov also takes an ironic view of the use of "local dialects" by the inhabitants of Sosnovo. This is how he characterizes the speech of Mikhail Ivanych, from whom the narrator in *The Sanctuary* rents a room in the village:[30]

> His speech was akin to classical music, abstract painting, or the singing of a goldfinch. Emotion clearly took precedence over meaning. [. . .] Misha's utterances reminded one of the sound patterning of the Remizov school.
>
> Rech' ego byla srodni klassicheskoi muzyke, abstraktnoi zhivopisi ili peniiu shchegla. Emotsii iavno preobladali nad smyslom. [. . .] Mishiny vystupleniia napominali zvukopis' remizovskoi shkoly. (*SS* 2:214)

Mikhail Ivanych is presented as a typical representative of the village folk; the narrator has only seen him sober twice during the whole summer. His character is a combination of cruelty and unexpected kindness, and is implicitly compared with the blacksmith Arkhip in Pushkin's story *Dubrovskii* (*Dubrovsky*). Dovlatov introduces *Dubrovskii* into *The Sanctuary* through an anecdote about the informer Lenia Gur'ianov's student days.[31] In Pushkin's *Dubrovskii,* Arkhip is watching a burning house in which people are trapped: "In a minute the whole house was in flames. Red smoke curled above the roof. Windowpanes cracked and fell out; burning beams began to collapse; there were pitiful wails and screams: 'Help, we're burning! Help!' 'Not on your life,' said Arkhip, eyeing the blaze with a malicious smile."[32] However, when Arkhip notices a cat on the roof of the burning house, he risks his own life to save it: " 'Why are you laughing, you little devils?' said the blacksmith angrily. 'Aren't you afraid of the Lord? One of God's creatures is dying, and you blockheads rejoice.' He placed a ladder against the burning roof and climbed up."[33] As with Arkhip, it is difficult to understand Mikhail Ivanych's mentality. He has not burned anybody alive himself, but he approves of the Germans killing Jews and Gypsies. These are not the humane and ethical values that village writers were keen to promote, but both Pushkin and Dovlatov revealed the narrow line dividing good and evil in human nature.

> I never did understand what sort of person he was. On the surface he was ridiculous, kind, muddleheaded. Once he hanged two cats on the rowan tree. He made the noose out of fishing line.
>
> "They multiply everywhere," he said, "the bastards . . ."
>
> Once I inadvertently bolted the door from inside and he sat on the porch the whole night, not wanting to wake me . . .
>
> Chto za lichnost', ia tak i ne ponial. S vidu—nelepyi, dobryi, bestolkovyi. Odnazhdy povesil dvukh koshek na riabine. Petli smasteril iz rybolovnoi leski.
>
> — Rasplodilis',—govorit,—shumovki, sopsiudu luzgaiut . . .
>
> Kak-to raz ia nechaianno zadvinul iznutri shchekoldu. I on do utra prosidel na kryl'tse, boialsia menia razbudit' . . . (*SS* 2:214–15)

The ethical ambiguity which Dovlatov shows in Mikhail Ivanych is a topic that runs through some of his other stories, notably *The Zone.* One thing that fascinated Dovlatov in Pushkin was the latter's ability to rise above moral judgments, above the antagonism of good and evil: "Like the moon which lights the way to predator and victim alike" ("Podobno lune, kotoraia osveshchaet dorogu i khishchniku i zhertve"; *SS* 2:212). Here he echoes the sentences in *The Captain's Daughter* (*Kapitanskaia dochka*) that had struck him with its apparent indifference: "The night was quiet and cold. The moon and the stars shone brightly, lighting the square and the gallows."[34]

Igor' Sukhikh considers that in *The Sanctuary* Dovlatov is presenting a portrait of an unsuccessful contemporary writer, shown in contrast with Pushkin: "He shows a portrait of an unsuccessful writer contrasted with Pushkin. With Pushkin from the Pushkin Sanctuary and his attendants (who are also partly portraits)."[35] It can be argued, however, that it is not so much a question of using Pushkin as a background, but rather of Dovlatov drawing an elaborate comparison of the restrictions under which Russian writers lived in the past and the present. Informers, denunciation, and betrayal have long held a fascination for Russian writers, and not only in the Soviet period. Pushkin's works contain references to an earlier antecedent, the novelist, critic, and informer for the Third Department, Faddei Bulgarin, with whom he came into conflict. Bulgarin was a prolific and successful writer whose novel *Ivan Vyzhigin* was a sellout, while Pushkin's work did not enjoy commercial success. Bulgarin was also a publisher, and the editor of *Severnaia pchela* (*The Northern Bee*), in which capacity he manipulated the Third Department and used it to destroy his competition and impede other talented writers.

The theme of censorship and surveillance is introduced by Dovlatov not only as a contemporary feature, but also as a parallel with Pushkin's times. It gives him the opportunity to look at the eternal Russian question of the relationship between the intelligentsia and the Establishment from a different historical angle. The theme of creativity and conflict with the State runs through the whole story and it is interesting to follow its escalation, with the State's inevitable victory.

The first meeting with the informer in the story is at the beginning, when the narrator arrives in the Sanctuary:

> "Everything here lives and breathes Pushkin," said Galia, "literally every branch, every blade of grass. You keep expecting to see him coming round the corner . . . Top hat, cloak, the familiar profile . . ."
>
> Meanwhile round the corner came Lenia Gur'ianov, the police informer from university days.

— Tut vse zhivet i dyshit Pushkinym,—skazala Galia,—bukval'no kazhdaia vetochka, kazhdaia travinka. Tak i zhdesh', chto on vyidet seichas iz-za povorota . . . Tsilindr, krylatka, znakomyi profil' . . .

Mezhdu tem iz-za povorota vyshel Lenia Gur'ianov, byvshii universitetskii stukach. (*SS* 2:179)

This omnipresence of the informer mirrors the omnipresence of Faddei Bulgarin in Pushkin's life.[36] The narrator in *The Sanctuary* is also under constant police surveillance (of course, Pushkin was under surveillance in Mikhailovskoe). "I knew you were coming" (*SS* 2:179), the university informer Gur'ianov greets him; and the local KGB man at an informal gathering volunteers information about the narrator:

> The security agent concentrated his attention on the braised duck. Then he raised his head and made a brief utterance:
>
> "There is evidence that he is coming to Pushkinskie Gory . . ."
>
> Chekist sosredotochenno poedal tushenuiu utku. Zatem pripodnial golovu i korotko vyskazalsia:
>
> — Est' dannye—sobiraetsia v Pushkinskie Gory . . . (*SS* 2:180)

Eventually, when at the end of the story the narrator's wife and daughter receive their visa to emigrate, it is clear that the local KGB man Beliaev has been informed about it first, but that he also knows about the narrator's every step. It is not surprising that the narrator has excuses ready: "Rumors were reaching us about publications in the West. I tried not to think about it. After all, it does not concern me what goes on in the other world. That's just what I'll say if I am questioned" (*SS* 2:216). The reaction of the bleached blond Galia to the departure of Alikhanov's wife is typical. The narrator wants to borrow some money to return to Leningrad and say farewell to his family, but does not want to tell her. However, she knows already: "I know anyway. Your wife has betrayed our Motherland" (*SS* 2:263), says Galia.

The narrator is summoned to the KGB, whose duty it is (like the Third Department's in the last century) to educate citizens who go astray. At the KGB offices the narrator again bumps into Gur'ianov:

> "Oh, hello . . . Beliaev is expecting you . . ." He wanted to show that everything was all right. As if we had bumped into each other in the doctor's surgery and not in the Gestapo headquarters.
>
> I asked him: "Is he your superior?"
>
> "Who?"

> "Beliaev. Or is he your subordinate?"
> "Less of your irony," said Gur'ianov.
> His voice acquired a strict tone of authority.
> "And remember. The KGB is nowadays the most progressive organization. It's the only real force in the state. And, by the way, the most humane. If only you knew those people!"
>
> — Nu, zdravstvui, zdravstvui . . . Tebia Beliaev zhdet . . . On zakhotel pokazat', chto vse normal'no, kak budto my stolknulis' v poliklinike, a ne v gestapo.
> Ia sprosil:
> — On—tvoi nachal'nik?
> — Kto?
> — Beliaev . . . Ili podchinennyi? . . .
> — Ne ironizirui,—skazal Gur'ianov.
> V golose ego zvuchali strogie rukovodiashchie notki.
> — I pomni. KGB seichas—naibolee progressivnaia organizatsiia. Naibolee real'naia sila v gosudarstve. I kstati, naibolee gumannaia . . . Esli by ty znal, kakie eto liudi! (*SS* 2:265)

The "humaneness" of the KGB consisted in the fact that in the late 1970s they did not on the whole imprison writers simply for their writing, particularly the ones who had publications abroad, but "humanely" hounded them out of the country. Only a few years before the events in the story, Solzhenitsyn was similarly "humanely" transported abroad. The KGB officer Beliaev, who significantly now has a portrait of Makarenko[37] above his desk rather than Dzerzhinsky, tries to educate and influence the narrator.[38] The essence of suppression and its manifestations for Pushkin and Dovlatov were barely distinguishable.[39] However, these considerations were common in the lives of most Russian writers through the centuries.

Shortly before his death, Dovlatov gave an interview to John Glad in which he discussed Russian traditions of storytelling. At their basis is Pushkin's refined and laconic prose, but according to Dovlatov this tradition was interrupted, and in spite of the brilliance of Tolstoy, Dostoevsky, Turgenev, and many others, and the respect and admiration that their prose commands, the style of writing that they developed in the decades following Pushkin's death cannot be called laconic.[40] However, such a tradition in Russia does continue to exist.

> From time to time we can see sparks of Pushkinian refinement and Pushkinian laconism (laconism and refinement are almost synonyms, because one can do something faultlessly only by sweeping aside all that is redundant). In

> many ways, "laconic" does not mean just using few words. [. . .] There were flashes of the Pushkin tradition in the person of Zoshchenko, who wrote very concisely and clearly.[41]

Among writers continuing the Pushkin tradition, apart from Zoshchenko, Dovlatov singles out Venedikt Erofeev, Fazil' Iskander, and Georgy Vladimov in *Vernyi Ruslan* (*Faithful Ruslan*). To write concise and laconic Russian, following the criteria established by Pushkin, was the task Dovlatov set himself in *The Sanctuary*.

Pushkin's dissatisfaction with the state of contemporary prose is well known. He found it flowery, poeticized, and affected. He demanded that prose should be clear, precise, laconic, but not without ideas. "Precision and brevity are the two foremost merits of prose. It requires ideas and more ideas. Without ideas brilliant expressions serve no purpose."[42] Pushkin's writings about the style of prose fiction are often perceived as symptomatic of his tendency toward realism. In equal measure, though, they can be seen as an attempt to create a specific poetics of prose fiction. Lotman draws attention to the specific literary circumstances in which this process took place. In that period the dominance of poetry was overwhelming. This demonstrated itself among other things in the poeticization of prose. It was in opposition to this that the poetics of the *Tales of Belkin* became so clearly defined: "the aesthetic perception of prose becomes possible only against the background of poetic culture."[43] A parallel can be drawn here with the period in which Dovlatov reached maturity as a writer. In the 1960s poetry took precedence over prose, as is demonstrated not only by the popularity of such "semiofficial" poets as Evtushenko, Voznesensky, and Akhmadulina, whose poetry recitals filled entire sports stadiums, but also by the immense flourishing of guitar poetry and the growth of underground alternative poetry. In terms of prose, the most popular writers (as has been described in chapter 1) were Aksenov and Gladilin, whose romantic qualities made them the idols of the younger generation of writers.

The description of scenery is considered by A. Lezhnev to be a touchstone of a writer's stylistic skill. He shows that Pushkin distances himself from the prevailing descriptive tradition of Russian prose of the time. In Dovlatov's writing we will also look in vain for verbose and extensive descriptions of landscape or detailed descriptions of surroundings and interiors. And if in Dostoevsky we just note the absence of nature descriptions, then Pushkin and, following in his footsteps, Dovlatov put scenery in a subordinate position, reducing its function and extent. There is no need to quote the well-known passage with the terse, laconic description of the onset of the blizzard in *The Captain's Daughter*. The smells and sounds of a summer's day are outlined by Dovlatov in short, minimalist strokes:

> Summer in childhood had a soundtrack of train whistles. Holiday houses . . . The smell of soot in the station and warm sand . . . table tennis under the trees . . . the taut, resonant tapping of the ball.
>
> The sun-scorched beach . . . Spiky sedge grass . . . Long swimming trunks, and elastic marks on your calves . . . Shoes full of sand . . .

> V detstve leto bylo ozvucheno gudkami parovozov. Prigorodnye dachi . . . Zapakh vokzal'noi gari i nagretogo peska . . . nastol'nyi tennis pod vetkami . . . Tugoi i zvonkii stuk miacha . . .
>
> Vyzhzhennyi solntsem pliazh . . . Zhestkaia osoka . . . Dlinnye trusy i sledy rezinok na ikrakh . . . Nabivshiisia v sandalii pesok. . . . (*SS* 2:183)

Distinctive characteristics of Pushkin's style find a continuation in Dovlatov's work. "He uses short, firm, swift phrases, and prefers to avoid subordinate clauses," says Lezhnev of Pushkin.[44] Just such an alternation of short, energetic phrases creates the swift pace of Dovlatov's prose. This deliberate restraint became his hallmark. Dovlatov's conscious continuation of Pushkin's style is expressed in a number of stylistic devices. Lezhnev notes how the sparing use of epithets in Pushkin's prose combines with a great wealth and variety of verbs. He observes that an overabundance of epithets slows the phrase down and makes it static. The use of verbs, on the other hand, adds liveliness and intensity. The absolute limit Pushkin is aiming for is described as: "it is a noun plus verb, the naked phrase without adornments."[45]

Dovlatov's own expressiveness is likewise achieved by a predominant emphasis on the verb over all other parts of speech. Like Pushkin, he reduces his sentences to a bare expressive minimum, using noun-plus-verb constructions: "I *walked* across the village, then *returned.* I *lingered* by one of the houses. A door *banged.*" ("Ia *peresek* derevniu, *vernulsia. Pomedlil* vozle odnogo iz domov. *Khlopnula* dver' "; *SS* 2:190.) Or take the following description of the narrator's day:

> My days *passed* monotonously. The tours usually *finished* around two. I *had lunch* in the Lukomor'e and *went* home. Mitrofanov and Pototsky *asked* me out for a drink a few times. I *refused* . . .

> Dni moi *prokhodili* odnoobrazno. Ekskursii *zakanchivalis'* v dva. Ia *obedal* v 'Lukomor'e' i *shel* domoi. Neskol'ko raz Mitrofanov s Pototskim *zvali vypit'.* Ia *otkazyvalsia* . . . (*SS* 2:213)[46]

This stylistic feature even attracts an admiring comment from the narrator when it is observed in his semiliterate landlord: "Misha only uttered nouns and verbs" ("Misha vygovarival lish' sushchestvitel'nye i glagoly"; *SS* 2:214).

It was pointed out by Lezhnev that "in Pushkin's prose the metaphor is strictly subordinate and establishes a particular feature of the object."[47] Dovlatov's metaphors and comparisons are similarly specific:

> I headed for Sosnovo. The road led to the summit of a hill, curving round a melancholy field. Dark boulders lay in shapeless heaps around its edges. On the left gaped a ravine, overgrown with bushes. As I went down the hill I caught sight of a few huts surrounded by birch trees. Some monochrome cows, two-dimensional-like stage scenery, were ambling around nearby. Dirty sheep with decadent physiognomies were languidly nibbling the grass. Jackdaws were flying around over the roofs.

> Ia napravilsia v Sosnovo. Doroga tianulas' k vershine kholma, ogibaia unyloe pole. Po kraiam ego besformennymi grudami temneli valuny. Sleva ziial porosshii kustami ovrag. Spuskaias' pod goru, ia uvidel neskol'ko izb, okruzhennykh berezami. V storone brodili odnotsvetnye korovy, ploskie, kak teatral'nye dekoratsii. Griaznye ovtsy s dekadentskimi fizionomiiami vialo shchipali travu. Nad kryshami letali galki. (*SS* 2:189–90)

The means of depiction convey the essential qualities of the landscape: its static nature, the squalor of the village and the surrounding field. The sobriety of description is emphasized by "prosaic" details such as "I caught sight of a few huts" ("ia uvidel neskol'ko izb") and by somewhat ironic comparisons: "two-dimensional-like stage scenery" ("ploskie, kak teatral'nye dekoratsii").

The breakthrough Pushkin made in adapting the Russian language by combining its different layers into a single literary language is a commonplace of literary history. Beyond this, however, his particular achievement was in the creation of lively dialogues and the conversational intonation of much of his prose. Dovlatov's stories are similarly written in an everyday language. Their ordinariness is such that many perceive his writing as made up of direct quotes or verbatim renderings of actual conversations, rather than fiction. But just like Pushkin's dialogue, Dovlatov's has a descriptive function as well as a function in the plot. This, too, is brought out clearly in *The Sanctuary*. Pushkin made a point of using simple, "democratic" language. He distanced himself from Karamzin's abstractness of expression and, more importantly, from Dal's stylized naturalism.[48] In this respect, too, Dovlatov differs from his contemporaries. The discussion of village prose, introduced into *The Sanctuary*, is a pointer to Dovlatov's rejection not only of its ideological stance, but also of the idea of the artificial conservation of language.[49] Stylistic reorientation of such a kind requires a simultaneous reassessment of the persona of the narrator. The moralizing tone that Pushkin ridiculed in Bulgarin has its parallel in the didacticism of much poetry and prose in the 1960s, such as the rhymed journalism of Evtushenko or (at an entirely different level of seriousness) the much-quoted conclusion of Solzhenitsyn's "Matrenin dvor" ("Matriona's Home"), from which village prose is often thought to stem. Both Pushkin and Dovlatov avoid cautionary tales and allegories, never allowing their narrators to utter obiter dicta of a moral nature. The place of moralizing is taken by irony.

V. V. Vinogradov remarked that "Pushkin's contemporaries were struck by the author's intention to make the image of the storyteller [*povestvovatel'*] the constructive and stylistic center of *Tales of Belkin.*"[50] The text of *Tales of Belkin* is divided between several types of narrators. Pushkin went out of his way to prove the "authenticity" of the narrators and place the image of the storyteller at the forefront of *Tales of Belkin.* "Pushkin leaves the dividing line between author and characters flexible . . . He does not become one with them and does not dissolve the characters in the author's voice."[51] The consciousness of the "publisher" constantly merges with Belkin's. The relationship of Belkin and the narrators is similar. The texts of the "original" stories are oral: each story bears Belkin's inscription "heard by me from such and such a person."[52] It could equally be said of the relationship between Dovlatov's semi-fictitious narrator, Alikhanov, and the biographical author that the boundary between the two is unstable. The narrator is not distanced from the author by any so complicated mechanism as is the case with Belkin, and it is often impossible to tell for certain which voice is the bearer of a particular utterance. That is why a number of scholars have been inclined to read his prose as purely autobiographical. However, Pushkin in *Tales of Belkin* and Dovlatov in *The Sanctuary* share the crucial feature of ironically subverting a tradition of naive, romantic sentimentality.

Writing later in the United States, Dovlatov admitted that he would not have written such a work as *The Sanctuary* in emigration: "In 1982 I wrote *The Sanctuary,* and many people consider that this is the most tolerable of my books. Now I would not have written *The Sanctuary.* It is a typically Russian story and the chances of successful publication in English are minimal" (*SS* 4:385). It is apparent that Dovlatov exploited the almost anecdotal episode of his sojourn in Pushkinland to develop a number of related topics, each of which displays a particular aspect of that "typically Russian story," which he felt would not be appreciated in the West. On the level of the action, perhaps the most "typically Russian," and in that sense untransportable, aspect of the story is the unchanging relationship between the writer and the state. Both Pushkin in the 1820s and Dovlatov in the 1970s were under police surveillance at Mikhailovskoe, suspected of seditious intentions and a wish to leave the country. The state organizations of both periods used other writers to assist in that ignoble task, creating divisions between writers and offering opportunities to the unscrupulous. There is a continuity in Russian life and culture revealed here which is at variance with the relationship of past and present as embodied in the theme park itself, where, for ideological reasons, a distorted and fictionalized version of the past is casually retailed to a largely indifferent public. This is paralleled in the work of the *derevenshchiki,* the village prose writers who bewail the passing of a rural Russia, embellished in their imagination, which can be used as a stick with which to beat the present. I have suggested that behind the text itself stand also the typical literary modes of the 1960s, the flamboyant prose of Aksenov and the rhetorical poetry of Evtushenko. Alikhanov/Dovlatov, the narrator/author of *The Sanctuary,* stands aloof from all these tendencies. His open polemic with the *derevenshchiki,* and his implicit rejection of the 1960s, have much in common with Pushkin's opposition to the archaicizing tendencies of his own time. In his quest for the narrative manner appropriate to his own purpose, it is to Pushkin that Dovlatov turns, finding in Pushkin's prose both a style of writing and an approach to the persona of the narrator that serve him well.

Lotman wrote of the Pushkin period:

> The Pushkin period, as the initial period, was marked by considerable internal contradiction, which allows us to see in it both the origins of Tolstoy and the roots of Dostoevsky. At the same time there is no doubt that this period is not exhausted by those two tendencies, which came to occupy such a dominant role in Russian literature. The richness of this period (the Pushkin period) consists in the depiction of potential, hitherto unrealized models, which are perhaps still waiting to reveal themselves in the future.[53]

It seems no exaggeration to claim that in writing *The Sanctuary* Dovlatov recuperated the Pushkin tradition for his own time in just such a way as to create one of those "hitherto unrealized models" of which Lotman spoke.

Chapter Six

The Suitcase and *The Fridge*

THE STORIES comprising *Chemodan* (*The Suitcase*) were written in the 1980s in New York and published in full there in 1986.[1] A preliminary publication, "Rasskazy iz chemodana" ("Tales from a Suitcase"), lacking the story "Kurtka Fernana Lezhe" ("Fernand Léger's Jacket"), had been published a year before in the periodical *Grani* no. 137, 1985. The English translation of *The Suitcase* appeared just a few days after Dovlatov's death in 1990.

The pretext for this collection of stories is the author's discovery, some time after emigrating from the Soviet Union, of a battered old suitcase he had brought with him and which is now gathering dust in his wardrobe. Rummaging through the suitcase provides the impulse for the eight stories that make up this cycle.[2] "I am writing about my clothes. Something akin to Erenburg's *Thirteen Pipes*," as Dovlatov put it.[3] Each of the items found in the suitcase serves as the basis for a story about a bizarre event connected with the item's acquisition (similar to stories from the lives of protagonists of different nationalities in Erenburg's novella). "The Finnish Nylon Socks" describes Dovlatov's attempt to become a black market dealer while still at university.[4] In "A Decent Double-Breasted Suit" he is working as a journalist and is approached by the KGB to spy on a Swede. "A Poplin Shirt" examines the narrator's troubled relationship with his wife and her decision to leave the Soviet Union.

T. V. Tsiv'ian in her article "*Veshchi* iz chemodana Sergeiia Dovlatova i byvshaia (?) sovetskaia model' mira" ("*Things* from Sergei Dovlatov's Suitcase and the Former (?) Soviet Model of the World") suggests that the story cycle begins with a relatively positive notion of ownership, while it very quickly transpires that what is owned is a pile of old rags, and that belongings as such do not exist.[5] The next logical step is that there is no need to have any belongings. Tsiv'ian considers this to be Dovlatov's protest against the Soviet "veshchevoi/veshchnyi" (material[istic]) world. However, this argument can be taken a step further. Those emigrating from the Soviet Union were allowed to take no more than three suitcases each. In the event, the narrator managed with one. In the United States it transpired that the things he had brought were unnecessary, and that only the intangible things enclosed in the suitcase retained their value: "On the bottom was Karl Marx. On the lid was Brodsky. And between them, my lost, my precious, my only life." ("Na dne—Karl Marks. Na kryshke—Brodskii. A mezhdu nimi—propashchaia, bestsennaia, edinstvennaia zhizn' "; *SS* 3:289.) Mark Lipovetsky considers that in this introduction to the cycle "a perfectly postmodernist narrative frame is established."[6]

Contemplating the contents of the suitcase, the narrator remarks with sadness that this is all that he has managed to accumulate in thirty-six years of life, eighteen of which were spent working. As the stories progress, the reader gradually realizes that none of the items was in fact purchased for money earned: the socks were obtained as the result of black marketeering, the shoes the narrator admits to having stolen from the mayor of Leningrad, the suit is a "present" from the newspaper administration/KGB, the poplin shirt is a parting gift from his wife, and so on.

In her article "O nazvaniiakh dovlatovskikh knizhek" ("On the Titles of Dovlatov's Books"), Ksana Mechik-Blank argues that the title *The Suitcase* is a symbol of all Dovlatov's wanderings.[7] The following final paragraph was added in the "Afterword" to the English translation of the novel:

> The journey doesn't end. And when my turn comes I will come to some other gates. And I will hold in my hand a cheap American suitcase. And I will hear:
>
> What did you bring to us?
>
> Here, I will reply, look.
>
> And I will also add:
>
> Not without reason—any book, even the least serious, has the shape of a suitcase.[8]

Igor' Smirnov argues that in the postwar period wanderings (*strannichestvo*) became as much a literary phenomenon as an existential matter, citing as examples Jack Kerouac's *On the Road* (1957) and John Steinbeck's *Travels with Charley* (1962). "For the wanderer no earthly boundaries have any meaning; what is relevant to him is the threshold dividing being from other-being," writes Smirnov.[9]

The influence of American literature, as noted in previous chapters, was of paramount importance in forming the attitudes of the postwar generation of Soviet writers; however, French existentialism also had an impact, particularly in Leningrad. The official translation of Albert Camus' *L'étranger* (*Postoronnii, The Stranger*) was published in 1969 in the U.S.S.R. The stranger of the title is condemned to death, not so much for killing a person, as because he refuses to conform in the way society expects. At about the same time (according to Boris Ivanov), Rid Grachev's translation of Camus' *Le mythe de Sisyphe* circulated in samizdat.[10] Both these works deal with the feeling of the absurd and the position adopted by someone who has become aware of the absurd. *The Myth of Sisyphus* is viewed as an explanation of the central idea of Absurdity, which was developed in *The Stranger.* In *The Myth of Sisyphus* Camus writes: "Under the fatal lighting of that destiny, its uselessness becomes evident. No code of ethics and no effort are justifiable *a priori* in the face of the cruel mathematics that command our condition."[11] At the center of this notion of the absurd lies the inevitable fact of death, which, according to Camus, makes all human life senseless.

Existentialism in its atheistic variety is an attempt to define the metaphysical status of man in a world without God. Metaphysical alienation is a recurrent theme in Dovlatov's work, to which he returns in a number of stories. It can clearly be seen in some of the stories mentioned in earlier chapters of this study. In a later story, "Vstretilis', pogovorili" ("They Met for a Chat"), one of the characters remarks: "What is it all for? OK, I'll eat another two thousand cakes. I'll wear out twelve pairs of shoes. I'll make ten trips to the Baltic . . ." (*SS* 1:201). In the same story, Golovker, who has achieved his ambition and become rich in America, exclaims: "You live without knowing what it is for. What do you earn money for? What do you acquire possessions for? What do you switch over to English for?" (*SS* 1:201). The story "Lishnii" ("Superfluous") from *The Compromise* and written at the same time as the *Suitcase* stories provides another example, as Bush, the protagonist, destroys all his own prospects by refusing to conform to society's expectations.

For Camus the only certainty in life is one's own inevitable death, and he has his fictional protagonist face the death penalty in order that he shall overcome all inauthentic existence. Truly authentic existence is to be found only by living through the fact of unavoidable death. There are many instances in Dovlatov's work that illustrate a similar attitude.

In many of his stories Dovlatov "experiences" his own death:

> The grave was surrounded by strangers in dark coats. I could smell the stifling odor of flowers and pine needles. The edges of the uncomfortable bed pressed against my shoulders. The fallen petals tickled my hands, crossed on my chest. Above my head a TV cameraman was fussing with something. A faraway voice sounded, colored by self-admiration: "I didn't know this man . . ." (*C*, 95–96)

Mogilu okruzhali neznakomye liudi v temnykh pal'to. Ia pochuvstvoval udushlivyi zapakh tsvetov i khvoi. Borta neuiutnogo lozha davili mne plechi. Opavshie lepestki shchekotali slozhennye na grudi ruki. Nad moim izgolov'em suetlivo peremeshchalsia teleoperator. Zvuchal dalekii, okrashennyi samoliubovaniem, golos: '. . . Ia ne znal etogo cheloveka . . .' (*SS* 1:386)

And further in the same story from *The Compromise:*

What am I thinking of, standing beside this grave? Of the mysteries of the human soul. Of overcoming death and spiritual grief. Of the laws of existence born in the depth of millennia which will live till the extinction of the sun . . . (*C*, 96)

O chem ia dumaiu, stoia u etoi mogily? O tainakh chelovecheskoi dushi. O preodolenii smerti i dushevnogo goria. O zakonakh bytia, kotorye rodilis' v glubine tysiacheletii i prozhivut do ugasaniia solntsa . . . (*SS* 1:387)

Lipovetsky considers that in his prose Dovlatov expressed better than anyone else this "fundamentally absurdist consciousness."[12] The questions of existence and of wandering come together: as an émigré (Who am I in a foreign country?) and as a wanderer (Who am I in my own country?). In Dovlatov this unease turns into a feeling of extreme loneliness and alienation. The word *suitcase* is an all-embracing symbol here, not just of lonely wandering and alienation but also of the senselessness of life. This sense of existential loneliness also evokes an essential element of the Petersburg text: "In the Petersburg text of Russian literature the quintessence of life in a 'liminal' condition is reflected, on the edge, over the abyss, on the border of death, and paths to salvation are indicated."[13]

Although the interest in existentialism and problems of estrangement in the Soviet Union from the 1960s to the 1980s most probably had its origins in Western literature, nevertheless the fact that this became one of the main topics for many authors indicates that such a sense of absurdity had a basis in Soviet reality itself. If Kafka's *Trial,* for instance, is for most Western readers an extreme case, the limit of absurdity, existential angst, and surrealist nightmare, then for a Soviet citizen it was sometimes perceived as everyday reality—the whole life was such a trial. It was not without reason that Dovlatov/Bakhchanian's motto "We were born to make Kafka a reality" ("My rodilis', chtob Kafku sdelat' byl'iu") became so popular. In Kafka's works such as *The Trial* or *The Castle* the monster that man fights is not inside him; man in these works is determined from outside. The power of the invisible tribunal in *The Trial,* for example, traps the human being. This is one of the points that emerges naturally from the world Dovlatov depicts in *The Suitcase:* history for Russians is concrete, palpable.

Ar'ev recalls that during his last meeting with him in 1989 in New York, Dovlatov mentioned many times that he was more and more taken with Kafka: "It's some kind of fantasy—a writer who is most cruelly deprived of a sense of humor suddenly obsesses me" (*SS* 1:19). At about the same time, Dovlatov also wrote to Sagalovsky that Kafka's "Letter to His Father" was something "stupendous."[14] Ar'ev writes that Dovlatov quoted to him a passage from Kafka's letter to his father about waking up every morning and lowering himself from bed with the thought: "I do not know why I should go on living" (*SS* 1:19). Ar'ev was not able to locate this actual passage in Kafka's "Letter to His Father," and suggests that Dovlatov was succinctly summing up the general tone of the letter.

In terms of composition *The Suitcase* is one of Dovlatov's most well-wrought works. The eight stories are united not only by the voice and persona of the narrator, but also by the topos of the rediscovered articles in the suitcase. In preparing the *Grani* publication, Dovlatov had written to Vladimov that he wanted to present the stories in the journal as a selection of stories rather than as a complete "*povest'* " (novella).[15] However, in the book edition of 1986 he made it clear that he saw the stories as constituting a unity: "Some minimal introduction is essential, to make clear the connecting idea, the little trick that holds it all together."[16]

This "connecting idea" is revealed in the foreword that Dovlatov wrote for the book edition. The author looks back at his life in the Soviet Union. He tells how after many years of wandering from place to place his family was finally reunited. His daughter became a "young American woman" (*iunaia amerikanka*), and his son was born. In fact, it is this American-born son who discovers the suitcase and the author's reminiscences that it contains. At the top is the "Decent Double-Breasted Suit," which the author brought with him for attending interviews, lectures, conferences. It would have come in handy for Nobel Prize ceremonies, too. Under this is the shirt, the shoes wrapped in paper, and the velvet jacket with artificial fur. The winter hat, the gloves, and the leather belt are all there. The suitcase is lined with a copy of *Pravda* from May 1980 with the article "The Great Teaching Shall Live!" (*SS* 3:289) and a portrait of Karl Marx on the front page. This article that the author finds at the bottom of the suitcase evokes all sorts of contradictory feelings that he wants to share with his daughter and son. Each story in the novel serves as the subversion of this "great teaching." A parallel motif in the novel is also indicated in the foreword: that of belonging to the brotherhood of painters and poets. Asked about the picture of Brodsky on the suitcase lid, the author identifies him as a distant relative.

The Suitcase is not simply a catalog of things, enclosed in a frame, as is typical of others of Dovlatov's works, but it has a plot and even "culminates in a denouement."[17] Tsiv'ian considers that *The Suitcase* is not simply a cycle of stories, but "a novel with a plot running right through (the more so as

Dovlatov himself uses the designation 'chapter') . . . This plot is not the author's biography, or, to be more precise, not an image of the author created by separate episodes that fuse into a complete and integral life (or, at all events, not only that)."[18] Developing her argument about Dovlatov's rejection of the Soviet material model of the world, Tsiv'ian sees the main axis of the plot in the conflict between the initial impulse toward possession and the burgeoning realization that possessions are squalid and unnecessary. Undoubtedly such a development can be seen in the work as a whole, though one might argue that it is too implicit to be regarded as a plot in the customary sense. The internal links between the stories in *The Suitcase* are more associative than plot-based. Each story assumes a relationship with other stories in the collection. *The Suitcase* is constructed as a fictional world where characters in one tale can be at home in another. Some of the characters and things do indeed migrate from one story to another, while the common denominator of them all is the authorial point of view. For example, the story of the colorful criminal Chipa is partially told in several different stories, so that his whole character can be drawn together at the end of the cycle. Similarly, Fernand Léger's jacket also appears in different stories, so that its meaning as a whole is likewise only fully understood at the end. In many ways this structure corresponds to the definition given by A. Bocharov of the story cycle: "The stories of a cycle are truly like a system of mirrors placed in a particular way to create a sense of expanse that permits a full vision of the world."[19] However, Tsiv'ian is surely right in her observation that these stories are unified above and beyond the requirements of a story cycle. A distinguishing feature of *The Suitcase* is the specific form of authorial presence in these stories, a kind of author participation peculiar to contemporary fiction. This has the effect of foregrounding the varying intensity of the author's attitude to depicted events, which takes precedence over the system of internal reflections as defined by Bocharov. Once collected, the stories in *The Suitcase* lost their separate existence as periodical pieces and became parts of a sequence. In the end the attempt to find a fully satisfactory generic definition of *The Suitcase* is probably idle, particularly since the Russian word *povest'* has no adequate English equivalent, and the English word *novel* can cover a great multitude of sins. The essential fact is that Dovlatov achieved in this work a degree of internal coherence beyond what had been realized in any other of his story cycles.

The Suitcase has a literary epigraph (*SS* 4:455): "But even like that, my Russia, you are dearer to me than all other lands" ("No i takoi, moia Rossiia, / ty vsekh kraev dorozhe mne . . ."; from Blok's 1914 poem, "Greshit' besstydno, neprobudno . . ." ["To sin without shame or awakening . . ."]).[20] As Sukhikh remarks:

> Blok's image is one of contrast. It is built upon the juxtaposition of righteousness and venality, spiritual generosity and miserliness, kindness and indifference. Dovlatov replaces Blok's affirmative "Yes" in the quotation with a doubtful "but." It is addressed not so much to Blok's poetic subject as to the ubiquitous subject of his own prose.[21]

Sukhikh is surely right to emphasize that this questioning "but" is important for Dovlatov's attitude to the events depicted in the story cycle. As Dovlatov explains in his letter to Vladimov: "Ideally I wanted the whole of Russia, so to speak, to be contained in this suitcase, in various dimensions and aspects."[22] The stories in *The Suitcase* present, indeed, a cross-section of life in the Soviet Union which might well be compared with the catalog of venality in Blok's poem, though with the essential distinction that Dovlatov's author-figure, unlike Blok's poet, is a full participant in that life, not a dispassionate, lofty observer.

Such a juxtaposition of contrasting elements is typical of Dovlatov's later prose. Several themes and techniques come together in *The Suitcase.* The narrator once again acquires the name Dovlatov, and the chronology of the stories corresponds to the extra-textual biography of the author. The difficulty has been noted earlier of distinguishing Dovlatov the writer from Dovlatov the protagonist: even those who knew him well had difficulty in following for certain where documentary left off and invention began.[23] Or as Nikita Eliseev put it: "He was often taken for the person he pretended to be."[24]

The confessional intonation of the first-person narration intensifies the illusion of intimacy with the reader, and this intimacy in turn promotes the identification of the storyteller with the author, or perhaps more precisely with what Galina Belaia termed the "authorial mask."[25] This "authorial mask" is not the real, biographical author but a reflection of his existential being, of his personality, created by Dovlatov in the stories. Here is just one example of this intimate narrative tone from the foreword to *The Suitcase:*

> The suitcase was plywood, covered with fabric, and had chrome reinforcements at the corners. The lock didn't work; I had to wind clothesline around it.
>
> Once I had taken it to Pioneer camp. It said in ink on the lid: "Junior group. Seryozha Dovlatov." Next to it someone had amiably scratched: "Shithead." The fabric was torn in several places.
>
> Inside, the lid was plastered with photographs: Rocky Marciano, Louis Armstrong, Joseph Brodsky, Gina Lollobrigida in a transparent outfit. The customs agent tried to tear Lollobrigida off with his nails. He succeeded only in scratching the picture. But he didn't touch Brodsky. He merely asked, "Who's that?" I said he was a distant relative . . . (*S*, 4)

Chemodan byl fanernyi, obtianutyi tkan'iu, s nikelirovannymi krepleniiami po uglam. Zamok bezdeistvoval. Prishlos' obviazat' moi chemodan bel'evoi verevkoi.

Kogda-to ia ezdil s nim v pionerskii lager'. Na kryshke bylo chernilami vyvedeno: 'Mladshaia gruppa. Serezha Dovlatov.' Riadom kto-to druzheliubno natsarapal: 'govnochist.' Tkan' v neskol'kikh mestakh prorvalas'.

Iznutri kryshka byla zakleena fotografiiami. Rokki Marchiano, Armstrong, Iosif Brodskii, Lolobridzhida v prozrachnoi odezhde. Tamozhennik pytalsia otorvat' Lolobridzhidu nogtiami. V rezul'tate tol'ko potsarapal.

A Brodskogo ne tronul. Vsego lish' sprosil—kto eto? Ia otvetil, chto dal'nii rodstvennik . . . (*SS* 3:288)

In *The Suitcase* Dovlatov masterfully reproduces various linguistic registers: official newspaper style, youth slang, intellectual conversation, criminal and obscene language. All the layers he uses have equal status and coexist beside each other. No single register has predominance.

Dovlatov created the stories that comprise the novel over a number of years. There is a tension within the stories between the time of the action, the time of writing, and the time of publication. Changes come about in the author's attitude toward the events narrated, toward the characters depicted, and toward the historical period in which a given story is set.

The time span of the stories is between the 1960s and the 1980s. The chronological frame is established by the author's indicating the period of the first story and the last: "This happened eighteen years ago" (*S*, 7; this is the beginning of the first story, "The Finnish Nylon Socks," *SS* 1:291); and "Let all Forest Hills know me as 'that crazy Dovlatov, the guy who has no car!' " (*S*, 125; the ending of the last story, "The Driving Gloves," *SS* 1:404). As the author-narrator, Dovlatov differentiates between the author then and now, but in characteristic style does not pass judgment on any of the events. All other participants-protagonists in the stories are seen through the eyes of the author-narrator, and their relationships are characterized by dialogue. As a rule, Dovlatov does not introduce his author-narrator to the reader; no individual traits are attributed to him, and he begins his story immediately. If in *The Zone,* in *The Compromise,* and in *Ours* Dovlatov removes the titles under which these stories appeared in other publications, then *The Suitcase* is the only novel in which Dovlatov preserved the titles of the stories in the novel itself. It has the same textual coherence as *The Sanctuary,* which was written as an independent novella.

The novel begins with "Krepovye finskie noski" ("The Finnish Nylon Socks"). It is based on certain extra-textual biographical facts, namely Dovlatov's student years at Leningrad State University, his first love, Asia, and his attempts to impress her. Dovlatov sets the story within the Petersburg text: "The combination of water and stone creates a special, majestic atmosphere here" (*S*, 7; *SS* 1:291).

In this story, the reason the author-narrator signs up to work for a black-market dealer in the first instance is to buy back his winter coat from the pawnshop. Anyone who lived in the Soviet Union remembers how important clothes, foreign stereo equipment, and so on were. Asia is introduced in the story first by the fact that she wears imported shoes and only later by name. Very little is said about Asia, except that she belongs to a circle of well-to-do people, wears French scents, and has plenty of money. The black-market dealer, Fred Kolesnikov, is from Asia's circle. The protagonist is initiated into the workings of the Soviet shadow economy, in which many people were involved to a greater or lesser extent. Dovlatov demonstrates how the shadow economy functioned by the example of Fred Kolesnikov, who used to work as a clerk in a dispatch office, earning ninety rubles a month. Fred admits that he does not have any talents but says he was not prepared to live a miserable life on such a salary: "And die without scratching the earth's surface. Is that it? . . . I'd rather live only a minute, but live it right!" (*S*, 11; *SS* 1:295).

One example of how the Soviet shadow economy worked is described in the story in detail. Fred buys fashionable nylon socks that are smuggled into the U.S.S.R. from Finland at sixty kopecks a pair. Such socks are in demand, but are not produced in the Soviet Union and can be sold at six rubles a pair. In this way the black-market dealer gets a 900 percent return on his investment. This first attempt to get rich did not work out for Dovlatov simply because all of a sudden the Soviet economy started to produce almost identical socks at eighty kopecks a pair. "Who could have expected such a dirty trick from a socialist economy?!" exclaims the author. The large unsold supply of pea-green Finnish socks serves the author as a reminder of his criminal youth.

Several critics have commented upon Dovlatov's skill in storytelling; his secret, according to Lev Losev, was not in the plot.[26] Nikita Eliseev expands on this, adding that everything hinges on the language, on the intonation of the story and its timing.[27] Dovlatov is particularly adept at conveying information about characters through vivid and precise dialogue. Black marketers, students, the intelligentsia—all have their own language, appropriate to the psychological portrait of the characters that Dovlatov is depicting. Here is an example of a mysterious exchange between Fred and a young man in a "silvery Dacron jacket":

> "Greetings."
> "My respects," said Fred.

"Well?"
"Nothing."
The young man's eyebrows rose in disappointment. "Absolutely nothing?"
"Absolutely nothing."
"But I asked you."
"I'm very sorry."
"But I can count on it?"
"Indubitably."
"It would be good sometime this week."
"I'll try."
"What about a guarantee?"
"No guarantees. But I'll try."
"Will it be a name brand?"
"Naturally."
"So, call me."
"Of course."
"Do you remember my phone number?"
"Unfortunately I don't."
"Please write it down."
"With pleasure."
"Even though this is not a conversation for the phone."
"I agree."
"Maybe you'll just come by with the wares?"
"Gladly."
"Do you remember my address?"
"Afraid not." (*S*, 10)

Privetstvuiu vas.
Moe pochtenie,—otvetil Fred.
Nu kak?
Da nichego.
Iunosha razocharovanno pripodnial brovi.
Sovsem nichego?
Absoliutno.
Ia zhe vas prosil.
Mne ochen' zhal'.
No ia mogu rasschityvat'?
Bessporno.
Khorosho by v techenie nedeli.
Postaraius'.
Kak naschet garantii?
Garantii byt' ne mozhet. No ia postaraius'.

> Eto budet—firma?
> Estestvenno.
> Tak chto—zvonite.
> Nepremenno.
> Vy pomnite moi nomer telefona?
> K sozhaleniiu, net.
> Zapishite, pozhaluista.
> S udovol'stviem.
> Khot' eto i ne telefonny razgovor.
> Soglasen.
> Mozhet byt', zaedete priamo s tovarom?
> Okhotno.
> Pomnite adres?
> Boius', chto net. (*SS* 3:294)

This superficially innocuous conversation establishes Fred's reputation as a dealer to be reckoned with. Fred's replies are clipped and exceedingly polite. The young man in the silver jacket is in a subordinate position, although he is trying to show his importance; he wants to show that he is able to buy a shipment of some special watches, to show he is a businessman. Fred Kolesnikov can afford to keep cool: he has everything. He really lives for the moment. He has money and authority. At the end of the story Dovlatov comments that after spending two years in jail (probably because one of his own people betrayed him), Fred was killed on his Chezet motorbike, one of the most coveted motorbikes for young people in the Soviet Union.

In *Novyi Amerikanets* Dovlatov has a different ending for this story. He bumps into a former black marketeer friend on Queens Boulevard in New York:

> "Well," I ask, "what are you up to?"
> "I'm a driver," he replies, "slaving away from morning to night."
> I was astonished.
> "You used to be good at business, the enterprising type!" My friend smiled: "America has shown who's good at business, and who isn't . . . Really, America has made me look again at lots of things in myself and in life. Everything's different here. Here the notions of 'businessman' and 'crook' aren't the same. To put it simply, here you have to work." (*SS* 2:469–70)

The methods Dovlatov employs to individualize his characters' language are fresh and varied. This is not stylization, which would indicate an intention, but creates the impression of live recording of inventive and dynamic speech. Dovlatov also uses slang and colloquialisms of the 1960s and

'70s, which help to evoke the spirit of the time the story is set in. There are many examples: "Take a cab" (*S*, 12) ("Berite tachku" [slang] / "Beri motor"); "Looks like an idiot" (*S*, 13) ("Idiotskaia kharia" [mug—popular]); "What a couple of dogs!" (*S*, 13) ("Nu i khari!"); "Boy, they look pissed off!" ("Nu i mrachnye fizionomii!"; *SS* 3:298); "With a mug like that!" ("Eto s ego-to rozhei!"; *SS* 3:301); "You can always get out" ("Mozhno i soskochit' " [slang]; *SS* 3:296); "Where is that guy?" (*S*, 13) ("Gde etot tip?"); "What's he trying to pull?" (*S*, 13) ("Chego on nam golovu morochit?"); "By the way, they dig Russian" (*S*, 14) ("Kstati, oni volokut po-russki" [criminal and student slang]); "Let's ball these Finns" (*S*, 16) ("Davaitc trakhnem etikh finok"); "I'd send Rymar, but he'll keep part of the money" (*S*, 16) ("On zazhilit chast' deneg [zazhilit'—fail to return (colloquial)]); "Who would have expected a low blow from a socialist economy?" (*S*, 19) ("Kto mog zhdat' takoi podlianki ot sotsialisticheskoi ekonomiki?!" [podlianka—slang]); "I know our bloody industry! All the stores are filled with the same crap." ("Znaiu ia nashu bliadskuiu promyshlennost'! Vse magaziny zabity kakoi-nibud' odnoi khrenovinoi." [colloquial]; *SS* 3:302).

The illusion that the dialogues and the language that the characters use are taken word for word from "real life" is, of course, misleading. As Lidia Ginzburg insists, characters in literature do not speak as in "real life," because direct speech in literature is organized: "It constitutes an artistic structure, subordinated to requirements that genuine conversational language does not know. Any representation of direct speech, even the most naturalistic, is (to a greater or lesser extent) conventional."[28] In a literary dialogue, writes Ginzburg, the character's speech is required by the author in order to add to the depiction of the character or the character's world outlook, or to reveal the author's opinion or move the plot along.[29] Dovlatov's dialogues were taken to be so true to real life that when he read his stories, some of the characters that appear in them felt impelled to make corrections in order to assert what was said in reality. Dovlatov was very pleased when people mistook his stories for recordings of real events: "He set far greater store by mystification than by truth to life. He wouldn't have been in the least offended to be caught out in some untruth, some lie, some bad action, which did happen. But he would have been terribly offended if he had been caught out in some literary mystification, in some literary invention of his own."[30]

The second story in the sequence is "Nomenklaturnye polubotinki" ("The *Nomenklatura* Half Boots"). If "The Finnish Nylon Socks" is about Soviet aspirations to acquire foreign goods, then "The *Nomenklatura* Half Boots" is about the eternal Russian and Soviet problem of theft. Here again Dovlatov establishes a link to the Petersburg text by quoting Karamzin, who, according to V. N. Toporov, was the first in the history of Russian culture to appreciate the autonomous value of the city and to single it out as such an independent object of feeling.[31] The story opens with a confession by the first-person narrator that the shoes in the suitcase were stolen. Theft in Russia is endemic. Dovlatov cites Karamzin's response of two hundred years ago when he was asked by Russian émigrés in France what the news was from home, and he allegedly replied with one word: "Thieving!" ("Voruiut!").

This story is also based to a certain extent on Dovlatov's extra-textual biography: weary of working for the factory's newspaper, the narrator becomes an apprentice to a monumental sculptor at an Applied Arts Complex.[32] He chooses to become a monumental sculptor because they made a good living in the Soviet Union; as the narrator explains, each town had to have a sculpture of Lenin. The narrator becomes part of a team that has been given the task of putting up a frieze depicting Lomonosov, to coincide with the opening of a new underground station bearing Lomonosov's name. As was usual in Soviet workplaces, there is a great deal of discussion and drinking, followed by a last-minute rush to finish the work on time. Everything is in place for the opening event, though there is one small worry: the epoxy resin may not be strong enough to hold the frieze, which might therefore fall down. The tension in the story builds up as the reader is led to believe that this will happen when all the dignitaries arrive and deliver the customary speeches. However, the reception takes place in a side room underground, and the story culminates in the narrator stealing the mayor's elegant shoes, which, although made in the Soviet Union, are produced for export and therefore are of much better quality than the ordinary shoes available for purchase by ordinary Soviet citizens. The reader is aware of the shoes' fate: the author has taken them with him to America. However, the reader is not told whether the shoes fit the narrator, or whether he needed a pair of shoes in the first place. The shoes, it seems, are stolen just for the sake of stealing. The fate of the frieze was more unfortunate: it had to be taken down, allegedly because a group of Leningrad scholars complained to the paper that this sculpture "is unworthy of the great man" ("prinizhaet velikii obraz"; *SS* 3:317). The real reason for taking the sculpture down, however, is ideological: the globe that Lomonosov was depicted holding in one hand, symbolizing Science, was turned to the viewer with its side showing America. Many details of American geography were lovingly sculpted, although such detailed maps did not exist in Lomonosov's time.

"Prilichnyi dvubortnyi kostium" ("A Decent Double-Breasted Suit") is a story about the acquisition of a suit. In the Soviet Union it was not easy to purchase a good-quality suit in a shop. If one required a nonstandard size, it became virtually impossible. The narrator of the story is reproached for not dressing smartly enough. This is a perennial problem, and he recalls that when he worked in the Pushkin Museum as a guide, the administration used to rebuke him: "Your trousers, comrade Dovlatov, disrupt the festive atmosphere of this place . . ." ("Svoimi bruikami, tovarishch Dovlatov, vy narushaete prazdnichnuiu atmosferu zdeshnikh mest . . ."; *SS* 3:318).

The story has a frame: at the beginning the narrator is arguing his case with the editor of the newspaper as to why the paper should buy him a suit. The editor tells him that he should write some stories with "broad socio-political resonance" (*S*, 37) and then the paper would be able to reward him. However, this presents difficulties for the narrator. Not a single word in Soviet papers could be published without the censor's permission. Since all the stories in the paper have to be approved, there seems to be a lack of material to base them on. It proves very difficult for the narrator to find topics for articles with "broad socio-political resonance." Even a story about a Soviet heroine-mother, a "winning number" (*S*, 37) as journalists call it, under the narrator's pen turns into something unpublishable, because he attempts to describe matters truthfully. Some of the ideas on the selection process for story material, the various taboos imposed on journalists in Soviet papers, and the problems of censorship are similar to those described in *The Compromise.* The narrator has to find someone suitable for a feature on Constitution Day: an Uzbek, for instance, as a representative of one of the fifteen republics; or write a story on the occasion of the Day of the Rationalizer (people who invent something to improve production methods). For Constitution Day the narrator finds an Uzbek who is a musician. Unfortunately, he has just come out of prison and is consequently no good as material. For an inventor the narrator finds a truly remarkable person who skillfully restores antique cars. However, it transpires that his ancestry is not Russian but English, which similarly disqualifies him from being the subject of a newspaper article.

The story "A Decent Double-Breasted Suit" ends with the editor arranging to buy an imported suit for the narrator so that he will not be disgraced when he takes a Swede, in whom the KGB has developed an interest, to the theater. The story reflects the eternal Russian problem of cronyism (*blat*): if you know the right person, then you can obtain a smart, good-quality suit, even if you require a nonstandard size (as in the case of the protagonist, who is one meter ninety-four centimeters tall). There is a discernible plot in this story: Artur, a Swede, who has studied Russian language and culture, comes to the Soviet Union to research a book. He speaks very good Russian and the narrator, a Soviet newspaper correspondent, meets him by chance at the newspaper premises. The correspondent and Artur get on well; they have a lot in common: jazz, American literature, theater, and Russian culture. From the official Soviet point of view, anybody who is interested in Russian culture is likely to be a spy, and Artur, therefore, is forced to leave the Soviet Union. Meetings with foreign nationals were discouraged, and if they did occur, then the KGB inevitably tried to control events. So in this story, when the KGB learns about the informal friendship between Artur and the narrator, it attempts to persuade him to compromise the Swede so that he can be blackmailed. As usual, Dovlatov makes no overt judgment. The narrator in the story makes only one remark, when the KGB officer takes out a fat file with the inscription "Dovlatov": "I felt what a pig might feel in the meat department of a store" (*S*, 48) ("Ia ispytyval to, chto chuvstvovala by, dopustim, svin'ia v miasnom otdele gastronoma"; *SS* 3:331).

Despite a similarity in the milieu depicted, this story differs from the stories in *The Compromise* in that it does not "quote" a "real" newspaper article. This allows the author to weave into the story several narrative lines and thus make it fit into the pattern of the other *Suitcase* stories.

The action of "Ofitserskii remen' " ("The Army Belt") dates back to the summer of 1963, when the narrator was serving as a camp guard in the Soviet Army. There is a correspondence here too to the extra-textual biography of Dovlatov. The setting is the southern end of the Komi Republic. This story also has a plot: the narrator is given the task of accompanying a prisoner, who is said to be deranged, to the psychiatric clinic for a medical examination. The prisoner has to be accompanied by two armed guards. It is a four-kilometer journey, and during a rest (with a couple of bottles of vodka, which they share with the prisoner) the other guard, Churilin, becomes very drunk and nearly kills the narrator. This incident serves to show that it is the guard Churilin who is deranged, while the allegedly disturbed prisoner behaves with perfect common sense. In fact, it becomes clear to both guards that there is psychologically nothing wrong with the prisoner, and it is they themselves who behave in an abnormal way. (This can be compared with the story of Fidel in *The Zone,* where the guard drives a group of prisoners into an icy river for no particular reason; *SS* 2:50.) The army belt of the title with its red star on the buckle is the one that all army personnel wore as standard. This belt is turned into a dangerous weapon by soldering tin on to the reverse side of the buckle. This was a popular device for self-defense among the guards (although they were allowed to use firearms). The guards received, the narrator informs us, only three weeks' training for coping with the dangerous situations that arose and defending themselves. The army and the state were clearly neglectful of their duty of care toward guards and prisoners alike, despite protestations to the contrary.

If "The Finnish Nylon Socks" is characterized by the slang of the 1960s and the argot of petty criminals, then in "The Army Belt" Dovlatov uses the specific language of the camp criminals: "What's all the ruckus about?"[33] ("Chto za shukher na banu?"; *SS* 3:339); "Why are you giving me trouble, you bastard? I can stick one into you too, you know." ("Khuli zhe ty mne, suka, plesh' raz"edaesh'?! Mogu ved' i tebia poshchekotit'!"; *SS* 3:346).

During his army service as a camp guard, Dovlatov had noted down words and expressions that were in use in that environment. In one of his letters to his father, he wrote that he had come to know life in many types of camps quite well and that he had heard many stories from the criminal world and even learned their language.[34] Certainly, the often coarse expressions he uses in the stories are carefully used to evoke atmosphere and character. Dovlatov noted in one of his fictitious letters to the publisher in *The Zone* that the prisoners did not swear in vain and that some of the more lexically "neutral" expressions were more powerful in their hierarchy of abuse. He writes that "the disgusted 'You belong by the piss bucket' is worth more than ten choice swear words" (Z, 93) ("Brezglivoe: 'Tvoe mesto u parashi'—stoit desiatki otbornykh rugatel'stv"; *SS* 2:88). Just what importance was attached not only to the right word, but even to the right stress, is illustrated in *Zapisnye knizhki* (*Notebooks*). One of the sergeants from an educated Muscovite family is trying hard to fit in by using swear-words he is obviously not familiar with, which serves only to emphasize even more his "otherness." He receives a lesson from a prisoner: "You can say that someone's 'fucking off,' 'fucked up,' or 'getting fucked.' But 'fucked off'—that doesn't exist, pardon me, in the Russian language" (Z, 92). ("Po-russki mozhno skazat'—**ë**bnulsia, eban**u**lsia ili naebn**u**lsia. A 'ebn**u**lsia'—takogo slova v russkom literaturnom iazyke, uzh izvinite, net"; *SS* 4:138.)[35] As Benedikt Sarnov commented on a different example many years later: "By a shift of stress in one single word you can create a clear and exhaustive picture of the entire organization of our—unique—Soviet society."[36]

There are two other stories woven into "The Army Belt." One is about Private Churilin, who, along with the narrator, accompanies the prisoner to the psychiatric clinic. The reader meets Churilin at the moment when he is soldering the tin onto his buckle, with which he later injures the narrator. Churilin is quite uneducated and, as the narrator puts it: "What do you say to a guard who uses after-shave only internally?" (*S*, 59) ("Chto mozhno skazat' okhranniku, kotoryi los'on 'Gigiena' upotrebliaet tol'ko vnutr'?"; *SS* 3:341). For wounding a fellow soldier Churilin is tried by a "comrades' court." He hopes to avoid the severe punishment of service in a disciplinary battalion and has the cheek to ask the narrator (who is recovering in the hospital from the injuries inflicted by Churilin) to help him out. The narrator takes pity on him and ends up writing out a whole scenario of such hearings, attempting to foresee all the possible questions and reactions. At the hearing itself, chaired by Major Afanas'ev, Churilin tries to read the script the narrator has written for him, but the questions do not correspond to the scripted answers. This is used in the story to great comic effect. Churilin is sentenced to one year in a disciplinary battalion, and the narrator does not see him again. There is an almost identical story in Dovlatov's *Notebooks* about a

Private Babichev who is due to be tried for fighting while drunk. He wakes the author up on the night before the hearing and asks for help. In a similar way, the author and Babichev write a script. At the actual hearing the lieutenant colonel asks: "Well, Babichev, explain what happened there" ("Nu, Babichev, ob"iasnite, chto u vas tam proizoshlo?"). Babichev feverishly looks through the script, but not finding this precise question, answers: "Why the hell should I explain it to you, you idiot?" ("A khuli tebe, kozlu, ob"iasniat'?"; *SS* 4:140). As a result, he gets three years in a disciplinary battalion. In "The Army Belt" there are two contrasted dialogues. The first is the discussion between the narrator and Churilin in the hospital ward when the narrator comes up with an idea of how to rescue Churilin:

> I said, "I don't know what to do. There is one possibility . . ."
> Churilin perked up. "What?"
> "At the trial I'll ask you a question. I'll say, 'Churilin, do you have a civilian profession?' You'll reply, 'No.' I'll say, 'What is he supposed to do after his discharge—steal? Where are the promised courses for chauffeurs and bulldozer drivers? Are we any worse than the regular army?' And so on. This will create a stir, of course. Maybe they'll let you out on bail." (*S*, 60)

> — Ne znaiu, chto tut mozhno sdelat'. Est' odin variant . . .
> Churilin ozhivilsia:
> — Kakoi?
> — Ia na sude zadam vopros. Sproshu: 'Churilin, u vas est' grazhdanskaia professiia?' Ty otvetish': 'Net.' Ia skazhu: 'Chto zhe emu posle demobilizatsii—vorovat'? Gde obeshchannye kursy shoferov i bul'dozeristov? Chem my khuzhe reguliarnoi armii?' I tak dalee. Tut, konechno, podnimetsia shum. Mozhet, i voz'mut tebia na poruki. (*SS* 3:342)

The special prison camp guards (VOKHR) had the same rights in law as the regular army, which meant that they were supposed to have an opportunity to acquire some skills such as driving, typing, and so on.[37] Although it would not have occurred to Churilin to enroll in any such course, he is happy to go along with this suggestion in the hope of escaping punishment in a disciplinary battalion. He asks the narrator to write down all the questions and answers. The second dialogue is what actually happens when Major Afanas'ev opens the meeting:

> "Let's begin. Tell us how it happened, Churilin."
> Everyone looked at Churilin. A crumpled paper appeared in his hands. He turned it this way and that, looked it over, and mumbled to himself.
> "Tell us," Major Afanasiev repeated.

Churilin looked at me in bewilderment. We had not foreseen this. We had left something out of the scenario.

The major raised his voice. "We're waiting!"

"I'm in no rush," Churilin said.

He looked grim. His face was turning meaner. At the same time the major's voice was growing more irritated. I had to raise my hand. "Let me tell it."

"Drop it," the major shouted. "You're a fine one to talk!"

"Aha," said Churilin. "Here . . . I want . . . whatchamacallit . . . I want to take bulldozer driving courses."

The major turned to him. "What have courses got to do with it, damn your eyes! You got drunk, mutilated your friend, and now you dream about courses! . . . How about going to college while you're at it? Or the conservatory?"

Churilin looked at the paper once more and said grimly, "Why are we worse than the regular army?"

The major choked with rage. (*S*, 65)

Nachnem! . . . Rasskazyvaite, Churilin, kak vse eto proizoshlo.

Vse posmotreli na Churilina. V rukakh u nego poiavilas' izmiataia bumazhka. On vertel ee, razgliadyval i chto-to bezzvuchno sheptal.

— Rasskazyvaite,—povtoril maior Afanas'ev.

Churilin rasterianno vzglianul na menia. Chego-to, vidno, my ne predusmotreli. Chto-to upustili v stsenarii.

Maior povysil golos:

— Ne zastavliaite sebia zhdat'!

— Mne toropit'sia nekuda,—skazal Churilin.

On pomrachnel. Ego litso stanovilos' vse bolee zlym i ugriumym. No i v golose maiora kreplo razdrazhenie. Prishlos' mne vytianut' ruku:

— Davaite, ia rasskazhu.

— Otstavit',—prikriknul maior,—sami khoroshi!

— Aga,—skazal Churilin,—vot . . . Zhelaiu . . . eto . . . postupit' na kursy bul'dozeristov.

Maior povernulsia k nemu:

— Pri chem tut kursy, mat' vashu za nogu! Napilsia, ponimaesh', druga iskalechil, teper' o kursakh mechtaet! . . . A v institut sluchaino ne khotite postupit'? Ili v konservatoriiu? . . .

Churilin eshche raz zaglianul v bumazhku i mrachno proiznes:

— Chem my khuzhe reguliarnoi armii?

Maior zadokhnulsia ot beshenstva. (*SS* 3:346)

Churilin's inability to utter a single unscripted word (at the same time asking a question to which Afanas'ev would not have had an answer), juxtaposed with Afanas'ev's ironic question, which Churilin takes at face value, increases the comic effect of the dialogues.

The other story within the story is about the "deranged" prisoner, who has been sentenced for theft of state property: he attempted to steal a tractor from a heavily guarded site. He calculated that if he attached to the tractor a barrel of lubricating grease, it would be the barrel that would attract the guard's attention. His assumption proved correct. The noise made by the barrel of lubricating oil does indeed attract the watchman's attention. The prisoner is made to leave the barrel behind and can then drive out on the tractor as planned. This was a typical Soviet story, the same malaise as in "The *Nomenklatura* Half Boots," and a different angle to stealing. There was nothing at all "deranged" about the prisoner. All this seems to the author very remote now, viewed from across the ocean. All this past world has disappeared: "And only the belt is still in one piece" (*SS* 3:347). And it is Churilin's belt with the heavy tin buckle that Dovlatov takes with him to America.

"Kurtka Fernana Lezhe" ("Fernand Léger's Jacket") is a story about a prince and a pauper, and was added at a later date to the *Suitcase* stories, where it is placed roughly in the middle of the cycle.[38] In a letter to Efimov, who published the book version of *The Suitcase,* Dovlatov explains this decision by saying that this will ensure that the first and last stories in the cycle are of higher quality.[39] Nevertheless, in his article "Chelovecheskii golos" ("The Human Voice"), Nikita Eliseev expresses the view that the Fernand Léger story is pivotal, showing that "it is Dovlatov who is the prince: he is the one who acquires the mantle of the king—'the jacket of Fernand Léger,' the great artist, who dreamed of painting on the walls of buildings and railway carriages. Can any Ph.D. in physics or mathematics compare with that gift?"[40]

The background Russian theme to this story is cronyism and betrayal of a different kind from what we find in the previous stories. The narrator is a childhood friend of the son of a famous actor, Cherkasov.[41] The Cherkasovs lead the lives of privileged people: they have a chauffeur-driven car (a Bugatti), a dacha, and a big government flat on Kronverksky Street. The family has an array of servants. Many famous people come to visit the Cherkasovs' house (in the story Mravinsky, Raikin, and Shostakovich are among the visitors). It was through their mothers' friendship (both actresses who studied together) that the boys, Andriusha and Sergei (the narrator), came to know each other and grow up together. Their lives are told in parallel. Sergei lives in a communal flat and goes to school on public transport, his parents do not have a dacha, and so on. The model for this contrast is taken from Mark Twain's *Prince and the Pauper,* which tells the story of two young boys who have misconceptions about each other's lifestyles. In Twain's story the poor boy is brought into the palace and the prince goes to live with the poor boy's abusive father. In Dovlatov's story the protagonist is taken to live in the dacha and goes to visit the Cherkasovs.

This story is also based on certain extra-textual biographical facts. Dovlatov's family was friendly with the Cherkasovs in real life. In one of his radio scripts, "Ordinary People: *Blat* in the Soviet Union Is Now a Norm of Daily Life," Dovlatov explained that he owed his birth to Cherkasov's patronage:

> You could say that I was born through *blat*. This is how it happened. My parents were friends with an outstanding actor—Cherkasov. They worked in the same theater . . . it was 1941. In Ufa. My mother was evacuated there. I was about to be born.
>
> Finally my mother was taken to the maternity hospital. The friends who accompanied her found unimaginable filth there. The medical staff were rude. Terrible drafts. They approached Cherkasov. He phoned some local officials. Reminded them of his achievements. My mother was transferred to a special hospital for the elite. And as a result I made a safe appearance in the world.[42]

In this same radio script Dovlatov discusses the nature and significance of *blat* in the Soviet Union: "In a country where there is a chronic shortage of everything, *blat* acquires an immense significance. Behind this little slang word lies an immense phenomenon of diverse character. The workers' and peasants' state is permeated with it from top to bottom." *Blat* had the power of turning quite ordinary people without a great deal of talent into a special elite that possessed everything the Soviet Union could offer: good living accommodation, access to education, holidays, and much more.

The loss of *blat* produces quite the opposite effect. When Cherkasov dies, his widow finds that all the privileges are gradually withdrawn. The prizes her husband received are taken away, and famous people are no longer so keen to know her. She loses her job at the theater. The only people who maintain friendship with her are a group of French left-wing artists, Yves Montand, Sartre, Léger, and the narrator's mother. Cherkasova, dispirited by the betrayals of Soviet friends, later travels to Paris where she is well received by the friends of her husband. One of the people she meets there is the widow of Fernand Léger. She tells Léger's widow about Dovlatov, by now a nonconformist writer. Léger's widow presents her with the painter's jacket to give to Dovlatov, saying that Fernand instructed her in his will to befriend all kinds of riffraff.

The whole story is told in a series of contrasts. It continues the debates, so fashionable in the 1960s, about the relative importance of physicists and lyricists; throughout Dovlatov's cycle, but particularly in "Fernand

Léger's Jacket," the lyricists are clear winners.[43] It was believed by many at that time that thanks to scientific and technical progress, a new man with new spiritual parameters could be formed, as Bocharov notes: "A leap forward in psychology was seen as a direct and necessary consequence of the leap forward in science and technology."[44] However, this leap forward in the human psyche did not quite materialize.

This jacket, inherited by the author from the cubist painter, is mentioned in another story in *The Suitcase.* In "A Decent Double-Breasted Suit" the editor of one of the papers complains that Dovlatov compromises the paper by wearing unsuitable clothes at the funeral of a general.

> "You're compromising us, clear and simple. We sent you to the funeral of General Filonenko, and I have been informed that you showed up without a suit."
>
> "I was wearing a jacket."
>
> "You wore some old cassock."
>
> "It's not a cassock. It's an imported jacket. And incidentally, it was a present from Léger." (*S*, 35)

> My okazali vam doverie. Delegirovali vas na pokhorony generala Filonenko. A vy, kak mne stalo izvestno, iavilis' bez pidzhaka.
>
> — Ia byl v kurtke.
>
> — Na vas byla kakaia-to staraia riasa.
>
> — Eto ne riasa. Eto zagranichnaia kurtka. I kstati, podarok Lezhe. (*SS* 3: 318–19)

No doubt Eliseev is right in considering that the word "cassock" (*riasa*) was used deliberately to represent a sign of belonging to the brotherhood of painters and poets.[45]

The story "Poplinovaia rubashka" ("A Poplin Shirt") is about the author-narrator's difficult relationship with his wife and is one of the most moving in the cycle.[46] It describes in flashback how the narrator met his wife, who is called Lena, just like Dovlatov's real-life wife.[47] "We met twenty five years ago [in Leningrad]. I even remember that it was a Sunday. February 18. Election Day" (*S*, 82). ("Poznakomilis' my dvadtsat' let nazad. Ia dazhe pomniu, chto eto bylo voskresen'e. Vosemnadtsatoe fevralia. Den' vyborov"; *SS* 3:362.) The narrator was then a young writer wishing to impress the young woman who came canvassing to persuade him to vote. From that time on they stayed together, simply because they were indifferent to each other and too lazy to part. This was a convenient way for the narrator to achieve his aim of avoiding unnecessary worries: "We simply turned out to be at home together. That was twenty years ago." ("Prosto my okazalis' doma. Eto bylo dvadtsat' let nazad"; *SS* 3:362.)

In the frame of the story, the narrator is alone in his New York apartment looking through various papers in quest of a particular document, and he comes across his wife's photo album, in which he all of a sudden sees his own photograph. This is quite a normal thing for a wife to do, but it touches the narrator: "I didn't have the strength to think it through. I never knew that love could be so strong, so sharp" (*S*, 92). ("U menia ne khvatalo sil obdumat' proiskhodiashchee. Ia ne znal, chto liubov' mozhet dostigat' takoi sily i ostroty"; *SS* 3:372.) Love has not been mentioned before; various other expressions are used to describe the tenderness felt by the narrator and his wife. The ending of "A Poplin Shirt" is similarly tender and laconic:

> And Lena went for the tickets. She came back with a box. She walked up to me and said, "I had some money left over. This is for you."
>
> Inside the box was an imported poplin shirt. (*S*, 93)

> I vot Lena poekhala za biletami. Vernulas' s korobkoi. Podoshla ko mne i govorit:
>
> — U menia ostavalis' lishnie den'gi. Eto tebe. V korobke lezhala importnaia poplinovaia rubakha. (*SS* 3:374)

"Zimniaia shapka" ("The Winter Hat") is a story about the metamorphosis of an ugly ski cap into a new sealskin hat, about anti-Semitism in the Soviet Union, and about the narrator's relationship with Boris, his first cousin, whom he often uses in other stories as a kind of alter ego.[48] In the story the narrator is disgusted by his colleagues' reaction to the suicide of a Jewish woman who worked as a secretary in the newspaper office. The narrator is deeply upset by the hypocritical atmosphere and decides he needs to talk to somebody, so he calls Boris.

It is well known that in the Soviet Union the authorities actively encouraged anti-Semitism. The death of millions of Jews in the Nazi concentration camps was a forbidden topic for a long time, and that is why Evtushenko's *Babii Iar* (*Babi Yar*) made such an impact on the reading public: he was the first to broach the topic openly. Shostakovich then set the poem to music, which also provoked controversy. Shostakovich had worked on Jewish themes before. He had used the emotional ambivalence of Jewish folklore, which expresses despair and grief through dance. Such psychological and emotional identification with the Jews was characteristic of many Russian intellectuals. Dovlatov was half Armenian and half Jewish, and his cousin Boris was half Armenian and half Russian. When Boris's father (Boris was the illegitimate child of a high-ranking party functionary) dies, Boris refuses to look for the relatives of his biological father. He confesses that he does not need anybody else, since he has Sergei. Lipovetsky notes that the argument the cousin uses for this declaration of kinship is quite absurd, but that it could not be otherwise: "How strange! Both of us with Armenian mothers, and I'm half Russian, you're half Jewish. But we both like vodka with beer" (*O*, 97). ("Kak stranno! Ia—napolovinu russkii. Ty—napolovinu evrei. No oba liubim vodku s pivom.")[49]

The relations between the cousins form the main substance of "The Winter Hat": "in counterpoint with the cousin's story, the story of Dovlatov himself runs through the entire tale."[50] Boris is successful, while the narrator is a failure, although the narrator manages to attract the sympathy of the women surrounding Boris, even if only briefly and only because he was beaten up. Dovlatov remarks that in the end he managed to grasp his cousin's main characteristic: he was "an unconscious elemental existentialist" (*SS* 2:352). Lipovetsky concludes that "in essence it is not only Dovlatov's lyrical hero who turns out to be a version of the author's biography, but all his other characters appear in the same function."[51]

Many themes come together in "Shoferskie perchatki" ("The Driving Gloves"): the insanity of Peter and of Petersburg, authority and the elements, the state and the individual, Russia and history, victory and defeat, belief and unbelief. The dominant motif is that of the Russian state and the individual. One of the narrator's newspaper colleagues, Iury Schlippenbach,[52] a descendant of General Wolmar Anton von Schlippenbach[53] (a real historical figure mentioned in Pushkin's *Poltava*), decides to break out of the newspaper production routine and make a short film about Peter the Great suddenly finding himself in Soviet Leningrad. It is the narrator's stature of one meter and ninety-four centimeters that attracts Schlippenbach's attention and persuades him to cast the narrator in the role of the tsar.

The narrator is dressed in what to modern eyes is a most ridiculous outfit: tall black boots, a frock coat, a cloak, a broad-brimmed hat, a pair of velvet breeches with gold braid, and a sword. He also receives a black wig and he glues on a moustache. In this outfit he walks around the streets of Leningrad and stands in a queue, but nobody pays the slightest attention to him. No event, not even the appearance of Peter the Great, can distract the people from their aim: to cure their hangover (*opokhmelit'sia*). The crowd only reacts when they think this person is trying to jump the queue. Dovlatov's dialogue is vivid, and each person in the queue is characterized by distinctive expressions, using a mixture of slang and officialese with the occasional element of criminal jargon:

> "Excuse me," said the railroad man to Filimonov. "You're jumping the line."

"I'm carrying out my work responsibilities," Filimonov replied, thinking fast.

"So are we all," mumbled someone in the crowd.

The dissatisfaction grew. The voices got more aggressive.

"There's all kinds of wise guys and jokers around here."

"They take your picture and then they use it as a bad example, like 'Another Troublemaker.' " "We're just getting a drink in a perfectly civilized way, and these people come stirring up trouble." "A bum like that should be sent to the camps." (*S*, 124)

Izviniaius',—obratilsia k Shlippenbakhu zheleznodorozhnik,—vas zdes' ne stoialo!

— Nakhozhus' pri ispolnenii sluzhebnykh obiazannostei,—chetko reagiroval Shlippenbakh.

— Vse pri ispolnenii,—doneslos' iz tolpy.

Nedovol'stvo roslo. Golosa delalis' vse bolee agressivnymi:

— Khodiat tut vsiakie satiriki, bliad', iumoristy . . .

— Sfotografiruiut tebia, a potom—na dosku . . . V smysle—'Oni meshaiut nam zhit' . . .'

— Liudi, mozhno skazat', kul'turno pokhmeliaiutsia, a on nam tiul'ku gonit . . .

— Takomu barmaleiu mesto u parashi . . . (*SS* 3:402–3)

Tsiv'ian argues that this indifference is not at all a sign of the carnivalization of life: "this is its *Soviet essence,* with its fundamental admixture of violence."[54] People show no surprise, because fear and self-preservation are the dominant emotions: it is better not to delve deeply; asking questions will only make matters worse.

Everywhere are grey, apathetic people, aloof, "as if at a stranger's grave" (*S*, 121), and the only colorful person the narrator comes across is the former criminal Chipa in his striped T-shirt and top hat, who recognizes in the narrator a former prison camp guard. This is one of the dialogues that in one form or other recur in Dovlatov's fiction; in "The Driving Gloves":

"Did you work as a prison guard?"

"Why?"

"Remember the isolation cell in Ropcha?"

"Yeah."

"Remember the prisoner who hanged himself with his belt?"

"Vaguely."

"That was me. They worked on me for two hours, the bastards." (*S*, 116)

— Ty v okhrane sluzhil?
— A chto?
— Pomnish' shtrafnoi izoliator na Ropche?
— Nu.
— A pomnish', kak zek na remne udavilsia?
— Chto-to pripominaiu.
— Tak eto byl ia. Dva chasa otkachivali, suki . . .[55] (*SS* 3:395–96)

It is the Russified Swede who is angered by the crowd's preoccupation with drink:

> The crowd's energy was close to bursting point. But Filimonov was angry himself.
>
> "You've boozed Russia away, you vipers! You've lost the last remnants of conscience! Up to your eyeballs in vodka from morning 'til night!" (*S*, 123–24)[56]

> Energiia tolpy rvalas' naruzhu. No i Shlippenbakh vdrug rasserdilsia:
>
> — Propili Rossiiu, gady! Sovest' poteriali okonchatel'no! Vodiaroi zalili glaza, s utra poran'she! (*SS* 3:402–3)

Among the details of Russian life that are depicted with great care is the institution of the queue, with its special rules: it is legitimate, for instance, to save a place for somebody else: "No, the tsar was in line, I saw him. And the ass with the camera is with him, so it's okay, it's legal!" (*S*, 124). ("Tsar' stoial, ia videl. A etot pidor s fonarem—ego druzhok. Tak chto, vse zakonno!")

The Soviet queue is described most vividly in Vladimir Sorokin's novel *Ochered'* (*The Queue*), where life in the Soviet Union is rendered in the form of dialogue as one long queue. People queue for days on end for some item of clothing, but it is not revealed what exactly they are queuing for. In the end a central character in the story has sex with a warehouse worker and thus obtains the desired, but still unnamed product. This method of obtaining desired goods in the Soviet Union recalls Dovlatov's story "A Decent Double-Breasted Suit." It is also described in his story "Labirint" ("The Labyrinth"), published in *Russkaia mysl'*, but not included in the most complete edition of Dovlatov's work.[57]

The juxtaposition of Peter the Great and an ordinary man inevitably recalls the founding text of the Petersburg tradition, Pushkin's *Bronze Horseman.* In this poem Pushkin makes no definitive judgment between the Tsar and Evgeny: each is right in his way, and they are even equal inasmuch as the Tsar leaves his pedestal to pursue the little man. In Dovlatov's text, Shlippenbakh is intending to surround the Tsar with Soviet reality: a policeman attempts to fine him, two drunks invite him to join them for a drink, the KGB takes him for a spy, and a girl takes him for a wealthy foreigner. Shlippenbakh's intention is for the Tsar to express his horror at his creation: "What have I done? . . . Why did I ever start this whorish city?" (*S*, 114). ("Chto ia nadelal? Zachem ia osnoval etot bliadskii gorod?"; *SS* 3:393.)

Shlippenbakh is very excited as he prepares to shoot a scene by the beer kiosks: "It'll be terrific—the monarch among the lowlifes" (*S*, 120) ("Eto budet potriasaiushche. Monarkh sredi podonkov"; *SS* 3:399). However, the crowd in the beer queue does not react in any way; all are equal, monarch or plebs, in the queue for beer. There is no conflict between them, despite Shlippenbakh's desire to create conflict, to show the "antagonism of the masses" toward the Tsar. What happens is that antagonism is evoked not by the Tsar, but by the man with the movie camera, in whom the people see a figure of authority. For a moment things become quite uncomfortable for the filmmaker. Afraid that the crowd's anger is about to spill over onto him, he struggles for words: " 'It was something like . . .'—'the Battle of Poltava,' I finished his sentence for him" ("Eto bylo chto-to vrode . . .—Poltavskoi bitvy,—zakonchil ia"; *SS* 3:403).

This mention of the Battle of Poltava invites a comparison between the eighteenth century, when that battle established the newly won status of Russia as a full-fledged European power (as every Soviet schoolchild knew), and the twentieth, the time of writing, when the political significance of the Soviet Union was such as to instill fear in the world.

It was mentioned earlier that in writing *The Suitcase* Dovlatov was trying to emulate the idea behind Il'ia Erenburg's *Trinadtsat' trubok* (*The Thirteen Pipes*).[58] Each of the stories in Erenburg's collection tells the story of how a particular pipe was acquired by the narrator: each story ends with the narrator smoking one of the pipes that belonged to different characters in different countries. This gives the author the opportunity to describe the life and customs of various countries. In the story of the tenth pipe, Erenburg expresses the idea that perhaps his book, "with its reliable information on the life of thirteen pipes," will provide an impulse for the serious investigation of the psychology of the *thing*.[59] Some of the stories have a philosophical coloring, others give priority to social factors, while others again are about love, or good and evil. For example, the narrator's favorite thirteenth pipe tells a story about love. The narrator inherits this pipe from convict number 348: "I smoke this one in order to learn how to love with a love that is faithful and selfless."[60] However, Dovlatov is not so much following Erenburg's idea as polemicizing not only with Erenburg, but also with other Soviet stories of the 1920s and '30s about things (*o veshchakh*). Writers of that time looked at things as being perhaps of greater value than their owners. An example might be Konstantin Vaginov's passion for collecting books, coins, and various ephemera.[61] For Dovlatov in *The Suitcase,* the ownership of a thing is reduced to a trivial and absurd event. It is testimony to the narrator's personal history and not to the history of the revolution. Dovlatov turns the value of ownership upside down; he uses elements of parody and irony in his stories in order to repudiate the value of owning the objects that were coveted in the Soviet Union.

E. S. Shevchenko considers the specifics of what she calls Dovlatov's theatrical code in *The Suitcase,* finding them in a combination of conventional theatrical elements with elements of constructivism:

> The specificity of Dovlatov's theatrical code is in evidence at every level of the text—from its structure to its semantics. It is particularly worthy of attention that the verbal method of text construction is complicated by the iconic, and that the theatricality is realized in its first and fundamental meaning—as spectacle.[62]

The Russians in *The Suitcase* are ordinary Russians, not dissidents, not the government, but characters from the bottom layer of society. The Soviet Union appears in *The Suitcase* in all its aspects, truly as if it was a "magician's suitcase": "It is as though before us were a conjuror's box of tricks, from which ever new things miraculously emerge, each one of which is capable of revealing its own (and our) history, of creating its own story."[63]

Eliseev is right that *The Suitcase,* if not the "pinnacle" of Dovlatov's creativity, is certainly a work most typical of Dovlatov:

> In *The Suitcase* Dovlatov freed himself entirely from "literariness," from the descriptive. What is left is a human voice, telling stories. Nothing else . . . . But just try retelling one of Dovlatov's stories—and you will realize how difficult that is, how deceptive is the illusion of simple, primitive, "unmarked" language.[64]

It is this laconic, deceptively simple "human voice" that creates this illusion of reality, which is particularly acute in his later stories.

The Suitcase is a short novel or a collection of interconnected stories. The pieces that make up this collection are linked by such elements as shared settings (the Soviet Union), plots, the narrator and some of the characters, and themes. Many authors, both American and Russian (such as Sherwood Anderson, Ernest Hemingway, Isaac Babel), used tightly integrated stories that served Dovlatov as distant models, although Dovlatov uses the linking devices of setting, the protagonist-narrator, and theme to integrate the individual pieces into a whole that is greater than the sum of its parts. In this way he made the short-story cycle his own distinctive genre. Dovlatov intended these *Suitcase* stories to be read sequentially and in their entirety. His other collections, such as *The Compromise* and *Ours,* can be approached randomly and piecemeal, read out of sequence, even excerpted for anthologies. In *The Sanctuary* and in *The Suitcase* he achieved a coherence of the whole text.

Dovlatov planned a sequel to *The Suitcase,* and in April 1990 he wrote to Ar'ev about it. It was to be a book about food, "in the manner of *The Suitcase*" (*SS* 3:457). It had several working titles, such as *The Menu,* or *Notes of a Hungry Man,* but he most frequently referred to it as *The Fridge.* Dovlatov only managed to complete two stories before his death: "Vinograd" ("Grapes") and "Staryi petukh, zapechennyi v gline" ("An Old Cockerel Baked in Clay").[65] The first version of "An Old Cockerel Baked in Clay" was entitled "Gus': Rozhdestvenskaia istoriia" ("Goose: A Christmas Story") and was published earlier in *Novyi Amerikanets.* A Christmas story has its own traditions: the events have to take place on New Year's Eve, and it has to be sentimental. In his introduction to this story, the author assures the reader that it is truthful. "Goose: A Christmas Story" is dated 1964, and the action takes place at Piskarevka camp. The basic outline of "An Old Cockerel Baked in Clay" remains the same as "Goose: A Christmas Story," with the cockerel taking over the role played by the goose in the earlier version.

The opening story, "Grapes," is set, rather like the opening story of *The Suitcase,* in the protagonist's student days at Leningrad State University. Fifteen first-year students are sent to help out at a fruit and vegetable storehouse. This was a common event in the life of all students in the Soviet Union. As in "The Finnish Nylon Socks," the protagonist, who is a student of philology, learns about the workings of the shadow economy and the need to steal in order to make a living. He also has his first sexual experience. All within one day of working at the vegetable storehouse: "In a word, in a single day I completed a miraculous journey: from theft—to literature. Not to mention fornication . . ." ("Koroche, za den' ia prodelal chudodeistvennyi marshrut: ot vorovstva—k literature. Ne schitaia preliubodeianiia . . ."; *SS* 3:419).

The foreman Mishchuk (who, it transpires, is also a philology graduate of Leningrad State University) uses the students to cover up (for a large sum of money) the embezzlement by a Caucasian, named Bala, of sixteen tons of grapes. Dovlatov portrays in vivid terms the bargaining process between the foreman and the Caucasian, but Bala has in fact no choice. He will have to give Mishchuk whatever bribe he asks for, since if he is found out, he will be sent to prison. This is how the foreman explains the task to the students, who also stand to gain:

> "The patriarch's short of sixteen tons. We'll have to sketch them in, lads. The chap's playing hard to get at the moment, but in fact he's on the hook. Sixteen tons means the jug . . ."
>
> My fellow student Zaichenko asked, "What do you mean, sketch them in?"
>
> The foreman replied, "Sketching in—that's a trick."
>
> "And what does jug mean?" Lebedev inquired.
>
> "Jug," said the foreman, "means prison." And he added, "What on earth do they teach them at university?"
>
> — Etomu aksakalu ne khvataet shestnadtsat' tonn. Pridetsia ikh narisovat', rebiatki. Muzhik poka chto zhmetsia, khotia fakticheski on na kriuchke. Shestnadtsat' tonn—eto vily . . .
>
> Moi odnokursnik Zaichenko sprosil:
>
> — Chto znachit—narisovat'?
>
> Brigadir otvetil:
>
> — Narisovat'—eto sdelat' fokus.
>
> — A chto znachit—vily?—pointeresovalsia Lebedev.
>
> — Vily,—skazal brigadir,—eto tiur'ma.
>
> I dobavil:
>
> — Chemu tol'ko ikh v universitete obuchaiut?! (*SS* 3:413)

In the course of the story, the narrator is told that Mishchuk has a degree with distinction from Leningrad State University, and he cannot conceal his surprise at finding the foreman in such a lowly position, but Mishchuk is quite sanguine about it:

> "Where should I be? Where do you think I ought to be working? In a school? What could I steal there, blotting paper? When you're looking for a job the first thing you have to think about is: what, where, and how? What shall I be able to steal? Where will I be able to steal it? And how shall I be able steal it?" (*SS* 3:415)

Like Fred Kolesnikov in "The Finnish Nylon Socks," Mishchuk weighs up the risks, understanding that he can and probably will go to prison, but there is no moral dilemma about stealing, because he is stealing from the State. In fact, everybody involved, including the students, benefits financially from the proceeds of this swindle. The topic of bribery and corruption, as mentioned earlier, is a topic to which a good deal of space is also devoted in Dovlatov's unpublished work *Fiveways*.

Apart from "The Finnish Nylon Socks," "Grapes" also has affinities with "The Driving Gloves": in "Grapes" the protagonist loses his innocence with "an extravagant married woman called Regina Britterman," the same who inherits the frock coat that Dovlatov wore in the role of Peter the Great in "The Driving Gloves": "An extravagant woman called Regina Britterman wore the frock coat in place of an autumn overcoat" (*SS* 3:404). In "Grapes" there is also a dubious victory over the physicists: Regina Britterman's cuckolded husband has a Ph.D. in physics.

If "Grapes" is Dovlatov's farewell to his youth, then "An Old Cockerel Baked in Clay" is a kaleidoscope of the narrator's life. The protagonist of the story is a well-known Russian writer living in New York. Many of his books have been translated into English and other languages. He receives a phone call in the middle of the night from the American police, who have caught red-handed a thief trying to steal a ladies' fur coat. The thief is a Russian criminal whom the narrator guarded in the distant past when he was serving in the Soviet Army. The criminal is asking the narrator to post bail for him, and the narrator reluctantly agrees. As he sets off to the police station, the thought strikes him that this story is so incredible that nobody would believe it if he told it.

Eliseev argues that in "An Old Cockerel Baked in Clay" Dovlatov is using the classical story of King Lear to tell a contemporary phantasmagorical story about the unpredictability of fate. Eliseev takes the view that in this story Dovlatov formulated a crucial point in terms of plot and meaning, hinging on the word *lishnee.*[66] He points to Dovlatov's sentence "*It's just the superfluous I need, you bastards*" ("*Da lishnego-to mne kak raz i nado, suki vy pozornye*") as a "a reduced quotation from *King Lear*": "Reduce the whole life to necessity—and there's nothing to tell a man from an animal" ("Svedi k neobkhodimosti vsiu zhizn'—i chelovek sravniaetsia s zhivotnym"). Eliseev considers this to be the moral of this story and furthermore "possibly of the whole of Dovlatov's work. The superfluous is freedom. The overcoming of the necessary—that is what is meant by freedom."[67]

There is a passage in Dovlatov's essay "Literatura prodolzhaetsia" ("Literature Goes On") which is subheaded "Kul'tura nachinaetsia s izlishestv" ("Culture Begins from Excess") and which corroborates this argument:

> Necessary superfluity—there's a precise metaphysical formulation.
>
> Remember King Lear. His daughters wanted him to be satisfied with what was necessary. But he obstinately sought the superfluous. And therein lay his terrible tragedy. The tragedy of a former dictator who had been robbed of everything superfluous. The tragedy of a man standing on the very edge of civilization.[68]

However, as the narrator exclaims in the story: "Who knows what is the main thing in life, and what is superfluous" (*SS* 3:426). The story is about the narrator's attempts to escape from his past, from the chaos and absurdity that haunt him: "I realized that I had to protect myself from the chaos that was assailing me. It had pursued me in the Soviet Union, and I had left. Now it had caught up with me in America. Chaos and absurdity" (*SS* 3:426–27). What remains is art, in which the author strives to re-create the past as a way of deceiving oblivion and death. The aim of art can be seen in outliving death and oblivion. The narrator's quasi-autobiographic personality, which is deliberately falsified in other stories, appears less obscured here. The narrator and the writer become the same.

In one of his radio scripts, Dovlatov declared that it was easier to tell about the phantasmagorical Soviet life of the past and about the strangeness and volatility of the émigré's "second" existence in precisely such a kaleidoscopic form.[69] "An Old Cockerel Baked in Clay" is an attempt to defend himself from chaos and bring back a feeling of normality to this mad world.

Chapter Seven

Ours

NASHI (*OURS: A RUSSIAN FAMILY ALBUM*) is an autobiographical collection of character sketches providing an engaging glimpse of four generations of a Soviet family.[1] It consists of twelve chapters written in the early 1980s as separate stories and published separately in various journals. The thirteenth chapter was specially added for the book edition and is about Dovlatov's son, Nicholas, born in the United States as an American citizen. All the stories were translated into English, and of the ten stories Dovlatov published in the *New Yorker* between 1980 and 1989, five were from *A Russian Family Album:* "My First Cousin," "The Colonel Says I Love You," "Uncle Aron," "Uncle Leopold," and "Father."[2] Donat Mechik recalls that in one of his letters Dovlatov wrote about the significance of being published by the *New Yorker:* "I read in a book the following sentence about Nabokov: 'In 1941 he was published by *The New Yorker,* which was equivalent to worldwide recognition.' So you see!"[3] In another letter to his father written while publication in the *New Yorker* was still pending in the early months of 1980, Dovlatov said how fortunate he felt it to be, and expressed the hope that this publication would radically change his situation.[4]

Not long after his arrival in the United States in November 1979, Dovlatov wrote that he was about to finish *Ours,* which was to consist of fourteen stories about close relatives: "An indirect self-portrait, through relatives and friends."[5] He sometimes refers to this work as *Svoi* (*Ours*), and the excerpts published in *Novyi Amerikanets* are subtitled "Iz povesti *Svoi.*" However, he kept on rewriting it, and only in November 1982 did he bring it to completion:

> It is the history of the family plus politics, the war, the state, and some kind of philosophy of life. In general, through the family larger things are shown. I've been writing all this for a long time, and at first I didn't like it at all, then I suddenly wrote three more successful chapters: about my father, my cousin, and Lena. And the whole thing got evened out.[6]

The author is looking back in order to understand his present, his own self. In her article "The Family Chronicle Revisited," Karen Ryan-Hayes approaches *Ours* through an analysis of the family chronicle as a genre, beginning in the nineteenth century with such works as Aksakov's *Family Chronicle,* Tolstoy's *Childhood,* and Saltykov-Shchedrin's *Golovlev Family* and *Old Days in Poshekhonie.* She writes that Dovlatov's use of the genre was quite a traditional way of using family chronicles: "The family chronicle served in the past as a means of delving into the writer's self, his or her individual nature. As an autobiography or pseudo-autobiography (gaining in popularity in the middle of the nineteenth century as well), tracing one's ancestry was a way to understand the forces that shaped one's personality and character."[7] Among the reasons for the popularity of the genre, Ryan-Hayes points to increased interest in historical themes and memoir literature in general, but she sees one of the main reasons for relevance to Dovlatov's text in the appearance of the literary "little man." Dovlatov's narrator and his extended family are, as Dovlatov emphasizes, "ordinary people." However, as Ryan-Hayes concludes, "In *Ours,* Dovlatov subverts and parodies these canonical aspects of the family chronicle genre even as he adopts them. He relies on the readers' knowledge of nineteenth-century models in reshaping their form and content to his own ends."[8]

Ryan-Hayes also notes that the boundaries of the genre of family chronicle are mobile and that it can fluctuate between sketches of a memoir nature and a full-fledged novel. "*Ours* occupies middle ground between history and pseudo-autobiography; its apparent authenticity encourages the reader to accept it as documentary, but its status as fiction leaves the issues unresolved and ambiguous."[9] This ambiguity suits Dovlatov's intention particularly well. In all the stories comprising *Ours,* Dovlatov emphasizes how much he has inherited of the particular relative's character traits, often concluding the chapter by saying that when his grandchildren leaf through the family album, it will not be hard "to mistake us for one another" (*SS* 2:283). He finds common traits not merely with the members of the family but even with his dog Glasha. For example, Glasha performed a number of heroic feats: "First of all, she saved a puppy from drowning by dragging it out of a pool of water. Also, she had been the first one to catch the scent of a bear on the prowl. Finally, she strangled a fox." ("Vo-pervykh, spasla shchenka, kotoryi tonul. Vytashchila ego iz luzhi. Krome togo, pervaia vziala sled medvedia-shatuna. I nakonets, zadushila lisitsu"; *SS* 2:356.) The author had similarly saved an Estonian from drowning: "Some twenty-five years ago I saved a drowning man. Heroism is so uncharacteristic of me that I even remembered his name—Seppen." ("Let dvadtsat' piat' nazad ia spas utopaiushchego. Prichem geroizm mne tak neisvoistvenen, chto ia dazhe zapomnil ego familiu—Seppen"; *SS* 4:217.) The author and his dog share some allergic reactions: "The tinned 'Tourist's breakfast' caused her an allergic reaction. As it did me too . . ." ("Konservy 'Zavtrak turista' vyzyvali u nee allergiiu. Kak i u menia . . ."; *SS* 2:404). In many other ways, too, the author and his dog are similar: "No longer youthful, irritable foreigners with complexes . . . We collaborate in stealing sausages from the fridge." ("Nemolodye razdrazhitel'nye chuzhestrantsy s kompleksami . . . Soobshcha taskaem kolbasu iz kholodil'nika . . ."; *SS* 2:361.) Glasha did not become an American, and she often dreamed of her homeland: "Glasha often sleeps at my feet. Sometimes she moans quietly. Perhaps she's dreaming of home. Sprats in tomato sauce, for instance. Or the little square in Shcherbakov Lane . . ." ("Glasha chasto spit u moikh nog. Inogda ona tikhon'ko stonet. Vozmozhno, ei snitsia rodina. Naprimer, melkii chastik v tomate. Ili skver v Shcherbakovom pereulke . . ."; *SS* 2:361).

As in other works of Dovlatov's, the narrative technique of *Ours* is relatively straightforward and simple. Except in the earlier chapters, the narrator is a participant in the events he relates. Ryan-Hayes writes:

> Even when he was not a direct participant, Dovlatov's use of the conventions of the family chronicle allow him to report events as if he participated in them or witnessed them because they constitute family lore. This should not obscure the tension, which is nonetheless present, between the realm of the author and the literary realm of his text.[10]

The work as a whole ranges from prerevolutionary times to the present day. It is a portrait of an entire society and culture and a vehicle through which the author comments on some of the central historical events of his time. He depicts his parents and grandparents, his aunts, his aunt's husband Aron, his uncles, his cousin Boris, himself and his wife, their daughter Katia, and their family dog Glasha. Each chapter tells the reader the family gossip and the sayings or legends surrounding a particular relative. First we meet grandfather Isaak, who is described in folk epic style: he was notable for his height (he was about seven feet tall), his strength (during the war with Japan the tsar personally chose him to serve in the artillery; when the horses got tired, the grandfather dragged the gun across the swamp), his voracious appetite, and for the fact that he had three sons.[11] This good-humored story suddenly veers into horror when in the late 1930s the grandfather is shot, sentenced as a foreign spy, simply because his émigré son's friend had come from Belgium to visit him. As it happens, the Belgian is a great admirer of Stalin.

The fairytale-folkloric intonation of the opening chapters of *Ours* is reminiscent of Babel's *Odesskie rasskazy* (*Stories from Odessa*). The warmth and closeness of family relationships in the patriarchal world described by

Babel, where the robbers from the Moldavanka belonged to the same family as the victims, are also felt in Dovlatov's description of his grandparents.

Ours is symbolically "framed" by an American connection between the first story and the last. In the first an American firm is exporting folding beds to prerevolutionary Russia. The American salesman is trying to demonstrate the usefulness of this novelty. He offers customers an opportunity to try the bed out, and Grandfather Isaak breaks one bed after another by lying down on them:

> Soon the hall was littered with the wreckage of wonder beds. Tatters of colorful canvas drooped to the floor, twisted frames gleamed dimly.
>
> After some haggling, Grandpa bought a sandwich and went home.
>
> The reputation of the American firm was severely damaged. Merkher, Merkher and Co. began trading in crystal chandeliers. (*O*, 6; *SS* 2:282)

The closing story shows America from an entirely different perspective, introducing the American descendant that Isaak never lived to see, the author's son Kolia—Mr. Nicholas Dowley—and the author comments: "That is what my family and our country have come to" ("Eto to, k chemu prishla moia sem'ia i nasha rodina"; *SS* 2:380). Ksana Mechik-Blank describes the reaction of the real Grandpa Isaak's brother Anisim, who had managed to emigrate to the United States in the 1930s and lived in Florida, where he died at the age of 104 in 1991. Anisim was outraged that Dovlatov had described his brother in such "dark colors" and he "corrects" some "facts" in Dovlatov's story, asserting, for example, that his brother did not serve in the artillery, but was a foot soldier, and that the tsar did not visit the Far East during the Russo-Japanese War.[12]

Dovlatov's grandfather on his mother's side is "Ded Stepan" (Grandfather Stepan).[13] He has a difficult character, and his mysterious exclamation "ABANAMAT!" has all the family members paralyzed with fear. He was obeyed by the whole family and by the celestial forces to boot. One of grandfather's duels with God ended in a draw. Of course, God eventually won and grandfather Stepan died a terrible death: he walked into a ravine at the edge of Tiflis. The intonation of this story is still folkloristic, and it has the mark of a story "heard from so-and so." It is a family legend, retold by the author.

The next four stories are about three uncles and an aunt: "Uncle Roman" (related on his mother's side), "Uncle Leopold" (one of Grandpa Isaak's three sons), "Uncle Aron" (Aunt Mara's husband), and "Aunt Mara" herself (Dovlatov's mother's sister). Dovlatov's parents' generation, at least the members who made a career under Stalin, are later beset by doubts. Aunt Mara acknowledges the bitter truth that many of her literary friends were informers. This acknowledgment only comes on her deathbed, and even then she has difficulty in facing it.

In *The Zone* Dovlatov had explained that serving as a camp guard helped him to understand certain banal truths:

> I understood that greatness of spirit does not necessarily accompany physical power. It is usually just the opposite. Spiritual strength is most often contained in a frail, awkward covering, while physical prowess often comes with inner impotence.
>
> The ancients used to say, "Sound of body, sound of mind."
>
> In my opinion, this isn't so. It seems to me that it is precisely the physically healthy who are most often spiritually blind, most often in the healthy body that moral apathy reigns. (*Z*, 39; *SS* 2:40)

The story about his uncle Roman in *Ours* serves as an illustration of this point. Roman is a person who was unable to find his place in society. Without being a complete drunkard, he was inclined to drink too much and get into brawls. His attempt to enter the university to study philosophy comes to nothing since he fails the compulsory exam in Russian literature, having never read even the standard classics. He comes into his own at the outbreak of war. "Even in peacetime he loved to raise hell. He returned a lieutenant colonel. War had made a man of him" (*O*, 17; *SS* 3:289). As a lieutenant colonel Roman was a trusted man, and was able to find a job as head of the personnel department in a large factory. His real test comes, however, when his wife is nearly murdered and is in desperate need of his help: he is the last to arrive on the scene and spends the evening in tears. At the same time he considers himself entitled to despise people like his nephew, because he does not perform morning exercises or wash in cold water.

This disparity between body and soul is a matter which Dovlatov also addresses in one of his reviews in *Grani*, where he explains more fully what it means for his own generation:

> For this generation Hemingway was a little simple and even infantile; his basic tenets struck a chord with the ancient Greek "a healthy mind in a healthy body," whereas Russian society had more and more occasion to conclude that in the healthiest of bodies a slavish rabbit-heart could be nestled, while a weak and frail physical frame often turned out to be the vessel of true spirituality.[14]

Chapter 4 of *Ours* is the story of "Uncle Leopold." Uncle Leopold had escaped from the Soviet Union in 1925 and gone to live in Belgium. It is his friend who comes from Belgium to visit Grandfather Isaak and causes his arrest and death. Although he was born in Russia, Uncle Leopold has no real experience of the Soviet Union. This is the issue at the forefront of Dovlatov's attention in this chapter: the inability of people who have not lived in the Soviet Union to understand the system that operates there. He gives examples of Uncle Leopold's naive understanding of Russia. The narrator meets him in Vienna after his own emigration, and is shocked by his comments on Russia.

> "What a savage country! I've been in America, Israel, I've traveled all round Europe . . . But I shan't go to Russia. There's nothing there but chess, ballet, and the 'black Maria' . . . Do you like chess?"
> "Not much."
> "And ballet?"
> "I don't know much about it."
> "It's just some kind of nonsense with ghosts," my uncle said.

> — Kakaia dikaia strana! Ia byl v Amerike, Izraile, ob'ezdil vsiu Evropu . . . A v Rossiiu ne poedu. Tam shakhmaty, balet i 'chernyi voron' . . . Ty liubish' shakhmaty?
> — Ne ochen'.
> — A balet?
> — Ia v nem malo razbiraius'.
> — Eto kakaia-to chepukha s privideniiami,—skazal moi diadia. (*SS* 2:301)

His conception of the difference between Russia and the West shows that he has no real knowledge of Russia:

> "Look at all those cars! Have you ever seen foreign cars before? . . . There are far more cars in America. And what shops they have there! Are there department stores in Leningrad?"

> — Posmotri, skol'ko mashin! Ty kogda-nibud' videl zagranichnye mashiny? [. . .] V Amerike mashin gorazdo bol'she. A kakie tam magaziny! V Leningrade est' bol'shie magaziny? (*SS* 2:301)

If someone who was born in the country has such difficulty fathoming it, what can one expect from American citizens born and bred? In the author's experience, the average American confuses Brezhnev and Baryshnikov and is petrified of the "Reds."[15] (In a number of his letters to the Soviet Union, Dovlatov also shows his awareness of Soviet people's failure to understand life abroad, but this topic is not discussed in *Ours*.)

Dovlatov sees Uncle Aron's biography as a particular reflection of the recent history of Russia. In his youth Uncle Aron was a soldier in the Red Army; then he changed sides and fought against the Red Army; then later he joined the Reds once more out of political conviction. He loved all the leaders, particularly Stalin. When they fell, he simply transferred his allegiance to the next leader, but when Brezhnev came to power he wearied of loving different leaders and, typically for the 1970s, concentrated his love upon Lenin. As a party member, he would constantly press his point of view in argument with the narrator. However, when Uncle Aron fell ill and believed he was about to die, his doubts got the upper hand, and he asked the narrator, his nephew, to smother him. He was only able to express his doubts in clichés: "I don't believe communism can be built in one country. I've slid into the swamp of Trotskyism" (*O*, 50). ("Ia ne veriu, chto kommunizm mozhet byt' postroen v odnoi strane. Ia skatilsia v boloto trotskizma"; *SS* 2:315.) However, when he recovered he reverted to his old beliefs and resumed his arguments with his nonconformist nephew. In real life Dovlatov writes that his uncle was a highly educated and kind-hearted person: "My uncle only ever struck me once (there is nothing about this in *Ours*) for some anti-Soviet comment . . . in about 1963."[16]

Dovlatov's Aunt Mara is included in the family album, although her sister Anelia is not, because she is so decent and nice that it is "boring to write about her." Aunt Mara was an editor and worked for many years in literary associations, educating young writers. She edited the works of many Soviet writers, although in one of his letters Dovlatov expresses astonishment at her inability to understand metaphor: "She asks what 'lively blue-eyed targets' are, how it is possible to be 'afraid of a close stare,' what is meant by 'the excitement of the angler,' and so on . . . How did she have the effrontery to conduct a literary association for the young?" ("Ona sprashivaet, chto takoe 'zhivye sineglazye misheni', kak mozhno 'boiat'sia pristal'nogo vzgliada', chto takoe 'volnen'e rybaka' i t.d. [. . .] Kak ona otvazhilas' vesti molodezhnoe litob"edinenie?")[17] This is reflected in *Ours*. The young author, just beginning his literary career, asks his experienced aunt for advice on his work. The author's amusement at his aunt's limitations is summed up in the following dialogue:

> She said things like, "In this passage you write, 'the kinship of silence and frost.' It's inaccurate. Frost and silence are two different kinds of phenomena. You should write, 'in the forest it was cold and quiet.' Without making it fancy . . ."
>
> "Why do you say 'in the forest'?" I asked in surprise. "The action takes place in a penal isolation cell." (*O*, 42)

> — Zdes' napisano: '. . . rodstvo tishiny i moroza . . . Eto netochno. Moroz i tishina—iavleniia razlichnogo poriadka. Sleduet pisat': 'V lesu bylo morozno i tikho.' Bez vykrutasov . . .—Kak eto—v lesu?—udivlialsia ia.—Deistvie proiskhodit v shtrafnom izoliatore. (*SS* 2:309)

Dovlatov's preoccupation with such questions is seen also in the many anecdotes about Aunt Mara in his *Zapisnye knizhki* (*Notebooks*).

The younger generation of Dovlatov's relatives, those who grew up during the thaw, are concerned to rid themselves of their parents' fear, and they adopt a more cynical attitude toward the regime (as is illustrated by the story of his cousin). His parents are still not fully able to free themselves, although Dovlatov's real mother (according to correspondence) had a deep hatred of Stalin and the Soviet regime: "On the other hand, life never offered her the enticements and temptations of the *nomenklatura*."[18] His father, however, retained his belief: "All his life he was (and in some sense still remains)[19] a right-thinking Soviet man, despite the execution of his father."[20]

In *Ours* chapter 7 is entitled "Mother" and chapter 8 "Father." His parents grew up in the shadow of the Great Terror. They were very different:

> Like all frivolous men, Father was a kind-hearted person. Mother was outspoken and sharp-tongued. Her exceptional honesty allowed for no compromises. Her slightest gesture took on the quality of self-sacrifice. In the merciless light of her moral purity, my father's shortcomings stood out catastrophically. (*O*, 70; *SS* 2:330)

His father viewed life as a great theatrical spectacle, but the author exonerates him, as it were, just by enumerating what he lived through: "So my father lived through the cult of personality, through war, evacuation. Then divorce, hackwork, women . . ." (*O*, 70). ("Itak, kul't lichnosti, voina, evakuatsiia. Zatem—razvod, khaltura, zhenshchiny . . ."; *SS* 2:330.)

In describing each member of this extensive family, Dovlatov throws light not so much on his own biography as upon the character traits that he inherited: his voracious appetite from Grandfather Isaak, his misanthropy from Grandfather Stepan, Uncle Roman's love of blonde women and wine, and Aunt Mara's dedication to literature (despite her limitations). From his father he acquired democratism and a tolerance even toward enemies and informers.

A characteristic feature of many of Dovlatov's stories has been described by Lipovetsky and Leiderman: "Repetitions, not only in plot, but also in structure, are characteristic of Dovlatov's style. Many of his stories are built as a series of episodes of a single structural type."[21] A striking example of this in *Ours* is the story "My First Cousin" (which has many similarities with the story "Superfluous" from *The Compromise*). It tells a repeated tale of his cousin Boris's immense success, which is followed on each occasion by some senseless offense which destroys his prospects, compelling him to start again. This pattern is repeated several times. Similarly to "Kuptsov and Others" (in *The Zone*), there are two as it were superimposed stories: the narrator, who at first glance leads a very ordinary life, is measured against the more extraordinary, almost fairy-tale deeds of his cousin. It is the interplay between their lives that creates the underlying structure of the story. As mentioned earlier, Dovlatov was a great admirer of jazz, and became very knowledgeable about it. It is apparent that in this story he set out to create the pattern of ragtime. In 1982 he published a number of articles about jazz, in one of which he explains the originality of ragtime:

> The pianist who plays in this style creates with his right hand rhythmic variations of a single theme, syncopating it more and more and adding melodic figures to it. Meanwhile the left hand pursues a precise rhythmic formula in two-four time, keeping to a single, constantly repeated harmonic scheme.[22]

The stories of the two cousins are told in parallel and set off against each other. This is a technique which can be regarded as such a "rhythmic variation," and which Dovlatov employed in several stories ("Fernand Léger's Jacket" from *The Suitcase* is one example). Boris was born in mysterious circumstances. He is the son of Aunt Mara, who had an affair with a high-ranking Communist Party official, Kirov's deputy, and Boris was his illegitimate son. Soon after Boris's birth this official was arrested as an "enemy of the people," so it was fortunate that he and Aunt Mara were not formally married. The narrator was born to a perfectly ordinary couple. Boris grew up into an exemplary, handsome Soviet youth. His achievements are enumerated in contrast with the narrator's modest feats: "Borya put together a detector receiver (to this day I have no idea what this is)" (*O*, 77) ("Boria sobral detektornyi priemnik. [Ia do sikh por ne znaiu, chto eto takoe . . ."]; *SS* 2:336). Then Boris destroys his own prospects, and when asked why he did such a senseless thing, " 'I did what every student secretly dreams of doing,' he replied. 'When I saw the Stoolie that day, I realized it was now or never! I'll do it—or I'll stop respecting myself' " (*O*, 78). ("Ia sdelal to, o chem mechtaet vtaine kazhdyi shkol'nik. Uvidev Legavogo, ia ponial—seichas ili nikogda! Ia sdelaiu eto! . . . Ili perestanu sebia uvazhat' . . ."; *SS* 2:337.) This echoes almost word for word the episode in *The Compromise* when Bush spectacularly and senselessly ruins his chances of getting the full-time position in the newspaper that he so much wanted. In answer to the narrator's inquiry as to why he did this, he similarly replies: "And then I realized—the decisive moment had come. This will decide who I am. Whether I'm a knight in shining armour, as Galia thinks, or a turd, as everyone else asserts. And then I stood up and set off . . ." ("I tut ia ponial—nastupila otvetstvennaia minuta. Seichas reshitsia—kto ia. Rytsar', kak schitaet Galka, ili der'mo, kak utverzhdaiut vse ostal'nye? Togda ia vstal i poshel . . ."; *SS* 1:358).

In their student years Boris and the narrator have diametrically opposing views on women; the narrator outlines his own views, but then stops himself: "However, this story is not about me" (*O*, 79) ("Vprochem, rech' idet ne obo mne . . ."; *SS* 2:338). The cousin graduates from the university, while the narrator drops out and ends up in the army. His cousin once again builds up an enviable career, but then again destroys it by committing a criminal act. Here they metaphorically cross paths: "So I was a guard. And Borya was a prisoner" (*O*, 83). ("Tak chto ia byl okhrannikom. A Boria—zakliuchennym"; *SS* 2:340.) They return home to Leningrad simultaneously, and each of them has to build his life again. Boris does it more successfully. He works at the Leningrad film studio; he is energetic and merry: "It was impossible to believe that he had been in prison. People who knew us only slightly thought I was the one who had done time" (*O*, 85). ("Nevozmozhno bylo poverit', chto on sidel v tiur'me. Mnogie iz chisla ne ochen' blizkikh znakomykh dumali, chto v tiur'me sidel ia . . ."; *SS* 2:342.) As was noted in the case of the story of Kuptsov, the two become interchangeable. "What follows will sound familiar" (*O*, 97) ("Dal'she ia vynuzhden povtoriat'sia"; *SS* 2:352), writes Dovlatov. Boris is imprisoned again, and when he is released he once more restores his reputation and builds a new career, whereas the narrator's life is in tatters: "Just about the same time, I was laid off from work, this time for good. I wrote short stories and lived off my mother's pension" (*O*, 97). ("Primerno v eti zhe dni menia okonchatel'no uvolili s raboty. Ia sochinial rasskazy i zhil na maminu pensiiu . . ."; *SS* 2:352.) Their interchangeability is expressed in a seemingly irrational remark: "How strange! Both of us with Armenian mothers, and I'm half Russian, you're half Jewish. But we both like vodka with beer" (*O*, 97; *SS* 2:353). Dovlatov's real cousin Boris was offended when he read the story, which caused Dovlatov some puzzlement:

> My book *Ours*, which so offended Boria—I don't know why, will be coming out in English soon. It's not my job to judge the quality of the prose, but what I write about all my relatives is written with love. That has been noted many times in all the reviews. And the story about my cousin has been printed separately in the best journals in several languages. I'm very sorry if I've hurt someone's feelings.[23]

In letters, however, Dovlatov openly admits that his cousin is not quite such an exemplary character. He writes to Anne Frydman, his translator:

> I am sending you a story about my cousin. I swear to you that every last word of it is true. If he ever comes to America, you will like him. Although he is one of the most awful people in the world. That was just the task I set myself in the story—to write about an absolutely awful person, whom everybody likes. Simply—to depict a human character.[24]

And nevertheless, the narrator is full of admiration for his cousin himself, and the gifts he receives from him are among his most treasured possessions.

On January 21, 1983, Efimov wrote to Dovlatov that he had particularly enjoyed the story about Borya and was wondering where the strength of the story lay:

> You have managed to do something there so that suddenly, out of a cluster of anecdotes I already knew, something complete and dramatic has arisen. I liked the one about Lena, too, though I'm a bit afraid on your account: to write about your nearest and dearest while still living with them is a dangerous business, harmful for relationships.[25]

Efimov, who was acquainted with Dovlatov's wife, appears to have read the story "The Colonel Says I Love You" as autobiographical. No doubt there are some characteristic traits of the real person in the story, but Dovlatov uses it as a vehicle to create an indirect self-portrait, to create the feeling of a real document, without it actually being a real document. As mentioned earlier, the real meeting between Dovlatov and his wife took place in quite different circumstances. In his interview with John Glad, Dovlatov admits that the history of his meeting with his wife is depicted in different works in various ways: "Masses of attempts were made to explain to me how it all happened in fact."[26] For Dovlatov the truthful flight of fantasy became the basic credo of his aesthetics, as Ar'ev sums up: "A truthful invention is more convincing in art than the truth of any fact."[27]

In *Ours* Dovlatov writes that he came to the United States with one dream: to divorce his wife. The only reason he gives for this is "my wife's extreme imperturbability. Her serenity had no limits" (*O,* 111) ("krainiaia stepen' nevozmutimosti moei zheny. Ee spokoistvie ne imelo granits"; *SS* 2:362). He recalls why they came together: "It was not love, and it was certainly not a 'momentary weakness.' It was an attempt to ward off chaos" (*O,* 118). ("Eto byla ne liubov'. I tem bolee—ne minutnaia slabost'. Eto byla popytka zashchitit'sia ot khaosa"; *SS* 2:368.) For Dovlatov this was the usual dichotomy:

> In this way, my life came under the rule of two opposing elements. An ocean of nonconformism rose to the left. To the right stretched the untroubled calm of bourgeois well-being. And I stumbled along in between. (*O*, 119)

> V zhizni moei, takim obrazom, tsarili dve protivobortsvuiushchie stikhii. Sleva busheval okean zarozhdaiushchegosia nonkoformizma. Sprava rasstilalas' nevozmutimaia glad' meshchanskogo blagopoluchia.
>
> Tak ia i brel, spotykaias', uzkoi poloskoi zemli mezhdu etimi dvumia okeanami. (*SS* 2:369)

"The mixture of the everyday and the absurd" (*O*, 114) ("Smes' obydennosti i bezumiia"; *SS* 2:364) is a formulation that Dovlatov repeats in many of his stories.

Both "A Poplin Shirt" and chapter 11 of *Ours* end with his fictional wife and daughter leaving for the United States. In *Ours* the author-narrator joins his family in New York. His wife's indifference is emphasized by having the narrator arrive in an empty apartment, welcomed only by a note: "We are at the health club. We will be home around eight. There is food in the refrigerator. Lena." As if there had been no months of separation and he had just gone out for a walk. The story about his wife in *Ours* is framed by a similar event at the beginning and the end. At the beginning it is early morning when the narrator wakes up with a hangover and realizes that there is a living creature next to him in the room:

> I asked, "Who are you?"
> "Let's say Lena," a calm female voice answered unexpectedly.

> Ia sprosil:
> Vy kto?
> Dopustim, Lena,—otvetil neozhidanno spokoinyi zhenskii golos. (*SS* 2:362)

At the end of the story when the narrator arrives in his wife's New York apartment, he falls asleep before she arrives home from the health club. Next morning, as before, he realizes there is somebody next to him:

> I asked, "Who's [that]?"
> "Lena," answered a calm, female voice. (*O*, 125)

> Ia sprosil:
> Kto eto?
> Lena,—otvetil spokoinyi zhenskii golos. (*SS* 2:374)

In between these statements the realization comes: "In our case, it's no longer a matter of love, but of fate" (*O*, 126) ("Tut uzhe ne liubov', a sud'ba . . ."; *SS* 2:375).

It has been mentioned that in "A Poplin Shirt" the narrator is all of a sudden overcome by love for his wife: "I never knew that love could be so strong and so sharp" (*S*, 92; *SS* 2:372). In *Ours* (in chapter 11 about his wife) Dovlatov remarks that "love is for teenagers" and that the relationship between a woman and a man is more complex. Dovlatov—and he was not alone in this—found it difficult to describe love scenes. "In our prose the clumsiest passages, the most shameful failures, are connected with love scenes," writes Aleksandr Kushner.[28] Ar'ev recalls in his interview with Ivan Tolstoy that one of the most frequently discussed topics between himself and Dovlatov was how to write about love.[29] Discussing the translation of the chapter in *Ours* titled "Polkovnik govorit—liubliu" ("The Colonel Says I Love You"), Dovlatov wrote to his translator:

> "This is the only love story in the world completely lacking in eroticism. I think this is quite a serious story. It isn't a story about love, it's a story about fate. It says that if a young woman is given to you by fate, then anybody can say the word "love," even a colonel in the KGB, it doesn't matter, and in general, fate cancels all other qualities and motives.[30]

This is a development of a theme from one of Dovlatov's early stories, "Interv'iu" ("The Interview"), one of the stories published in the Soviet Union in *Iunost'*. There a worker, who is being interviewed by the narrator, a journalist on the factory newspaper, quotes the words of a writer:

> A certain writer said that people don't get married because they're made for one another, and not even because they're attracted to each other, but they just happen to find themselves together. It's as though an invisible hand had thrown a handful of chips on to the baize, and two of them fell side by side. . . .
>
> Odin pisatel' govoril, chto liudi zheniatsia ne potomu, chto sozdany drug dlia druga, i dazhe ne potomu, chto ispytyvaiut vzaimnoe raspolozhenie, a prosto sluchaino okazyvaiutsia vmeste. Kak budto nevidimaia ruka vybrosila na sukno gorst' fishek, I dve iz nikh upali riadom. . . .[31]

The journalist in the story refutes this idea: "Rubbish, it's pigeons that live like that. The human being can choose. That's why it's so terrible to get it wrong . . ." ("Bros'te, eto u golubei takaia zhizn'. A chelovek, on mozhet vybirat'. Poetomu i oshibit'sia strashno . . .").[32]

Love and marriage often assume an accidental nature in Dovlatov's work, for example in his story "Tretii povorot nalevo" ("Third Turn on the Left") and in the newspaper article "Brak po-emigrantski" ("Marriage Émigré Style"). In *The Zone* Dovlatov writes: "A thousand times I heard: 'The main thing in marriage is to share spiritual interests.' A thousand times I answered: 'The way to virtue lies through deformity' " (*Z*, 39; *SS* 2:40). In *The Sanctuary* the protagonist asks his wife whether they are ever going to see each other: "Yes, if you love us . . ." (*SS* 2:276), replies his wife, but the protagonist does not understand: "What's love got to do with it?" (*SS* 2:276). In *Ours* it is the KGB officer who makes the assertion: " 'After all, you love them, don't you?' 'Who is "them"?' 'Your wife and daughter. Well, of course you love them.' It was in this way that my love for my wife and daughter became a fact. And the person to stand witness to it turned out to be a KGB colonel" (*O*, 123). ("Vy zhe ikh liubite?—Kogo—ikh?—Zhenu i dochku . . . Nu, konechno, liubite . . . Tak moia liubov' k zhene i dochke stala faktom. I zasvidetel'stvoval ego—polkovnik MVD . . ."; *SS* 2:372.)[33] Dovlatov considered marriage something mysterious and fantastic ("Brak—iavlenie tainstvennoe i fantasticheskoe").[34] Why do people start living together? The protagonist's difficult relationship with his wife is, as mentioned, a topic that frequently arises in Dovlatov's works. In his article "Marriage Émigré Style" he gives many examples of how people come together, but gradually comes to the conclusion that the standard explanation—that marriage in emigration is a voluntary and independent union of loving people—is simply banal. In one of his last interviews, though, Dovlatov expressed the realization that marriage and family are after all the most important things in life:

> It turned out that I had a family, that marriage wasn't simply a fact, it was a process. It turned out that children are not a capital investment, not an object for your sententious speeches, and not underrated creatures whom you are for some reason obliged to bring up, whatever you may be like yourself, but that they are god's creations, on whom you are dependent, who criticize you and with whom you must maintain normal human relations at any price. That turned out to be the most important thing. (*SS* 4:394)

In one of his letters, Dovlatov comments on Joyce's *A Portrait of the Artist as a Young Man*: "*A Portrait of the Artist as a Young Man* is a work of genius about how a beginning writer consistently repudiates his family, his country, and his religion for the sake of his writing."[35] In the course of his career Dovlatov too had to make many sacrifices, and it took him some time to realize how important his family was to him.

In each chapter of *Ours* Dovlatov summarizes succinctly the main features of the central character and through this characterization develops a panoramic view of Russia:

> Every chapter of the book is a human fate in its most compressed exposition. Where another author would have overwhelmed us with details, Dovlatov selects just that which expresses the character of that hero. And this character is important not in itself, but inasmuch as it defines a person's fate.[36]

The structure of *Ours* is chronological, covering four generations of the family. The last brief chapter is dedicated to the narrator's son Kolia. It is chapter 13 in the Russian edition, where it also has a subtitle, "Conclusion." The English version is slightly different from the original. In the English version his son is described as "our own round-the-clock, fully operational, dear little factory of positive emotions" (*O,* 133). In many letters to his friends Dovlatov writes that there are two achievements of which he is especially proud: the first is his son and the second is the fact that he managed to buy a house on his earnings from literature.[37] He expresses sadness, though, that "our seven-year-old son Kolia is a typical American, with a permanent smile on his face and not a problem in the world" ("Nash semiletnii syn Kolia—tipichnyi amerikanets, a imenno—postoiannaia ulybka na litse i nikakikh problem").[38] The concluding chapter of the English version ends with the sentence: "I hope it is clear to everyone that it has been his story" (*O,* 133).

The English translation of *Ours* was to be promoted, as Dovlatov wrote to Ar'ev, as "non-fiction" ("Budet prodavat'sia po riazriadu 'non-fiction' ").[39] However, it is not the real life of his family that Dovlatov depicts. Despite the similarity between real-life events and an abundance of biographical material, including photographs of various members of the family, this is a form of "pseudo-documentalism," and its generic character is not entirely simple to define. Addressing this issue, Ryan-Hayes cites the case of Leskov's *Old Times in the Village of Plodomasov,* in which he utilizes the family chronicle to give the illusion of factual, documentary accuracy.[40] Lidia Ginzburg describes the lengths Leskov went to in order to achieve this pseudo-documentalism, particularly in his stories about righteous men (*pravedniki*), when his narrative could have appeared implausible.[41] Dovlatov uses photographs for this purpose: however implausible the story, once it is supported by a real photograph of the person, it turns the story into a document. Ginzburg comments that Leskov was not depicting the typical, but the extraordinary. For this reason he referred his readers, who might have difficulty in understanding his characters or the surprising events he described, to an index of concrete, ostensibly historical facts:

> The recognition of the hero thus possesses its own typology. The hero appears as a traditional literary role or a quotation from another's text, sometimes a text hallowed through centuries, as a type or a character oriented toward social status, as a historically and biographically truthful "documentary" phenomenon and even as a pseudo-documentary fact.[42]

In "My First Cousin" the narrator is helping his cousin to choose a prison where the regime is more lenient and one can rely on some *blat* (Boris's success in life extends to choosing his own prison!). In the course of this quest the narrator introduces him to a certain Captain Deriabin, an alcoholic whom Dovlatov used to know while serving as a prison guard. Deriabin, having heard that Dovlatov has become a writer, decides to tell him a story that is completely out of place, but which he thinks may have some literary value for Dovlatov. The story is about a prisoner who attempted to escape by being catapulted out of the camp on a bent-down pine tree which was then released. The prisoner flew out of the prison zone all right, but miscalculated and landed by the military registration and enlistment office:

> They bent down a pine tree, see, and buckled the guy to the top branch with a rigging belt. Then let go. And then in mid-flight the zek unbuckles himself, and it's good-bye! He flies just short of the railway crossing. However, it turns out he was just a little off his reckoning. He was hoping to land in the snow by the sawmill. But it turns out he bangs down in the yard of the Regional Military Committee. And there's also this detail, pure literature: When they grabbed him, he bit the commanding officer in the nose. (*O*, 90)

> Nagnuli, ponimaesh' sosnu. Pristegnuli zeka k verkhushke montazhnym remnem—i otpustili. A zek v polete rasstegnulsia—i s kontsami. Uletel chut' ne za pereezd. Odnako malost' ne rasschital. Nadeialsia v sneg prizemlit'sia u lesobirzhi. A poluchilos', chto ugodil vo dvor raivoenkomata . . . I eshche takaia chisto literaturnaia detal'. Kogda ego brali, on voenkoma za nos ukusil . . . (*SS* 2:347)

This notion of the detail that is "pure literature"—the prisoner biting the commanding officer's nose—is similar to Leskov's illustration of "truth" in his story about a man saving a child from a mad dog. The unlikely or irrelevant fact is interpreted as a guarantee of the story's veracity. According to Ginzburg, Leskov went out of his way to prove that this child was he himself.[43]

What function did such quasi-autobiographical discourse have for Dovlatov? It is perhaps not fanciful to approach this question through what we know of his lifelong concern with existential problems. The typical existential situation (best exemplified, perhaps, by Camus) entails the moment when a man faces the mystery of his own being. Dovlatov hardly depicts such situations directly (though there are intimations of death in his work which inevitably raise similar questions), but the quest for the self, which underlies *Ours*, implies a similar kind of self-interrogation. What is taking place here is a search for the integrity of the personality, for the true irreducible self. It comes from a desire on the author's part to understand better the basis of his own experience and to make this personal experience compelling to others. There is nothing confessional in Dovlatov's writing; his writing is subjective but never narcissistic.

In December 1989 Dovlatov proudly informed Ar'ev that according to a *New York Times* report, "*Ours* has found its way into the best books of the year list."[44] *Ours* was Dovlatov's most successful English book, selling more copies than the translations of *The Zone* and *The Compromise* put together.[45] It was not the exoticism of a strange country that attracted American readers, but the recognition of their own human qualities, of their own weaknesses, passions, compromises, and failings. "A luminous gem by a gifted Russian émigré with the sense of humor of an American," writes Joseph Heller on the dust jacket of the English translation of *Ours*. "Dovlatov reminds us with wit that each life is unique, and all lives are familiar to us. The brief account of his courtship and marriage is a rarity to savor."

Chapter Eight

Tales of Émigré Life

THE SHORT NOVEL *Inostranka* (*A Foreign Woman*) was written in New York in 1985 and published there by Russica in 1986. It has a dedication: "To lonely Russian women in America with love, sadness and hope." The novel is about Russian émigré life in Forest Hills, New York, where Dovlatov depicts a community of former dissidents, bibliophiles, and lawyers who have to grapple with the problem of starting again from scratch. The narrative centers on Marusia Tatarovich, the spoiled daughter of party functionaries. Marusia emigrated not for political reasons, but because there was something exotic and fashionable about emigration. She has several marriages behind her: one with the son of a general, another with a famous singer called Razudalov, who is the father of her son Liova, and a third, which was a marriage of convenience contracted with a Jew, Tsekhnovitser, so that she could emigrate. In Austria they part: Tsekhnovitser flies to Israel (Marusia shows some concern for him: "How are you going to survive in Israel? It's full of Jews!" ["Kak ty budesh' zhit' v Izraile? Ved' tam odni evrei!"; *SS* 3:209]); Marusia departs for the United States.

In the Soviet Union Marusia never did any real work in her life, since she was provided for by her party functionary parents. In a vain attempt to gain some qualifications in the United States, she attends a jewelry workshop. After an equally unsuccessful attempt to return to the Soviet Union, she then takes up with a middle-aged Hispanic man, Rafael, and his parrot Lolo. The novel is a kaleidoscope of portraits of third-wave émigrés, whose lives and hopes are barely different from what they were in the Soviet Union. Like all Latin Americans, Rafael is a puzzle to the Russians: "enigmatic people with transistors. We don't know them. But just to be on the safe side we fear and despise them" (*SS* 3:182).

Dovlatov first published a version of this novel in the Russian-language American weekly *Almanac Panorama.*[1] He wrote to Vladimov:

> I forgot my honor and sold to the newspaper "Panorama" a nonexistent erotic story about the love of an émigré woman Musia Tatarovich and a Latin

> American gangster Rafael. This dissipated, but agreeable woman Tatarovich represents the emigration and even Russia, while Rafael represents the West. I assure you that it is frightful drivel and could not in any circumstances have appeared in *Grani*.[2]

As usual, Dovlatov is self-deprecating about his work. By the time the novel was published in book form, he had reworked it several times, and he later wrote to Sagalovsky:

> I'm sending you *A Foreign Woman* with a restrained dedication. So far—sorry—everyone has been praising it, including at least two intelligent people—the film producer Slava Tsukerman, the author of the monstrous film "Liquid Sky," and a certain writer called Sumerkin, who is astute and clever [. . .] Boria Shragin [. . .] said, "After this book I want to live." So there you are. In a word, *The Captain's Daughter* it isn't, but all the same, if you can muster the strength, have a read of it.[3]

As has been shown to be the case with a number of Dovlatov's stories, the roots of *A Foreign Woman* (apart from the publication in *Almanac Panorama*) are in a newspaper feature Dovlatov published in three issues of *Novyi Amerikanets*.[4] The story, "Telezhka s khlebnym kvasom" ("A Cart Selling Kvass"), had a subtitle: "Kartinki russkogo N'iu-Iorka: Forest Khills" ("Pictures of Russian New York: Forest Hills"). Some incidents that occur in *A Foreign Woman* are described in *Novyi Amerikanets* in "Sentimental'nyi marsh" ("A Sentimental March"): "I started attending jewelry courses. I remember some little metal bits and pieces. There were some little glass balls . . . I've forgotten the details. I remember a piece of white-hot metal dropping into my shoe . . ."[5] This incident is reproduced almost word for word in the description of the courses the heroine attends in *A Foreign Woman*.

New York in Dovlatov's vision is like an independent state: people from Texas appear as foreigners, and inhabitants of Iowa look as if they had arrived from another planet, so the Russians are just as much at home as many other foreigners, since everybody speaks English with an accent. In "The Invisible Newspaper" Dovlatov summed up his feelings about New York: "There is no sense of place here. It feels like a ship crammed with millions of passengers. This city is so multifarious that you realize there's a corner here for you, too" (*SS* 3:110). This article in *Novyi Amerikanets* is accompanied by photographs of the main road in Forest Hills—108th Street, with its Russian inhabitants. Many of the characters depicted under different names in this article appear in *A Foreign Woman:* the Russian taxi drivers, the supermarket owner, the publisher, and the hairdresser who left the Soviet Union as a protest against Karl Marx's hairstyle: "How can you trust a man with a hairstyle like that?"[6] People of many different nationalities live in Forest Hills: Germans, Latin Americans, Indians, Armenians, and so on, but the main language of communication is Russian. There are about seven thousand Russians living there, and it is said that they are predominantly members of the intelligentsia. It is Vysotsky's baritone voice that can be heard from the windows, and "if you shout out 'Sasha!' in the street, a dozen people will instantly turn round. And for every milling-machine operator you will find eight university lecturers."[7] So this is the Russian emigration's corner of New York: "America all round, and us in the middle. And in New York's polyphony a distinct Russian note rings out with ever greater confidence."[8] All social classes are present in Russian Forest Hills: poor poets, rich merchants, gangsters, lawyers, doctors, writers, and even a "blind musician." Local people are considered to be foreigners: "If we hear English being spoken, we prick up our ears. In such instances we earnestly request: 'Speak Russian!' " ("Esli my slyshim angliiskuiu rech', to nastorazhivaemsia. V takikh sluchaiakh my ubeditel'no prosim: 'Govorite po-russki!' "; *SS* 3:182.)

In both *A Foreign Woman* and in the article "A Cart Selling Kvass" the author recommends that if you wish to get to know Russian Forest Hills you need to stand on the corner of 108th and 64th Street. This is the place where Dovlatov himself lived. From this vantage point he describes each character in the story. As is the case in other stories, the characters are based on real people. In "A Cart Selling Kvass" most of them are given their real names. For example, Grigory Poliak, who in the Soviet Union worked as a refrigeration engineer, founded a publishing house in the United States—Serebrianyi vek (Silver Age). A number of Dovlatov's works were published there. For the fifth anniversary celebrations of this publishing house Dovlatov prepared a broadcast for Radio Liberty. This is how he describes Poliak in it: "Grigory Poliak had a physical love of books. He took delight in the texture of antique embossed bindings. In the grainy firmness of satin paper. In the calligraphy of a Meyer typeface."[9] In "A Cart Selling Kvass" there is even a photograph of Poliak. Dovlatov writes that he published around thirty books, including some unique ones, such as Khodasevich's memoirs, as well as previously unpublished works by Bulgakov, Platonov, and Erofeev: "His creditors give Poliak no peace. Aggrieved authors scowl at Poliak. But the publisher has a satisfied expression on his face. Such are the paradoxes of our district."[10] He is the prototype of Fima Druker in *A Foreign Woman,* who is described as a slightly crazy, obsessive publisher whose first publication was Lion Feuchtwanger's *Jud Süss* (*Jew Suess*), with a misprint on the cover: "FEIKHTVAGNER" (FEUCHTWAGNER). He is so absorbed in his books that his wife cannot stand it any longer and leaves him. He is erudite and altruistic, and has made the acquaintance of a number of leading American philologists. He corresponds with Nabokov's wife: "He carefully preserved the telegrams he had received from her: 'I strongly object.' 'I am in categorical disagreement.' 'I regard the conditions as unacceptable.' " ("Berezhno khranil poluchennye ot nee telegrammy: 'Reshitel'no vozrazhaiu.' 'Kategoricheski ne soglasna.' 'Uslovia schitaiu nepriemlemymi' "; *SS* 3:185.) Druker's lack of business acumen reduces him in *A Foreign Woman* to sleeping on boxes of Feuchtwanger's *Jew Suess* and even to trying to exchange copies of the book for sausage in the local supermarket.

Another real-life prototype in *A Foreign Woman* is Mark Popovsky,[11] who figures as the publicist Zaretsky.[12] Mark Aleksandrovich Popovsky was a Russian writer, journalist, and essayist. He had published a number of works in the Soviet Union, some of book length, mainly on scientific issues. During the 1970s two of Popovsky's books, *Delo akademika Vavilova* (*The Vavilov Affair*) and *Zhizn' i zhitie Voino-Iasenetskogo* (*The Life of Voino-Iasenetskii*) were rejected by the censor and subsequently circulated in samizdat. Popovsky also signed several letters in support of Russian dissidents. He was persecuted by the KGB and left the country in 1977, settling in New York. In emigration he contributed to numerous Russian-language periodicals. He worked for Radio Liberty, contributed to *Novyi Amerikanets*, and worked briefly at *Grani. The Vavilov Affair* was published in the United States by Grigory Poliak's publishing house. Dovlatov thought very highly of Popovsky's works, but it is his qualities as a human being that find a humorous reflection in *A Foreign Woman.*

This is how Popovsky is described in a letter to Vladimov:

> He's a decent, conscientious journalist with, for the most part, sensible ideas. He is straightforward, not cunning, devoid of treachery, on the contrary, he is direct, honest (within the limits of his outlook) and so on. But at the same time he is ridiculously militant, mistaken about his own role, coarse and tactless with women, and for that matter with men too [. . .]. Back at home he fought against Soviet power—a huge target, perfect visibility, everything was clear. Here it's all more complicated. [. . .] Apart from anything else he's a great ladies' man, an *homme fatal,* who declared to one peroxide blond who brought her monstrous stories to him as a *maître:* "Give me complete power over you, and I will make you famous!"[13]

This last phrase (*SS* 3:224) is quoted in a slightly modified form in *A Foreign Woman* when Zaretsky interviews the central heroine Marusia, allegedly for his research project, "Sex in the Totalitarian State," an unfinished copy of which circulated in samizdat. In the course of this project, Zaretsky also visits Aleksandr Solzhenitsyn: "It is known, incidentally, that Zaretsky made a secret visit to Solzhenitsyn. He was accorded a conversation of two minutes' duration. He inquired what Isaich thought about sex. And received the answer: 'That is all a foreign delusion, the fabrication of the Antichrist . . .'" ("Izvestno, mezhdu prochim, chto Zaretskii taino ezdil k Solzhenitsynu. Byl udostoen razgovora prodolzhitel'nost'iu v dve minuty. Pointeresovalsia, chto Isaich dumaet o sekse? Poluchil otvet, chto 'vse sie est' blazh' zamorskaia, antikhristova lzha . . ."; *SS* 3:244.)

The background of the "the enigmatic man of religion Lemkus" ("zagadochnyi religioznyi deiatel' Lemkus"), mentioned in *A Branch Office,* is explained more fully in *A Foreign Woman.* It transpires that Lemkus did not originally change his profession when he emigrated to the United States. In the Soviet Union he had been quite a loyal professional entertainer (*zateinik*). He wrote a cantata celebrating the sixtieth anniversary of the armed forces, and the author recalls the following lines from this cantata:

As you protect our peaceful sleep
You have become firmer than granite.
For that our beloved Party
Will generously reward the worthy.

I, son nash mirnyi zashchishchaia,
Vy stali tverzhe, chem granit.
Za eto partiia rodnaia
Dostoinykh shchedro nagradit! (*SS* 3:189)

After an incident which aroused the suspicions of the KGB, Lemkus had difficulties with the authorities and emigrated. In the United States he started working as an entertainer, writing couplets like these:

Suffering all our lives from the KGB,
We remember the bitterness of all the insults!
So let our beloved America
protect us from our enemies!

Ot KGB vsiu zhizn' stradaia,
My pomnim gorech' vsekh obid!
Puskai Amerika rodnaia
Nas ot vragov predokhranit! (*SS* 3:190)

So nothing changed in his life. However, in America this did not pay so well, and when Lemkus's second child was born and he was short of money, he was introduced to the Baptists, who were trying to penetrate émigré circles: "He became devout and sad. He would lower his eyes and whisper, 'If it pleases the Lord, Fira will cook some veal for dinner . . .' In our district he is firmly regarded as a crook." ("On stal nabozhnym i pechal'nym. To i delo sheptal, opuskaia glaza.—Esli Gospodu budet ugodno, Fira prigotovit na obed teliatinu . . . V nashem raione ego uporno schitaiut moshennikom . . ."; *SS* 3:191.)

Of the three fictional taxi drivers on 108th Street, Leva Baranov, Esilevsky, and Pertsovich, only Pertsovich has a real-life prototype in "A Cart Selling Kvass":

> At the wheel of a huge egg-yellow "Checker" is the former Kharkovan Kormer . . . "I was a taxi-driver in Kharkov, too. There you had a crowd of parasites. Grease the mechanic's palm. Grease the controller's palm. The foreman of the shift. The workman, so that he washes the car properly. If you don't, you lose good work. Always having to twist and turn. Getting up to various tricks, trips on the sly. Taking risks and worrying. But here I'm my own master . . ."[14]

So Kormer-Pertsovich is one whose life has changed for the better.

The dissident Karavaev, some of whose features were derived from Kirill Vladimirovich Kostsinsky,[15] is another of the characters appearing in this novel. However, Ar'ev has rightly warned against becoming too concerned to identify Dovlatov's "prototypes" and attempting to compile a *Who's Who* of his prose:

> An artist's attitude to people depends on his scrutiny of his own soul. If Sergei Dovlatov does spy or snoop on anyone, then only on himself.
>
> It is only by listening to himself that Dovlatov learned so incredibly well to listen to others. And when he had learned that, he still insisted that the storyteller had more sins to answer for than all the other characters. (*SS* 1:7)

At the same time, it is also true that Dovlatov used absolutely everything as material for his fiction.

Dovlatov as author also appears as a figure in the text, where he is truthfully depicted as an established Russian writer with many books to his credit in Russian, English, and other languages. He is described as a friend of Marusia Tatarovich. Like all the rest of the characters to be met on the corner of 108th Street, the author too is shown in his relation to Marusia, to emigration, and to the fortunes and misfortunes of life in the United States. Despite her lack of accomplishments, Marusia remains attractive and is a magnet to all the male characters in the novel. Alla Marchenko sees both her and the whole third wave of émigrés, despite the humor of the novel, as living in a state of permanent insecurity: "What laughter? There's nothing but tears . . ."[16] She considers that it is Dovlatov's old-fashioned sentimentality that turns the laughter into sadness: "The comical is instantly transformed into the sad, and anti-life, without ever managing to turn into life, leaps across into the fairy tale about the Russian Cinderella, Musia-Marusenka, who finally gets her lawful protector."[17]

This "lawful protector" is the Latin American Rafael whom Marusia ultimately marries. Having failed to find work in New York, she fails even to return to the Soviet Union. The officials at the Soviet embassy tell her she has to earn the right to return and be pardoned for her treason. By this they mean she has to write a letter denouncing life in the United States, which she is not willing to do. She is weary of her fellow countrymen's lofty ideals, and when, at a low ebb in her life, Rafael makes her a present of the parrot Lolo, her fate is decided. This is indeed the fairy-tale happy ending. All the inhabitants of 108th Street, including the author, come to the wedding, each with an appropriate wedding present: a white double bed from the taxi drivers, a cage for Lolo, food from the supermarket owner, and from Druker 118 volumes of the "World Library of Adventures and the Fantastic." The human rights activist Karavaev surprises everybody:

> He arrived with a hangover and in a foul mood. He proposed to organize in Marusia Tatarovich's honor a small personal auto-da-fe. Literally beside the lift to Musia's flat.
>
> They managed to put Karavaev out with some French brandy called Luamel. It turned out that his green synthetic jacket was flame-resistant.

> On iavilsia neoopokhmelivshiisia i mrachnyi. Zakhotel ustroit' v chest' Marusi Tatarovich nebol'shoe lichnoe samosozhzhenie. Bukval'no vozle Marusinogo lifta.
>
> Karavaeva uspeli potushit' frantsuzskim brendi 'Liuamel'.' Zelenyi sinteticheskii pidzhak ego, kak vyiasnilos', byl ogneupornym . . . (*SS* 3:282)

The parrot flies away. Vladimov suggests that it does so in protest at the heroine's attempt to return to the Soviet Union.[18] Be that as it may, the fairy tale ends appropriately with the parrot's successful recapture by Rafael and his fourteen brothers.

In *The Craft* Dovlatov recounts an episode that illustrates well his attitude to ideological intransigence and moral preaching:

> I called Naiman, "Tolia," I said, "let's go and visit Liova Ryskin."
> "I don't want to. He's too Soviet."
> "How do you mean, Soviet? You're mistaken!"
> "Well, anti-Soviet then. What's the difference?" (*SS* 3:20)

As mentioned before, Dovlatov saw the spirit of Pushkin's work "in his sympathy for the movement of life as a whole" ("v sochuvstvii dvizheniiu zhizni v tselom"; *SS* 2:212). He was attracted by Pushkin's willingness to express any point of view: "His literature is above morality. It overcomes morality and even replaces it. His literature is akin to prayer, or nature" (*SS* 2:212). In *A Foreign Woman,* Dovlatov as author within the fiction speaks out in response to other émigrés' censure of Marusia's life. Zaretsky says of Marusia:

> "A perfectly healthy woman, doesn't work, lives with some savage . . . She's free all day. Dresses in furs and suede. Drinks like a fish. And not a care in the world . . . In Afghanistan, incidentally, blood is flowing, and here it's champagne that's flowing in torrents! . . . In Nepal children are starving, and here some horrid parrot is gobbling sardines! . . . Where's the justice?"
>
> At that I tactlessly laughed.
>
> "You cynic!" Zaretsky cried.
>
> So I had to say to him, "There's something higher than justice!"
>
> "Aha!" said Zaretsky. "That's interesting! Speak up, I shall enjoy listening to you. Attention, please, gentlemen! So what is it that's higher than justice?"
>
> "All sorts of things," I replied.
>
> "Can you be more specific?"
>
> "If you want something more specific—mercy . . ."

> — Zdorovaia, prostite, baba, ne rabotaet, zhivet s kakim-to dikobrazom . . . Tselyi den' svobodna. Odevaetsia v mekha i zamshu. P'et stakanami. I nikakikh zabot . . . V Afganistane, mezhdu prochim, l'etsia krov', a zdes' rekoi techet shampanskoe! . . . V Nepale deti golodaiut, a zdes' kakoi-to merzkii popugai sardiny zhret! . . . Tak gde zhe spravedlivost'?
>
> Tut ia bestaktno zasmeialsia.
>
> — Tsinik!—vykriknul Zaretskii.
>
> Mne prishlos' skazat' emu:
>
> — Est' koe-chto povyshe spravedlivosti!
>
> — Ogo!—skazal Zaretskii.—Eto interesno! Govorite, ia vas s udovol'stviem poslushaiu. Vnimanie, gospoda! Tak chto zhe vyshe spravedlivosti?
>
> — Da chto ugodno, otvechaiu.
>
> — Nu, a esli bolee konkretno?
>
> — Esli bolee konkretno—miloserdie . . . (*SS* 3:254)

If in *The Suitcase* Dovlatov's world is constructed from the individual items, united in a suitcase, that the narrator takes with him on his journey, then in *A Foreign Woman* his world is made up of fellow émigrés: each of them tells a story which relates to Marusia Tatarovich and to the author, Dovlatov. The author hears the stories from Marusia, with whom he is acquainted. The other characters are also his acquaintances, since he lives in the same area of the city. The author in this way becomes a participant in the text at the same time as standing outside it; the author and the protagonist become the same person. This state of affairs is "realized" when at the climactic moment of Marusia's wedding the "real live" author enters the pages of the story: "And the music was starting to play. And they were all waiting for someone. And, to be quite honest, I can more or less guess who. The real live author. And at that point I arrived with my wife and daughter." ('I muzyka naigryvala. I vse kogo-to zhdali. I ia, chestno govoria, dogadyvaius', v obshchem-to,—kogo. Zhivogo avtora. I tut iavilis' my s zhenoi i dochkoi"; *SS* 3:283.)

Instead of an epilogue, the author writes a letter to his heroine, "Pis'mo zhivogo avtora Marii Tatarovich" ("Letter to Marusia Tatarovich from the real live author"):

> You are a character, I am the author. You are a figment of my imagination. Everything that you hear is spoken by me. Everything that happens has been experienced by me. I am the vindictive, chastened, untalented, bad-tempered, what you will—author.
>
> Those whom I have known go on living within me. They are my neurasthenia, my anger, my self-assurance, my lack of care. And so on.
>
> And the bloodiest of wars is the battle of ghosts.
>
> I am the author, you are my heroes. And if you were living people I would not love you so much.

> Ty—personazh, ia—avtor. Ty—moia prichuda. Vse, chto slyshish', ia proiznoshu. Vse, chto sluchilos', mnoiu perezhito. Ia—mstitel'nyi, prinizhennyi, bezdarnyi, zloi, kakoi ugodno—avtor.
>
> Te, kogo ia znal, zhivut vo mne. Oni—moia nevrasteniia, zlost', aplomb, bespechnost'. I t.d.
>
> I samaia krovavaia voina—boi prizrakov.
>
> Ia—avtor, vy—moi geroi. I zhivykh ia ne liubil by vas tak sil'no. (*SS* 3:284)

The resulting state of affairs has been succinctly described by Karen Ryan-Hayes:

> The source of creativity or the transformation of experience into fiction is now located within the author himself. The battle may have been bloody, but the implied author has now attained a position that is at once broadly philosophical, sophisticated and psychologically insightful. Both formally and thematically, then, *A Foreign Woman* represents a significant advance in Dovlatov's narrative praxis.[19]

This conclusion is clearly one of the ways in which Dovlatov sought to realize the ambition he had written to Efimov about in 1982: "The author and the hero gradually merge into a single documentary person, and that person is the writer."[20] The same intention can be seen to underlie a set of three stories that he wrote in the summer of 1988: "Rasskazy o minuvshem lete" ("Stories of Last Summer"). In the same letter to Efimov, he had written that he would like to complete the novel *Fiveways* with a chapter in which the action takes place in the West ("It's essential to write one more part, where the action takes place in the West").[21] The three "Stories of Last Summer" might be regarded as an initial sketch for this last part of the novel. They realize the fusion of author and hero in quite a different way from *A Foreign Woman.* They all describe episodes from the life of a writer, Grigory Borisovich Koshits, who spends the summer in a bungalow in the Russian colony near Monticello in upstate New York. They are written in the third person, and the narrator is given no individual features: he is the traditional omniscient third-person narrator. The words of the writer-hero are given only in direct speech. On the technical level, therefore, there is nothing to identify the author with the hero. The reader familiar with earlier works of Dovlatov's, however, will easily recognize autobiographical references. When somebody unexpectedly calls out his name, the writer jumps: "He shuddered. The writer always shuddered when his name was unexpectedly called out. This had started long ago, during his army years, when the writer was a guard in Mordovia." ("On vzdrognul. Kogda ego neozhidanno oklikali, pisatel' vzdragival. Eto nachalos' davno, eshche s armeiskikh let, kogda pisatel' byl okhrannikom v Mordovii"; *SS* 3:444.) Another quirk that can be recognized from earlier work is his anxiety at the sight of a clean piece of paper: "He saw a clean sheet of paper. He was seized by a familiar fear." ("Uvidel chistyi list bumagi. Privychnyi strakh okhvatil ego"; *SS* 3:443.)

The setting of these stories is also very recognizably that in which Dovlatov lived at that time. It is noticeable that the émigré community is now more settled and more acclimatized (even to the extent of coining new Russian swear-words from English roots). The third story, "The Gynecologist Budanitsky and I," is mainly about the trivial material preoccupations of people around the writer, and the silly advice his neighbors give him on what he should write about. One of them lists every item that he has eaten in the course of a day, and suggests that readers in Russia would be so astonished at its richness and variety that the writer would be awarded a Lenin Prize for his revelations. The wife of one Bernovich, Faina, who imagines herself to be an intellectual, confides in Koshits, telling him of her loneliness and her contempt for her husband. Telling the writer that she has met a cultured man, she explains: "our relations are purely pathological" ("otnosheniia mezhdu nami chisto patologicheskie"; *SS* 3:453). (The writer realizes that she means "platonic.") Bernovich requests the writer to hide him in his bungalow during his wife's tryst, and Koshits, though somewhat perturbed, agrees to play his allotted part. The description of his decision encapsulates succinctly much of Dovlatov's perception of the writer's function:

> The writer came to his senses. He felt a broad smile flitting across his face. He suddenly felt an acute sympathy for the course of life as a whole. [. . .] And then, now addressing himself: "What will it be called? Let's say 'The Gynecologist and I'? Have to change the name . . . Well, what about 'The Gynecologist Budanitsky and I' "?

> Pisatel' ochnulsia. Pochuvstvoval na litse svoem shirokuiu bluzhdaiushchuiu ulybku. Ispytal neozhidanno ostroe sochuvstvie khodu zhizni v tselom. [. . .] I dal'she, uzhe obrashchaias' k sebe: 'Kak zhe eto budet nazyvat'sia? Dopustim—'My i ginekolog . . .' Nado zamenit' familiiu . . . Nu, skazhem 'My i ginekolog Budanitskii.' (*SS* 3:455)

The first two stories, "Ariel' " and "Igrushka" ("The Toy"), are concerned with the writer's acquaintance with a child called Ariel, whom he meets near his bungalow.[22] Ariel is a young boy who is excluded from the company of other children because he has lice. Exclusion is something he shares with the writer, and in the first story the writer explains to him the nature of the lice that afflict him. In the second story Ariel visits the writer again, bringing him a mechanical toy car, which he wants to share with the writer: "I've played with it enough. It's your turn" ("Ia naigralsia. Vasha ochered' "; *SS* 3:445), says Ariel. The writer accepts the car, but in his preoccupation with his own thoughts, he loses it, and Ariel makes tiresome daily visits in the attempt to find it. No other substitute car, not even a real 1981 "Buick Regal," will do.

These two stories have a metaphorical character that has not previously been in evidence in Dovlatov's writing, suggesting that, as well as in some sense completing a development he had long foreseen, they could have marked the beginning of a new manner, had he lived to pursue it. This feature is seen clearly in a short exchange between Koshits and the boy Ariel, when the writer asks the child what has happened to his wings:

> "Where are your wings, Ariel?" asked the writer. "Haven't got any," the boy replied brusquely and without surprise, "What's yours?" "I don't understand, my what?" "What's your name?" "My name's Grigory Borisovich. And I must admit I haven't got any wings either."

> — Gde zhe kryl'ia tvoi, Ariel'?—sprosil pisatel'.—Netu,—korotko i bez udivleniia otvetil mal'chik, a tebia?—Ne ponial, chto—tebia?—A kak tebia zovut?—Menia zovut Grigorii Borisovich. I kryl'ev u menia, priznat'sia, tozhe net . . . (*SS* 3:441)

In the context of Dovlatov's observations in his last works of the changes coming about in émigré society, these words can well be read as an acknowledgment that the intense spiritual concerns the émigrés brought with them were giving way to more material preoccupations. Four other stories written in New York in the 1980s deserve a brief mention: "Tretii povorot nalevo" ("Third Turn on the Left"), "Zhizn' korotka" ("Life Is Short"), "Vstretilis', pogovorili" ("They Met for a Chat"), and "Na ulitse i doma" ("In the Street and at Home"). They all take their subject matter from émigré life, showing various more or less successful adaptation strategies. Dovlatov was scathing about their quality, writing to Ar'ev in 1989: "The story in *Continent* is crap, you're right. It's just that last summer I suddenly wrote five stories and published them all, I was in too much of a hurry, and they all turned out rubbish, all five of them."[23] Nevertheless it is "They Met for a Chat" that is perhaps the most interesting of these, in that it addresses the burning question of the perestroika period: whether and on what terms to go back to the Soviet Union. The Soviet press is no longer so hostile to the émigrés, who are now described as "our compatriots abroad" ('nashi zarubezhnye sootechestvenniki'). And also: "people who for a variety of reasons have found themselves abroad" ('litsa, v silu mnogikh prichin okazavshiesia za rubezhom'; *SS* 1:212). The hero of this story is an émigré man of no special distinction, who has become wealthy in America but is lonely. He makes a visit to the Soviet Union in this new climate, hoping to reestablish contact with his former wife, with whom he has found it impossible to correspond: "It was too difficult to write from one world to another. From one planet to another." ("Slishkom uz trudno bylo pisat' iz odnogo mira—v drugoi. S odnoi planety—na druguiu"; SD 1:203.) Much of the story is concerned with his anticipations, his imagined meetings and conversations, the generosity he will be able to bestow. In the event everything turns out differently; his ex-wife has no interest in him or his presents, and he ends up drunk in the arms of a prostitute. On his return to the United States he is interviewed by an émigré journalist, who finally asks him why he has returned to America. In reply the hero is able only to mouth the standard cold war cliché: "I chose freedom" (*SS* 1:216). It is apparent that his loneliness and his lack of inner freedom are things that he carries with him, and it makes no difference whether he lives in Russia or America.

At about this time, Dovlatov wrote in a letter to Donald Fiene that his attitude to events in the Soviet Union—perestroika and glasnost—was a mixture of "mistrust, skepticism, hope, self-interest, and a growing indifference."[24] Like the characters in his fiction of the 1980s, Dovlatov was aware of an increasing gulf between himself and the country he had left behind.

Dovlatov's last major work arose from a conference that had been held several years previously. In May 1981 a number of Russian writers, all recent émigrés from the Soviet Union who were living in various parts of the United States and Europe, were invited to the conference "Russian Literature in Emigration: The Third Wave" at the University of Southern California. Dovlatov attended the conference in two capacities: both as a writer and as a journalist covering the event for Radio Liberty. There were a large number of participants, including Aksenov, Aleshkovsky, Bobyshev, Gladilin, Korzhavin, Limonov, Viktor Nekrasov, Sasha Sokolov, Siniavsky, Voinovich, many Western Slavicists, and others. The conference proceedings were published by Ardis in 1984.[25] Dovlatov participated in two roundtable discussions: "Two Literatures or One?" and "The Russian Émigré Press." He also gave a paper, "Kak izdavat'sia na Zapade?" ("How to Publish in the West?").[26] Dovlatov's paper at this conference is also reproduced in the recent four-volume edition of his works. This event is the basis of Dovlatov's novel *Filial: Zapiski vedushchego* (*A Branch Office: Notes of an Anchorman*). In a letter to Vladimov, Dovlatov defines this work as an "ideological satire": "I have now written an ideological satire, the action takes place in Los Angeles at the dissident symposium 'The New Russia,' there are masses of prototypes, barbed remarks, unpardonable mockery, or, as Zoshchenko put it—'laughter, lies, and merriment.' "[27] In his correspondence with Sagalovsky he speaks of *A Branch Office* as a novel, mentioning it in his usual self-deprecating manner:

> The novel—complete with love, politics, and all manner of stupidity, is called *A Branch Office,* the action takes place in Los Angeles around the émigré symposium 'The New Russia,' the hero meets the love of his youth, and as a result—the past, the present, and the future get tied up in an ugly knot. All in all, it's what you might call a load of twaddle.[28]

It was in fact *A Branch Office,* a story written in the United States, which became Dovlatov's first postemigration publication in the Soviet Union. An earlier and different version of *A Branch Office* was published in the Russian-language American weekly *Almanac Panorama* beginning with issue no. 350 (January 1, 1988). However, this edition is quite different from the reworked edition published in *Zvezda.*

A Branch Office is a first-person narrative. The present-tense action takes place in the United States, but it is interspersed with reminiscences about Leningrad. The protagonist, Dalmatov, is a journalist at a radio station called The Third Wave. He finds working as a journalist in America not so different from the same work in the Soviet Union. The advice the narrator receives from his employer in the United States echoes the advice from the editor of *Soviet Estonia* in *The Compromise:*

> Barry Tarasevich continued: "Don't write about the Kremlin's frenzied saber-rattling and don't say that the Kremlin gerontocracy are holding their sclerotic fingers . . ."
> I interrupted him: "on the trigger of war?"
> "How do you know?"
> "I have been writing about it in Soviet papers for ten years."
> "About the Kremlin gerontocracy?"
> "No, about the hawks from the Pentagon."
>
> Barri Tarasevich prodolzhal:
> — Ne pishite, chto Moskva isstuplenno briatsaet oruzhiem. Chto kremlevskie gerontokraty derzhat skleroticheskii palets . . .
> Ia perebil ego:
> — Na spuskovom kriuchke voiny?
> — Otkuda vy znaete?
> — Ia desiat' let pisal eto v sovetskikh gazetakh.
> — O kremlevskikh gerontokratakh?
> — Net, o iastrebakh iz Pentagona. (*SS* 4:9)

Tarasevich was formerly a TV producer in the Soviet Union, and the narrator tells us that he made a successful TV serial called "Budushchee nachinaetsia segodnia" ("The Future Begins Today"). When he emigrated, he adapted to émigré life extremely well: "He took up mushroom growing. That wasn't a slip of the tongue, I do mean mushrooms. I don't know the details." ("Uvleksia vyrashchivaniem gribov. Ia ne ogovorilsia, imenno gribov. Podrobnostei ne znaiu"; *SS* 4:12.)

It is Tarasevich who asks Dalmatov to cover the symposium. The narrator protests that he still has difficulty in understanding Russia's past and has not put a great deal of thought into ideas about its future. The fictional symposium is organized by the Californian Institute of Human Rights and has three sections: sociopolitical questions, religious problems, and culture. Dalmatov has to report on the work of all three sections. The topics are wide-ranging (from "Fet as the Herald of Eurocommunism" ["Fet—Provozvestnik evrokommunizma"] to "Ecumenical Centers in a Future Russia" ["Ekumenicheskie tsentry v budushchei Rossii"]), and the symposium is planned to close with the symbolic election of a president in exile. The whole event is presented as quite absurd, but the narrator's interest is at least in part in unraveling the past, not so much the past of Russia as that of his own life. On his arrival in Los Angeles he takes a taxi. His past, in fact, is relentlessly pursuing him. One of Dovlatov's special vignette conversations that serve as leitmotifs in a number of works and migrate from story to story is found here. It is a meeting with somebody from his army days, the beginning of an absurd event. This is the past he is attempting to escape:

> The taxi driver was dressed in a baseball cap with "Yankees" written on it, a checked shirt, and jeans. There was a cigar puffing away between his teeth. Finally I asked, "Is it much further?" (I am able to say a sentence like that without an accent.)
>
> The driver glanced at me in the mirror and asked: "Hey, mate, weren't you a screw in Ustvymlag? Around 1960?"
>
> "Not a screw. I was in charge of the punishment block."
>
> "Camp number two, twelve kilometers from Yosser?"
>
> "Could be."
>
> "Astonishing. That's where I did my ten-year stretch. What a meeting, chief!"

> Taksist byl odet v zhokeiskuiu shapochku s nadpis'iu 'Iankis', kletchatuiu rubashku i dzhinsy. V zubakh u nego dymilas' sigara. Nakonets ia sprosil:
>
> — Daleko eshche?
>
> (Takuiu frazu ia sposoben vygovorit' bez aktsenta.)
>
> Taksist pogliadel na menia v zerkalo i sprashivaet:
>
> Zemliak, ty v Ust'vymlage popkoi ne sluzhil? Godu v shestidesiatom?
>
> — Sluzhil. Ne popkoi, a kontrolerom shtrafnogo izoliatora.
>
> Vtoroi lagpunkt, dvenadtsat' kilometrov ot Iossera?
>
> — Dopustim.
>
> — Potriasaiushche! A ia tam svoi chervonets ottianul. Kakaia vstrecha, grazhdanin nachal'nik! (*SS* 4:18–19)

There is a similar scene in "The Driving Gloves," where the narrator is recognized while walking round a Leningrad film studio, and another in "An Old Cockerel Baked in Clay," where his meeting in America with the criminal Strakhuil takes the same form.

The cool and detached pose that the narrator adopts in these exchanges is a deliberate part of his characterization. Ar'ev recalls that in his early youth Dovlatov sought to emulate Hemingway, but when he started thinking about literature seriously, he took as a model Sergeant X from Salinger's story "For Esmé—with Love and Squalor":

> It was as just such a sullen, unshaven Sergeant X that Serezha appeared in our literature. What was it that he understood in the first place? That there are no angels or villains in life, and that life is nothing but compromise. This compromise has to be taught in its real sense, not in the political sense to which everyone hypocritically summons us; you have simply to understand life's warmth and its ordinary pattern, in which there are no villains, no angels, neither sinners nor righteous men.[29]

It has been observed by some critics that Dovlatov's prose is constructed rather like poetry: "They [his stories] are written like poems: the plot has only a secondary significance, it is merely the pretext for speech. It is more like singing than storytelling," writes Brodsky.[30] Viktor Kulle expands on this, arguing that some of the mysteries of Dovlatov's prose can be explained by his manner of constructing prose according to laws of poetry:

> It is his structuring of prose by the rules of poetry that explains certain of the enigmas of Dovlatov's prose, such as plots that are repeated from one work to another with endless variations, thumbnail descriptions, or character-masks, like the "enigmatic man of religion Lemkus." This is how a poet constantly returns to his favorite images. The role of metaphor is played for Dovlatov either by the character himself, or by a story that contains new information about the absurdity of the universe and man's reaction to it.[31]

Many examples could be adduced from all of Dovlatov's works to confirm the accuracy of such observations. These features are, however, particularly in evidence in *A Branch Office* for reasons that are not far to seek. The double time frame of the story—Los Angeles in the 1980s and Leningrad in the 1960s—motivates a system of constant flashbacks, many of which naturally recapitulate elements from other works. "In hindsight I saw every detail" ("Obratnym zreniem ia videl kazhduiu meloch' "; *SS* 4:34), the narrator writes. This hindsight is generated not only by the conference itself, but specifically by the unexpected appearance of the narrator's first wife, Tasia, whom he has not seen for twenty years. The ironic sketches of the conference events alternate with the narrator's reminiscences about his first meeting with Tasia in his student days at Leningrad State University. This is based on Dovlatov's extra-textual biography and his brief marriage to Asia Pekurovskaia.[32] She had the reputation of "the first beauty of 1960s Petersburg" ("pervaia Piterskaia krasavitsa" 60–kh godov)[33] and many were in love with her,[34] including Brodsky (who in fact met Dovlatov through Pekurovskaia): "At that time we were besieging the same good-looking fortress with short hair, located somewhere in the Peski district. When I came back two months later, I discovered that the fortress had fallen."[35] In real life she married Dovlatov, but evidently their happiness did not last long:[36] Pekurovskaia left Dovlatov the day after their wedding. This was part of the reason why Dovlatov abandoned his studies and was expelled from the university. Their first meeting is dramatically described in *A Branch Office* as fatal:

> And immediately the famous Leningrad cannon fired. As though an invisible exclamation mark had resounded. Or a mysterious chronometer had started working.
>
> And so began my downfall.
>
> I totchas zhe vystrelila znamenitaia leningradskaia pushka. Kak budto prozvuchal nevidimyi vosklitsatel'nyi znak. Ili zarabotal tainstvennyi khronometr.
>
> Tak nachalas' moia pogibel'. (*SS* 4:37)

This relationship also figures in "The Finnish Nylon Socks" from *The Suitcase.* The frivolous heroine of that story is Asia, who wears French scent and imported shoes. It is because of her that the protagonist of the story is in debt. In *A Branch Office,* too, her demands are quite absurd, and Dovlatov marks this by reference to a popular song from the 1960s: "Podari mne lunnyi kamen', Talisman moei liubvi . . ." (*SS* 4:43) ("Give me a moonstone, talisman of my love").[37] This is how L. Shtern, who knew the real Pekurovskaia in Leningrad, describes her: "Asia Pekurovskaia—'dressed from abroad,' vivid, elegant, her eyes made up right to her temples, unrestrained, self-confident, accustomed to admirers, sharp-tongued."[38]

The material concerning the narrator's relationship with his former wife and first love (both in *The Suitcase* and in *A Branch Office*) was taken from "Odin na ringe" ("Alone in the Ring"), a chapter of the unpublished novel *Piat' uglov* (*Fiveways*). In the unpublished version the heroine is called Tania, while the protagonist is a boxer, with only a minimal interest in literature. The black-market system in the Soviet Union is described in great detail in "Alone in the Ring," and this part is reused in *The Suitcase.* This was the novel Dovlatov was referring to in a letter to Vladimov:

> As regards my unwritten novel, in the first place it is written, and in the second it is written so badly that, reading those 650 pages, I was even surprised. I really did write a novel entitled *Fiveways* back in the Soviet Union and got it across to America with the greatest difficulty. That wonderful, quarrelsome man David Iakovlevich Dar once made a good comment about it: "How did you manage to write a novel which is at the same time frightfully pretentious and unbelievably boring?"[39]

In the same letter Dovlatov says that he would not even be able to reduce it to a hundred-page story, because it is ruined "at the level of its chemistry" ("na khimicheskom urovne"). Nevertheless, some of the ideas and dialogues from it found their way into other works. For example, the narrator's limited intellectual ability is illustrated in this telling passage:

> We got into the train. The girl took from her bag a book in English. I asked:
> "What's it called?"
> "*The Myth of Sisyphus* by Camus."
> "It's a story, or rather, an essay. Do you know what an essay is?"

> My seli v elektrichku. Devushka vynula iz sumki knizhku na angliiskom iazyke. Ia sprosil:
> — Kak nazyvaetsia?
> — Mif o Sizife Kamiu.
> — Eto rasskaz, vernee esse. Vy znaete, chto takoe esse?[40]

This dialogue is slightly modified and reused in the final version of *A Branch Office,* where the narrator Dalmatov is now a fellow philologist with only a minor interest in boxing: " 'Is it true, you're a boxer?' I nodded faintly." ("Pravda, chto vy bokser?—Ia vialo kivnul"; *SS* 4:39.) As happened in numerous instances, Dovlatov rewrote this episode many times. There are recognizable elements in the unpublished parts that made their way into the final text, but the final version is a completely different text.

It is the breakdown of their relationship and the narrator's despair at Tasia's irrational behavior that link the two time planes of *A Branch Office.* She is just as unpredictable in Los Angeles as she was in Leningrad: "It can happen that you're talking to a woman, using eloquent arguments and making a convincing case. But she doesn't care about your arguments. She's sick of the sound of your voice." ("Byvaet, ty razgovarivaesh' s zhenshchinoi, privodish' krasnorechivye dovody i ubeditel'nye argumenty. A ei ne do argumentov. Ei protiven sam zvuk tvoego golosa"; *SS* 4:95.) An almost identical passage is to be found in *The Sanctuary:* "In conversation with a woman there is one painful moment. You cite facts, reasons, arguments. You call upon logic and common sense. And all of a sudden you discover that she can't stand the sound of your voice . . ." ("V razgovore s zhenshchinoi est' odin boleznennyi moment. Ty privodish' fakty, dovody, argumenty. Ty vzyvaesh' k logike i zdravomu smyslu. I neozhidanno obnaruzhivaesh', chto ei protiven sam zvuk tvoego golosa . . ."; *SS* 2:175.) Twice in *A Branch Office* the narrator tries to recall where he has read the following lines:

Maybe the whisper was born before the lips
and leaves swirled round when there were no trees,
and those to whom we dedicate our experience,
acquired their features prior to experience.

Byt' mozhet, prezhde gub uzhe rodilsia shepot
i v bezdrevesnosti kruzhilisia listy,
i te, komu my posviashchaem opyt,
do opyta priobreli cherty![41] (*SS* 4:91 and 94)

In real life, Dovlatov understood that he had to get out of this relationship, and in January 1962 he wrote to Pekurovskaia:

> I know, Asia, how deep your bitterness and surprise are, I know that it will take you a long time to forgive me . . . How I would like you, my dear, to understand the most important things in life, to understand my hatred of people to whom you are well-disposed . . . Don't listen to the wisdom of failures. Be clever, kind, beautiful, honest, and humane.[42]

There is also a real-life postscript to this story: Pekurovskaia published her own version of their relationship, long after Dovlatov's death.[43]

There is a difference in intonation between the reminiscences and the descriptions of the writers' symposium, as V. Kuritsyn remarks: "In the 'Russian' passages the 'temperature of sadness' rises perceptibly."[44] The author casts a nostalgic look back upon the Russia of his youth, aware that his perspective is from the periphery, the "branch office," toward the center. As Kuritsyn puts it, Dovlatov's America is a branch office of Dovlatov's Russia.[45]

The patchwork nature of Dovlatov's compositional technique creates an effect that can be compared with montage in the manner of Eisenstein. Many scholars, such as Ar'ev and Kulle, have noted the episodic nature of *A Branch Office.* I. A. Mart'ianova sums it up like this:

> Dovlatov uses the frames of film perception, which in his works function rather as clichés: such are the happy ending of *A Foreign Woman* and the episodic perception of reality in *A Branch Office.*[46]
>
> [. . .] Dovlatov inclines not toward the metaphor of the cinema, but toward the metaphor of life's film-reel, cut into individual shots, toward the metaphor of cinematic perception, which resurrects the archetype of cinema. [. . .] It is possible that in this withdrawal from cinematic metaphor Dovlatov the storyteller was revealing his jealousy of such a virtuoso storyteller as the cinema, where montage all too openly sets the tone for the perception of the world.[47]

It is the elaborate intertwining of two realities, the reality of the fictional physical world and the reality of Dalmatov's recollected life, that give this montage-like narrative structure its justification. Its product is his memory, whose function is to explore the various layers of his inner experience. The narrator's image is sketched more vaguely than in other stories. Ryan-Hayes notes that "his role as a journalist allows him to don the cloak of a witness-observer and remove himself somewhat from the farce he recounts. He stands apart, describing his compatriots with bemused mockery (never sharpening his tone to serious attack or exposure)."[48] But what is true of Dalmatov the narrator is not true of Dovlatov the author. Dovlatov cannot "remove himself" and "stand apart"; his memories and his concern about his friends left behind in the Soviet Union are reflected more passionately in his journalism. In October of the same year as the conference, in one of his editorials in *Novyi Amerikanets,* Dovlatov tells about a letter ("This letter arrived by a miracle"—"Eto pis'mo doshlo chudom") that he had supposedly received from friends in the Soviet Union. Ar'ev takes the view that this letter is fictional and was written by Dovlatov himself.[49] In it Dovlatov's "friends" tell him that he cannot remove himself, he cannot be impartial:

> Your emigration is not a private matter. Otherwise you are not a writer, but a lodger. And it's immaterial where—in America, in Japan, in Rostov . . . You got out in order to tell about us and about your own past. Everything else is trivial. Everything else simply besmirches the dignity of a writer. Although the chances of success may increase. You didn't go there for jeans or for a used car. You went there in order to tell. So remember us . . .
>
> You can't become an American. And you can't escape your own past. It may seem that you are surrounded by skyscrapers. You are surrounded by the past. Us, that is. Crazy poets and artists, drunks and lecturers, soldiers and convicts.
>
> I say again—remember us. We are many, and we are alive. They kill us, but we live and write poems. In this nightmare, in this hell we recognize each other not by our names. How—is no concern of ours! (*SS* 2:418)

In the second part of *Remeslo* (*The Craft*), Dovlatov also quotes this letter in a modified form ("Pis'mo ottuda"—"A letter from there") and sums up his attitude to "past, future, and present," trying to define exactly what he means by the word "native land" (*rodina*):

> If our native land has rejected our love? Humiliated and tortured us? Betrayed our interests?
>
> Then a decent man says:

"You don't choose your mother. This is the only native land I have. I love America, I admire America, I am grateful to America, but my native land is far away. Impoverished, starving, mad and drunken! Having lost, destroyed, and rejected its best sons! How can you expect it to be kind, cheerful, and gentle?

"It turns out that birch trees grow everywhere. But does that make you feel better?

"Our native land is us ourselves. Our first toys. Hand-me-downs from older brothers. Sandwiches wrapped in newspaper. Girls in severe brown skirts. Change out of Dad's pocket. Exams, cribs . . . Ridiculous, horrendous poetry . . . Thoughts of suicide . . . A glass of 'Agdam' in the archway . . . Army *makhorka* . . . Daughter, mittens, leggings, the crumpled back of a tiny shoe . . . Lines crossed out diagonally . . . Manuscripts, militiamen, OVIR . . . Everything that has happened to us is our native land. And everything that has happened will stay forever."

Esli rodina otvergla nashu liubov'? Unizila i zamuchila nas? Predala nashi interesy?

Togda blagorodnyi chelovek govorit:

— Materei ne vybiraiut. Eto moia edinstvennaia rodina. Ia liubliu Ameriku, voskhishchaius' Amerikoi, blagodaren Amerike, no rodina moia daleko. Nishchaia, golodnaia, bezumnaia i spivshaiasia! Poteriavshaia, zagubivshaia i otvergnuvshaia luchshikh synovei! Gde uzh ei byt' dobroi, veseloi i laskovoi?! . . .

Berezy, okazyvaetsia, rastut povsiudu. No razve ot etogo legche?

Rodina—eto my sami. Nashi pervye igrushki. Pereshitye kurtochki starshikh brat'ev. Buterbrody, zavernutye v gazetu. Devochki v strogikh korichnevykh iubkakh. Meloch' iz ottsovskogo karmana. Ekzameny, shpargalki . . . Nelepye, uzhasaiushchie stikhi . . . Mysli o samoubiistve . . . Stakan 'Agdama' v podvorotne . . . Armeiskaia makhorka . . . Dochka, varezhki, reituzy, podvernuvshiisia zadnik kroshechnogo botinka . . . Koso perecherknutye stroki . . . Rukopisi, militsiia, OVIR . . . Vse, chto s nami bylo,—rodina. I vse, chto bylo,—ostanetsia navsegda . . . (*SS* 3:164)

As many critics have noted, *A Branch Office* is Dovlatov's last tribute to the idol of the 1960s, Hemingway. The influence of American fiction on Dovlatov's early prose was discussed in chapter 1, and, as Ar'ev has noted in his introduction to the collected works, its traces can be found in later works as well, such as *A Branch Office:*

This last of Dovlatov's stories ends with a passage which is as effective as it is familiar: "I lit a cigarette and went out of the hotel into the rain." Anybody who has read Hemingway will immediately recall (and with justification) the

> ending of *A Farewell to Arms:* "After a while I went out and left the hospital and walked back to the hotel in the rain." (*SS* 1:21–22)

Viktor Kulle in his article "Bessmertnyi variant prostogo cheloveka" ("The Immortal Variant of an Ordinary Person") remarks that "the echo of these last words is very significant. *A Branch Office* is Dovlatov's most 'Hemingwayan' work and at the same time it is a farewell to the master, an assertion of his own way."[50] Dovlatov himself, in one of his shorter reviews of Raisa Orlova's book *Hemingway in Russia,* "Papa i bludnye deti" ("Father and His Prodigal Children"), expresses the sentiments of his generation: "Hemingway was our idol. He was not only loved as a writer, but many of us tried to emulate him in life. Our disappointment in him was particularly acutely felt, because a person is able truly to despise and hate only his own weaknesses and sins."[51]

Dovlatov's narrator in this work muses over his immature behavior in his relationship with his first wife, experiencing the same bewilderment he is undergoing in relation to the gathering of writers who are discussing Russia's fate and trying to elect a president in exile. After long and heated discussions between the Slavophiles and Westerners, Tasia, "the most Hemingwayan heroine," as Kulle calls her, is absurdly elected president.

Introducing Soviet readers to *A Branch Office,* Ar'ev wrote in "Teatralizovannyi realism: O povesti Sergeia Dovlatova *Filial*" ("Realism Adapted for the Stage: On Sergei Dovlatov's novel *A Branch Office*"):

> Life here is dependent on the author-producer, it is turned into a series of mise-en-scènes. Dovlatov created the theater of a single storyteller. His prose has an additional dimension: an oral equivalent. It is senseless to consider each of its fragments only in a subordinate context, which might be necessary and sufficient to clarify the general idea of the work. Because its vocal arrangement and its sound are so fascinating. [. . .] In terms of its composition, *A Branch Office* is not divided into chapters, but into paragraphs, into micro-novellas. As in Chekhov's theater, the boundary between them is a pause.[52]

A notion which can help in appreciating the specific character of some of Dovlatov's works, and especially, perhaps, of *A Branch Office,* is the notion of minimalism. Introduced in the 1960s to describe art (painting, sculpture, or music) in which all elements of expressiveness and illusion are minimized, it can be applied equally to literary forms. As Vladislav Kulakov explains, it is not necessarily restricted to short forms, but does of necessity relate to the aesthetics of small elements: "Minimalism is of course not simply the aesthetics of small forms. The forms can be as unwieldy as you like. But undoubtedly minimalism is the aesthetics of the small. It is a particular type of aesthetic strategy, put into effect precisely by the postmodernist period."[53] The essential characteristic of minimalist art is simplicity of both content and form. Dovlatov had the following to say about these stalwarts of Marxist aesthetics:

> In Russia they used to tell us that form and content are indivisible. In the West many people think differently. Bakhchanian is a formalist, he is concerned solely with form, with combinations, with the invention of forms and devices. He has no content, if you can imagine that, and if he has, then only as an inalienable manifestation of form. His books [. . .] are designed not for reading, but for astonishment. Philistines in such circumstances will say, "I'll go and shit on a clean sheet of paper, and everyone will be even more astonished." That's nonsense. It is unbelievably difficult to astonish someone.[54]

The aim of minimalism is to allow the viewer to experience the work more intensely without the distractions of composition, theme, and so on. There exists in fact a tradition of miniature minimalist stories in twentieth-century Russian literature, exemplified by such writers as Babel, Kharms, and Goliavkin. The episodic miniature portraits in *A Branch Office* add a new dimension to this tradition. Dovlatov's stories are punctuated by what Ar'ev calls micro-novellas. Dovlatov evinces here his tremendous sense of drama, using these micro-novellas to postpone the climax of the story. It is in this work that Dovlatov adopted this stripped-down, matter-of-fact prose style to the greatest effect.

Chapter Nine

Dovlatov's Posthumous Reputation

IN ONE OF HIS LETTERS from the mid-1980s, Dovlatov wrote to Naum Sagalovsky:

> Bulgakov's hero says: "Fame will never come to a man who writes bad poems." This sentence also works in reverse. Sooner or later everything will work out. Is it not a miracle that Bulgakov and Platonov, who had been among the literary extras in their lifetime, became the undisputed leaders of the new Russian prose? Everything was rediscovered, Platonov's tiniest newspaper articles were unearthed, up to and including the letters to the editor of a Voronezh newspaper in 1924, which he had edited.[1]

Something very similar has happened with Dovlatov himself. Unknown except to a narrow circle of friends and virtually unpublished when he left the Soviet Union in 1978, he achieved recognition in America, paving the way for his triumphant, but alas, largely posthumous return to the Soviet Union and post-Soviet Russia. He has since become one of the most widely discussed authors in contemporary Russia and Estonia.[2] A vivid example of the rediscovery of unknown work by him took place in December 2003, when the puppet theater in Pskov premiered Dovlatov's play "Chelovek, kotorogo ne bylo" ("The Man Who Never Was"), the text of which had been found in 2001 in the theater's archives.[3] This discovery became a great sensation and was reported in major Russian newspapers such as *Moskovskie novosti* (no. 45, December 2–8, 2003) and *Nezavisimaia gazeta* (December 1, 2003, p. 8). Dovlatov's *Kompromiss* (*The Compromise*) provided the basis for a documentary film by Kristina Davidjants, *Intimate Town,* which was shown during the Twenty-sixth Moscow International Film Festival in the summer of 2004 (June 18–27).[4] Most of the characters whom Dovlatov used as prototypes play themselves in the film (or as the program put it, "the story is told by witnesses of his life"), while the role of Dovlatov is played by an actor. This is a particularly interesting illustration of the Dovlatov myth, of the way his artistic fantasy has come to be taken for reality. There is a lively debate about *The Compromise* on the Internet under the heading "Po sledam klassika" ("In the Footsteps of a Classic"), in which a number of interviewees dispute the extent to which Dovlatov's account of them corresponds to the truth.[5] Not only prototypes whom Dovlatov used under their real names are interviewed, but also other colleagues from the various papers Dovlatov worked on, who did not quite make it into Dovlatov's stories: "The former journalist of the *Youth of Estonia,* Vladimir Vel'man, did not become a protagonist in *The Compromise.*"

The house in which Dovlatov lived in Tallinn now has a plaque in Estonian and Russian: "The Russian writer Sergei Dovlatov lived in this house in 1972–1975."[6] According to *Petrovskii kur'er* (*Petrovskii Courier*), a plaque was unveiled in January 2004 in the Shipbuilding Institute in St. Petersburg, where Dovlatov worked between 1965 and 1967.[7] The author of the article claims to have seen Dovlatov once in his life in 1972 on Nevsky Prospekt, and he comments: "But that 'one time' was very powerful." Apparently Dovlatov was in the company of Anatoly Naiman and was expressing himself in witticisms (he was "shooting" caustic comments in all directions). This article is a telling example of the way in which myths about Dovlatov have developed and been embellished.

September 2006 saw the sixty-fifth anniversary of Dovlatov's birth. This provided the occasion for a collection of Dovlatov's editorials from the newspaper *Novyi Amerikanets* (*The New American*), entitled *Rech' bez povoda . . . ili Kolonki redaktora* (*Speech for No Occasion: Editorials*), published by Dovlatov's widow and daughter to commemorate the event. Both widow and daughter were extensively interviewed, and many articles appeared in the Russian media: *Ogonek, Rossiiskaia gazeta, Komersant, Izvestia, Vzgliad, Radio Rossia, Radio Svoboda, Novoe vremia, Nezavisimaia gazeta,* and others. Discussion raged on the Internet on such sites as rosbalt.ru, fontanka.ru, gorod-spb.ru, konkretno.ru, and many more. The whole twenty-five-thousand-copy print run of the book *Rech' bez povoda . . .* was sold out in two days. In this connection Radio Rossia prepared a special literary radio serial, *The Prose of Sergei Dovlatov,* in which Dovlatov's stories, read by famous actors, were transmitted twice a day on weekdays. Readings included stories from *Demarsh entuziastov* (*Démarche of the Enthusiasts*), *The Suitcase,* and *The Compromise.* This anniversary was also marked by an evening in the Meyerhold Center, jointly arranged by the International Dovlatov Fund and the Praktika Theater (directed by Vyrypaev), where, similarly, actors such as Ingeborga Dapkunaite, Tatiana Drubich, Evgeny Grishkovets, Gosha Kutsenko, and others read stories by Dovlatov. This event was recorded for television and has served as the basis for a TV film on Dovlatov shown on various channels. A further documentary film on Dovlatov was made by Sergei Gureev with the title *Ostanovka na mestnosti* (*A Halt in the Landscape*). Many of Dovlatov's works such as *The Zone* and *The Sanctuary* have been dramatized and are successfully performed in major Russian theaters. (*The Sanctuary,* for example, is still at the time of writing in the repertoire of the Mossovet Theater in Moscow.) The stories concerning the rise and fall of *Novyi Amerikanets,* with extracts from *The Zone* and *The Sanctuary,* have also been dramatized and performed by the Moscow Arts Theater. This production has been playing to full houses since the opening performance in 1994.

A considerable number of poems have been dedicated to Dovlatov, and often set to music. Iunna Morits, for instance, wrote a poem on the occasion of his death, "Dovlatov in New York," recalling him walking around New York in a Panama hat shortly before he died:

Everyone laughs at his jokes
And women dissolve in his presence,
And his heart will only fail
On a Friday in August in the afternoon.
But now it's only a Saturday in July,
He's young and handsome and famous,
New York, like a great saucepan
Rings out beneath the roof of his Panama.

I vsiak ego shutke smeetsia
I zhenshchiny mleiut pri nem,
I serdtse ego razorvetsia
Lish' v piatnitsu, v avguste, dnem.
A nynche subbota iiulia.
On molod, krasiv, znamenit.
N'iu-Iork, kak bol'shaia kastriulia,
Pod kryshkoi panamy zvenit.

This poem has been set to music by Pavel Matveiko.[8] Oleg Gorodetsky's song "Ozhidaniem leta napolnen moroznyi ianvar' . . ." ("Frosty January is filled with the anticipation of summer . . .") develops images from Dovlatov's *Zone* and quotes the following passage from it as its epigraph: "The 'Turkish March' was playing on the radio. Katia imagined the Turkish army wandering through the deep snow in their heavy turbans . . . Their curved daggers were frozen to their sheaths and their turbans were covered in ice."[9] Masha Shkol'nik's poem "Piter," celebrating a visit to St. Petersburg, introduces Dovlatov as one of the city's famous literary sons.[10]

And to feel you are in touch
With the giants of literary exploits,
Why here, for certain, have walked
Dovlatov, Brodsky, Kushner, Bitov.

I oshchushchat' sebia prichastnoi
K gigantam pis'mennykh kul'bitov,
Ved' zdes', konechno, prokhodili
Dovlatov, Brodskii, Kushner, Bitov.

This poem has also been set to music. Vladimir Nikolaevich Durkin from Nizhny Novgorod writes songs on texts inspired by Dovlatov, while Igor' Belyi has written a song using Dovlatov's *Sanctuary* as his theme. It is clear from these examples that Dovlatov has entered the popular consciousness without any restriction of cultural level; rather like Vladimir Vysotsky a couple of decades earlier, he is felt to embody something that all Russians share.

The city of Dovlatov's birth, Ufa, submitted a request to be allotted the formal title "city of Dovlatov."[11] In his article "Khronicheskii emigrant" ("A Chronic Émigré"), Shamil Valeev writes that the house where the Dovlatovs lived during the wartime evacuation still stands and that many people would like to mark No. 56 Gogol Street "with a memorial plaque to the Ufa writer Sergei Dovlatov."[12] Valeev asserts that Dovlatov himself "attributed a mystical significance to the fact of his birth in this city, and described his semi-mythical meeting with Andrei Platonov."[13] This refers to the story "Sud'ba" ("Fate") in Dovlatov's *Remeslo* (*The Craft*), where Dovlatov tells about a fictional meeting with Andrei Platonov in Ufa when he was three weeks old (the fictional Dovlatov in the story has a birthday in October).[14] His mother was taking him for a walk in a baby carriage when a stranger came up to her and asked if he could give the little boy a pinch. The impression this man made on the narrator's mother was so great that she remembered the event for the rest of her life. The narrator indignantly refutes his friends' doubts about the story's veracity: "What nonsense! In the story described here even I am an indubitable figure! So what can be said about Platonov?" ("Kakaia chepukha! V opisannoi istorii dazhe ia—figura nesomnennaia! Tak chto zhe govorit' o Platonove?!"; *SS* 3:11.) What is important, Valeev insists, is that "in his thought he [Dovlatov] raised this stranger to the status of a classic and lived for many years in the certainty that it was precisely then that he had received the baton from Platonov, who was in Ufa that very autumn."[15] Determined to prove that Ufa had made an impression on Dovlatov during the first three years of childhood, Valeev resorts to rudimentary psychology: "Any psychologist will confirm that the events of the first years of life are in no way of lesser significance than all subsequent universities."[16]

As part of the celebrations for the sixty-fifth anniversary of Dovlatov's birth, the newspaper *Pskovskaia zemlia* (*The Pskov Land*) published an article called "In Quest of the Pskov Dovlatov—Selected Quotations from *The Sanctuary* with Commentary and Evidence from the Prototypes."[17] In this article the putative prototypes of characters in *The Sanctuary* are interviewed and given the opportunity to comment on the truthfulness of their description in the novel. The author of the article is Aleksandr Donetsky, who a few years earlier had made a television film about Dovlatov's life in Pushkinskie Gory. According to Donetsky, Dovlatov entered forever "the calendar of literary saints of the Pskov region. Sergei Dovlatov's *Sanctuary* is a kind of apocrypha, a text which reproduced the unrepeatable coloration of life alongside the museumified *genius loci.*"[18] Donetsky also interviews Andrei Ar'ev, who admits that it was he who recommended Dovlatov to try working as a guide in the Pushkin Museum. However, Donetsky claims this was not fortuitous; Dovlatov could not have done otherwise. It was fate. "New generations of pilgrims come to Mikhailovskoe in order, besides their communication with Pushkin's muse, to walk also on 'Dovlatov's path' and to glance at the sanctuary through his magic crystal."[19]

Among the characters interviewed by Donetsky is one Stanislav Igorevich Mal'chonkov, a KGB officer who reputedly served as prototype for the character Beliaev. In *The Sanctuary* Beliaev summons Dovlatov to his office and over a glass of vodka discusses with him various issues, such as the state of Soviet agriculture. Beliaev gives Dovlatov his "friendly" advice to leave the country. In his interview with *Pskovskaia zemlia,* Mal'chonkov admits that the KGB did show an interest in Dovlatov, but categorically denies that such a conversation could have taken place: "That is all very far from reality. Dovlatov invented all that to arouse the readers' interest."[20]

Donetsky also conducted an interview with Ekaterina Sergeevna Evdokimova, the neighbor of the colorful fictional character Mikhail Ivanych from whom Dovlatov rented a room (the real-life prototype was called Vania; he died very recently). Ekaterina Sergeevna tells how she met Dovlatov by the well, but explains that they did not have a conversation: "We had different work systems: he had his, in the sanctuary, and I had mine, in agriculture. So we didn't have any special conversation."[21]

Writing similarly on the occasion of Dovlatov's sixty-fifth birthday, the critic Pavel Basinsky claimed that for some time Dovlatov became the "only" writer for the Russian reader: "Dovlatov's books were snatched from the bookstalls, he was quoted by heart just as Zoshchenko was in his own time, but the main thing is that people swore by his name their fidelity to fine literature, precisely to fine literature, with the word 'fine' underlined three times."[22]

On the sixty-sixth anniversary of Dovlatov's birth, September 3, 2007, a memorial plaque, designed by Aleksei Arkhipov, was unveiled amidst wide publicity on the house where Dovlatov lived in Leningrad. Many of Dovlatov's friends and relatives were present, including his widow Elena Dovlatova and his daughter Katia. The governor of St. Petersburg, Valentina Matvienko, and Elena Dovlatova jointly performed the unveiling ceremony. On the same day, the new season of the program *Zhivaia istoriia* (*Living History*) on the St. Petersburg TV station Piatyi kanal (Channel Five) opened with a two-part documentary film on Dovlatov's life, which was filmed in St. Petersburg, Tallinn, New York, and Boston. The author and anchorman of the program was Lev Lur'e. The program describes Dovlatov as "one of the Leningrad-Petersburg 'brands,' one of the greatest writers of the second half of the twentieth century. He is a genuine writer of the people. His stories are scattered everywhere in the form of proverbs and sayings. Leningrad of the '70s is above all the Leningrad of Dovlatov."[23]

Dovlatov's reputation was first established in the United States, where he published a number of books in Russian, and his work was translated, already during his lifetime, not only into English but also into French, German, Swedish, Finnish, Japanese, Danish, Hungarian, and other languages. He won the American PEN Club prize for the best short story written in 1986, and was the only Russian writer (if one discounts Nabokov) to publish in that most prestigious of American magazines, the *New Yorker.* In the United States Dovlatov enjoyed considerable critical acclaim: his books in English translation received hundreds of positive reviews. *The New York Review of Books* published an extended article on Dovlatov, with his photograph on the front page. In one of the reviews of the American translation of *The Compromise,* published in the *Village Voice,* a review of which Dovlatov was said to be particularly proud, the reviewer Adam Gussov wrote: "Dovlatov's characters burn just as brightly as Dostoevsky's, but in a considerably more frivolous hell." Gradually during the perestroika period his work came to be known in Russia. One of his colleagues from *Novyi Amerikanets,* Petr Vail', wrote: "When his books first appeared in Russia at the end of the 1980s, interest in them and their popularity could easily be explained. At that time everything 'Made in USA,' all the more so of Russian origin and in the Russian language, was received with enthusiasm."[24] Dovlatov himself flippantly enumerated possible reasons for his growing popularity: " 'It's the fashionable Russian topic,' 'He is easy to translate,' 'Dovlatov is a liberal, this is why the American intelligentsia sympathizes with him,' 'Sergei's Caucasian charm affects sixty-year-old women.' "

Gratified as Dovlatov undoubtedly was by his reception in America, it was to Russia that his work was ultimately addressed. His death in 1990 coincided with radical changes in Russian literary culture. He lived to see some of his work published in the Soviet Union in the late 1980s, and he became the subject of some critical acclaim in the last few years of his life. His posthumous reputation has grown apace. Publications relating to him have become a substantial industry. Many of his letters have been published both in literary journals and in popular magazines. Dovlatov has become the subject of many books, such as Mikhail Veller's *Nozhik Serezhi Dovlatova* (*Serezha Dovlatov's Penknife*), Aleksandr Genis's "philological novel" *Dovlatov i okrestnosti* (*Dovlatov's Surroundings*), Vladimir Evseev's *Ne tol'ko Dovlatov* (*Not Only Dovlatov*), Vladimir Aleinikov's *Dovlatov i drugie* (*Dovlatov and Others*), and *Golos i svet, ili SMOG—Samoe Molodoe Obshchestvo Geniev* (*Voice and Light, or SMOG—the Youngest Association of Geniuses*). There is also a curious book by Aleksei Del'nov which uses Dovlatov's name in its title, but has in fact little to do with him, *Kod zastoia, ili zadushevnaia dovlatovshchina (The Stagnation Code, or Heartfelt Dovlatovism*). The list of memoirs written by close and not so close friends of Dovlatov's is also constantly growing: Evgeny Rein, *Mne skuchno bez Dovlatova* (*I Miss Dovlatov*); Liudmila Shtern, *Dovlatov, dobryi moi priiatel'* (*My Good Friend Dovlatov*); Vladimir Solov'ev and Elena Klepikova, *Dovlatov vverkh nogami: Tragediia veselogo cheloveka* (*Upside Down Dovlatov: The Tragedy of a Cheerful Man*); Vladimir Solov'ev, *Roman s epigrafami: Varianty liubvi: Dovlatov na avtootvetchike* (*A Novel with Epigraphs: Varieties of Love: Dovlatov on the Answerphone*), and more. His reputation is also attested by the creation in St. Petersburg in 1993 of a short-story prize carrying his name.

As A. Genis has written: "In contrast to other famous émigrés, perestroika did not return Dovlatov to Russian literature, but introduced him into it. He fell upon it with such force that he conquered it in a single hour. However, the phenomenon of Dovlatov's popularity, which so swiftly turned into universal fame, still requires explanation."[25]

In one of his literary essays, Dovlatov remarks: "Thoughts, ideas, not to speak of plot, are precisely the things that interest me least of all in literature" (*SS* 4:352). His fundamental preoccupation was with the texture of language. He worked tirelessly at his style, constantly rewriting his stories. As he explained to John Glad, "I have to tell you that like all talkers I repeat my stories thousands of times, and in the process of telling everything superfluous is removed, all unnecessary details are taken out. So I write slowly."[26] The oral substratum of Dovlatov's prose not only affects this constant process of refining the linguistic surface, but is of fundamental importance for his attitude to his role as author. He defined his position in literature as that of a storyteller, distinguishing this title from the traditional Russian notion of the writer: "I'm not sure that I regard myself as a writer. I would like to think of myself as a storyteller. These are not the same thing. A writer is concerned with serious problems; he writes about the things people live for, how people ought to live. But a storyteller writes about HOW people live" (*SS* 4:393). As a storyteller in this definition, Dovlatov avoids the customary moral and ethical stance that over the years has been more or less obligatory for a Russian man of letters.

> Like philosophy, Russian literature took upon itself the intellectual interpretation of the surrounding world . . . And like religion, it took upon itself the spiritual and moral education of the people. What has always most impressed me in literature, however, is that which is most immediately literary, i.e., a given piece of text which either casts us into sadness or arouses a feeling of joy.[27]

One of Dovlatov's literary ideals was Pushkin's *Kapitanskaia dochka* (*The Captain's Daughter*). P. Vail' reports Dovlatov as saying that every time he reached his favorite passage in *The Captain's Daughter*—Pugachev's words "Who dares hurt an orphan?"—he felt a lump in his throat.[28] Dovlatov wanted his readers to experience similar feelings when reading his books. He held the highest possible opinion of Pushkin. "The work of Pushkin was the victory of pure aestheticism over the sociopolitical tendencies of preaching and moralizing in literature" (*SS* 4:357). Dovlatov considered that the generation of writers that followed Pushkin, the four giants of Russian literature, Tolstoy, Dostoevsky, Turgenev, and Gogol, fell foul of their attempts to engage in sociopolitical or spiritual and religious issues. It was Chekhov, the first truly European Russian writer, who resisted this temptation and despite criticism "preserved the artist in himself and immortalized his name" (*SS* 4:359). Chekhov became his great ideal for emulation. "You can bow in respect before the intelligence of Tolstoy. You can take delight in the elegance of Pushkin. You can admire Dostoevsky's moral quest. Or Gogol's humor. And so on. But it is only Chekhov that you want to be like" (*SS* 4:168).

It is clear, then, that no matter how well Dovlatov's work could be translated and how much success he could enjoy in other countries, it was his place in Russian literature that mattered to him most. Many of the English translations are heavily edited to remove passages that would not be fully comprehensible to an audience unfamiliar with the Russian background. The posthumous reputation that he has earned in his native country is the true measure of his achievement. His popularity has had a noticeable impact on the contemporary literary process in Russia. P. Vail' points in this connection to the pseudo-documentalism of his work, the deceptive ease with which reality is reproduced.[29] He notes that many authors think it must be easy to write like Dovlatov, since all it requires is to listen and record what is heard. Their failure in practice shows the error of this judgment. Nor is it enough simply to tell funny stories. Dovlatov understood this well, pointing out that the sense of drama is even more important than the sense of humor:

> If a writer is lacking in a sense of humor that is a great misfortune, but if he is lacking in something opposite to it, say, a sense of drama, then it is an even greater tragedy. After all, Tolstoy wrote *War and Peace* hardly applying the humor pedal at all, but did not create anything great without a sense of drama. Teffi had a sense of drama, so did Averchenko, not to mention Zoshchenko or Bulgakov.[30]

Besides the precision and conciseness of his language and his insistence that mercy is a higher value than justice, the third distinguishing feature of Dovlatov's prose is precisely that pseudo-documentalism of which Vail' writes. The way in which his work has given rise to a headlong quest for prototypes shows how important this aspect is perceived to be. His stories create the impression of using material taken directly from real life. And indeed, autobiographical facts do underlie practically all his fictions. In *The Zone* his military service is reflected, in *The Compromise* his work as a journalist, in *The Sanctuary* his period at the Pushkin estate; *Ours* is the epic of his family, *The Suitcase* presents reflections on Russia and what was left behind, *The Craft* is the chronicle of a "literary failure," and *A Branch Office* and *A Foreign Woman* show the life and work of the émigré community. It seems that his whole life is spelled out in detail, while in his correspondence and articles on literature his creative methods are similarly described. In all these works there is an awareness, which can, if one so wishes, be called "postmodernist," of the extent to which any recorded fact is also a fiction. Much of Dovlatov's work examines the ways in which fictions, or myths, are created. Perhaps this is most clearly seen in *The Compromise,* where conflicting fictions, based on the same events, are juxtaposed with each other. Dovlatov's work is not, of course, truly documentary. Nevertheless, its "pseudo-documentary" character succeeds in creating what he himself termed a "feeling of reality" (*oshchushchenie real'nosti*). The atmosphere of Leningrad in the 1960s, the absurdity of Soviet reality seen in its punitive institutions, the hardships of émigré life in New York become real and precise. Dovlatov described his intention as follows:

> I try to arouse in the reader a sense of the norm . . . One of the most serious sensations associated with our times is the sense of the approaching absurd, when madness becomes a more or less normal phenomenon . . . In this way, madness and the absurd become something entirely natural, while the norm, that is to say, normal, natural, well-intentioned, calm, restrained, intelligent behavior—becomes an absolutely extraordinary thing.[31]

There is a substantial volume of serious critical comment on Dovlatov's work. Brodsky declared that Dovlatov was the only contemporary prose writer he had managed to read through to the end, and that the only essay he ever wrote about prose was about Dovlatov's prose. (His comments on its structural resemblance to poetry have been cited above.) Vladimov, who was an early admirer of Dovlatov's prose, showed an astute appreciation of the techniques involved: "I like your unstrained natural humor and your precise, simple, and elegant style—all those qualities that are attained with far greater effort and experience than any avant-garde 'inventions.' "[32]

Some critics have emphasized what they see as the "universality" of Dovlatov's writing. Sergei Vladimirovich Dediulin[33] compares him with the recent past in these terms:

> The phenomenon of samizdat is now history. We inherited from it a unique experience of free self-expression, which was heard in spite of the muteness imposed by officialdom. Time has shown the vitality of independent creativity, based not on the ideological and aesthetic criteria or the defunct premises of socialist realism, but on the personal experience of spiritual freedom and the realization of being part of world culture.[34]

Il'ia Serman finds a similar quality in his depiction of life in America, seeing one of the merits of Dovlatov's prose in the fact that the author relates to America as his natural habitat and allows his heroes to feel at home there:

> This is one of the indubitable virtues of Dovlatov's prose, which gives it that unusual complexion that is so difficult to achieve [. . .]. In Dovlatov the Western reader recognizes himself too, those mean little passions common to all men, those weaknesses, compromises, concessions, of which there are so many on life's paths. And it is perhaps in this universality of Dovlatov's humor that the principal quality of his prose lies.[35]

Dovlatov's narratives defy attempts to classify them. All comparisons of Dovlatov's prose with that of his contemporaries in the Soviet Union have led only to the rediscovery of its singularity. His particular combination of characteristics resulted in what is essentially a new genre. There are affinities with certain writers of the past, with Zoshchenko or Babel, perhaps, in his succinctness and his often vivid metaphors, or indeed with Chekhov, whom he wished to resemble. On the other hand, there is no resemblance to the "literature of fact" of the 1920s, which a superficial glance might see in his pseudo-documentalism. That was based on a far simpler epistemology, where "fact" was seen as an unproblematic category that could be directly juxtaposed with "invention." Dovlatov's work, in contrast, shows a network of competing fictions.

Critics are in broad agreement that Dovlatov has proved one of the most enduring, if not the most enduring, writer of his generation. Ian Shenkman argues that of the Leningrad writers of the time, only Dovlatov and Valery Popov stand out from the general background.[36] Mikhail Berg argues that in the 1970s and '80s the emigration was in competition with the underground culture in the Soviet Union, which also became a kind of internal emigration. However, with the end of the Soviet Union, this competition also ended. When this happened, practically all the participants in the underground culture disappeared from view. He names only three who did not: Joseph Brodsky, Boris Grois (who made the most successful academic career), and Sergei Dovlatov:

> Dovlatov returned to Russia after his death, but not as the author of *Novyi Amerikanets* (not an émigré product), but as a writer who had published in the *New Yorker,* and he came to occupy the only possible position for writers of the final wave of emigration—he became a star of mass literature. All the rest disappeared from view.[37]

Notes

CHAPTER 1

1. Arlen V. Bljum, ed., *Zensur in der UdSSR. Archivdokumente 1917–1991: Tsenzura v SSSR. Dokumenty 1917–1991* (Bochum: Projekt Verlag, 1999), 375 (emphasis in the original).

2. I. Erenburg, "O rabote pisatelia," *Znamia* 10 (1953).

3. V. Pomerantsev, "Ob iskrennosti v literature," *Novyi mir* 12 (1953).

4. V. M. Piskunov, *Chistyi ritm mnemoziny* (Moscow: Al'fa-M, 2005), 446.

5. Vladimir Maramzin, "Uroki Nabokova. Leningrad, 60–e gody," *Zvezda* 7 (2000): 202.

6. Boris Eikhenbaum, "O. Genri i teoriia novelly" ("O. Henry and the Theory of the Novella"), in *Literatura: Teoriia, kritika, polemika* (Chicago: Russian Language Specialties, 1969), 166.

7. Maurice Friedberg, *A Decade of Euphoria: Western Literature in Post-Stalin Russia, 1954–1964* (Bloomington and London: Indiana University Press, 1977).

8. This is discussed in detail in Raisa Orlova, *Kheminguei v Rossii* (*Hemingway in Russia*) (Ann Arbor, Mich: Ardis, 1985).

9. Petr Vail' and Aleksandr Genis, *60–e: Mir sovetskogo cheloveka* (*The Sixties: The World of Soviet Man*) (Moscow: Novoe Literaturnoe Obozrenie, 1996), 280.

10. There was an open polemic in the Soviet Union against such a standpoint, as can be seen, for example, in Mikhail Sholokhov's *Sud'ba cheloveka* (*The Fate of a Man*) which polemicizes with *The Old Man and the Sea.* In Viktor Nekrasov's *V okopakh Stalingrada* (*In the Trenches of Stalingrad*) one of the stories is called *Posviashchaetsia Khemingueiu* (*Dedicated to Hemingway*). Iurii Kazakov in his *Goluboe i zelenoe* (Blue and Green) also pays tribute to the Hemingway theme.

11. Konstantin Chugunov, "Soviet Critics on J. D. Salinger's Novel *The Catcher in the Rye*," *Soviet Literature* 5 (1962).

12. Slobodanka Vladiv-Glover, "Rediscovery of the Other," in *Russian*

Postmodernism: New Perspectives on Post-Soviet Culture, ed. Mikhail Epstein, Alexander Genis, and Slobodanka Vladiv-Glover (New York and Oxford: Berghahn Books, 1999), 32.

13. Alexander Genis, "Paradigms of Contemporary Culture," in Epstein, Genis, and Vladiv-Glover, *Russian Postmodernism,* 411.

14. Harvey Swados, "Must Writers Be Characters?" in *J. D. Salinger: Reviews, Essays and Critiques of "The Catcher in the Rye" and Other Fiction,* ed. M. Laser and N. Fruman (New York: Odyssey, 1963), 119–20.

15. Andrei Ar'ev, "Nasha malen'kaia zhizn'," in *Sergei Dovlatov, Sobranie prozy v trekh tomakh* (St. Petersburg: Limbus, 1993), 1:16.

16. Aleksandr Genis, "Sad kamnei: Sergei Dovlatov," *Zvezda* 7 (1997): 236.

17. Katerina Clark, *The Soviet Novel: History as Ritual* (Bloomington and Indianapolis: Indiana University Press, 2000), 189–234.

18. Benedikt Sarnov, *Nash sovetskii novoiaz: Malen'kaia entsiklopediia real'nogo sotsializma* (Moscow: Materik, 2002), 185–86.

19. B. I. Ivanov, "Evoliutsiia literaturnykh dvizhenii v piatidesiatye-vos'midesiatye gody," in *Istoriia leningradskoi nepodtsenzurnoi literatury: 1950–1980–e gody,* ed. B. I. Ivanov (St. Petersburg: Dean, 2000), 21–22.

20. R. Lachmann, *Demontazh krasnorechiia: Ritoricheskaiia traditsiia i poniatie poeticheskogo* (St. Petersburg: Akademicheskii proekt, 2001), translation from German; M. O. Chudakova, *Literatura sovetskogo proshlogo* (Moscow: Iazyki Russkoi Kul'tury, 2001); Evgenii Dobrenko, *The Making of the Soviet State Reader: Social and Aesthetic Contexts of the Reception of Soviet Literature* (Stanford, Calif.: Stanford University Press, 1997).

21. Piskunov, *Chistyi ritm mnemoziny,* 464.

22. In his later writing Vasilii Aksenov experimented with the grotesque. Aksenov himself dates this change to a meeting between members of the Soviet intelligentsia and Khrushchev in December 1962, when apparently Khrushchev shouted at the writers and painters, "Eto pederastia v iskusstve, a ne iskusstvo" (Irada Zeinalova, "40 let nazad Khrushchev ustroil raznos avangardistam," *Vesti nedeli* [December 14, 2002], http://www.vesti7.ru/news?id=1676). Aksenov left the Soviet Union in 1980 after the *Metropol'* affair.

23. Deming Brown, *The Last Years of Soviet Russian Literature* (Cambridge: Cambridge University Press, 1993), 60.

24. Sergei Dovlatov, "Literatura prodolzhaetsia," *Zvezda* 3 (1994): 117, first published in *Sintaksis* 10 (1982), Paris.

25. Sergei Dovlatov, *Skvoz' dzhungli bezumnoi zhizni: Pis'ma k rodnym i druz'iam* (St. Petersburg: Zvezda, 2003), 101.

26. "A spot of humanity is needed" ("Chelovechinka nuzhna"), says the editor to the protagonist in the story "An Interview." Sergei Dovlatov, "Interv'iu," *Iunost'* 6 (1974): 42.

27. Igor' Efimov, "Rasshiriaia granitsy vozmozhnogo: Interv'iu Alekseia Mi-

taeva," *Novyi bereg* 10 (2005), http://magazines.russ.ru/bereg/2005/10/ef19-pr.html (accessed March 27, 2006). I am grateful to Aleksei Mitaev for pointing this interview out to me.

28. Sergei Dovlatov, . . . *posledniaia kniga* . . . (St. Petersburg: Azbuka-klassika, 2001), 385.

29. Aleksei Khvostenko and Anri Volokhonsky were VERPA's most active participants. For details of this literary group, see Konstantin K. Kuzminsky and Gregory L. Kovalev, comp., *Antologiia noveishei russkoi poezii "U Goluboi Laguny"* [*The Blue Lagoon: Anthology of Modern Russian Poetry*], 5 vols. (Newtonville, Mass.: Oriental Research Partners, 1981–86), 2:226–390 and 679–735.

30. Vladimir Erl' was associated with this group. He continued to promote the Khelenukty after the group disintegrated around 1970. See S. Savitskii, "Khelenukty v teatre povsednevnosti. Leningrad: Vtoraia polovina 60–kh godov," *Novoe literaturnoe obozrenie* 30, no. 2 (1998): 210–59.

31. K. Iu. Rogov, ed., *Semidesiatye kak predmet istorii russkoi kul'tury* 1, no. 9 (1998): 18–19.

32. Andrei Bitov, "Prizraki i dushi," *Nezavisimaia gazeta* no. 17 (May 23, 2003): 14–15.

33. John Glad, *Besedy v izgnanii: Russkoe literaturnoe zarubezh'e* (Moscow: Knizhnaia Palata, 1991), 294.

34. Iurii Andropov, report to the Central Committee of the Communist Party of the U.S.S.R., marked "Top Secret," on December 21, 1970, no. 3461-A, p. 2, RFE/RL, document no. V119, unit 300/85/9/1, Open Society Archives, Budapest.

35. Clark, *The Soviet Novel*, 232–33.

36. Efimov, "Rasshiriaia granitsy vozmozhnogo."

37. See also Nikolai Mitrokhin, *Russkaia partiia: Dvizhenie russkikh natsionalistov SSSR, 1953–1985 gody* (Moscow: *Novoe Literaturnoe Obozrenie*, 2003), 624.

38. V. V. Ovechkin (1904–68), *Trudnaia vesna* (Moscow, 1956). E. I. Dorosh (1908–72), *Derevenskii dnevnik* (Moscow, 1958). I. A. Iashin (1913–68), "Rychagi," *Literaturnaia Moskva* no. 2 (1956).

39. Glad, *Besedy v izgnanii*, 255. (There were, of course, works by urban writers published in *Novyi mir*, such as V. T. Semin's (b. 1927) *Semero v odnom dome* (1965), or Georgii Vladimov's (1931–2003) *Bol'shaia ruda* (1961). Maksimov's views have to be taken with caution. The significance of Tvardovsky's editorship of *Novyi mir* is more complex and possibly not as narrow as Maksimov suggests. Lakshin, one of Tvardovsky's colleagues on the journal, describes the atmosphere of *Novyi mir* differently: "The critical section of *Novyi mir* consistently attacked the principal dogmas of socialist realism: the hierarchy of themes, associated with allegiance to class and party, the priority of the positive hero as a 'model for imitation,' the cult of 'organizers' and 'inspirers of society'; the

contrast between the 'great' and the 'small' truth, the apologia of the heroic feat at the expense of the heroism of daily life, and so on" (Vladimir Lakshin, *Puti zhurnal'nye. Iz literaturnoi polemiki 60–kh godov* [Moscow: Sovetskii Pisatel', 1990], 22). This view is echoed in a recent evaluation of the journal by Hosking: "As principal editor of the number-one journal of the Soviet Writers Union, Tvardovskii implemented the official doctrine of 'socialist realism,' but he gave it a twist that ultimately undermined it. He repudiated the aesthetic of the heroic rejection of *byt* (routine everyday life) in the name of the future" (Geoffrey Hosking, *Rulers and Victims: The Russians in the Soviet Union* [Cambridge, Mass., and London: Belknap Press of Harvard University Press, 2006], 342).

40. Vladimir Maramzin, " 'A vy kuda, rebiata?' Pamiati Vladimira Gubina," *Zvezda* 5 (2003): 232.

41. Application by B. B. Vakhtin, V. A. Gubin, I. M. Efimov, and V. R. Maramzin to Sovetskii Pisatel', January 6, 1965, East European Research Institute, Historical Archive, University of Bremen, F. 120.

42. Ibid.

43. The first *Gorozhane* collection contained 544 typewritten pages and, apart from D. Ia. Dar's introduction, included the following stories: By Vakhtin: "U pivnogo lar'ka" ("By the Beer Pavilion"), "Chelovek iz Vyshnego Volochka" ("The Man from Vyshnii Volochek"), "Mimo teplogo dyma" ("Past the Warm Smoke"), "Ee lichnoe delo" ("Her Private Business"), "Shiroka strana moia rodnaia" ("Wide Is My Native Land"), "Ochen' temnaia lichnost' " ("A Very Dark Horse"), "Nozhnitsy v more" ("Scissors in the Sea"), "Paporotnik i landyshi" ("Fern and Lily of the Valley"), "Anabioz" ("Anabiosis"), "Tri povesti s tremia epilogami" ("Three Novellas with Three Epilogues"), "Letchik Tiutchev, ispytatel' " ("Test Pilot Tiutchev"), "Van'ka Kain" ("Van'ka Cain"), "Abakasov—Udivlennye glaza" ("Abakasov—Amazed Eyes"), "Epilogi" ("Epilogues"); by Gubin: "Vosem' rasskazov iz tsikla 'U nas v mekhanicheskom tsekhe . . ." ("Eight Stories from Our Mechanical Workshop . . ."), "Zhen'ka s inoi planety" ("Zhen'ka from Another Planet"), "Tsvet neba" ("The Color of the Sky"), "Povest' " ("A Story"); by Efimov: "Skrytyi smysl zhizni" ("The Hidden Meaning of Life"), "Ia zabyl nazvanie" ("I Have Forgotten the Title"), "Avtomatika" ("Automation"), "Montekki i Kapuletti" ("Montagues and Capulets"), "Nachal'nik stenda" ("The Test Rig Supervisor"); and by Maramzin: "Den' zhizni polotera" ("A Day in the Life of a Floor-Polisher"), "Ia, s poshchechinoi v rukakh" ("Myself, Holding a Slap in the Face"), "Istoriia zhenit'by Ivana Petrovicha" ("The Story of Ivan Petrovich's Marriage"), "Povest' " ("A Story").

44. Nison Aleksandrovich Khodza (1906–78) wrote mainly stories for children, such as *Prodelki Khitriushkina* (*Mischievous Khitriushkin*) and a number of stories about V. I. Lenin, such as *Samyi chelovechnyi chelovek* (*The Most Humane of Humans*).

45. Reply to B. B. Vakhtin, V. A. Gubin, I. M. Efimov, and V. R. Maramzin

from Sovetskii Pisatel', East European Research Institute, Historical Archive, University of Bremen, F. 120.

46. This edition of *Molodoi Leningrad* was passed for typesetting on August 13, 1965, and it was approved for printing on December 1, 1965.

47. N. Khodza, "Retsenziia na rukopis' *Gorozhane,*" typescript, p. 3, courtesy of I. V. Vakhtina, St. Petersburg, 2002.

48. Ibid., 4.

49. Ibid.

50. Ibid.

51. Ibid., 11.

52. Vera Ketlinskaia (1906–76), a Soviet writer who also worked in the State Publishing House (Gosizdat) as an editor.

53. Vera Ketlinskaia, "Zametki na poliakh sbornika *Gorozhane,*" Perm', 1965, typescript, p. 17, courtesy of I. V. Vakhtina, St. Petersburg, 2002.

54. Emphases in original.

55. Ketlinskaia, "Zametki," 3.

56. Sergei Vol'f (1935–2005) was a journalist and a writer of children's stories, short stories, and poems, mainly circulated in samizdat, but his children's stories were published in the Soviet Union, and most of his poetry was first published in Russia in the 1990s.

57. Sergei Dovlatov, *Nevidimaia kniga (Epilog),* 1976. Typescript consulted at St. Petersburg "Memorial" Foundation.

58. Clark, *The Soviet Novel,* 232–33.

59. *Gorozhane o sebe,* typescript, p. 4, courtesy of I. V. Vakhtina, St. Petersburg, 2002.

60. Ibid., 5.

61. D. I. Dar (1910–80) was a writer and journalist. Toward the end of the 1950s he organized the literary association Golos iunosti (The Voice of Youth), which was very popular among the young writers and poets of the time. V. Sosnora, A. Kushner, B. Vakhtin, V. Maramzin, D. Bobyshev, I. Efimov, and many others attended the association's meetings. Many Leningrad poets and writers acknowledge Dar as their teacher. He was the husband of Vera Panova and the stepfather of Boris Vakhtin. In 1977 he was forced to emigrate to Israel. He was one of the most colorful and courageous figures in the alternative culture of Leningrad.

62. D. Ia. Dar, "Po povodu etogo sbornika" ("Concerning This Collection"). Introduction to *Gorozhane,* typescript, courtesy of I. V. Vakhtina, consulted in St. Petersburg, 2002.

63. Boris Shvartsman is a photographer. He was a friend of the writers and designed the covers of both collections of *Gorozhane.* Conversation with Boris Shvartsman, September 2002, St. Petersburg.

64. *Gorozhane,* vol. 2, Leningrad, 1966, typescript, courtesy of Nikolai

Borisovich Vakhtin, St. Petersburg, 2002. According to Oleg Iur'ev, Vakhtin's most popular works in Leningrad of the 1960s to the 1980s were "Letchik Tiutchev" and "Abakasov."

65. *Gorozhane,* vol. 2.

66. D. Dar's letter to the Presidium of the Fourth All-Union Congress of Soviet Writers (with copy to *Literaturnaia gazeta*), May 17, 1967, RFE/RL, document no. AC184, unit 300/85/9/4, Open Society Archives, Budapest.

67. *Gorozhane,* vol. 2.

68. Sergei Dovlatov, unpublished letter to V. Maramzin, April 8 (no year). Dovlatov's family archive, consulted in April 2007.

69. Brodsky was tried in 1964 on charges of parasitism and had been subjected to psychiatric examination. The judge decided that five years of forced labor in the "remote locality" of the Archangel forced-labor camp was the proper cure for his illness.

70. Ol'ga Sedakova, "O pogibshem literaturnom pokolenii—Pamiati Lioni Gubanova," *Volga* 6 (1990): 141.

71. Evgenii Dobrenko, *Formovka sovetskogo pisatelia: Sotsial'nye i esteticheskie istoki sovetskoi literaturnoi kul'tury* (St. Petersburg: Akademicheskii Proekt, 1999), 13.

72. Viacheslav Dolinin, "Nepodtsenzurnaia literatura i nepodtsenzurnaia pechat' (Leningrad 1950–80–kh godov)," in Ivanov, *Istoriia leningradskoi nepodtsenzurnoi literatury,* 10–11.

73. Abram Terts [Andrei Siniavskii], *Literaturnyi protsess v Rossii* (Moscow: Rossiiskii Gosudarstvennyi Gumanitarnyi Universitet, 2003), 21.

74. Radio Free Europe Research, 0953, April 1971, Open Society Archives, Budapest.

75. In *Formovka sovetskogo pisatelia,* Evgeny Dobrenko discusses the question of where people like Markov come from. He does not identify anybody in particular but calls them "prorabotchiki." His conclusion is that: "And so lack of talent became a fact of huge, fundamental social importance" (474).

76. Il'ia L'vovich Dvorkin (1937–1978) was a Leningrad writer.

77. This story was finally published in *Neva* 5 (1973): 8–19.

78. Evgeny Vsevolodovich Voevodin (1928–1981), a Leningrad prose writer, represented the Leningrad branch of the Union of Writers at Joseph Brodsky's trial.

79. Bljum, *Zensur in der UdSSR,* 459–60.

80. Aleksandr Fedorovich Popov was editor in chief of *Neva* from 1964 to 1979.

81. Dovlatov, *Nevidimaia kniga (Epilog),* 1976, 33.

82. *Avrora* is a monthly journal published since 1969.

83. Bljum, *Zensur in der UdSSR,* 443–47.

84. Ibid., 445.

85. Ibid., 446.

86. Ibid.

87. Ibid.

88. Ibid., 446–47.

89. Piskunov, *Chistyi ritm mnemoziny*, 429.

90. *Tamizdat* means publication "over there" (*tam*) and is the term used for the Soviet writers' illicit publication of their works in the West.

91. Alexei Yurchak, *Everything Was Forever, Until It Was No More: The Last Soviet Generation* (Princeton, N.J., and Oxford: Princeton University Press, 2006), 181.

92. Maramzin, "Uroki Nabokova. Leningrad, 60–e gody," 206.

93. Yurchak, *Everything Was Forever*, 127.

94. "Sometimes it turns out that in literature that is subject to censorship even the best things are bad, since the writer is unable or unwilling to speak the whole truth at the top of his voice, in the way that émigré or dissident authors do." Terts [Siniavskii], *Literaturnyi protsess v Rossii*, 347.

95. Ivanov, "Evoliutsiia literaturnykh dvizhenii v piatidesiatye-vos'midesiatye gody (Tezisy)," in Ivanov, *Istoriia leningradskoi nepodtsenzurnoi literatury*, 24.

96. Ibid., 23.

97. "Alesha Lavrent'ev" is a reference to Andrei Cherkasov, son of the actor Nikolai Cherkasov (see *The Suitcase*). Dovlatov spent summers at Cherkasov's dacha in Komarovo. In one of the earliest letters to his father written from there in 1954, he asks his father to bring him some plasticine and some table tennis balls. Sergei Dovlatov, "Iz pisem Sergeia Dovlatova k ottsu" ("Sergei Dovlatov's Letters to His Father"), published by Ksenia Mechik-Blank in *Zvezda* 1 (2008): 98. This correspondence also throws light on Dovlatov's relationship with his daughter Katia, whom he adored.

98. Dovlatov, unpublished letters to Donald Fiene, November 8 and 10 (ca. 1989). Dovlatov's family archive.

99. Donat Mechik, *Vesnushki: Naedine s synom* (St. Petersburg: Iskusstvo Veka, 1993), 19.

100. According to Ksana Mechik-Blank, Dovlatov's half sister, the family returned to Leningrad in 1944. In a personal letter to the author, she writes that shortly after Dovlatov's birth in Ufa, his mother and he moved to Novosibirsk, where the Pushkinsky Theater (Aleksandriisky), in which his father had worked since 1938, had been evacuated. Dovlatov's mother, Nora Sergeevna, had worked in a different theater in Leningrad, which had been evacuated to Ufa.

101. Dovlatov, unpublished letter to Donald Fiene, November 8 (ca. 1989). Dovlatov's family archive.

102. Ibid., November 10 (ca. 1989). Dovlatov's family archive.

103. Dovlatov, *Skvoz' dzhungli bezumnoi zhizni* (army letters to his father).

104. Dovlatov, *Skvoz' dzhungli bezumnoi zhizni*, 59.

105. Ibid., 85.

106. Ibid., 89–90.

107. Ibid., 70.

108. In conversation with Andrei Ar'ev, St. Petersburg, September 2002.

109. Dovlatov, *Skvoz' dzhungli bezumnoi zhizni,* 80.

110. Ibid., 96.

111. Ibid.

112. Valerii Khait, "Istoki muzyki: O pis'makh Sergeia Dovlatova ottsu iz armii," The World Odessit Club, http://www.odessitclub.org/reading_room/hait/dovlatov.htm (accessed January 17, 2007).

113. Mechik, *Vesnushki,* 26.

114. Dovlatov, *Skvoz' dzhungli bezumnoi zhizni,* 106.

115. Tat'iana Vol'tskaia, "Otkrytie pamiatnoi doski Sergeiu Dovlatovu v Peterburgskom morskom tekhnicheskom universitete," http://archive.svoboda.org/ll/cult/0104/ll.013104-1.asp. (accessed January 17, 2007).

116. Liudmila Shtern, *Dovlatov, dobryi moi priiatel'* (St. Petersburg: Azbuka-klassika, 2005), 38.

117. Ibid., 72.

118. In 1974 Dovlatov reports to his father that a prepublication copy of his book has been sent to Glavlit in Moscow, and that he has made "the final distortions recommended to me. Previously, the collection was called *Fiveways* (*Piat'uglov*)—after the place where I lived; I was ordered to change the name. Now it will be *City Tales* (*Gorodskie rasskazy*)." In Dovlatov, "Iz pisem Sergeia Dovlatova k ottsu," letter 11, p. 103.

119. *Petropol'* 5 (1994), St. Petersburg, 98.

120. In a letter to Georgy Vladimov (November 2, 1985, in Dovlatov, *Skvoz' dzhungli bezumnoi zhizni*), Dovlatov writes that he has written a 650-page novel called *Piat' uglov,* and sent it with great difficulty to the United States. The novel Dovlatov wrote in the 1970s in Leningrad also had the title *Odin na ringe* (*Alone in the Ring*). *Piat' uglov* (*Fiveways*) was just one of the possible titles. The typescript of this novel is kept in the family archive. The 1981 reworking of *Piat' uglov* has a subheading: "(roman v 3–kh chastiakh s epilogom)." Part 1 is "Odin na ringe," part 2 is "Boi s ten'iu," part 3 is "Sudeiskii protocol," and the last part is simply "Epilog: Nevidimaia kniga."

121. Tamara Zibunova, "Sergei Dovlatov's letters from Leningrad (1975–1978)," http://zibunova.narod.ru/dovlatov/DVLTRLEN.htm (accessed August 29, 2002).

122. Ibid.

123. Ibid. A copy of this play, *Chelovek, kotorogo ne bylo* (*The Man Who Never Was*), with the subtitle "P'esa dlia mladshikh shkol'nikov s fokusami, no bez obmana" ("A Play for Primary School Children with Tricks, But No Deception"), was discovered by chance in the archives of a theater in Pskov in 2001 and was performed in the same year to great critical acclaim.

124. I. P. Uvarova and K. Rogov, "Semidesiatye: Khronika kul'turnoi zhizni," in Rogov, *Semidesiatye kak predmet istorii russkoi kul'tury*, 55.

125. V. E. Dolinin, B. I. Ivanov, B.V. Ostanin, and D. Ia. Severiukhin, *Samizdat Leningrada, 1950–e–1980–e: Literaturnaia entsiklopediia* (Moscow: Novoe Literaturnoe Obozrenie, 2003), 497.

126. Zibunova, "Sergei Dovlatov's letters from Leningrad (1975–1978)." A mistake has evidently occurred at some point in the reporting of this episode. "Literatorskie mostki" (not "Literaturnye") is in fact part of the Volkovo cemetery, not the Aleksander Nevskii lavra (Alexander Nevsky Monastery).

127. Zibunova, "Sergei Dovlatov's letters from Leningrad (1975–1978)."

128. Sergei Dovlatov, *Nevidimaia kniga* (*The Invisible Book*) (Ann Arbor, Mich.: Ardis, 1977).

129. Zibunova, "Sergei Dovlatov's letters from Leningrad (1975–1978)."

130. Ibid.

131. Ibid.

132. Ibid.

133. Sergei Dovlatov, *Epistoliarnyi roman: Perepiska Sergeia Dovlatova s Igorem Efimovym* (Moscow: Izdatel'stvo Zakharov, 2001) (letter to Efimov, February 20, 1982).

134. Sally Laird, *Voices of Russian Literature: Interviews with Ten Contemporary Writers* (Oxford: Oxford University Press, 1999), 81.

CHAPTER 2

1. AC no. 1635, p. 1, box no. 300/85/9/5, Open Society Archives, Budapest. This text was published in *Russkaia mysl'*, April 11, 1974. In Moscow on March 5, 1974, Viktor Nekrasov made a statement ("Komu eto nuzhno?") to the press condemning the Soviet authorities for persecuting the intelligentsia and expressing deep regret about the drain of talented people abroad. The case of Nekrasov was interesting. He was a member of the Communist Party (joined in Stalingrad in 1943) and was given an official reprimand in 1972 on the grounds that he had his own opinion which differed from the party line.

2. NTS—Narodno-Trudovoi Soiuz was founded in 1930. It was a strongly anti-Soviet organization and was publisher of the journals *Posev* and *Grani*.

3. Iurii Andropov, to the Central Committee of the Communist Party of the U.S.S.R., July 16, 1978 (no. 1439), document 24-330A/4, Open Society Archives, Budapest.

4. John Glad, *Russia Abroad: Writers, History, Politics* (Tenafly, N.J.: Hermitage and Birchbark, 1999), 395.

5. Maria Rozanova, for example, describes the First Wave of Russian emigration as a "colossal cemetery." Siniavsky criticised Bunin's extremely conservative opinions, his view of Blok as a madman and a graphomaniac, and his

condemnation of the postsymbolists as a mass of hooligans and syphilitics. These, considers Siniavsky, were the prevailing views of the First Wave. In Glad, *Besedy v izgnanii,* 188.

6. L. D. Rzhevsky (1905–86), writer and critic, was taken prisoner by the Germans in 1941. After the war he settled in Germany and in the 1960s moved to the United States.

7. L. D. Rzhevskii, "Natsional'naia kul'tura i emigratsia: Doklad, prochitannyi na rasshirennom soveshchanii 'Poseva' 7–12 sentiabria 1951 g. v g. Limburge (Germania)," *Posev* (1952): 18.

8. Ibid., 25.

9. Ibid., 30.

10. Dolinin et al., *Samizdat Leningrada, 1950–e-1980–e,* 36.

11. The samizdat journal *Pamiat'* and later *Minuvshee* (published abroad) dedicated their issues to the study of Russian culture abroad.

12. *Kollektsiia: Peterburgskaia proza (leningradskii period), 1970–e* (St. Petersburg: Izdatel'stvo Ivana Limbakha, 2003), 8.

13. Glad, *Besedy v izgnanii,* 189–90.

14. Boris Khazanov, "Lotova zhena," *Literaturnaia gazeta* no. 5 (February 4, 1998): 10.

15. S. Karlinsky and Alfred Appel Jr., eds., *The Bitter Air of Exile: Russian Writers in the West, 1922–1972* (Berkeley: University of California Press, 1977), 6–7.

16. According to Ksana Mechik-Blank, Dovlatov exaggerated his own lack of English. He had studied English in his youth and read American literature in the original. He spoke English no worse than the average émigré, a standard he regarded as insufficient.

17. Dovlatov, unpublished letter to Raisa Orlova, February 4, 1988. Dovlatov's family archive. R. Orlova (wife of Lev Kopelev) was a specialist in American literature and the author of *Kheminguei v Rossii* (*Hemingway in Russia*) (Ann Arbor, Mich.: Ardis, 1985).

18. Dovlatov, *Skvoz' dzhungli bezumnoi zhizni,* 157 (letters to L. Shtern).

19. Ibid., 284 (letters to G. Vladimov).

20. Ibid.

21. Ibid., 157 (letters to L. Shtern).

22. Ibid., 196 (letters to Elena Dovlatova: "I liked both articles in *Russkaia mysl'* ").

23. See chapter 2, note 16.

24. Dovlatov, *Skvoz' dzhungli bezumnoi zhizni,* 208 (letters to Elena Dovlatova).

25. Prose writer, born 1937, emigrated in 1978.

26. Dovlatov, *Epistoliarnyi roman,* 7 (letter to Efimov, December 16, 1978).

27. Ibid., 8 (letter to Efimov, December 16, 1978).

28. Dovlatov, . . . *posledniaia kniga* . . . , 561. The text of the Russian translation of the interview is taken from *Sem' dnei* no. 48 (October 5, 1984), New York. In English this interview was published in *Threepenny Review* (Berkeley, California) (Winter 1985).

29. Dovlatov, *Skvoz' dzhungli bezumnoi zhizni,* 159 (letters to L. Shtern).

30. Dovlatov, *Epistoliarnyi roman,* 51 (letter to Efimov, August 27, 1979).

31. Sergei Dovlatov, *Marsh odinokikh* (Holyoke, Mass.: New England Publishing, 1983).

32. Sergei Dovlatov, "Posledniaia kolonka . . ." *Zvezda* 3 (1994): 54.

33. *Novyi Amerikanets* no. 24 (July 25–August 1, 1980): 2.

34. *Novyi Amerikanets* no. 34 (September 27–October 2, 1980): 2.

35. "Slovo i delo gosudarevo" was a system of criminal investigation in sixteenth- to eighteenth-century Russia. Every citizen was obliged to inform authorities of any known intention by any other citizen to discredit the tsar or the members of his family. The informer and the person informed on were then cross-examined and even tortured to obtain a confession.

36. Sergei Dovlatov, "Ispytanie svobodoi," *Novaia gazeta,* April 23–29, 1983, pp. 17–18.

37. Glad, *Russia Abroad,* 427.

38. Dovlatov, "Ispytanie svobodoi," 17–18.

39. Dovlatov, *Skvoz' dzhungli bezumnoi zhizni,* 315 (letters to I. Gubareva).

40. Lev Losev, "Russkii pisatel' Sergei Dovlatov," in "Pamiati Sergeia Dovlatova," special issue, *Petropol'* 5 (1994): 196.

41. Kurt Vonnegut, "Letter to Sergei Dovlatov," *Zvezda* 3 (1994): 173.

42. Dovlatov, unpublished letter to Anne Frydman. Dovlatov's family archive.

43. Dovlatov, unpublished letter to Donald Fiene. Dovlatov's family archive.

44. Dovlatov, unpublished letter to Anne Frydman. Dovlatov's family archive.

45. Ibid.

46. Dovlatov, unpublished letter to Anne Frydman. Dovlatov's family archive.

47. Ibid.

48. Ibid.

49. Dovlatov, unpublished letter to Donald Fiene. Dovlatov's family archive.

50. Ibid.

51. Sergei Dovlatov, "Kak izdavat'sia na Zapade," in *The Third Wave: Russian Literature in Emigration,* ed. Olga Matich and Michael Heim (Ann Arbor, Mich.: Ardis, 1984), 239.

52. Ibid., 239.

53. Ibid., 241.

54. Dovlatov, unpublished letter to Andrei Ar'ev. Dovlatov's family archive.

55. Andrei Ar'ev, unpublished letter to Sergei Dovlatov. Dovlatov's family archive.

56. Dovlatov, unpublished letter to Donald Fiene. Dovlatov's family archive.

57. Ibid.

58. Dovlatov, . . . *posledniaia kniga* . . . , 560–61.

59. Ibid., 559.

60. This excerpt by G. Vladimov was enclosed in an unpublished letter to Naum Sagalovskii, and the quotation cited here was later published in *Slovo(Word)* no. 9 (1991): 95 (translation by Brian Baer). This issue of *Slovo(Word)* was dedicated to the memory of Sergei Dovlatov.

61. Dovlatov, unpublished letter to Leva. Dovlatov's family archive.

62. Dovlatov, unpublished letter to Donald Fiene. Dovlatov's family archive.

63. Dovlatov, unpublished letters to Andrei Ar'ev and Donald Fiene. Dovlatov's family archive.

64. Glad, *Besedy v izgnanii,* 91.

CHAPTER 3

1. For a discussion of this point, see Igor' Sukhikh, *Sergei Dovlatov: Vremia, mesto, sud'ba* (St. Petersburg: Kul'tInform, 1996).

2. Israel Metter, "Ia rad, chto my s Vami dozhili do strannykh vremen . . . Vosem' poslednikh pisem Sergeia Dovlatova," *Iunost'* 5 (1993): 71.

3. When in 1989 Eesti Raamat wanted to publish the old collection, Dovlatov was horrified and wrote to Zibunova (January 6, 1989) that those stories that comprised the 1973 collection simply did not exist. (Zibunova, "Sergei Dovlatov's letters from Leningrad [1975–1978].")

4. Dovlatov, *Epistoliarnyi roman* (letter to Efimov, May 21, 1981).

5. Ibid. (letter from Efimov, May 30, 1981).

6. Ibid. (letter to Efimov, June 4, 1981).

7. Ibid. (letter to Efimov, January 21, 1982).

8. This line of Pushkin's is translated by Avril Pyman in A. Pushkin, *Selected Works* (Moscow: Progress, 1974), 61.

9. Dovlatov, *Skvoz' dzhungli bezumnoi zhizni,* 239 (letter to Naum Sagalovskii, June 21, 1986).

10. Dovlatov, *Epistoliarnyi roman* (letter from Efimov, June 18, 1982).

11. Miroslav Drozda, "Narrativnaia maska v khudozhestvennoi proze," in *Russian Literature,* vol. 12 (Amsterdam: North-Holland, 1982), 274–75.

12. Karen Ryan-Hayes, "Narrative Strategies in the Works of Sergej Dovlatov," *RLJ* 16, no. 153 (1992): 159.

13. Ibid., 160.

14. Dovlatov, *Skvoz' dzhungli bezumnoi zhizni,* 93.

15. Ibid., 18–19.

16. Ibid., 101.

17. In the Soviet Union, Constitution Day was celebrated on December 5.

18. Dovlatov, *Skvoz' dzhungli bezumnoi zhizni,* 39.

19. The poem is called "Leningradtsy v Komi," in Dovlatov, *Skvoz' dzhungli bezumnoi zhizni,* 41.

20. Dovlatov, *Skvoz' dzhungli bezumnoi zhizni,* 32.

21. See, for example, A. Solzhenitsyn's *GULAG Archipelago* and Shalamov's *Kolyma Tales.*

22. Dovlatov, *Skvoz' dzhungli bezumnoi zhizni,* 49. In a large number of his letters, Dovlatov discusses the process of writing poetry. He seeks his father's opinion on the poems he has written and also offers his own criticism of them. In the special issue of *Peterburgskii literator* dedicated to Sergei Dovlatov, there is an article by Mark Shlafman, who served in the same regiment as Dovlatov. He recalls that at the compulsory study time Dovlatov was always busy writing poems. In the same article, Shlafman also tells the story of how Dovlatov became acquainted with Svetlana Men'shikova, with whom Dovlatov became very friendly and to whom he dedicated a number of poems.

23. Sergei Dovlatov, "SSSR—Bol'shaia zona," *Novyi Amerikanets* no. 72 (July 5–11, 1981): 20–22. (This article is illustrated by contemporary artists.) Reprinted in Sergei Dovlatov, *Rech' bez povoda . . . ili Kolonki redaktora: Ranee neizdannye materialy* (Moscow: Makhaon i mezhdunarodnyi fond Sergeia Dovlatova, 2006), 177–86.

24. Dovlatov, *Rech' bez povoda,* 178.

25. Ibid., 181.

26. Ibid.

27. V. Shklovskii, *Energiia zabluzhdeniia* (Moscow: Sovetskii Pisatel', 1981), 349.

28. Eikhenbaum, "O. Genri i teoriia novelly," 177.

29. The title *Marsh odinokikh* (*March of the Lonely*) in the four-volume collected works now refers to a collection of editorials Dovlatov wrote for the newspaper *Novyi Amerikanets.*

30. Dovlatov, *Nevidimaia kniga (Epilog),* 1976, pp. 30–31.

31. Ibid., 32.

32. Mark Lipovetskii, "Uchites', tvari, kak zhit': Paranoia, zona i literaturnyi kontekst," *Znamia* 5 (1997): 208.

33. Dovlatov, *Skvoz' dzhungli bezumnoi zhizni,* 103.

34. Dovlatov, *Rech' bez povoda,* 181.

35. A. N. Latynina, "Dostoevskii i ekzistentsializm," in *Dostoevskii—Khudozhnik i myslitel'* (Moscow: Khudozhestvennaia Literatura, 1972), 210–58.

36. Sergei Dovlatov, "Made in USA: Mini-istoria dzhaza," *Novyi Amerikanets* no. 107 (March 2–8, 1982): 15.

37. Ibid.

38. Il'ia Serman, "Teatr Sergeia Dovlatova" ("The Theater of Sergei Dovlatov"), *Grani* 136 (1985): 149–50.

39. I. A. Mart'ianova, *Kinovek russkogo teksta. Paradoks literaturnoi kinematografichnosti* (Saga: St. Petersburg, 2001), 127.

40. Ar'ev, "Nasha malen'kaia zhizn' "; Sukhikh, *Sergei Dovlatov;* Genis, "Sad kamnei," 235–38.

41. L. S. Vygotskii, *Psikhologia iskusstva* (Moscow: Iskusstvo, 1968), 191.

42. Viktor Kulle, "Bessmertnyi variant prostogo cheloveka," in *Sergei Dovlatov: Tvorchestvo, lichnost', sud'ba,* ed. Andrei Ar'ev (St. Petersburg: Zvezda, 1999), 243.

43. Anne Frydman received a prize for the best translation of 1986 for her translation of Dovlatov's *Zone.*

44. Sergei Dovlatov, "Straight Ahead," *New Yorker,* January 25, 1982, pp. 35–41.

45. Dovlatov, *Epistoliarnyi roman* (letter to Efimov, November 8, 1984).

46. Dovlatov, unpublished letter to Anne Frydman. Dovlatov's family archive.

47. Ibid. Much of the discussion in this letter is about the translation of the story "My First Cousin," which was published in the *New Yorker* on December 5, 1983, pp. 50–58.

48. Sergei Dovlatov, "Predstavlenie," *Kontinent* 39 (1984). This story was adapted for the theater in 1993 as *Komediia strogogo rezhima.* The plot is slightly different. The action is set in 1970 as the Soviet Union is preparing to celebrate Lenin's centenary. Not to be outdone, the camp commander decides to have the prisoners put on a play about Lenin's life. However, the ensuing preparations turn everything upside down and seem to offer a chance to plot an escape.

49. Dovlatov, *Epistoliarnyi roman* (letter to Efimov, November 1983).

50. On prison camp theater, see N. B. Kuziakina, "A byl li 'fol'klornyi' teatr v GULAGe?" in *Fol'klor i kul'turnaia sreda GULAGa,* comp. V. S. Bakhtin and B. N. Putilov (St. Petersburg: Fond Kul'turnaia Initsiativa, 1994).

51. Serman, "Teatr Sergeia Dovlatova," 159.

52. F. Dostoevskii, *Zapiski iz mertvogo doma: Sobranie sochinenii v 10 tomakh* (Moscow: Gosudarstvennoe Izdatel'stvo Khudozhestvennoi Literatury, 1956), 3:553.

53. To the best of my knowledge, there is no such playwright. One of the most successful attempts to put Lenin on stage was by the popular Soviet dramatist Nikolai Fedorovich Pogodin (pseudonym of N. F. Stukalov) in his historical trilogy *Chelovek s ruzh'em, Kremlevskie kuranty,* and *Tret'ia pateticheskaia.*

54. Bakhtin and Putilov, *Fol'klor i kul'turnaia sreda GULAGa,* 53.

55. N. L. Leiderman and M. N. Lipovetskii, *Sovremennaia russkaia literatura, 1950–1990-e gody* (Moscow: Akademia, 2003), 2:602.

56. Mark Lipovetsky, *Russian Postmodernist Fiction: Dialogue with Chaos* (Armonk, N.Y., and London: M. E. Sharpe, 1999), 282.

57. Dovlatov, *Skvoz' dzhungli bezumnoi zhizni,* 52.

58. This letter had previously appeared in Russian in an article in *Novyi Amerikanets.* See Dovlatov, *Rech' bez povoda,* 177–86.

59. Dovlatov, *Skvoz' dzhungli bezumnoi zhizni,* 97.

60. An earlier version of this article was called "Kirpich s pogonami" ("Blockhead with Epaulettes") and was published in *Russkaia mysl'.*

61. Sergei Dovlatov, "Kirpich s lampasami," *Novyi Amerikanets* no. 58 (March 17–23, 1981): 10.

62. Ibid.

63. Dovlatov, *Skvoz' dzhungli bezumnoi zhizni,* 51. See also "Razvod po-emigrantski," in Dovlatov, *Rech' bez povoda,* 311–18.

64. Lev Mak (b. 1939, Odessa) was a poet and weight lifter, mentioned in *Skvoz' dzhungli bezumnoi zhizni,* 42.

65. Dovlatov, *Skvoz' dzhungli bezumnoi zhizni,* 73.

66. Sukhikh, *Sergei Dovlatov,* 120.

67. Ibid.

68. Hemingway's novel was based on his personal experiences as a young ambulance driver during World War I. He falls in love with a nurse, Catherine. After many twists in the plot the couple escape to Switzerland, where Catherine gives birth to a stillborn child and hemorrhages to death.

69. This story was published with slight variations in *Russkaia mysl'* no. 3395.

70. Dovlatov, *Skvoz' dzhungli bezumnoi zhizni,* 288. In a letter to Vladimov, Dovlatov remarks that in Russia or among Russian émigrés, if somebody steals something and gets away with it, he is regarded as a real businessman.

71. The expression "It'll be stronger than Goethe's *Faust*" is also quoted in *The Sanctuary.* It refers, according to legend, to what Stalin inscribed on Gorky's quite ordinary *Devushka i smert',* but, like all Stalin's profundities, it was endlessly quoted.

72. Sukhikh, *Sergei Dovlatov,* 119. The various Mariks, Shuriks, and Toliks from whom Katia "escapes" by marrying Captain Egorov can be seen as Dovlatov poking fun at his "youth prose" colleagues (*SS* 2:77).

73. E. Markshtain, "Sovetskii iazyk i russkie pisateli," *Voprosy literatury* 1 (1995): 98–112.

74. P. Vail' and A. Genis, "Iskusstvo avtoportreta" ("The Art of Self-Portrait"), *Zvezda* 3 (1994): 180.

75. Igor' Sukhikh, "Golos: O remesle pisatelia D." ("The Voice: On the Craft of the Writer D."), *Zvezda* 3 (1994): 181.

76. Ar'ev, *Sergei Dovlatov: Tvorchestvo, lichnost', sud'ba,* 275.

77. Glad, *Besedy v izgnanii,* 90.

78. Iurii Karabchievskii, "Pamiati Sergeia Dovlatova" ("In Memory of Sergei Dovlatov"), *Literaturnaia gazeta,* no. 35 (August 29, 1990): 7.

79. Glad, *Besedy v izgnanii,* 90.

80. Boris Rokhlin recalls that Dovlatov used to tell his stories a couple of times to an informal gathering of his friends first, and only then put them down on paper. (See the special issue of *Zvezda* 3 [1994], dedicated to Sergei Dovlatov, pp. 132–33.)

81. Whether consciously or not, Dovlatov quotes this line from Zamiatin's story "Bich Bozhii"; see E. Zamiatin, *Povesti i rasskazy* (Munich: TSOPE, 1963), 254.

CHAPTER 4

1. Dovlatov, "Iz pisem Sergeia Dovlatova k ottsu," letter 6, p. 100.

2. Sergei Dovlatov, *Kompromiss* (New York: Serebrianyi Vek, 1981). This edition contains only eleven compromises, the story "Lishnii" [Superfluous] being omitted. References in this chapter are to Sergei Dovlatov, *Sobranie sochinenii v chetyrekh tomakh,* 4 vols., ed. A. Iu. Ar'ev (St. Petersburg: Azbuka, 2000), in which the full text of *The Compromise* is published. Dovlatov's life in Estonia is also reflected in some stories in *Zona: Zapiski nadziratelia* (*The Zone: A Prison Camp Guard's Story*) (Ann Arbor, Mich.: Ermitazh, 1982) (this differs from the 1993 and 2000 editions in that "Predstavlenie" was not included). Dovlatov also refers to life in Estonia in *Nevidimaia kniga* (*The Invisible Book*), first published in the United States in 1977 (Ann Arbor, Mich.: Ardis, 1977), and later incorporated into *Remeslo* (Ann Arbor, Mich.: Ardis, 1985). The dates of composition have not been fully ascertained. In 1984 Dovlatov also published some more stories about the phantasmagoria of Soviet journalism: "Dopolneniia k *Kompromissu,*" in *Almanac Panorama* no. 171 (July 20–27, 1984), which were not republished in any editions of the collected works.

3. The issues of *Sovetskaia Estonia* from 1972 to 1975 were consulted in the Estonian National Library in Tallinn in May 1999.

4. Vail' and Genis, *Mir sovetskogo cheloveka,* 283.

5. Dovlatov, *Nevidimaia kniga (Epilog),* 1976, title page.

6. Ibid., 65.

7. Ibid., 75.

8. Ibid.

9. Ibid., 76.

10. Ibid., 79.

11. Zibunova, "Sergei Dovlatov's letters from Leningrad (1975–1978)."

12. AC no. 2180, pp. 1–2, box no. 300/85/9/70; and AS no. 2342, box no. 300/85/9/75, Open Society Archives, Budapest.

13. Nevertheless Dovlatov writes: "I work at the newspaper cynically and without interest, for the money"; in Dovlatov, "Iz pisem Sergeia Dovlatova k ottsu," letter 7, pp. 100–101.

14. Totalitarian language (including German and Italian) has been discussed in many studies. Soviet clichés have been a constant source of parody, from such writers as Zoshchenko, Platonov, Mayakovsky, and Erdman in early years, to the later and bolder Solzhenitsyn and Voinovich, culminating in the sots-art movement in the period of stagnation, with Prigov, Kibirov, Sorokin, and others.

15. See, for example, Evgeny Popov's collages of Soviet phraseology in *Prekrasnost' zhizni: Glavy iz romana 'Romana s gazetoi', kotoryi nikogda ne budet nachat i zakonchen* (Moscow: Moskovskii Rabochii, 1999).

16. In conversation with M. Roginsky and E. Skul'skaia, Tallinn, May 1999.

17. According to Roginsky, everybody was encouraged to use different names to sign their articles. This would give the appearance that many contributors of different nationalities were contributing to the paper. This particular surname Ader occurs in Zhbankov's story in the "Eighth Compromise": "I [Zhbankov] was colonel Ader's orderly" (*SS* 1:316).

18. Sergei Dovlatov (signed S. Ader), "Na svoem meste," *Sovetskaia Estonia,* December 5, 1974, p. 3.

19. Sergei Dovlatov (signed S. Ader), "Ishchu cheloveka," *Sovetskaia Estonia,* January 16, 1975, p. 3.

20. Sergei Dovlatov (signed R. Must), "Dlia odnoi loshadinoi sily," *Sovetskaia Estonia,* April 24, 1973, p. 3.

21. Sergei Dovlatov (signed S. Ader), "Proektiruiutsia . . . noski," *Sovetskaia Estonia,* August 15, 1973, p. 3.

22. Sergei Dovlatov (signed S. Ader), "Vysokoe polozhenie," *Sovetskaia Estonia,* July 4, 1973, p. 3.

23. Sergei Dovlatov (signed S. Ader), "Chisto, svetlo . . . ," *Sovetskaia Estonia,* December 14, 1973, p. 4.

24. Sergei Dovlatov, "Polchasa v srednevekov'e," *Sovetskaia Estonia,* October 5, 1973, p. 4.

25. Ibid.

26. Sergei Dovlatov, "K zvezdam!" *Sovetskaia Estonia,* November 1, 1973, p. 4.

27. Sergei Dovlatov, "Ia khochu vam rasskazat' . . . ," *Sovetskaia Estonia,* August 20, 1973, p. 4.

28. Sergei Dovlatov, "Ia znaiu silu slov . . . ," *Sovetskaia Estonia,* November 20, 1973, p. 4.

29. Also reprinted in Dovlatov, *Rech' bez povoda,* 362.

30. In the family archive there is a 1976–77 version of *The Compromise,*

which had a subheading: "Povest'v 4–kh deistviiakh." This version did not include the newspaper quotations. Some of the titles in this version differ from those in the later published version, as do the names of some characters and the sequence of the stories. The four parts of the 1976–77 version had the following titles: (1) "Ch'ia-to smert'," (2) "Vysokie muzhchiny," (3) "Ishchu cheloveka," (4) "Chernym po belomu (Dokumental'naia povest')." Part 4 had an epigraph by Brodsky: "A garrulous and empty trade, / My oar can splash in any waters" ("Boltlivoe, pustoe remeslo, / V liuboi vode pleshchi moe veslo"). Two parts are dated: the first to February 1977, and the third to March 19, 1977.

31. *Grani* 135 (1985): 105–43.

32. *Kontinent* 19 (1979): 49–70.

33. There was no opportunity to consult these newspapers and confirm the existence of the articles quoted.

34. Compare *Sovetskaia Estonia,* August 1, 1974: "The thunder of the victory salute has long since died away, but time and again the war veterans take out yellowing newspaper cuttings and photographs, old notebooks, and mementos of times long past. These recollections are infinitely dear to us." ("Davno otgremeli pobednye zalpy saliuta, no veterany voiny snova i snova dostaiut *pozheltevshie gazetnye vyrezki* i fotosnimki, starye bloknoty i relikvii davnikh vremen. Nam beskonechno dorogi eti vospominaniia"; italics mine).

35. Glad, *Besedy v izgnanii,* 90.

36. Sergei Dovlatov, "Nariad dlia Marsianina," *Sovetskaia Estonia,* October 18, 1973.

37. Sergei Dovlatov (signed S. Ader), "Samaia trudnaia distantsiia," *Sovetskaia Estonia,* June 4, 1973.

38. Peter Henry and Katya Young, *Gazeta: Clippings from the Soviet Press* (London: Collets, 1983).

39. Roger Fowler, *Language in the News: Discourse and Ideology in the Press* (London and New York: Routledge, 1991), 120.

40. Ibid., 2.

41. In his *Zapisnye knizhki* (*Notebooks*) and then in a reworked form in *The Craft,* Dovlatov gives his definition of a compromise as "a system of reciprocal concessions for the sake of a common cause" (*SS* 3:150). The "common cause" in this case was the newspaper *Novyi Amerikanets* (*The New American*), which Dovlatov and his friends founded in the United States. One of the friends had his own idea of how a compromise should be achieved: "I know what a compromise is. My compromise is like this: Moker goes down on his knees and in the presence of everyone promises to work honestly. Then maybe I will forgive him . . ." (*SS* 3:150). This "public genuflection" is the Soviet ideological machinery's idea of a compromise. Dovlatov's description of "compromises" within the American system in his "Nevidimaia gazeta" ("Invisible Newspaper"), the sec-

ond part of *Remeslo* (*The Craft*), is a related but separate issue that goes beyond the scope of the present study.

42. Zhbankov also appears in *The Compromise* as a fictional character.

43. Sergei Dovlatov (signed S. Ader), "Moi beglyi papa," *Sovetskaia Estonia,* October 13, 1973.

44. In her article (read in typescript) "Bol'shoi chelovek v malen'kom gorode" ("A Big Man in a Small Town"), Elena Skul'skaia recalls that the editor in chief, Turonok, was very suspicious of poetry quotations, particularly from living poets. The longer the poet was dead, the less the threat he represented for the Soviet authorities: "One day someone quoted Arthur Rimbaud. He was summoned. In the doorway, full of self-confidence, he nonchalantly announced: 'Rimbaud is dead, Genrikh Frantsevich, long ago.' 'This is a provocation!' Turonok stamped his foot at him. 'You've been trying to drag into the pages of our party press propaganda for the American green beret Rambo.' "

45. In coversation with Elena Skul'skaia, Tallinn, May 1999.

46. According to Vail' and Genis, the phrase "Druzhba narodov" came to be exclusively used in a humorous context (Vail' and Genis, *Mir sovetskogo cheloveka*). See also, for example, Vladimir Vysotskii's song "Marafon" in Vladimir Vysotskii, *Pesni i stikhi* (New York: Literaturnoe Zarubezh'e, 1981):

And Sam Brook from Guinea beat me by a lap,
And all around people were saying to me: Sam's a friend
Sam, they said, is our friend from Guinea.

A gvineets Sem Bruk oboshel menia na krug,
A eshche vse vokrug mne govorili: Sem—drug
Sem—nash, govorili, gvineiskii drug.

47. According to Elena Skul'skaia, Boris Shtein was at that time the literary consultant of the Writers Union's Russian section in Estonia, to whom Dovlatov submitted his collection of *City Tales: Fiveways.* E. Skul'skaia, "Chto byvaet posle smerti" ("What Is There After Death"), introduction to Dovlatov's Esto nian edition (typescript).

48. On September 8, 1975, Dovlatov's and Zibunova's daughter Aleksandra was born. Dovlatov, too, wrote a poem:

There was a little slip-up,
We were expecting a son, and then
A little mite was born into the world
About seven days late.
She's not from the moon, she's not from Mars,
On about the seventh day,
From Karl Marx Prospect
They'll bring her home to us.

There is no greater reward for me,
Than this joint child of ours.
We are all very, very glad.
Goodbye for now, your Wino.

Vyshla legkaia promashka,
Zhdali syna, a zatem,
Rodilas' na svet bukashka
S opozdan'em dnei na sem'.
Ne s Luny ona, ne s Marsa,
Den' primerno na sed'moi
Nam s prospekta Karla Marksa
Privezut ee domoi.
Netu bol'shei mne nagrady,
Chem rebenok obshchii nash.
Vse my ochen', ochen' rady,
Do svidan'ia, tvoi alkash.

(Zibunova, "Sergei Dovlatov's letters from Leningrad [1975–1978]." Postcard sent to the hospital on September 8–12, 1975.)

49. In the *Notebooks* it is Sergei Vol'f who comments on "The Technology of Sex." He says it is not a good book, as it is deficient in humor: "I open the first page, and it says—'Introduction' ('Insertion'). What a way to start!" ("Otkryvaiu pervuiu stranitsu, napisano—'Vvedenie.' Razve tak mozhno?"] (*SS* 4:153).

50. Daniil Smirnov, "Sergei Dovlatov i ego kompromissy," *Literaturnoe rassledovanie* (November 15, 2004), http://www.sergeidovlatov.com/chas_15-11-2004.html (accessed March 17, 2005).

51. Vladimir Novikov, "Bednyi Eros: Nepod"emnaia tema sovremennoi slovesnosti," *Novyi mir* 11, no. 883 (1998): 180–91.

52. Ibid.

53. "Polveka v efire: Seks v sovremennoi russkoi literature" (roundtable discussion: Ivan Tolstoy, Sergei Dovlatov and Petr Vail'), Radio Free Europe, http://archive.svoboda.org/50/files.1988.html (accessed August 27, 2007).

54. The story "Lishnii" was written in 1984 and first published in *Grani* 135 (1985). This is what Dovlatov says: "I've written a huge story with the title 'Superfluous'—the old theme of the 'superfluous man': Onegin, Pechorin, Grigorii Melekhov, Ostap Bender . . . So far I've sent the story to Vladimov at *Grani* [. . .] The elder Serman has praised it fairly energetically." In Dovlatov, *Epistoliarnyi roman* (letter to Efimov, October 2, 1984).

55. Evgenii Rein, "Neskol'ko slov vdogonku," in *Maloizvestnyi Dovlatov* (St. Petersburg: Limbus, 1993), 398.

56. *Russkaia mysl,'* no. 3432 (September 30, 1982): 7. This title possibly refers to a song that was popular in the 1960s: "Kapitan, kapitan, ulybnites' / ved' ulybka eto flag korablia."

57. Fowler, *Language in the News,* 4.

58. Henry and Young, *Gazeta,* 10.

59. V. M. Boguslavskii, "O nekotorykh osobennostiakh iazyka gazety," *Russkii iazyk za rubezhom* 4 (1968).

60. Allan Bell, *The Language of News Media* (Oxford, Eng., and Cambridge, Mass.: Blackwell, 1991), 155.

61. Dovlatov, *Skvoz' dzhungli bezumnoi zhizni,* 156 (letters to L. Shtern).

62. Lydia Ginzburg, *On Psychological Prose,* trans. and ed. J. Rosengrant (Princeton, N.J.: Princeton University Press, 1991), 8.

CHAPTER 5

1. Dovlatov, *Skvoz' dzhungli bezumnoi zhizni,* 63–64.

2. Ivan Tolstoy, "Sergei Dovlatov po obe storony okeana" (interview with Andrei Ar'ev), Radio Free Europe, http://www.svoboda.org/programs/OTB/2001/OBT.092601.asp (accessed March 24, 2006).

3. Sergei Dovlatov, " 'Pskovskie otkrytki (iz romana *Piat' uglov*)," *Novyi Amerikanets* no. 34 (September 27–October 2, 1980): 26.

4. Ibid., 26.

5. Sergei Dovlatov, *Naslednik,* chapter 1, "Poslednee leto" (marked "Draft version, not for publication"). Typescript in Dovlatov's family archive, consulted April 2007.

6. The end of this first part was completed by Dovlatov in April 1978. The letter to Zibunova (see chapter 1) in which he informs her of his decision to leave is dated April 2, 1978.

7. Dovlatov, *Naslednik,* chapter 1, "Poslednee leto," 71.

8. Ibid.

9. Ibid., 32.

10. Sergei Dovlatov, "Tak pit' ili ne pit'?!" *Novyi Amerikanets* no. 6 (March 21–27, 1980): 7.

11. Dovlatov, *Epistoliarnyi roman* (letter to Efimov, June 4, 1981).

12. Ibid. (letter to Efimov, February 20, 1982).

13. Ibid. (letter to Efimov, January 31, 1983).

14. Ibid. (letter to Efimov, June 21, 1983).

15. Paul Debreczeny, *Social Functions of Literature: Alexander Pushkin and Russian Culture* (Stanford, Calif.: Stanford University Press, 1997), 219.

16. Ibid., 244.

17. Irina Rodnianskaia, *Literaturnoe semiletie (1987–1994)* (Moscow: Knizhnyi Sad, 1995), 264–72: "Dawn broke and on a distant path / the liberated prisoner walked" ("Vzoshla zaria, Tropoi dalekoi / *Osvobozhdennyi plennik shel*"). This quotation from one of Pushkin's early poems Rodnianskaia considers the key to understanding Siniavsky's notion of freedom.

18. "I wrote *Walks with Pushkin* in circumstances as subject to censorship

as can be imagined. I wrote it in 1966–68 as a continuation of my final statement at the trial (only in a different style)—in defense of free creativity. It isn't 'criticism' of any sort, and Solzhenitsyn is wrong to call me a 'critic' in this instance. It is the lyrical prose of Abram Terts, in which I attempt, in my own way, to declare my love for Pushkin and to express my gratitude to his shade, that saved me in the camp." A. Siniavskii, "Chtenie v serdtsakh," *Sintaksis* 17 (1987): 191–206.

19. Susanne Fusso, "The Romantic Tradition," in *The Cambridge Companion to the Classic Russian Novel,* ed. Malcolm V. Jones and Robin F. Miller (Cambridge: Cambridge University Press, 1998), 185.

20. This event is recorded as a true story by Evgenii Rein, *Mne skuchno bez Dovlatova: Novye stseny iz zhizni moskovskoi bogemy* (*I Miss Dovlatov: The Life of Moscow's Bohème*) (St. Petersburg: Limbus, 1997).

21. Dovlatov, *Skvoz' dzhungli bezumnoi zhizni,* 155.

22. Iu. M. Lotman, *Struktura khudozhestvennogo teksta* (Moscow: Iskusstvo, 1970), 288: "The movement of the hero *within* his allotted space does not constitute an event."

23. Brown, *Last Years of Soviet Russian Literature,* 80.

24. Sergei Dovlatov, "Derevnia v 'chernom spiske,' " *Russkaia mysl'* no. 3546 (December 6, 1984): 7.

25. Sergei Dovlatov, "Esli b garmoshka umela . . . ," *Almanac Panorama* no. 198 (January 25–February 1, 1985): 25.

26. Dovlatov, "Derevnia v 'chernom spiske,' " 7.

27. Ibid.

28. Ibid.

29. Dovlatov, "Esli b garmoshka umela . . . ," 25.

30. It was in the village of Berezino (Sosnovo in the novel) that Dovlatov rented a room from the forester, who is the prototype of Mikhail Ivanych in the story. According to Ar'iev, editor of *Zvezda* and Dovlatov's close friend, he was pleased with what Dovlatov wrote about him: "He has nothing bad to say about me as a forester."

31. Professor Bialyi is examining Gur'ianov:

> "Have you read *The Tales of Belkin*"?
> "Never got round to it somehow," Lenia replied. "Do you recommend it?"
> "Yes," Bialyi restrained himself, "I emphatically recommend you to read that book."
> Lenia came to see Bialyi a month later and said:
> "I've read it. Thank you. There was a lot I liked."
> "What exactly did you like?" Bialyi inquired.
> Lenia tensed himself, remembered, and answered.
> "The story *Dombrovskii.*" (*SS* 2:265)

32. A. S. Pushkin, *Sochineniia v trekh tomakh* (Moscow: Gosudarstvennoe Izdatel'stvo Khudozhestvennoi Literatury, 1958), 3:346–47.

33. Ibid., 3:347; A. Pushkin, *Dubrovsky,* trans. Robert Chandler (London: Hesperus, 2003), 32–33.

34. Pushkin, *Sochineniia v trekh tomakh,* 3:489.

35. Sukhikh, *Sergei Dovlatov,* 154.

36. The year 1998 saw the publication of Bulgarin's letters and denunciations: *Vidok Figliarin, Pis'ma i agenturnye zapiski Faddeia Bulgarina v III otdelenie,* compilation, introduction, and commentary by A. I. Reitblat (Moscow: Novoe Literaturnoe Obozrenie, 1998), 704; A. G. Altunian, *'Politicheskoe mnenie' Faddeia Bulgarina: Ideino-stilisticheskii analiz zapisok F. V. Bulgarina k Nikolaiu I.* (Moscow: Universitet RAO, 1998). A considerable polemic has since arisen in the press about the morality of informing (*Voprosy literatury, Novoe literaturnoe obozrenie, Nezavisimaia gazeta*).

37. A. S. Makarenko (1888–1939) was a Soviet educationalist. His main idea was the education of children through the collective.

38. E. A. Tudorovskaia describes this episode in her article "Putevoditel' po *Zapovedniku,*" in the special issue of *Zvezda* 3 (1994) dedicated to Sergei Dovlatov. The scene where the narrator is being "educated" by the KGB reminds Tudorovskaia of A. K. Tolstoy's satirical poem "Son Popova" ("Popov's Dream"). For detailed analysis, see pp. 197–98. The objectives of the Third Department are in no way different from those of the KGB, as Tudorovskaia indicates.

39. Pushkin, as his letters to A. N. Woolfe (of August 1825 and October 10, 1825, from Mikhailovskoe) testify, was hoping to travel abroad either illegally or under the pretext of having an operation abroad. Pushkin was advised to have his operation on an aneurysm in Pskov, which he declined. In *Perepiska A. S. Pushkina v dvukh tomakh* (Moscow: Khudozhestvennaia Literatura, 1982), 2:180, 181.

40. Pushkin is often considered by many critics as the founder (*osnovopolozhnik*) of Russian prose. However, reservations have also been expressed about Pushkin's prose. This is discussed in R. Gregg, "Pushkin's Novelistic Prose: A Dead End?" *Slavic Review* 57, no.1 (Spring 1998): 1–27.

41. Glad, *Besedy v izgnanii,* 94.

42. Quoted from A. Lezhnev, *Proza Pushkina: Opyt stilevogo issledovaniia* (Moscow: Khudozhestvennaia Literature, 1966), 22.

43. Iu. M. Lotman, "Analiz poeticheskogo teksta," in Iu. M. Lotman, *O poetakh i poezii* (St. Petersburg: Iskusstvo-SPB, 1996), 38.

44. Lezhnev, *Proza Pushkina,* 30.

45. Ibid., 33.

46. My italics.

47. Lezhnev, *Proza Pushkina,* 69.

48. Dal's *Russkie skazki—Piatok pervyi* (1832) are stylized fairy tales and were hailed by many (including Pushkin) for the invention of a folk narrator.

49. The parallel here is A. S. Shishkov (1754–1841) and his society Beseda Liubitelei Russkogo Slova and Shishkov's defense of the Russian literary language against Europeanization.

50. This issue is discussed in detail by S. Schwarzband, *The History of Belkin's Tales* (Jerusalem: Magness and Hebrew University, 1993).

51. V. V. Vinogradov, *Stil' Pushkina* (Moscow, 1941), 535.

52. Pushkin, *Sochineniia v trekh tomakh,* 232.

53. Iu. M. Lotman, *O russkoi literature: Stat'i, i issledovaniia: istoriia russkoi prozy, teoriia literatury* (St. Petersburg: Iskusstvo-SPB, 1997), 601.

CHAPTER 6

1. The Radio Free Europe Archive contains a sound recording of the *Suitcase* stories read by Dovlatov himself.

2. "In each instance and for every thing there is a corresponding focus on its provenance: a present, black market, theft, and so on." Dovlatov, *Epistoliarnyi roman,* 345 and 359 (letters to Efimov on January 4 and December 8, 1985).

3. Dovlatov, *Skvoz' dzhungli bezumnoi zhizni,* 274 (letters to the Vladimovs).

4. The published English translation gives the title as "The Finnish Crepe Socks," but it was, of course, nylon socks that were the deficit product in the Soviet Union of the time, and I have changed the translation accordingly. It seems likely that Dovlatov used this unusual formulation because otherwise he would have had two consecutive words beginning with the letter *n.*

5. T. V. Tsiv'ian, "*Veshchi* iz chemodana Sergeia Dovlatova i byvshaia (?) sovetskaia model' mira," *Russian Literature* 37 (1995): 647–58.

6. Mark Lipovetskii, "Zabudem slovo 'realism'?" *Literaturnaia gazeta* no. 48 (December 4, 1991): 10.

7. Ar'ev, *Sergei Dovlatov: Tvorchestvo, lichnost', sud'ba,* 289.

8. Ibid.

9. I. P. Smirnov, "Strannichestvo i skital'chestvo v russkoi kul'ture," *Zvezda* 5 (2005): 206.

10. Conversation with Boris Ivanov, St. Petersburg, September 2002. Boris Ivanovich Ivanov (b. 1928) is a nonconformist writer and critic; in the 1960s he published in official publications and later in samizdat.

11. Albert Camus, *The Myth of Sisyphus,* trans. Justin O'Brien (Harmondsworth: Penguin Books, 1979), 21.

12. Lipovetskii, "Zabudem slovo 'realizm'?" 10.

13. V. N. Toporov, *Peterburgskii tekst russkoi literatury* (St. Petersburg: Iskusstvo-SPb, 2003), 65.

14. Dovlatov, unpublished letter to Naum Sagalovskii, November 2. Dovlatov's family archive.

15. Dovlatov, *Skvoz' dzhungli bezumnoi zhizni,* 282 (letters to the Vladimovs).

16. Ibid., 274 (letters to the Vladimovs).

17. Tsiv'ian, "*Veshchi,*" 653.

18. Tsiv'ian, "*Veshchi,*" 656.

19. A. Bocharov, *Literatura i vremia: Iz tvorcheskogo opyta prozy 60–x-80–x godov* (Moscow: Khudozhestvennaia Literatura, 1988), 362.

20. In *Marsh odinokikh* (*March of the Lonely*) Dovlatov has an editorial which is full of nostalgia: "Zima k N'iu-Iorku podstupaet . . ." He uses the same quotation from Blok: "As Blok has it . . . 'But even as you are, my Russia, you are of all lands the dearest to me.' It's painful to finish the conversation on a sad note. Grigorii Ryskin was right when he wrote: 'What we had was a fate. Not a biography, a fate. And we didn't surrender . . .' Of course, Ryskin isn't Blok. But then we weren't beautiful ladies either" (*SS* 4:455).

21. Sukhikh, *Sergei Dovlatov,* 194. The quotation is from Blok's poem of 1914: "Greshit' besstydno, neprobudno . . ." ("To sin without shame or awakening . . .").

22. Dovlatov, *Skvoz' dzhungli bezumnoi zhizni,* 274 (letters to the Vladimovs).

23. See chapter 2 above; Vail' and Genis, "Iskusstvo avtoportreta," 177–80; E. Dovlatova, comp., *O Dovlatove: Stat'i, retsenzii, vospominaniia* (New York and Tver': Drugie berega, 2001), 7.

24. Nikita Eliseev, "Chelovecheskii golos," *Novyi mir* 11, no. 835 (1994): 212.

25. G. Belaia, *Don-Kikhoty 20–kh godov:'Pereval' i sud'ba ego idei* (Moscow: Sovetskii Pisatel', 1989), 167–68.

26. Dovlatov, . . . *posledniaia kniga* . . . , 383.

27. Eliseev, "Chelovecheskii golos," 212–25.

28. Lidia Ginzburg, *O literaturnom geroe* (Leningrad: Sovetskii Pisatel', 1979), 150.

29. Ibid., 165.

30. Andrei Ar'ev, "Sergei Dovlatov po obe storony okeana," Radio Free Europe, http://www.svoboda.org/programs/OTB/2001/OBT.092601.asp (accessed March 24, 2006).

31. Toporov, *Peterburgskii tekst,* 80.

32. In *Dovlatov, dobryi moi priiatel',* Shtern (p. 72) quotes one of Dovlatov's letters from the summer of 1969 in which he describes his work as a stonemason in a workshop at Piskarevka.

33. Sergei Dovlatov, "The Officer's Belt," trans. J. Turnbull, in *Russian*

Short Stories from Pushkin to Buida, ed. Robert Chandler (London: Penguin Books, 2005), 367.

34. Dovlatov, *Skvoz' dzhungli bezumnoi zhizni,* 90 (army letters to his father).

35. *SS* 4:138. This point also appears in *The Zone,* in one of the letters to the publisher (*SS* 2:88).

36. Sarnov, *Nash sovetskii novoiaz,* 594.

37. In one of his letters to his father, Dovlatov writes that he is preparing to take the driving test. In Dovlatov, *Skvoz' dzhungli bezumnoi zhizni,* 46 (army letters to his father).

38. Fernand Léger (1881–1955) was a French painter and architectural designer and one of the most influential cubist painters. He was fascinated by the workingman and by machinery.

39. Dovlatov, *Epistoliarnyi roman,* 362 (letter to Efimov, December 14, 1985).

40. Eliseev, "Chelovecheskii golos," 215.

41. Nikolai Konstantinovich Cherkasov (1903–66) was a Soviet People's (*narodnyi*) actor. He played many roles in cinema and theater and was a member of the Leningrad Drama Theater from 1933. He was the recipient of numerous state prizes and was a deputy to the Supreme Soviet of the U.S.S.R. in 1950–58.

42. Transcript of radio broadcast *Kaleidoskop,* January 14, 1981; author S. Dovlatov, editor V. Rossinskii. RFE/RL, document no. 41 700-R, unit 300/85/13/105, Open Society Archives, Budapest.

43. See also "Nobody is Perfect," in which Dovlatov discusses the inferiority complex that affects even geniuses. In Dovlatov, *Rech'bez povoda,* 161–72. The subtext of "Fernand Léger's Jacket" is from Mark Twain's *Prince and the Pauper,* which tells the story of two young boys who have misconceptions about each other's lifestyles.

44. Bocharov, *Literatura i vremia,* 221.

45. Eliseev, "Chelovecheskii golos," 221.

46. This story was translated into English by A. Bouis and published in the *New Yorker* as "The Photo Album," March 27, 1989, pp. 43–47.

47. Elena Dovlatova tells her own story of her acquaintance with Sergei Dovlatov in an interview, "Elena i Katia v okrestnostiakh Sergeia," published in *Ogonek* 35 (August 1998): 42–46.

48. In real life Dovlatov had a cousin Boris, who was three years older than Dovlatov. Boris died a few years ago in St. Petersburg. The Russian word *brat* can mean either "brother" or "cousin," and in the fictional text the relationship of the two remains somewhat ambiguous.

49. Leiderman and Lipovetskii, *Sovremennaia russkaia literatura,* 2:608.

50. See also an analysis of Boris's character in Leiderman and Lipovetskii, *Sovremennaia russkaia literatura,* 2:608.

51. Ibid., 2:609.

52. The descendant of von Schlippenbach in the story is proud, despite the Swedish defeat, to be mentioned in Pushkin's poem *Poltava,* which he quotes to the narrator:

Beaten back by gunshot, all confused.
Battalions roll back into dust.
Rosen escapes through the throng,
And impetuous Shlippenbakh surrenders.

Pal'boi otbitye druzhiny.
Meshaias', katiatsia vo prakh.
Ukhodit Rozen skvoz' tesniny,
Sdaetsia pylkii Shlippenbakh.

A real person called Nikolai Andreevich Shlippenbakh lives in Sestroretsk. He was Dovlatov's friend and did plan to make a film about Peter the Great. The rest of the story is invented. (Sof'ia Shirokova, interview with Katya Dovlatova, http://izvestia.ru/interview/article3096390 [accessed September 18, 2006].)

53. Wolmar Anton von Schlippenbach (1653–1721) took part in the Battle of Poltava (1709). He was captured, kept imprisoned, and when he was released in 1712, entered the service of the tsar.

54. Tsiv'ian, "*Veshchi,*" 655.

55. Such situations where the narrator is recognized by former camp inmates recur frequently in Dovlatov's stories. An example is his meeting with the criminal Strakhuil in America. See *SS* 3:433 .

56. In the translation the name Schlippenbach is changed to Filimonov, and the whole theme of the role of Russia/U.S.S.R. is cut out.

57. Sergei Dovlatov, "Kapitan ulybnites'," *Russkaia mysl'* no. 3432 (September 30, 1982): 7.

58. Il'ia Erenburg (1891–1967) was a prolific Russian writer and journalist. *The Thirteen Pipes* was written in 1922, published in 1923.

59. Il'ia Erenburg, *Sobranie sochinenii v deviati tomakh* (Moscow: Khudozhestvennaia Literatura, 1962), 1:477.

60. Ibid., 1:516.

61. Vaginov (Wagenheim) Konstantin Konstantinovich (1899–1934) was a poet and prose writer. The author of *Novels Goat Song* (1928), *Works and Days of Svistunov* (1929), and *Bambochada* (1931), Vaginov was an avid collector. He collected anything from old coins to candy wrappers and cigarette packets.

62. E. S. Shevchenko, " 'Teatral'nyi kod dovlatovskoi prozy," *Vestnik SamGU* 10/2, no. 50 (2006): 65.

63. Tsiv'ian, "*Veshchi,*" 652.

64. Eliseev, "Chelovecheskii golos," 223.

65. "Vinograd" was first published in *Slovo(Word)* 9 (1991), and "Staryi petukh, zapechennyi v gline" ("An Old Cockerel Baked in Clay") was first published in the special issue of *Zvezda* 3 (1994) dedicated to Sergei Dovlatov, pp. 55–63.

66. Eliseev, "Chelovecheskii golos," 220.

67. Ibid., 221. The quotation comes from *King Lear,* act 2, scene 2, in Pasternak's translation.

68. Dovlatov, *Rech' bez povoda,* 266.

69. Dovlatov's radio script for Radio Liberty, written on the occasion of the publication of I. Suslov's book *Vykhod k moriu* by the publishing house Serebrianyi vek. Hoover Institution Archives, RFE/RL, box no. 11402, folder ID: m-cop, February 3–4, 1983.

CHAPTER 7

1. I have used the title of the published translation, *Ours,* in order to avoid confusion, but would have preferred to translate it as *Our Folks.*

2. All of these stories were translated by Anne Frydman and published in the *New Yorker:* "My First Cousin" ("Moi starshii brat"), December 5, 1983, pp. 50–58; "The Colonel Says I Love You" ("Polkovnik govorit—Liubliu"), May 5, 1986, pp. 42–47; "Uncle Aron" ("Tetkin muzh—Aron"), October 20, 1986, p. 40; "Uncle Leopold" ("Diadia Leopol'd"), July 13, 1987, pp. 25–30; "Father" ("Otets"), November 30, 1987, pp. 34–36.

3. Mechik, *Vesnushki,* 29.

4. "I can't wait for the *New Yorker* journal to come out. After that everything will get easier. They may give me some kind of stipend. And altogether, it's like being awarded a medal. Or the Stalin prize." In Dovlatov, "Iz pisem Sergeia Dovlatova k ottsu," letter 16, p. 107.

5. Dovlatov, *Epistoliarnyi roman* (letter to Efimov, November 28, 1979).

6. Ibid. (letter to Efimov, November 24–25, 1982).

7. Karen L. Ryan-Hayes, "The Family Chronicle Revisited: Dovlatov's *Ours,*" in *Contemporary Russian Satire: A Genre Study* (Cambridge: Cambridge University Press, 1995), 161.

8. Ibid., 162.

9. Ibid., 161.

10. Ibid., 157.

11. The story "Moi ded Isaak" was first published in the Krug chteniia (World of Books) section of *Novyi Amerikanets* no. 2 (February 8–14, 1980).

12. Dovlatov, "Iz pisem Sergeia Dovlatova k ottsu," 111.

13. The story "Ded Stepan" was first published in the Krug chteniia (World of Books) section of *Novyi Amerikanets* no. 8 (March 28–April 3, 1980).

14. Sergei Dovlatov, “Papa i bludnye deti,” review of Raisa Orlova’s *Khem-inguei v Rossii,* in *Grani* 138 (1985): 294.

15. There is a story in *Novyi Amerikanets* which can be seen as a precursor of this chapter: Sergei Dovlatov, “Mister Tvister edet v Kostromu,” *Novyi Amer-ikanets* no. 97 (December 19–25, 1981): 24–26.

16. Dovlatov, unpublished letter to R. Orlova, February 4, 1988. Dovlatov’s family archive.

17. Dovlatov, *Skvoz’ dzhungli bezumnoi zhizni,* 43.

18. Dovlatov, unpublished letter to R. Orlova. Dovlatov’s family archive.

19. Dovlatov’s father, Donat Mechik, also emigrated and lived in the United States.

20. Unpublished letter to R. Orlova. Dovlatov’s family archive.

21. Leiderman and Lipovetskii, *Sovremennaia russkaia literatura,* 2:604.

22. Dovlatov, “Made in USA: Mini-istoria dzhaza,” 15.

23. Zibunova, “Sergei Dovlatov’s letters from New York (2),” letter October 8, 1987.

24. Dovlatov, unpublished letter to Anne Frydman, September 22. Dovlatov’s family archive.

25. Dovlatov, *Epistoliarnyi roman* (letter from Efimov, January 21, 1983).

26. Glad, *Besedy v izgnanii,* 90.

27. Dovlatov, . . . *posledniaia kniga* . . . , 289.

28. Aleksandr Kushner, *Apollon v snegu: Zametki na poliakh* (Leningrad: Sovetskii Pisatel’, 1991), 433.

29. Ar’ev, “Po obe storony okeana.”

30. Dovlatov, unpublished letter to Anne Frydman, March 8. Dovlatov’s family archive. *Ours* was published in 1989.

31. Dovlatov, “Interv’iu,” 47.

32. Ibid.

33. This is where the title “The Colonel Says I Love You” originates.

34. Dovlatov, *Rech’ bez povoda,* 300–307.

35. Dovlatov, unpublished letter to Naum Sagalovskii, December 31, ca. 1986. Dovlatov’s family archive.

36. Serman, “Teatr Sergeia Dovlatova,” 139–40.

37. Metter, “Ia rad,” 72.

38. Ibid.

39. Dovlatov, *Skvoz’ dzhungli bezumnoi zhizni,* 344.

40. Ryan-Hayes, “Family Chronicle Revisited,” 160.

41. Ginzburg, *O literaturnom geroe,* 86–87.

42. Ibid., 87.

43. Ibid., 86–87.

44. Dovlatov, *Skvoz’ dzhungli bezumnoi zhizni,* 357.

45. Ibid., 331.

CHAPTER 8

1. *Almanac Panorama* was a weekly, published in Los Angeles from 1980. *Inostranka* was published there beginning with no. 270, June 13, 1986. It proved impossible to locate and consult this publication.

2. Dovlatov, *Skvoz' dzhungli bezumnoi zhizni,* 290.

3. Dovlatov, letter to Naum Sagalovskii, February 27. Dovlatov's family archive.

4. Sergei Dovlavtov, "Telezhka s khlebnym kvasom," *Novyi Amerikanets,* September 28, 29, and 30, 1983.

5. Dovlatov, *Rech' bez povoda,* 138.

6. Dovlatov, "Telezhka s khlebnym kvasom," September 29, 1983, p. 5.

7. Ibid.

8. Dovlatov, "Telezhka s khlebnym kvasom," September 30, 1983, p. 6.

9. Hoover Institution Archives, Stanford, Calif., collection title: RFE/RL 11413, box no.: 06726509, folder ID: M-Copies, March 7–8, 1983.

10. Dovlatov, "Telezhka s khlebnym kvasom," September 29, 1983, p. 5.

11. Short biographical details of Mark Popovskii and a review of his book *Delo akademika Vavilova* (published by Serebrianyi vek) were published by S. Dovlatov: "V zhanre detektiva," *Sem' dnei* no. 54 (1984), New York.

12. Dovlatov, *Skvoz' dzhungli bezumnoi zhizni,* 281.

13. Dovlatov, *Skvoz' dzhungli bezumnoi zhizni,* 280 (letters to the Vladimovs).

14. Dovlatov, "Telezhka s khlebnym kvasom," September 28, 1983, p. 8.

15. Kirill Vladimirovich Kostsinsky (real name Uspensky; 1915–84) was a writer and mentor of young Leningrad writers and poets, including Brodsky and Dovlatov. He was arrested in the 1960s for anti-Soviet propaganda and spent four years in a Mordovian prison camp. In the camp he started compiling his dictionary of camp slang. In 1978, he emigrated to the United States. Kostsinky taught at Harvard University. His memoir, *V teni Bol'shogo doma* (*In the Shadow of the Big House*), was published in the United States (Tenafly, N.J.: Hermitage, 1987).

16. Alla Marchenko, ". . . Obratitsia v pechal'noe . . . ," *Literaturnaia gazeta* no. 20 (May 16, 1990): 4.

17. Ibid.

18. Dovlatov, *Skvoz' dzhungli bezumnoi zhizni,* 297.

19. Ryan-Hayes, "Narrative Strategies," 171.

20. Dovlatov, *Epistoliarnyi roman* (letter to Efimov, February 20, 1982).

21. Ibid.

22. Besides the obvious reference to Shakespeare's *Tempest,* Ariel' is also the title of a book by the fantasy writer A. Beliaev (1884–1942). Beliaev's *Ariel'*

(1941) is a story about a human being who can fly in reality as others can in their dreams. Beliaev's novels were among the most popular books in the U.S.S.R. in the 1940s and 1950s, and it is virtually certain that Dovlatov would have known them.

23. Dovlatov, *Skvoz' dzhungli bezumnoi zhizni,* 351; the story "Vstretilis', pogovorili" was published in *Kontinent* no. 58 (1988).

24. Dovlatov, letter to Donald Fiene, November 14 (ca. 1987). Dovlatov's family archive.

25. Matich and Heim, *The Third Wave.* In his correspondence with Vladimov, Dovlatov remarks that at the opening ceremony V. P. Nekrasov summed up the aim of the symposium as follows: "The purpose of this conference is for me to embrace Emka Korzhavin and have a drink with Aleshkovskii." The organizers of the conference, in Dovlatov's view, naively supposed its aim to be the "failure of totalitarianism."

26. Matich and Heim, *The Third Wave,* 53–62.

27. Dovlatov, *Skvoz' dzhungli bezumnoi zhizni,* 297.

28. Dovlatov, letter to Naum Sagalovskii, February 27. Dovlatov's family archive.

29. Petr Vail', "Geroi vremeni: Sergei Dovlatov—Tsentral'nyi personazh knig Sergeia Dovlatova," Radio Free Europe, http://www.svoboda.org/programs/cicles/hero/05.asp (accessed July 2, 2007).

30. Dovlatov, . . . *posledniaia kniga* . . . , 298.

31. Ibid., 489.

32. Asia Pekurovskaia, *Kogda sluchilos' pet' SD i mne* (St. Petersburg: Symposium, 2001).

33. Interview with A. Pekurovskaia in *Terra Nova* no. 4 (October 2005), http://muza-usa.net/2005_04/2005-04-03.htm (accessed July 2, 2007).

34. Andrei Ar'ev, "On vse vremia khotel vernut'sia domoi," Komsomol'skaia Pravda, http://www.sergeidovlatov.com (accessed January 17, 2007).

35. Dovlatov, . . . *posledniaia kniga* . . . , 296.

36. Ar'ev, "On vse vremia khotel vernut'sia domoi."

37. The author of the song is I. Kashezheva, and the composer is A. Ostrovskii.

38. Shtern, *Dovlatov, dobryi moi priiatel',* 130.

39. Dovlatov, *Skvoz' dzhungli bezumnoi zhizni,* 283–84.

40. *Piat' uglov,* chapter 1, "Odin na ringe," 34. Dovlatov's family archive, consulted May 2007.

41. The poem in question is O. Mandelstam, "I Shubert na vode, i Motsart v ptich'em game."

42. Dovlatov, letter to Asia Pekurovskaia, January 1962, Komi Republic, Nezavisimaia gazeta, http://exlibris.ng.ru/before/2001-08-16/8_box.html (accessed January 10, 2007).

43. Pekurovskaia, *Kogda sluchilos' pet' SD i mne.*

44. Viacheslav Kuritsyn, "Vesti iz *Filiala,* ili duratskaia retsenziia na prozu Sergeia Dovlatova," *Literaturnoe obozrenie* 12 (1990): 42.

45. Ibid.

46. I. A. Mart'ianova, *Kinovek russkogo teksta: Paradoks literaturnoi kinematografichnosti* (St. Petersburg: Saga, 2001), 127.

47. Ibid., 129.

48. Ryan-Hayes, "Narrative Strategies," 171.

49. Ar'ev, "Po obe storony okeana."

50. Dovlatov, . . . *posledniaia kniga* . . . , 489.

51. Sergei Dovlatov, "Papa i bludnye deti," 294.

52. Andrei Ar'ev, "Teatralizovannyi realism: O povesti Sergeia Dovlatova *Filial,*" *Zvezda* 10 (1989): 20.

53. Vladislav Kulakov, "Minimalism: Strategiia i taktika," *Novoe literaturnoe obozrenie* no. 23 (1997), http://magazines.russ.ru/nlo/1997/23/kulackov.html (accessed January 10, 2007).

54. Dovlatov, letter to Naum Sagalovskii, October 13, ca. 1984. Dovlatov's family archive.

CHAPTER 9

1. Dovlatov, letter to Naum Sagalovskii, February 28, ca. 1985–86. Dovlatov's family archive.

2. Aleksandr Genis in *Dovlatov i okrestnosti* asserts somewhat hyperbolically that Dovlatov's impact on Estonia was greater than that of the Soviet Union.

3. On December 20, 1969, Dovlatov mentions in a letter to Liudmila Shtern that he has written a children's story about the circus. Dovlatov, *Skvoz' dzhungli bezumnoi zhizni,* 150.

4. *Intimate Town,* film, directed by Kristina Davidjants, Tartu, Estonia, 2003.

5. Smirnov, "Sergei Dovlatov i ego kompromissy."

6. Ibid.

7. Vladimir Fedorov, "Priiatno poznakomit'sia: Pardon—ia Sergei Dovlatov," Petrovskii Kur'er, http://kurier.spb.ru/pk/home/20042003/st4.shtm (accessed November 17, 2006).

8. Pavel Efimovich Matveiko (b. 1952) lives in Moscow. He is a graduate of the Mendeleev University in Moscow, and leader of the musical ensemble "Svoiasi."

9. Oleg Vitalievich Gorodetskii (b. 1972), a graduate of the Moscow Medical Academy, works as a doctor. He is the organizer of a number of bard festivals.

10. Maria Leonidovnaa Shkol'nik (b. 1975), a graduate of the Moscow State University Faculty of Journalism, lives in New York and Moscow.

11. Shamil' Valiev, "Khronicheskii emigrant," *Novoe Vremia* no. 36 (2004), http://www.sergeidovlatov.com/update.html (accessed November 17, 2006).

12. Ibid. Bashinform reported that a plaque was to be placed on the house where Sergei Dovlatov lived in Ufa (capital of Bashkorstan) (Gulmara Khasanova, comp., "Tatar-Bashkir Report: August, 2001; Daily Review from Tatarstan," Radio Free Europe, http://www.rferl.org/reports/tb-daily-report/2001/08/0-310801.asp [accessed November 19, 2008]).

13. Valiev, "Khronicheskii emigrant."

14. Dovlatov, letter to Naum Sagalovskii, March 31, ca. 1986. Dovlatov's family archive.

15. Valiev, "Khronicheskii emigrant."

16. Ibid.

17. Aleksandr Donetskii, "V poiskakh pskovskogo Dovlatova," Pskovskaia zemlia, http://culture.pskov.ru/ru/persons/object/85/publications/57 (accessed November 17, 2006).

18. Ibid.

19. Ibid.

20. Ibid.

21. Ibid.

22. P. Basinskii, "Bukval'nyi Dovlatov," *Rossiiskaia gazeta,* http://www.rg.ru/2006/08/21/dovlatov.html (accessed September 7, 2006).

23. St. Petersburg TV Channel 5, "Avtoportret Sergeia Dovlatova v kamne," http://www.5-tv.ru/programs (accessed September 4, 2007).

24. Piotr Vail', "Sergei Dovlatov: Between Reality and Literature," Radio Free Europe.

25. Genis, "Sad Kamnei," 235.

26. Glad, *Besedy v izgnanii,* 89.

27. Ibid., 85.

28. "Geroi vremeni."

29. Ibid.

30. Dovlatov, *Skvoz' dzhungli bezumnoi zhizni,* 290 (letters to the Vladimovs).

31. Glad, *Besedy v izgnanii,* 93.

32. Dovlatov, *Skvoz' dzhungli bezumnoi zhizni,* 258.

33. Sergei Vladimirovich Dediulin (b. 1950) emigrated to Paris in 1981.

34. V. E. Dolinin and D. Ia. Severiukhin, "Preodolen'e nemoty," in Dolinin et al., *Samizdat Leningrada, 1950–e-1980–e,* 7–54.

35. Il'ia Serman, "Grazhdanin dvukh mirov," in Dovlatova, *O Dovlatove: Stat'i, retsenzii, vospominaniia,* 161.

36. Ian Shenkman, "Seks popolam s rybnoi lovlei: Na odnogo udachlivogo eksperimentatora prikhoditsia diuzhina neudachnikov," *Nezavisimaia gazeta,* June 3, 2004, p. 4.

37. Mikhail Berg, "Neofitsial'naia leningradskaia literarura i emigratsia (leningradskii underground 1970–e—pervaia polovina 1980–kh)," in *Ent-Grenzen/Za predelami: Intellektual'naia emigratsia v russkoi kul'ture XX veka*, ed. Lyubov Bugaeva and Eva Hausbacher (Frankfurt am Main: Peter Lang, 2006), 48.

Selected Bibliography

What follows has no pretensions to being a complete bibliography either of Dovlatov's own works or of secondary literature about him. It lists only the major publications of works by him and does not take account of the vast industry of popular editions that has burgeoned since his death. The sections on secondary literature include practically everything that has come to my attention in the course of research, but undoubtedly omits much of a purely popular nature. A greater attempt has been made to list as completely as possible his uncollected newspaper articles, archive materials that have been consulted, and the Internet sites of which I am aware. The scene is, of course, constantly changing, and even these sections can at best be only a snapshot at the time of writing.

PRIMARY TEXTS BY SERGEI DOVLATOV

Collected Editions

Marsh odinokikh. Holyoke, Mass.: New England Publishing, 1983.

Sobranie prozy v trekh tomakh. Edited by Andrei Ar'ev. St. Petersburg: Limbus, 1993 and 1995.

Maloizvestnyi Dovlatov. Edited by Andrei Ar'ev. St. Petersburg: Zvezda, 1995.

Sobranie sochinenii v chetyrekh tomakh. 4 vols. Edited by A. Iu. Ar'ev. St. Petersburg: Azbuka, 2000, reprinted 2004 and 2007.

. . . posledniaia kniga . . . Edited by Andrei Ar'ev. St. Petersburg: Azbuka-klassika, 2001. This is a collection of Dovlatov's selected short stories, memoirs of friends, reviews and criticism, illustrations, and translations of reviews of Dovlatov's books, published in American periodicals and translated into Russian. This book was published to coincide with Dovlatov's sixtieth birthday.

Rech' bez povoda . . . ili Kolonki redaktora: Ranee neizdannye materialy. Moscow: Makhaon i mezhdunarodnyi fond Sergeia Dovlatova, 2006. A selection of Dovlatov's contributions to *Novyi Amerikanets.* This book was published to coincide with Dovlatov's sixty-fifth birthday.

Correspondence

Published:

Skul'skaia, Elena. *Zapiski k N . . . Perekrestnaia rifma.* Tallinn: Antek-Koostöö, 1996.

"Pis'ma Dovlatova" (correspondence with Iulia Gubareva), *Ogonek* 22 (1997): 43–46; reprinted in Sergei Dovlatov. *Skvoz' dzhungli bezumnoi zhizni: Pis'ma k rodnym i druz'iam.* St. Petersburg: Zvezda, 2003.

"Armeiskie pis'ma k ottsu" ["Army Letters to His Father"]. Commentary by Ksenia Mechik-Blank. *Zvezda* 5 (1998): 108–42; reprinted in Sergei Dovlatov. *Skvoz' dzhungli bezumnoi zhizni: Pis'ma k rodnym i druz'iam.* St. Petersburg: Zvezda, 2003.

Metter, Israel. *Izbrannoe.* St. Petersburg: Russko-Baltiiskii informatsionnyi tsentr "Blits," 1999, p. 256. "Ia rad, chto my s Vami dozhili do strannykh vremen . . . Vosem' poslednikh pisem Sergeia Dovlatova" was first published in *Iunost'* 5 (1993): 71–75.

Dovlatov, Sergei. "Deviat' pisem Tamare Urzhumovoi." *Zvezda* 8 (2000): 137–47; reprinted in Sergei Dovlatov. *Skvoz' dzhungli bezumnoi zhizni: Pis'ma k rodnym i druz'iam.* St. Petersburg: Zvezda, 2003.

Dovlatov, Sergei. *Epistoliarnyi roman: Perepiska Sergeia Dovlatova s Igorem Efimovym.* Moscow: Izdatel'stvo Zakharov, 2001. Excerpts "Izvinite za mysli . . ." were published in *Ogonek* no. 43 (2000): 46–49.

Dovlatov, Sergei. *Skvoz' dzhungli bezumnoi zhizni: Pis'ma k rodnym i druz'iam.* St. Petersburg: Zvezda, 2003.

"Iz pisem Sergeia Dovlatova k ottsu" ["Sergei Dovlatov's Letters to His Father"]. Commentary by Ksenia Mechik-Blank. *Zvezda* 1 (2008): 98–114.

Unpublished, in Dovlatov's Family Archive:

Letters to and from Andrei Ar'ev, Donald Fiene, Anne Frydman, Vladimir Maramzin, Naum Sagalovskii, and Igor' Smirnov.

Fiction

Books:

Nevidimaia kniga. Ann Arbor, Mich.: Ardis, 1977.

Solo na undervude: Zapisnye knizhki. Paris: Tret'ia Volna, 1980.

Kompromiss. New York: Serebrianyi Vek, 1981.

Zona: Zapiski nadziratelia. Ann Arbor, Mich.: Ermitazh, 1982.

Zapovednik. Ann Arbor, Mich.: Ardis, 1983.

Nashi. Ann Arbor, Mich.: Ardis, 1983.

Solo na undervude. 2nd ed. Holyoke, Mass.: New England Publishing, 1983.

Demarsh entuziastov. With V. Bakhchanian and N. Sagalovskii. Paris: Sintaksis, 1985.

Remeslo: Povest' v dvukh chastiakh. Ann Arbor, Mich.: Ardis, 1985.
Inostranka. New York: Russica, 1986.
Chemodan. Tenafly, N.J.: Ermitazh, 1986.
Predstavlenie i drugie rasskazy. New York: Russica, 1987.
Filial. St. Petersburg: *Zvezda* no. 10, 1989.
Filial. New York: Russica, 1989.
Rasskazy iz knigi "Chemodan." Moscow: *Oktiabr'* no. 7, 1989.
Inostranka: Povest'. Moscow: *Oktiabr'* no. 4, 1990.
Ne tol'ko Brodskii: Russkaia kul'tura v portretakh i anekdotakh. With M. Volkova. New York: Word, 1990.
Zapisnye knizhki. New York: Word, 1990.
Filial. New York: Word, 1990.
Zapovednik. Leningrad: Vasilievskii Ostrov, 1990.
Zona; Kompromiss; Zapovednik. Moscow: PIK, 1991.
Remeslo; Nashi. Leningrad and Tallinn: Zvezda, 1991.
Rasskazy. Moscow: Renaissance, 1991.
Chemodan. Moscow: Moskovskii Rabochii, 1991.

Play:
Chelovek, kotorogo ne bylo. P'esa dlia mladshikh shkol'nikov s fokusami, no bez obmana (*The Man Who Never Was. A play for primary school children with tricks, but no deception*), typescript found at the Pskov Puppet Theater in 2001. The typescript is dated 1975, Leningrad.

Stories:
"Po sobstvennomu zhelaniu." *Neva* no. 5 (1973): 8–19.
"Interv'iu." *Iunost'* no. 6 (1974): 41–51.
"Po priamoi." *Kontinent* no. 11 (1977): 129–40.
"Golos; Na chto zhaluetes', serzhant?" *Vremia i my* no. 14 (1977): 59–82.
"Uroki chteniia." *Ekho* no. 3 (1978): 106–11.
"Kuptsov i drugie." *Vremia i my* no. 28 (1978): 19–31.
"Ishchu cheloveka." *Vremia i my* no. 36 (1978): 83–100.
"V goru." *Vremia i my* no. 38 (1979): 5–36.
"Chernym po belomu." *Vremia i my* no. 40 (1979): 58–73.
"Iubileinyi mal'chik." *Kontinent* no. 19 (1979): 49–70.
"Vysokie muzhchiny." *Tret'ia volna* nos. 7–8 (1979): 8–21.
"Doroga v novuiu kvartiru." *Ekho* no. 1 (1979): 86–96.
"Ch'ia-to smert' i drugie zaboty." *Chast' rechi* no. 1 (1980): 140–59.
"Soldaty na Nevskom." *Tret'ia volna* no. 10 (1980): 30–51.
"Predstavlenie." *Kontinent* no. 39 (1984): 42–70.
"Inaia zhizn': Sentimental'naia povest'." *Sem' dnei* no. 41 (1984): 42–49; no. 42 (1984): 42–48.

"Tretii povorot nalevo." *Sem' dnei* no. 57 (1984): 32–37.
"Lishnii." *Grani* no. 135 (1985): 102–43.
"Rasskazy iz chemodana." *Grani* no. 137 (1985): 5–95.
"Vstretilis', pogovorili." *Kontinent* no. 58 (1988): 78–97.
"Zhizn' korotka." *Vremia i my* no. 102 (1988): 54–62.
"Russkaia kul'tura v portretakh i anekdotakh." *Vremia i my* no. 104 (1989): 276–87.
"Solo na IBM. Iz zapisnykh knizhek." *Vremia i my* no. 107 (1989): 83–88.
"Solo na IBM." *Kontinent* no. 61 (1989): 188–99.
"Ariel': Igrushka." *Slovo* nos. 7–8 (1990): 59–66.
"Lishnii: Rasskaz." *Zvezda* no. 1 (1991): 101–19.
"Iz zapisnykh knizhek." *Zvezda* no. 2 (1992): 7–34.
"Dva esse." *Zvezda* no. 1 (1993): 123–26.
"Ariel': Igrushka. Rasskazy." *Zvezda* no. 8 (1993): 110–14.
"Zhizn' korotka." *Zvezda* no. 3 (1996): 69–73.
"Zhizn' korotka." *Ogonek* no. 1 (1997): 43–45.

Unpublished Novels:
Piat' uglov (*Fiveways*) or *Odin na ringe* (*Alone in the Ring*), 1976–77. (Chapter 1—"Odin na ringe" ["Alone in the Ring"]; chapter 2—"Boi s ten'iu" ["Battle with a Shadow"]; chapter 3—"Sudeiskii protocol" ["The Referee's Statement"]; chapter 4—"Nevidimaia kniga" ["The Invisible Book"] or "Epilog" ["Epilogue"].) In Dovlatov's family archive.
Naslednik (*The Heir*), chapter 1, "Poslednee leto," April 1978. Working title of *Zapovednik*. (Marked: "Draft version, not for publication.") In Dovlatov's family archive.
Nevidimaia kniga (Epilog) (*The Invisible Book: Epilogue*), 1976 manuscript. This was chapter 4 of the unpublished novel *Piat' uglov* but was substantially reworked several times and eventually published in 1977 by Ardis. Manuscript in the "Memorial" Foundation, St. Petersburg.

Works Translated into English

Books:
The Invisible Book. Translated by Katherine O'Connor and Diana Burgin. Ann Arbor, Mich.: Ardis, 1979.
The March of the Lonely. Edited by Roman Sonynn. Holyoke, Mass.: New England Publishing, 1983.
The Compromise. Translated by Anne Frydman. London: Chatto and Windus, 1983; New York: Alfred A. Knopf, 1983; Chicago: Academy Chicago, 1990.
The Zone: A Prison Camp Guard's Story. Translated by Anne Frydman. New York: Alfred A. Knopf, 1985.
Not Just Brodsky: Russian Culture in Portraits and Anecdotes. Photographs by

Marianna Volkov, text by Sergei Dovlatov, translated by Brian Baer. New York: Slovo, 1988.

Ours: Scenes from Russian Family Life. Translated by Anne Frydman. New York: Weidenfeld and Nicholson, 1989.

The Suitcase. Translated by Antonina W. Bouis. New York: Grove Weidenfeld, 1991.

A Foreign Woman. Translated by Antonina W. Bouis. New York: Grove Weidenfeld and Atlantic, 1991.

Stories in *Harper's Magazine:*

"The Seance" ["Chudo—'MI-6' "]. Translated by Anne Frydman. *Harper's,* October 1985, pp. 32–34.

"Grandpa Isaak" ["Moi ded Isaak"]. Translated by Anne Frydman. *Harper's,* May 1989, pp. 24–26.

"Grapes" ["Vinograd"]. Translated by Antonina W. Bouis. *Harper's,* September 1992, pp. 58–64.

Stories in the *New Yorker:*

"The Jubilee Boy" ["Iubileinyi mal'chik"]. Translated by Anne Frydman. *New Yorker,* June 9, 1980, pp. 39–47.

"Somebody's Death" ["Ch'ia-to smert' "]. Translated by Katherine O'Connor and Diana L. Burgin. *New Yorker,* October 19, 1981, pp. 42–52.

"Straight Ahead" ["Po priamoi"]. Translated by Anne Frydman with Jack Dennison. *New Yorker,* January 25, 1982, pp. 35–41.

"My First Cousin" ["Moi starshii brat"]. Translated by Anne Frydman. *New Yorker,* December 5, 1983, pp. 50–58.

"The Colonel Says I Love You" ["Polkovnik govorit—Liubliu"]. Translated by Anne Frydman. *New Yorker,* May 5, 1986, pp. 42–47.

"Uncle Aron" ["Tetkin muzh—Aron"]. Translated by Anne Frydman. *New Yorker,* October 20, 1986, pp. 40–41.

"Uncle Leopold" ["Diadia Leopol'd"]. Translated by Anne Frydman. *New Yorker,* July 13, 1987, pp. 25–30.

"Father" ["Otets"]. Translated by Anne Frydman. *New Yorker,* November 30, 1987, pp. 34–36.

"The Photo Album" ["Rasskaz o zhene"]. Translated by Antonina W. Bouis. *New Yorker,* March 27, 1989, pp. 43–47.

"The Driving Gloves" ["Shoferskie perchatki"]. Translated by Antonina W. Bouis. *New Yorker,* May 8, 1989, pp. 36–40.

Nonfiction in Russian

Articles in the *Almanac Panorama:*

"Dopolneniia k *Kompromissu.*" *Almanac Panorama* no. 171 (July 20–27, 1984): 20–22.

"Chto takoe tsenzura." *Almanac Panorama* no.191 (December 7–14, 1984): 12.
"Baryshnikov nachinalsia tak." *Almanac Panorama* no. 194 (December 28, 1984–January 4, 1985): 14.
"Rossia vo mgle." *Almanac Panorama* no. 195 (January 4–11, 1985): 12.
"Esli b garmoshka umela." *Almanac Panorama* no. 198 (January 25–February 1, 1985): 25.
"Dokumental'naia proza—Rastsvet ili krizis?" *Almanac Panorama* no. 200 (February 8–15, 1985): 24.
"Ottepel' (Sbornik 'Izbrannye rasskazy 60–kh godov' v izdatel'stve 'Ermitazh')." *Almanac Panorama* no. 206 (March 22–29, 1985): 18.
"Tainaia zhizn' Very Panovoi (K 80–letiiu so dnia rozhdeniia)." *Almanac Panorama* no. 207 (March 29–April 5, 1985): 32.
"Zabytyi Erenburg." *Almanac Panorama* no. 212 (May 3–10, 1985): 18.
"Neizdannyi Merezhkovskii." *Almanac Panorama* no. 218 (June 14–21, 1985): 30.
"Kremlevskie 'zvezdy." *Almanac Panorama* no. 220 (June 28–July 5, 1985): 10.
"My stali uznavat' sebia v amerikanskikh fil'makh." *Almanac Panorama* no. 290 (October 31–November 7, 1986): 12–13.

Articles in *Novyi Amerikanets* (*The New American*):
These articles have either not been reprinted or were only partially reprinted in *Rech' Bez Povoda.*
"Schastlivaia derevnia." *Novyi Amerikanets* no. 14 (May 16–22, 1980): 27–28.
"Pskovskie otkrytki (iz romana *Piat' uglov*)." *Novyi Amerikanets* no. 34 (September 27–October 2, 1980): 25–26.
". . . ne putat' rodinu s peizazhem." *Novyi Amerikanets* no. 40 (November 12–18, 1980): 19.
"Kirpich s lampasami." *Novyi Amerikanets* no. 58 (March 17–23, 1981): 10.
"Mister Tvister edet v Kostromu." *Novyi Amerikanets* no. 97 (December 19–25, 1981): 24–26.
"Made in USA: Mini-istoria dzhaza." *Novyi Amerikanets* no. 107 (March 2–8, 1982): 14–15.
"Ia govoriu vam russkim iazykom . . ." *Novyi Amerikanets* no. 111 (March 30–April 5, 1982): 27.
"Telezhka s khlebnym kvasom." *Novyi Amerikanets* (September 28–30, 1983): 5–7.

Articles in Other Newspapers:
"Mnoi ovladelo bespokoistvo . . ." *Russkaia mysl'* no. 3226 (October 19, 1978): 5.
"Kapitan ulybnites'." *Russkaia mysl'* no. 3432 (September 30, 1982): 7.
"Ispytanie svobodoi." *Novaia gazeta,* April 23–29, 1983, pp. 17–18.
"Derevnia v 'chernom spiske." *Russkaia mysl'* no. 3546 (December 6, 1984): 7.

"V zhanre detektiva." *Sem' dnei* no. 54 (1984). Published in New York and available online at: http://www.sergeidovlatov.com/books/v_zhanre-html (accessed August 3, 2006).

Articles in *Sovetskaia Estonia* (*Soviet Estonia*):
"Blagodarite moego konia . . ." *Sovetskaia Estonia,* December 8, 1972, p. 3.
"Sila ubezhdeniia." *Sovetskaia Estonia,* January 7, 1973, p. 4.
"Isporchennyi telefon." *Sovetskaia Estonia,* January 13, 1973, p. 4.
"Kak ia brosil pit'." *Sovetskaia Estonia,* February 11, 1973, p. 4.
"S Ivanovym shutki plokhi." *Sovetskaia Estonia,* April 1, 1973, p. 4.
"Ozhivshie kamni istorii." *Sovetskaia Estonia,* April 7, 1973, p. 3.
"Esli podruzhilis' dvoe . . ." *Sovetskaia Estonia,* April 14, 1973, p. 3.
"Uvidet' mir vpervye" (signed D. Sergeev). *Sovetskaia Estonia,* April 20, 1973, p. 4.
"Dlia odnoi loshadinoi sily" (signed R. Must). *Sovetskaia Estonia,* April 24, 1973, p. 3.
"Ostorozhno—Fantomas." *Sovetskaia Estonia,* April 24, 1973, p. 3.
"Samaia trudnaia distantsiia" (signed S. Ader). *Sovetskaia Estonia,* June 4, 1973, p. 3.
"Moshchnost' vozrastaet" (signed S. Ader). *Sovetskaia Estonia,* June 21, 1973, p. 3.
"Detektiv bez vystrelov, no s zhertvami" (signed S. Ader). *Sovetskaia Estonia,* June 29, 1973, p. 4.
"Vysokoe polozhenie" (signed S. Ader). *Sovetskaia Estonia,* July 4, 1973, p. 3.
"Pobeda nad Gennadiem Shatkovym" (signed S. Ader). *Sovetskaia Estonia,* July 7, 1973, p. 4.
"Vpered, k dinozavram!" *Sovetskaia Estonia,* July 8, 1973, p. 4.
"Vchera, 60 tysiach let nazad . . ." (signed S. Ader). *Sovetskaia Estonia,* July 15, 1973, p. 3.
"Ruka ob ruku" (signed S. Ader). *Sovetskaia Estonia,* July 22, 1973, p. 4.
"Proektiruiutsia . . . noski" (signed S. Ader). *Sovetskaia Estonia,* August 15, 1973, p. 3.
"Ia khochu vam rasskazat' . . ." *Sovetskaia Estonia,* August 20, 1973, p. 4.
"Obyknovennoe chudo." *Sovetskaia Estonia,* September 30, 1973, p. 4.
"Polchasa v srednevekov'e." *Sovetskaia Estonia,* October 5, 1973, p. 4.
"Vam pis'mo . . ." *Sovetskaia Estonia,* October 11, 1973, p. 3.
"Moi beglyi papa" (signed S. Ader). *Sovetskaia Estonia,* October 13, 1973, p. 2.
"Vrag pod mikroskopom." *Sovetskaia Estonia,* October 16, 1973, p. 3.
"Nariad dlia Marsianina." *Sovetskaia Estonia,* October 18, 1973, p. 3.
"Rozhdenie istiny." *Sovetskaia Estonia,* October 24, 1973, p. 3.
"Dvor byl uzkii." *Sovetskaia Estonia,* October 26, 1973, p. 2.
"K zvezdam!" *Sovetskaia Estonia,* November 1, 1973, p. 4.
"Ia znaiu silu slov . . ." *Sovetskaia Estonia,* November 20, 1973, p. 4.

"Nichego strashnogo!" (signed S. Ader). *Sovetskaia Estonia,* November 25, 1973, p. 4.
"Chisto, svetlo . . ." (signed S. Ader). *Sovetskaia Estonia,* December 14, 1973, p. 4.
"Takaia dolgaia putevka . . ." (signed S. Ader). *Sovetskaia Estonia,* December 27, 1973, p. 4.
"Frontoviki, naden'te ordena . . ." (signed S. Ader). *Sovetskaia Estonia,* August 1, 1974, p. 3.
"Stuchat kolesa" (signed S. Ader). *Sovetskaia Estonia,* August 2, 1974, p. 3.
"Skromnyi Nikodimov" (signed S. Ader). *Sovetskaia Estonia,* August 7, 1974, p. 4.
"Byvaiu zdes' vse chashche . . ." (signed S. Ader). *Sovetskaia Estonia,* October 18, 1974, p. 3.
"Na svoem meste" (signed S. Ader). *Sovetskaia Estonia,* December 5, 1974, p. 3.
"Ishchu cheloveka" (signed S. Ader). *Sovetskaia Estonia,* January 16, 1975, p. 3.

Radio Broadcasts:
"Kushat' podano" ["Dinner Is Served"]. *Prostye liudi* [*Ordinary People*]. Radio Svoboda [Radio Liberty]. 1988. Available online at: http://svobodanews.ru.webarchive.
"Voditeli bol'shikh dorog" ["Long-distance Drivers"]. *Prostye liudi* [*Ordinary People*]. Radio Svoboda [Radio Liberty]. 1988. Available online at: http://svobodanews.ru.webarchive.

Unpublished Radio Scripts, in Hoover Institution Archive:
"Al'manakh 'Chast' rechi" ["The Almanac 'Chast' rechi' "]. Collection title: RFE/RL 11 404, box no.: 06726500, folder ID: M-Copy, Feb. 8/9, 1983.
"Gor'kaia ulybka poeta" ["Selected Poetry of Nikolai Oleinikov"]. Collection title: RFE/RL, box no.: 11 397, folder ID: M-C 20/21, 1983.
"Iubilei 'Serebrianogo veka' " ["Anniversary of the Publishing House 'Serebrianyi vek' "]. Collection title: RFE/RL 11413, box no.: 06726509, folder ID: M-Copies, March 7/8, 1983.
"Komsomol'tsy-dobrovol'tsy" ["Members of Komsomol Volunteers, Auxiliary Police Brigades"]. *Prostye liudi* [*Ordinary People*]. Radio Svoboda [Radio Liberty]. Collection title: RFE, box no.: 11 393, folder ID: M-C 8/9 1983.
Kul'tura, sud'by, vremia [*Culture, Destinies, Time*], radio broadcast.
"Novaia kniga Il'i Suslova" ["Il'ia Suslov's New Book"]. Collection title: RFE/RL, box no.: 11 402, folder ID: M-C Feb. 3/4, 1983.
Prostye liudi [*Ordinary People*]. Radio Svoboda [Radio Liberty]. January–May 1988.
"Riadom s Nabokovym: Roman Ianovskogo 'Amerikanskii opyt' " ["Alongside Nabokov: Ianovskii's Novel 'The American Experience' "]. Collection title: RFE/RL inc., box no.: 11408, folder ID: M-Copies, 21/22, 1983.

"V Rossiiu—s liubov'iu. (Zhurnal *Grani* v 1982 godu)" ["To Russia—with Love. (The Journal *Grani* in 1982)"]. Collection title: RFE/RL 11394, box no.: 06726490, folder ID: M-COPIES, Jan. 11/14, 1983.

Unpublished Radio Scripts, in Open Society Archive, Budapest:

"Blat: Obyknovennye chudesa" ["*Blat* in the Soviet Union Is Now a Norm in Daily Life"]. Radio Free Europe. January 14, 1981. Box 300/85/13/105.

Prostye liudi [*Ordinary People:* Blat *in the Soviet Union Is Now a Norm of Daily Life*]. Radio Svoboda [Radio Liberty]. January 14, 1981. Box 300/85/13/105.

Prostye liudi [*Ordinary People*]. Radio Svoboda [Radio Liberty]. January–May 1988. Box 300/85/13/105.

SECONDARY WORKS ON SERGEI DOVLATOV

Articles

Abdulaeva, Zara. "Mezhdu zonoi i ostrovom: O proze Sergeia Dovlatova." *Druzhba narodov* no. 7 (1996): 153–66.

Akhmadulina, Bella. "Posviashchenie Sergeiu Dovlatovu." *Literaturnaia gazeta* no. 26 (August 16, 1995): p. 6.

Anastas'ev, N. "Slova—Moia professiia: O proze Sergeia Dovlatova." *Voprosy literatury,* 1995, pp. 3–22.

Ar'ev, Andrei. "Nasha malen'kaia zhizn'." In *Sergei Dovlatov, Sobranie prozy v trekh tomakh,* 5–24. St. Petersburg: Limbus, 1993.

———. "Obzor." *Neva* no. 1 (1990): 187.

———. "Sergei Dovlatov." In *Russkie pisateli XX veka: Biograficheskii slovar',* 236–38. Moscow: Randevu-AM, 2000.

———. "Sergei Dovlatov." In *Russkie pisateli XX vek: Bibliobiograficheskii ukazatel',* 438–42. Moscow: Prosveshchenie, 1998.

———. "Teatralizovannyi realism: O povesti Sergeia Dovlatova *Filial.*" *Zvezda* no. 10 (1989): 19–20.

Arpishkin, Iurii. "Geroi v poiskakh avtora." Introduction to *Chemodan,* 3–7. Moscow: Moskovskii Rabochii, 1991.

Bobyshev, Dmitrii. "Guliaia s Dovlatovym." In *Ia zdes' (Chelovekotekst),* 278–85. Moscow: Vagrius, 2003.

———. "Poniat' Dovlatova trudno . . ." *Nezavisimaia gazeta,* March 18, 1996, p. 8.

Bogdanova, O. V. "'Dikhotomicheskaia triada' prozy Sergeia Dovlatova." In *Postmodernism v kontekste sovremennoi russkoi literatury,* ed. O. V. Bogdanova, 163–81. St. Petersburg: Filologicheskii fakul'tet Sankt Peterburgskogo universiteta, 2004.

Bondarenko, Vladimir. "Plebeiskaia proza Sergeia Dovlatova." *Nash sovremennik* no. 12 (1997): 257–71.

Brodskii, Iosif. "O Serezhe Dovlatove." *Zvezda* no. 2 (1992): 4–6.

Davydov, Oleg. "Tiazhba o dedovskom nasledstve." *Novoe Russkoe Slovo,* September 11, 1990, p. 7.

Dovlatova, Ekaterina. "On mechtal o domike, shortakh i svoem ogorode." *Literaturnaia gazeta* no. 33 (August 16, 1995): 6.

Eliseev, Nikita. "Chelovecheskii golos." *Novyi mir* no. 11 (1994): 212–25.

Genis, Aleksandr. "Korova bez vymeni, ili metafizika oshibki." *Literaturnaia gazeta* no. 24 (1997): 11.

———. "Mif o Dovlatove." *Obshchaia gazeta* no. 28 (July 16, 1994): 32–34.

———. "Peterburgskie shkol'niki o Sergee Dovlatove." *Zvezda* no. 5 (1998): 217–22.

———. "Sad kamnei: Sergei Dovlatov." *Zvezda* no. 7 (1997): 235–38.

———. "Vokrug *Novogo Amerikantsa.*" *Moskovskie novosti* no. 33 (September 1, 2006): 27.

Gillespie, David. "The Booze and the Blues: Laughter and the 'Real' World in the Work of Sergei Dovlatov." *Australian Slavonic and East European Studies,* vol. 15, pts. 1–2 (2001): 21–37.

Glad, John. "Interview with Sergei Dovlatov, January 5, 1988." In *Besedy v izgnanii: Russkoe literaturnoe zarubezh'e,* 84–95. Moscow: Knizhnaia Palata, 1991.

———. "Pisat' ob absurde iz liubvi k garmonii, Interv'iu Dzhona Gleda s Sergeem Dovlatovym." *Vremia i my* no. 110 (1990): 159–73, published in New York; reprinted in John Glad, *Besedy v izgnanii.*

Kamianov, V. "Svoboden ot postoia." *Novyi mir* no. 2 (1992): 242–44.

Karabchievskii, Iurii. "Pamiati Sergeia Dovlatova." *Literaturnaia gazeta* no. 35 (August 29, 1990): 7.

Karpov, A. S. "Po techeniu: Chitaia povesti E. Limonova *U nas byla velikaia epokha* i S. Dovlatova *Filia'.*" *Literaturnaia gazeta* no. 51 (1989): 4.

———. "Svoi sredi svoikh (O proze Sergeia Dovlatova)." *Russkaia slovesnost'* no. 2 (1996): 41–45.

Kasack, Wolfgang. "Sergei Donatovich Dovlatov." In *A Dictionary of Russian Literature Since 1917,* 259–62. London: Overseas Publications Interchange, 1988.

Krotov, M. "Mir kak volia i predstavlenie." *Kontinent* no. 53 (1987): 407–10.

Kuritsyn, Viacheslav. "Vesti iz *Filiala,* ili duratskaia retsenziia na prozu Sergeia Dovlatova." *Literaturnoe obozrenie* no. 12 (1990): 41–42.

Kuznetsova, Natal'ia. "Pamiati Sergeia Dovlatova." *Kontinent* no. 65 (1990): back cover.

Lanin, Boris. "The Image of Women in the Prose of Sergei Dovlatov." In *Women and Russian Culture,* ed. Rosalind Marsh, 252–59. New York and Oxford: Berghan Books, 1998.

Leiderman, N. L., and M. N. Lipovetskii. "Sergei Dovlatov." In *Sovremennaia russkaia literatura, 1950–1990–e gody,* vol. 2, 598–610. Moscow: Akademia, 2003.

Leontieva, Alexandra. "Some Trends in Contemporary Russian Prose in the Light of Bakhtin's Genre Theory." In *Dialogue and Rhetoric,* ed. Ingunn Lunde, 132–46. Bergen: University of Bergen, 1999.

Lesnaia, Polina. "A khodil li Dovlatov na lektsii?" *Stena,* September 3, 2002, p. 10.

Lipovetskii, Mark. "Sergei Dovlatov." In *Russian Postmodernist Fiction: Dialogue with Chaos,* 281–83. Armonk, N.Y., and London: M. E. Sharpe, 1999.

———. "Uchites', tvari, kak zhit': Paranoia, zona i literaturnyi kontekst." *Znamia* no. 5 (1997): 199–212.

Losev, Lev. "Russkii pisatel' Sergei Dovlatov." *Russkaia mysl'* no. 3843 (August 31, 1990), http://www.sergeidovlatov.com/losev.html.

———. "Sergei Dovlatov." In *The Modern Encyclopaedia of Russian and Soviet Literatures,* vol. 5, 239–40. Gulf Breeze, Fla.: Academic International Press, 1981.

Madison, Andrei, and Andrei Tantsirev. "Radio imeni Dovlatova: Vozvrashchenie zhivogo pisatelia." *Soglasie* 39, no. 61 (September 24–30, 1990): 5 and 40; no. 62 (October 1–7, 1990): 5.

Mal'gin, Andrei. "Ia vstretilsia s pisatelem Sergeem Dovlatovym v New Yorke." *Nedelia* no. 3 (1990): 10.

———. "Sergei Dovlatov, kotorogo liubili vse." *Stolitsa* no. 3 (September 1990): 6.

———. "Voploshchenie svobody: Pamiati Sergeia Dovlatova." *Moskovskie novosti* no. 35 (September 2, 1990): 5.

Marchenko, Alla. ". . . Obratitsia v pechal'noe . . ." *Literaturnaia gazeta* no. 20 (May 16, 1990): 4.

Mart'ianova, I. A. " 'Nebrezhnaia' kinematografichnost' pis'ma S. Dovlatova." In *Kinovek russkogo teksta: Paradoks literaturnoi kinematografichnosti,* 126–33. St. Petersburg: Saga, 2001.

Morits, Iunna. "Predislovie k publikatsii rasskazov iz *Chemodana.*" *Oktiabr'* no. 7 (1989): 118–19.

Mydans, S. "Writing Without Roots." *New York Times Book Review,* September 23, 1984, pp. 38–39.

Nekhoroshev, Mikhail. "Veller i Dovlatov: Bitva geroev i prizrakov." *Neva* no. 8 (1996): 183–91.

Nekrasov, Viktor. "Kak vazhno byt' neser'eznym." Unpublished radio script.

Ogryzko, Viacheslav. "Razvenchanie mifov." *Literaturnaia Rossia* nos. 45–46 (November 17, 2006): http://www.litrossia.ru/article.php.

Pekurovskaia, Asia. "Dovlatov bez mifa." *Vremia i my* no. 139 (1998): 202–75.

Popov, Valerii. "Pobeda neudachnika Dovlatova." *Literaturnaia gazeta* no. 43 (1997): 12.

Radzishevskii, V. "Triumf bez tragedii: Tri dnia na druzheskoi noge s Sergeem Dovlatovym." *Literaturnaia gazeta* no. 18–19 (May 13, 1998): 8.

Rein, Evgenii. "Mne nekhvataet Dovlatova." *Ogonek* no. 35 (1995): 69.

Riskin, Andrei. "Chelovek, kotoryi byl." *Nezavisimaia gazeta* no. 18 (May 24, 2001): 4–5.

Ryan-Hayes, Karen. "The Family Chronicle Revisited: Dovlatov's *Ours*." In Ryan-Hayes, *Contemporary Russian Satire: A Genre Study*, 150–93. Cambridge: Cambridge University Press, 1995.

———. "Narrative Strategies in the Works of Sergej Dovlatov." *RLJ* 16, no. 153 (1992): 155–78.

Salmon, Laura. "Naimenee sovetskii gorod Rossii: khronotop dovlatovskikh rasskazov." *Zvezda* no. 8 (2000): 151–55.

———. "Neobychnoe v obydennom." *Vestnik MGU* no. 4 (1999): 59–75.

Semenenko, A. "Linda Peips kak zerkalo sovetskoi deistvitel'nosti ili o metode Sergeia Dovlatova." *Russkaia filologia* no. 9 (1998): 137–42, published in Tartu, Tartusskii gosudarstvennyi universitet.

Serman, Il'ia. "Teatr Sergeia Dovlatova." *Grani* no. 136 (1985): 138–63.

Shenkman, Ian. "Rossiia, pereekhavshaia v Ameriku: Sergei Dovlatov o svobode i kolbase." *Nezavisimaia gazeta* no. 30 (August 24, 2006): 1.

Shevchenko, E. S. "Teatral'nyi kod dovlatovskoi prozy." *Vestnik SamGU 10,* no. 2 (50) (2006): 59–66.

Smirnov, Igor'. "O smysle kratkosti (Pamiati Sergeia Dovlatova)." In *Russkaia novella: Problemy, teorii, i istorii,* ed. V. M. Markovich and W. Schmid, 5–13. St. Petersburg: Izdatel'stvo Sankt-Peterburgskogo universiteta, 1993.

Soboleva, Olga. " 'It Is Only Chekhov That One Wants to Be Like': Chekhov and Dovlatov—The Art of a Storyteller." *Essay in Poetics* 31 (2006): 305–18.

Sokolova, Nadia. "Snova o lagernoi teme: *Zona* Sergeia Dovlatova." *Australian Slavonic and East European Studies* 10, no. 2 (1996): 157–64.

Solov'ev, Vladimir. "Moi sosed Serezha Dovlatov." *Novoe Russkoe Slovo,* September 18, 1990, p. 7.

Tabachnikova, Olga. " 'The World Is Ugly and People Are Sad': On Chekhov's Ethics and Aesthetics in the Works of Sergei Dovlatov." *Essay in Poetics* 31 (2006): 319–55.

Taranov, M. "Vyzhivanie." *Kontinent* no. 36 (1983): 400–404.

Timofeeva, Ol'ga. "Elena i Katia v okrestnostiakh Sergeia." *Ogonek* no. 35 (1998): 42–48.

Tolstoy, Ivan. "Sergei Dovlatov glazami kollegi." *Russkaia mysl'* no. 4288 (October 14–20, 1999): 14.

Trifonov, Gennadii. "Pis'ma iz podvala." *Neva* no. 4 (1987): 145–47.

Tsiv'ian, T. V. "Veshchi iz Chemodana Sergeia Dovlatova i byvshaia (?) sovetskaia model' mira." *Russian Literature* 37 (1995): 647–58.

Tudorovskaia, Elena. "Na ozere Gennisaretskom." *Grani* no. 140 (1986): 138–49.

———. "Russkii pisatel' v Amerike." *Grani* no. 140 (1986): 303–9.

Ufliand, Vladimir. "Nepovtorimyi chelovek i pisatel' Sergei Dovlatov." *Gumanitarnyi fond* 9, no. 42 (1990): 4.

Vail', Petr. "Brodskii o Dovlatove." *Zvezda* no. 8 (2000): 148–50.

Vail', Petr, and Aleksandr Genis. "Iskusstvo avtoportreta." *Zvezda* no. 3 (1994): 177–80.

———. "Literaturnye mechtaniia: Ocherk russkoi prozy s kartinkami." In *Chast' rechi, Al'manakh,* vol. 1 (New York: Serebrianyi Vek, 1980): 204–33.

Vasil'eva, O. V. "Evoliutsiia lagernoi temy i ee vliianie na russkuiu literaturu 50–80x godov." *Vestnik Sankt-Peterburgskogo universiteta* no. 23 (1996): 54–63.

Young, Jekaterina. "The Aesthetics of the *Gorozhane* Group." *Slavonic and East European Review* 81, no. 1 (2005): 14–37.

———. "Dovlatov's *Compromise:* Journalism, Fiction, Documentary." *Slavonica* 6, no. 2 (2000): 44–68.

———. "Dovlatov's Reception of Salinger." *Forum for Modern Language Studies* 36, no. 4 (2000): 412–25.

———. "Dovlatov's *Sanctuary* and Pushkin." *Slavica* 30 (2000): 133–51. A revised version of this article appeared in *Two Hundred Years of Pushkin,* ed. J. Andrew and R. Reid (Amsterdam, 2003), 135–53.

———. "Sergei Dovlatov." In *Russian Literature Since 1980,* 48–60. Dictionary of Literary Biography 285. Detroit: Bruccoli Clark, 2003.

Zakurenko, Aleksandr. "Sergei Dovlatov kak Rasskazchik." *Topos (literaturnofilosofskii zhurnal),* October 17, 2005, http://topos.ru/article/4095.

Zverev, Aleksei. "Zapiski sluchainogo postoial'tsa." *Literaturnoe obozrenie* no. 4 (1991): 65–73.

Books

Ar'ev, Andrei, ed. *Sergei Dovlatov: Tvorchestvo, lichnost', sud'ba.* St. Petersburg: Zvezda, 1999. Proceedings of the first international conference "Dovlatovskie chteniia."

Dovlatova, Elena, comp. *O Dovlatove: Stat'i, retsenzii, vospominaniia.* New York and Tver': Drugie Berega, 2001.

Genis, Aleksandr. *Dovlatov i okrestnosti.* Moscow: Vagrius, 1999.

Matich, Olga, and Michael Heim, eds. *The Third Wave: Russian Literature in Emigration.* Ann Arbor, Mich.: Ardis, 1984.

Mechik, Donat. *Vesnushki: Naedine s synom.* St. Petersburg: Iskusstvo Veka, 1993.

Pekurovskaia, Asia. *Kogda sluchilos' pet' SD i mne.* St. Petersburg: Symposium, 2001.

Rein, Evgenii. *Mne skuchno bez Dovlatova: Novye stseny iz zhizni moskovskoi bogemy.* St. Petersburg: Limbus, 1997.

Shtern, Liudmila. *Dovlatov—dobryi moi priiatel'.* St. Petersburg: Azbuka-klassika, 2005.

Sukhikh, Igor'. *Sergei Dovlatov: Vremia, mesto, sud'ba.* St. Petersburg: Kul'tInform, 1996.

Internet Publications

Ar'ev, Andrei. "On vse vremia khotel vernut'sia domoi." http://www.sergei dovlatov.com.

———. "Sergei Dovlatov po obe storony okeana." Radio Free Europe. http://www.svoboda.org/programs/OTB/2001/OBT.092601.asp.

Basinskii, Pavel. "Bukval'nyi Dovlatov." *Rossiiskaia gazeta,* August 21, 2006, http://www.rg.ru/2006/08/21/dovlatov.html (accessed September 8, 2006).

Belotserkovskii, Vadim. "Puteshestvie v budushchee i obratno: Povest' zhizni i idei" (chapter 26 on S. Dovlatov). http://www.belotserkovsky.ru/journey/index.html.

Bogomolov, Iruii. "Privet nam ot starogo novogo amerikantsa Sergeia Dovlatova." Rossiiskoe agenstvo mezhdunarodnoi informatsii/Novosti. http://www.rian.ru/authors/2006.

Donetskii, Aleksandr. "V poiskakh pskovskogo Dovlatova." Pskovskaia zemlia. http://www.pskov.ru/ru/persons/object/85/publications/57.

Fanailova, Elena. "Rai—eto 'kamera obshchego tipa, gde mozhno vstretit' blizkogo cheloveka.' " Radio Free Europe. http://www.svobodanews.ru/Article/2006/09/04/20060904182205880.html.

Genis, Aleksandr. "New York bez Dovlatova." Radio Free Europe. http://archive.svoboda.org/programs/ut/2005/ut.082305.asp.

"Geroi vremeni: Sergei Dovlatov—Tsentral'nyi personazh knig Sergeia Dovlatova." Radio Free Europe. http://www.svoboda.org/programs/cicles/hero/o5.asp.

Glushkova, Elena. "Chitaia Dovlatova-redaktora." Radio Free Europe. http://www.svobodanews.ru/Article/2006/11/15/20061115000027627.html.

Kolesnikov, Andrei. "Mnogotochie Dovlatova: K 65–letiu pisatelia." Rossiiskoe agenstvo mezhdunarodnoi informatsii/Novosti. http://www.rian.ru/analytics/20060830/53320817.html.

Kostyrko, Sergei. "'Strannyi' dar." Vzgliad. http://www.vz.ru/print.html?id=48709.

Krokhin, Iurii. "Iz zony v zapovednik." Rossiiskaia gazeta. http://www.rg.ru/2006/08/25/dovlatov.html.

Nikitina, Larisa. " 'Zapovednik' bez Dovlatova: V Pushkingor'e turisty vse bol'she guliaiut po 'dovlatovskim mestam.' " http://www.segodnya.ru/w3s.nsf/Archive/2000_187_life_text_nikitina1.html.

Orlova, M. "Posle smerti nachinaetsia istoriia: Sergei Donatovich Dovlatov." http://www.peoples.ru/srt/literature/prose/roman/dovlatov/.

"Otkrytie pamaiatnoi doski Sergeiu Dovlatovu v Peterburgskom morskom tekhnicheskom universitete." Radio Free Europe. http://archive.svoboda.org/ll/cult/0104/ll.013104-1.asp.

"Pamiati Sergeia Dovlatova." Radio Free Europe. http://archive.svoboda.org/50/files/1990.html.

Pekurovskaia, Asia. "Interview with Petkurovskaia." *Terra Nova* no. 4 (October 2005): http://muza-usa.net/2005_04/2005-04-03.htm.

Vail', Petr. "Pis'ma Dovlatova: Po pravde i po pravu." Radio Free Europe. http://archive.svoboda.org/ll/cult/1102/ll.111002-2.asp (accessed September 8, 2006).

Sharyi, Andrei. "Dovlatov—'Obychnyi bol'shoi russkii pisatel'.' " Radio Free Europe. http://www.svobodanews.ru/Article/2006/09/05/20060905135111780.html.

Sipiagina, Marina. "V takoi odezhde legche perenosit' udary sud'by." Utro. http://www.utro.ru/articles/2006/08/30/579038.shtml.

Tolstoy, Ivan. "Vspominaia Dovlatova." Radio Free Europe. http://archive.svoboda.org/programs/otbl/2005/otbl.082105.asp.

Vail', Petr. "Poverkh bar'erov" (interview with Sergei Dovlatov, Aleksandr Genis, and Solomon Volkov). Radio Free Europe. June 1, 1989. Available at http://archive.svoboda.org/programs/otb/2003/obt.061703.asp.

Vail', Petr, with Veronika Bode and Ekaterina Dovlatova. "Za chto moskovskii izdatel' Zakharov dolzhen vyplatit' 825 tysiach rublei vdove pisatelia Dovlatova?" Radio Free Europe. http://archive.svoboda.org/ll/russia/1102/ll.110702-1.asp.

Viktorov, Pavel. "Leningradskii pocherk." http://www.fontanka.ru.

Zibunova, Tamara. Correspondence with Sergei Dovlatov. http://zibunova.narod.ru/dovlatov/DVLTRLEN.htm.

Internet Sites Dedicated to Sergei Dovlatov

http://www.dovlatov.org.ru/id-sa-autor-9/

http://www.geocities.com/SoHo/Workshop/4368/

http://sergdovlatov.narod.ru/

http://www.sergeidovlatov.com/

Doctoral Theses

Bourlatskaya, Mariya. "Soviet Prison Camp Literature: The Structure of Confinement (V. Shalamov, Sergei Dovlatov, G. Vladimov)." Ph.D. diss., University of Pennsylvania, 1999.

Galloway, David. "The Prison Camp Theme in Russian Literature as Reworked by Lev Razgon and Sergei Dovlatov." Ph.D. diss., Cornell University, 1999.

Mason, K. C. "The Family Chronicle and Modern America." Ph.D. diss., University of Nebraska-Lincoln, 1981.

Special Issues of Journals

Peterburgskii literator, December 30, 1992. Published in St. Petersburg.

Petropol' no. 5 (1994). Published in St. Petersburg.

Slovo(Word) no. 9 (1991). Published in New York.

Zvezda no. 3 (1994). Published in St. Petersburg.

Unpublished Documents

East European Research Institute, Bremen University, History Archive:

Application by B. B. Vakhtin, V. A. Gubin, I. M. Efimov, and V. R. Maramzin to Sovetskii Pisatel', January 6, 1965, F. 120.

Reply to B. B. Vakhtin, V. A. Gubin, I. M. Efimov and V. R. Maramzin from Sovetskii Pisatel', December 27, 1965, F.120.

Open Society Archives, in Budapest:

"Pis'mo D. Dara v Prezidium IV Vsesoiuznogo S"ezda Sovetskikh pisatelei" (with copy to *Literaturnaia gazeta*), May 17, 1967.

Vakhtin's Family Archive, in St. Petersburg:

Dar, D. Ia. "Po povodu etogo sbornika" ["Concerning This Collection"]. Introduction to *Gorozhane.*

Gorozhane, vol. 1. Leningrad, 1964, bound typescript.

Gorozhane, vol. 2. Leningrad, 1966, bound typescript.

Gorozhane o sebe, typescript.

Ketlinskaia, Vera. "Zametki na poliakh sbornika *Gorozhane.*" Perm', 1965, typescript.

Khodza, N. "Retsenziia na rukopis' *Gorozhane,*" typescript.

Index

absurdity: in *The Fridge,* 160–61; in *Ours,* 173; in *The Zone,* 81, 83, 86
aesthetic creativity and conflict with the State, 11, 24–25, 41, 123–25
Ageichik, A., 22
Akhmadulina, Bella, 126
Akhmatova, Anna, 22
Aksenov, Vasily: and Baltic republics, 87; in exile, 25, 191; as model for Dovlatov, 10; and point of view, 8, 214n22; and Pushkin, 130; and youth prose movement, 6, 7
alcohol use, articles on, 92–93
Aleksandra (Dovlatov's daughter), 30
Aleshkovsky, Iuz, 81, 191
allusion in Russian literature, 20
Almanac Panorama, 39, 119, 179, 180, 191
"Alone in the Ring" ("Odin na ringe"), 195. See also *Fiveways*
ambiguity: in *Ours,* 163; in *The Sanctuary,* 123
American literature: effect on literary process in Russia, 5; plot twists in, 65–66; role of writer in American culture, 51; storytelling in, 84. *See also* Western writers, publication of in Soviet Union
Anderson, Sherwood, 6, 157
anti-Semitism in the Soviet Union, 152–53
Ar'ev, Andrei, 52, 134, 174, 184, 200, 206
"Ariel'," 189–90, 242n22
"Army Belt, The" ("Ofitserskii remen'"), 145–49
Asia (first wife), 27, 138–39, 194–97
"At His Own Request" ("Po sobstvennomu zhelaniu"), 21
"Aunt Mara," 165–66, 168–69. *See also* Dovlatova, Margarita (Mara)
author and hero, relation of: in *Fiveways* (*Piat' uglov*), 34–35; in *A Foreign Woman,* 34, 188; in *The Zone,* 68. *See also* narrator and hero, boundary between
author and narrator, relation of: in *The Zone,* 60–62, 86
author as participant in text: in *A Foreign Woman,* 184–85, 186, 187
authorial point of view: in *Soviet Estonia* articles, 107; in *The Suitcase,* 136, 137, 138
authorship under Soviet Union, 20–21
autobiography in *Ours,* 177–78
Avrora (journal), 22–23, 31, 32, 218n82

Babel, Isaac, 4, 157
Bakinsky, Viktor, 11
Balter, B. I., 10
Belaia, G. A., 137, 237n25
Belanenko, V., 67–68
Beliaev, A., 242n22
Belyi, Igor', 205
Berggol'ts, Ol'ga, 31
Bezzubov, Valery Ivanovich, 88
Bitov, Andrei: as Leningrad dissident writer, 7, 12, 17, 22; in literary association with Dovlatov, 10; point of view in, 9; and Voznesensky, 28
Blank, Ksana. *See* Mechik-Blank, Ksana
blat (cronyism), 144–45, 149–50, 177
Blok, Alexander, 136–37, 237n20
Bobyshev, D. V., 191
body and soul in *Ours,* 166
Boris (cousin), 152–53, 164, 171, 238n48. *See also* "My First Cousin"
Bouis, Antonina, 48
boundaries, blurring of. *See* documentary illusion in fiction; pseudo-documentalism

Branch Office, A (*Filial*), 191–201; as autobiography, 210; first wife in, 194–97; influence of American literature on, 6, 199–200; literary devices in, 191, 194, 197, 198; minimalism, 200–201; narrator in, 193–94; prison camp experience in, 193; publication history, 52; storytelling in, 197, 200
bribery and corruption, 93, 158–59. *See also* theft and embezzlement as theme
Brodsky, Joseph: apolitical stance of, 41; censorship of mentions of, 31; as "distant relative," 135, 137; and Dovlatov, 48, 211; exile of, 19, 218n69; and inner freedom, 24
brotherhood of painters and poets, 135, 151
Bulgakov, Mikhail, 202
Bulgarin, Faddei, 123–24

Camus, Albert, 132–33
"Captains on Land" ("Kapitany na sushe"), 77–80
"Cart Selling Kvass, A" ("Telezhka s khlebnym kvasom"), 181–82, 184
censorship: in 1970s, 19–23; in Estonia, 88; and forced emigration, 25; in *The Sanctuary,* 123–25; in *The Suitcase,* 144
Chekhov, Anton: influence on Dovlatov, 118, 200, 208, 209, 211; prison camp writings, 59, 65, 86
Chelovek, kotorogo ne bylo. See *Man Who Never Was, The*
Chemodan. See *Suitcase, The*
Cherkasov, Andrei, 219n97
Cherkasov, Nikolai Konstantinovich, 149–50, 238n41
City Tales (*Gorodskie rasskazy*), 30, 220n118
Clark, Katerina, 7, 12, 17, 214n17, 215n35, 217n58
"Clothing for a Martian" ("Nariad dlia Marsianina"), 96–97
collaboration in Estonia, 97
"Colonel Says I Love You, The" ("Polkovnik govorit—Iiubliu"), 162, 172–174, 241n33
Compromise, The (*Kompromiss*): early versions of, 229n30; literary devices in, 93–95, 104–9, 170; in posthumous reputation, 202–3, 207, 210; prison camp stories in, 97–98; as story collection, 157; and *The Suitcase,* 138, 145; title for collection, 230n41; translation of, 49–50; and *The Zone,* 57
Compromise, The, individual stories in, 90–107; "Third Compromise," 90, 107; "Fourth Compromise," 97–98; "Fifth Compromise," 92, 94, 99–101; "Seventh Compromise," 96–97; "Eighth Compromise," 94, 102–4, 229n17; "Ninth Compromise," 94–95, 101–102, 232n49; "Tenth Compromise" (*see* "Superfluous"); "Eleventh Compromise," 94
contrasting elements: in *The Suitcase,* 137, 150–51, 153
Craft, The (*Remeslo*): as autobiography, 11, 210; on Brodsky, 24; and *The Compromise,* 100, 230n41; emigration in, 42, 46; on ideology, 185–86; on Platonov, 205; on role of writer, 198–99
cronyism (*blat*), 144–45, 149–50, 177
cultural legacy in Soviet Union, 116–17, 120–21

Daniel, Iu. M., 19
Danini, Maia, 17
Dar, David, 11, 18, 217n61
"Decent Double-Breasted Suit, A" ("Prilichnyi dvubortnyi kostium"), 135, 143–45, 149–50, 151, 155, 219n97
"Ded Stepan," 165, 240n13
Démarche of the Enthusiasts (*Demarsh entuziastov*), 203
Derzanie (Daring) (literary association), 12
description of landscape, 121, 126–28
dialogue: in Pushkin, 128; in *The Sanctuary,* 118; in *The Suitcase,* 139–41; in *The Zone,* 80
dissidence. *See* aesthetic creativity and conflict with the State
documentary illusion in fiction: in "The Colonel Says I Love You," 172; in *The Compromise,* 94–95, 104–5, 108–9; in *Ours,* 176; in *The Sanctuary,* 114; in *The Suitcase,* 142; in *The Zone,* 59–60, 71
Dodulat, Viktor, 28
Donetsky, Aleksandr, 206
Dorosh, Efim, 14
Dostoevsky, Fyodor, 59, 69, 72–73, 103
Dovlatov, Sergei: and America, 42, 53; and

American literature, 6; apolitical stance of, 43; biography, use of, 26 (*see also* autobiography *under specfic works*); birthplace in Ufa, 26, 150, 205, 219n100, 245n12; and Cherkasov family, 149–50, 219n97; childhood, 25–27, 219n100; children of (*see* Aleksandra; Katia; Kolia); dramas by, 31–32, 202; as editor of *Novyi Amerikanets,* 44–46; effect of samizdat on writing of, 24, 32, 219n94; emigration, 33–34, 41, 43, 46–47; in Estonia, 30, 87, 88, 228n2; facility in English, 42, 43, 222n16; family of (see *Ours*); films of works, 202–3, 204, 206; journalism of, 29–30, 90–92, 119–21, 229n13; marriages, 27, 30, 151–52, 172 (*see also* Pekurovskaia, Asia; Ritman, Elena Davidovna); poetry of, 61–64; posthumous reputation of, 202–10; as postmodernist, 210; as prison guard in army, 27–29, 62, 64–65, 145; at Pushkin Museum, 33, 110–12, 143–44, 206; as stonemason, 30, 143, 237n32; works (*see titles of specific works*); as writer in Leningrad, 10, 13, 16–17, 18–19, 31; writings about, 208, 211
Dovlatova, Elena (wife). *See* Ritman, Elena Davidovna
Dovlatova, Margarita (Mara), 10, 165. *See also* "Aunt Mara"
Dovlatova, Nora Sergeevna (mother), 26, 44. *See also* "Mother"
dramas, 31–32, 202, 220n123
dramatic elements in fiction, 197, 200–201
"Driving Gloves, The" ("Shoferskie perchatki"), 138, 153–56, 159–60, 193
Drozda, Miroslav, 60, 224n11
Durkin, Vladimir Nikolaevich, 205

Efimov, Igor': in Gorozhane, 12, 13; influence on Dovlatov, 10, 19; and publication of *The Zone,* 56–58; publications of, 17, 18
emigration as Soviet policy, 36–37
émigré community, 180–82. See also *Branch Office, A; Foreign Woman, A*
émigré literature, 38–41, 46–47
Erenburg, Il'ia, 3, 131, 156–57, 239n58
Erl', Vladimir, 215n30
Erofeev, Venedikt, 126
Estonia, liberal atmosphere of, 87–90
Estonian nationalism, 97–98
Etkind, Efim, 31
Evdokimova, Ekaterina Sergeevna, 206
Evtushenko, Yevgeny, 51, 126, 129–30, 152
existentialism: and *Ours,* 177–78; and *The Suitcase,* 132–34; in *The Zone,* 69

fact disguised as fiction. *See* documentary illusion in fiction; pseudo-documentalism
family chronicle as genre, 163, 176
"Father" ("Otets"), 162, 169, 240n2. *See also* Mechik, Donat
Faulkner, William, 6
"Fernand Léger's Jacket" ("Kurtka Fernana Lezhe"), 149–51, 170, 238n43
Fiene, Donald, 50, 52
Filial. See *Branch Office, A*
"Finnish Nylon Socks, The" ("Krepovye finskie noskie"), 131, 138–39, 195, 239n4
First Wave of emigration, 37–38, 221n5
Fiveways (*Piat' uglov*): banning of, 56, 88; bribery and corruption in, 159; fusion of hero and author in, 34–35; manuscript destroyed, 30; plans to complete, 188; reuse of material from, 111, 114, 195; as unpublished, 220n120
folkloric intonation of *Ours,* 164–65
Foreign Woman, A (*Inostranka*), 179–86; as autobiography, 210; fusion of author and hero, 34; prototypes for, 181–85; publishing history, 179–80; theatrical elements in, 197
Forest Hills, New York: émigré community in, 180–82
framing devices: in *The Compromise,* 106; in *Ours,* 165, 173–74; in *The Sanctuary,* 117–18; in *The Suitcase,* 132, 135, 144, 152, 157; in *The Zone,* 56–57, 59–60
freedom of the individual in thaw period, 24
freedom of the writer, coping with, 53–54
Fridge, The (proposed book), 158–61
Frydman, Anne, 48–50, 71–72, 172

genre substitution, 59–60
Gladilin, Anatoly, 7, 10, 191
Glasha (dog), 44, 163–64
"Golos" ("The Voice"), 32, 68, 71
good and evil: in *The Sanctuary,* 122–23; in Soviet press, 95; in *The Suitcase,* 156

Gor, Gennady, 11
Gorodetsky, Oleg Vitalievich, 244n9
Gorozhane (Urbanists) (literary association), 11–19
Grachev, Rid, 7, 17
"Grandpa Isaak" ("Moi ded Isaak"), 164–65, 240n11
Grani (*Facets*), 38
"Grapes" ("Vinograd"), 158–60, 240n65
Grin, Aleksandr, 4
Gubin, Vladimir, 13, 15–16, 18
"Gynecologist Budanitsky and I, The" ("My i ginekolog Budanitskii"), 188–89

Heir, The (*Naslednik*) (draft of *The Sanctuary*), 112
Heller, Joseph, 178
Hemingway, Ernest: body and soul in, 166; influence on Dovlatov, 6, 79–80, 157, 193, 199–200, 227n68; influence on Russian writers, 4, 5, 213n10
humor, 92–93, 210

I Don't Want to Be Famous (*Ne khochu byt' znamenitym*) (play), 31–32
Iashin, Aleksandr, 14
ideology, satire of, 191
"In the Street and at Home" ("Na ulitse i doma"), 190
Inostranka. See *Foreign Woman, A*
Inostrannaia literatura (journal), 6
intertextuality, 82–83
"Interview, The" ("Interv'iu"), 174, 214n26
Invisible Book, The (*Nevidimaia kniga*): autobiography in, 25, 29; on Leningrad writers, 16, 21; publication of, 32–33, 41, 44, 48; unpublished versions of, 34, 66, 88–89, 220n120; on Voznesensky, 28
irony, 17, 82, 84
Iskander, Fazil', 9, 22, 126
Iunost' (*Youth*) (journal), 7

jazz, 69, 100, 170
Joyce, James, 175
"Jubilee Boy, The" ("Iubileinyi mal'chik"), 92, 94, 99

Kafka, Franz, 134–35
Karamzin, N. M., 128, 142–43
Kataev, V. P., 11
Katia (Dovlatov's daughter), 27, 34, 41, 54, 135, 164, 207, 219n97
Kazakov, Iury, 7, 213n10
Ketlilnskaia, Vera, 11
KGB, 88–89, 124–25
Kheifits, Mikhail, 31
Khodza, Nison Aleksandrovich, 15, 216n44
Khronika tekushchikh sobytii (*The Chronicle of Current Events*) (journal), 24
Khrushchev, N. S., 3, 19
Khvostenko, Aleksei, 215n29
Kolia (Nicholas) (Dovlatov's son), 54, 135, 162, 165, 176
Kompromiss. See *Compromise, The*
Korzhavin, N. M., 191
Kostsinsky, Kirill Vladimirovich, 184, 242n15
Kotel'nikov, Vladimir, 88–89
Krivulin, Viktor, 31
"Kuptsov and Others" ("Kuptsov i drugie"), 66–70, 86, 106, 170–71
Kuraev, Mikhail, 86
Kuz'minsky, Konstantin, 31

"Labyrinth, The" ("Labirint"), 155
language and style: in "Aunt Mara," 168–69; in Dovlatov's newspaper articles, 91–92; in Gorozhane writers, 17; like poetry, 194; in posthumous reputation, 208–9; in Pushkin, 128; in *The Sanctuary*, 113; in Soviet newspaper articles, 107; in *The Suitcase*, 138, 139, 141–42, 145–46; in youth prose movement, 10
Léger, Fernand, 238n38. *See also* "Fernand Léger's Jacket"
Leningrad as cultural center, 10–11, 31–33, 38, 210. *See also* Petersburg text
Lepta (*Offering*) (collection), 31
Leskov, N. S., 176, 177
Lezhnev, A., 126–128
"Life Is Short" ("Zhizn' korotka"), 190
Likhonosov, Viktor, 119–120
Limonov, E. V., 191
"Lishnii." *See* "Superfluous"
literary associations, 10–11, 24, 168
literary style: changes in after resigning from newspaper, 30; in Gorozhane writers, 17; honed during army service, 28; influences on, 80, 127–28; as journalist, 90–92

literary techniques: contrasting elements, 137, 150–51, 153; no two words in sentence begin with same letter, 52, 57–58, 97, 111; plot, 65–66, 69, 135–36. *See also* dialogue; language and style; narrative structure; narrative voice; repetition of passages; writing process
"Lofty Men" ("Vysokie muzhchiny"), 31, 230n30
"Looking for a Man" ("Ishchu cheloveka"), 230n30

Mal'chonkov, Stanislav Igorevich, 206
Man Who Never Was, The (*Chelovek, kotorogo ne bylo*) (play), 202, 220n123
Mandelstam, Osip, 4
Mann, Thomas, 4
Maramzin, Vladimir: censorship of, 16, 31; influence on Dovlatov, 10, 19; writings of, 13, 18, 41
"March of the Lonely" ("Marsh odinokikh") (early title for "Kupsov i drugie"), 66
March of the Lonely, The (*Marsh odinokikh*) (editorials), 45, 225n29, 237n20
Markov, B. (censor), 21–22
marriage and love, 174–75
Marsh odinokikh. See *March of the Lonely, The* (editorials)
Marx, Karl, in *The Suitcase,* 132, 135
materialism, Soviet, 131–32, 136
materialism of émigrés, 190
Matveiko, Pavel, 204, 224n8
Mechik, Donat (Dovlatov's father), 26. *See also* "Father"
Mechik-Blank, Ksana (Dovlatov's half sister), 132, 165, 219n100, 222n16
metaphorical character of writing, 189–90, 194
Metter, Israel, 11, 56
minimalism in prose, 127, 200–201
"Miracle of MI-6, The"/"The Seance" ("Chudo—'MI-6'"), 81–83
"Moi ded Isaak" ("Grandpa Isaak"), 164–65, 240n11
Molodoi Leningrad (*Young Leningrad*) journal, 15, 16, 17
moral sympathies of writer, 7, 186, 209
Morits, Iunna, 204
"Mother," 169. *See also* Dovlatova, Nora Sergeevna (mother)
"My First Cousin" ("Moi starshii brat"), 162, 170–72, 177–78. *See also* Boris (cousin)

Nabokov, Vladimir, 4–5, 24, 41, 71, 162
narrative structure: in *A Branch Office,* 198; in *A Foreign Woman,* 187; in newspaper articles and in *The Compromise,* 107–8; in *Ours,* 164, 170–71, 176; in *The Sanctuary,* 117–18; in *The Suitcase,* 135–36
narrative voice: in *The Compromise,* 94; in "Stories of Last Summer," 188; in *The Suitcase,* 135, 137, 157; in youth prose, 7–8; in youth prose movement, 10; in *The Zone,* 60, 62, 63–64, 66, 84
narrator, role of: in *A Branch Office,* 198; in *Ours,* 164; in Pushkin, 129; in *The Suitcase,* 135; in *The Zone,* 82–83
narrator and hero, boundary between: in *The Compromise,* 106; in *Ours,* 170, 171; in Pushkin, 129; in *The Suitcase,* 157; in *The Zone,* 86. *See also* author and hero, relation of
Nashi. See *Ours: Scenes from Russian Family Life*
nationalism, 95, 97–98
Nekrasov, Viktor, 36, 191, 213n10, 221n1
Nevidimaia kniga. See *Invisible Book, The*
New York émigré community, 180–82
New Yorker, 47–48, 162, 207, 240n4
"*Nomenklatura* Half Boots, The" ("Nomenklaturnye polubotinki"), 142–43, 149
Notebooks (*Zapisnye knizhki*), 28, 95, 98, 100, 146–47, 169, 230n41
Novoe Russkoe Slovo (*New Russian Word*), 44, 46
Novyi Amerikanets (*The New American*): article on New York, 180–81; article on Soviet army officers, 78–79; articles on alcohol use, 92–93, 113–14; collection of editorials from, 203; editorial on role of writer, 198; excerpts from *A Foreign Woman* in, 180; excerpts from *Fridge* in, 158; excerpts from *Ours* in, 162; excerpts from *Sanctuary* in, 111; founding, 39, 44–46, 47; prison camp experiences in, 64–65; "The Finnish Nylon Socks," 141
Novyi mir (*New World*) journal, 13–14, 215n39

Novyi zhurnal (*The New Journal*), 38
NTS (Narodno-Trudovoii Soluz), 37, 43, 221n2

Okhapkin, Oleg, 31
"Old Cockerel Baked in Clay, An" ("Staryi petukh, zapechennyi v gline"), 158, 160, 240n65
Olesha, Iury, 4
"On the Way Up" ("V goru"), 94, 103
oral language, 84, 105, 129, 200, 208, 228n80. *See also* storytelling
Ours: Scenes from Russian Family Life (*Nashi*), 162–178; as autobiography, 172–73, 177–78, 210; existentialism in, 177–78; as family chronicle, 163–64; literary devices in, 158, 163–65, 168–71, 173–74, 176; publication history, 138, 178; and sexual topics, 167; as story collection, 157
Ours: Scenes from Russian Family Life, individual stories in: "Aunt Mara," 165–66, 168–69; "The Colonel Says I Love You," 162, 172, 174, 241n33; "Ded Stepan," 165, 240n13; "Father," 162, 169, 240n2; "Grandpa Isaak" ("Moi ded Isaak"), 164–65, 240n11; Kolia's story, 162, 165, 176; "Mother," 169; "My First Cousin," 162, 170–72, 177–78; "Uncle Aron," 162, 165, 168; "Uncle Leopold," 162, 165, 166–67; "Uncle Roman," 165, 166, 240n13
Ovechkin, Valentin, 14

Panova, Vera, 6, 11, 30
past, fictionalized versions of, 130
Pasternak, Boris, 23
Pekurovskaia, Asia (first wife), 27, 138–39, 194–97
perestroika period and Gorbachev, 52, 54, 190
"Performance, The" ("Predstavlenie"), 52, 72–77, 226n48
Petersburg text, 134, 139, 142–43, 204–5. *See also* Leningrad
"Photo Album, The" ("Rasskaz o zhene"), 238n46. *See also* "Poplin Shirt, A"
Piat' uglov (*Fiveways*). *See* "Alone in the Ring"; *Fiveways; Invisible Book, The*
Piskunov, V. M., 4, 7, 8, 23
Platonov, Andrei, 4, 16–17, 202, 205
plot: in *The Suitcase,* 135–36; in *The Zone,* 65–66, 69
poetry: brotherhood of painters and poets, 135, 151; and Dovlatov's prose, 194; poeticized prose in Pushkin, 126; precedence over prose, 126; as therapy, 64, 225n22; writing constraints in, 59
point of view. *See* narrative voice
Poliak, Grigory, 181–82
Pomerantsev, V., 3
"Poplin Shirt, A" ("Poplinovaia rubashka"), 131, 151–52, 173–75, 238n46
Popov, Aleksandr Fedorovich, 21, 218n80
Popov, Evgeny, 25
Popov, Valery, 9–10, 17, 22, 212
Popovsky, Mark, 182
possessions, 157, 160. *See also* materialism, Soviet
press, role of in Soviet Union, 95–96, 107, 230n41
prison camp experience: in *A Branch Office,* 193; in *Ours,* 177; in "Stories of Last Summer," 188; in *The Suitcase,* 154–55, 239n55. See also *The Zone*
prison camp literature, 58–59, 86, 145
Proffer, Carl and Ellendea, 41
pseudo-autobiography and existentialism, 177–78
pseudo-documentalism: in *Ours,* 176; in posthumous reputation, 209–10; in *The Zone,* 71. *See also* documentary illusion in fiction
Pushkin, Alexander: distorted quotation of, 58; *Dubrovsky,* 122; *Eugene Onegin,* 102–3; exploitation of, 114–16, 118; influences on Dovlatov, 186, 209; parallels to Dovlatov, 123–27, 129–30, 235n40. See also *Sanctuary, The*

Radio Liberty, 33, 44, 103, 181
Rein, Evgeny, 31
Remarque, Erich Maria, 4
Remeslo. See *Craft, The*
repetition of passages: as characteristic of Dovlatov's work, 169–71; in *The Compromise,* 92–93, 98–99, 100, 192; in *A Foreign Woman,* 180, 182
reuse of material. *See* repetition of passages
rhythmic variation in narrative structure, 170

Ritman, Elena Davidovna (second wife): in "A Poplin Shirt," 151–52, 238n47; marriage to, 27; in New York, 30, 34, 41; in *Ours,* 164; at sixty-sixth anniversary celebration, 207
Robbe-Grillet, Alain, 4
Roginsky, Mikhail, 88–90
Russia: in *Ours,* 176; posthumous reputation in, 209. *See also* Soviet Union
Russian literature, Dovlatov's place in, 211–12
"Russian Literature in Emigration: The Third Wave" (conference), 191, 243n25
Russkaia mysl' (*Russian Thought*), 38
Rzhevsky, L. D., 37–38

Sagalovsky, Naum, 57, 135, 180, 191, 202, 224n60, 224n9, 237n14, 241n35, 242n3, 243n28, 244n54, 244n1, 245n14
Saint-Exupéry, Antoine de, 4
Salinger, J. D., 4, 5–6, 193–94
samizdat publication, 12, 23–24, 32
Sanctuary, The (*Zapovednik*), 110–30; as autobiography, 123, 210; and *A Branch Office,* 196–97; and *The Compromise,* 93; drafts of, 110–13; on emigration, 42; literary techniques in, 58, 111, 126; on marriage, 175; posthumous reputation, 204, 205, 206; and restrictions on the writer by the State, 123–25, 227n71; and *The Suitcase,* 138, 158; as typically Russian story, 112–13, 129
Sarraute, Natalie, 4
"Seance, The"/"The Miracle of MI-6" ("Chudo—'MI-6'"), 81–83
Second Wave of emigration, 37–38
self-censorship, 20–21
Semenov, Gleb, 11
sexual topics: in *The Compromise,* 94–95, 102–3, 232n49; in *A Foreign Woman,* 183; in "The Colonel Says I Love You," 174
Shalamov, Varlam, 85
Shef, Genrikh, 10
Shkol'nik, Masha, 204–5, 224n10
Sholokhov, Mikhail, 213n10
shortwave radios for cultural production, 23–24
Shtein, Boris, 100–101, 231n100
Shukshin, Vasily, 9
Shvarts, Elena, 31
Shvartsman, Boris, 18, 217n63
Siniavsky, Andrei, 19, 39–40, 115–16, 191, 233nn17–18
Skul'skaia, Elena, 100, 229n16, 231nn44–45, 231n47
Slominsky, Mikhail, 11
socialist realism, 4, 7, 18. *See also* Soviet reality
Sokolov, S., 41, 191
Soldatov, Sergei, 88–90
"Soldiers on the Nevsky Prospekt" ("Soldaty na Nevskom"), 50
Solzhenitsyn, Aleksandr: appeal for greater creative freedom, 23; character in *A Foreign Woman,* 182–83; exile of, 125; influence on village prose movement, 129; *One Day in the Life of Ivan Denisovich,* 13–14, 19, 59, 84–85
"Somebody's Death" ("Ch'ia-to smert' i drugie zaboty"), 94, 230n30
Sorokin, Vladimir, 82
Soviet Estonia (*Sovetskaia Estonia*) (newspaper): article on address bureau, 91; article on Jubilee baby, 92, 94, 99–101; article on milkmaid and "Eighth Compromise," 103–4; article on sexual topics and "Ninth Compromise," 94–95, 101; characteristics of, 95–96; Dovlatov at, 29–30, 89; "Technology of Sex" and Ninth Compromise, 101–2, 232n49
Soviet press, 95–96, 107, 230n41
Soviet reality: and *The Compromise,* 97; and Lenigrad writers, 21, 23; in *The Sanctuary,* 115–16; in *The Suitcase,* 134, 155. *See also* socialist realism
Soviet Union: anti-Semitism in, 152–53; *Ours* as metaphor for, 167; outsider's understanding of, 167; perestroika period and Gorbachev, 52, 54, 190; queuing in, 155; shadow economy in, 139, 158, 195; under Stalin, 15, 116; status of writers in, 51–52; in *The Suitcase,* 137, 157; thaw period, 3–35. *See also* Russia
Soviet writers, restrictions on, 123–25, 227n71
Speech for No Occasion (*Rech' bez povoda*), 203
state and the individual, 153
"Stories of Last Summer" ("Rasskazy o minuvshem lete"), 34, 188–91

storytelling: and Aksenov, 8; in *A Branch Office,* 197, 200; in *The Compromise,* 94; in *A Foreign Woman,* 186–87; in posthumous reputation, 208–9; in Pushkin, 129; in *The Sanctuary,* 126; in *The Suitcase,* 137; in *The Zone,* 84, 228n80. *See also* oral language
"Straight Ahead" ("Po priamoi"), 32, 57, 68, 71, 79–80
subtexts in Russian literature, 20
Suitcase, The (*Chemodan*), 131–58; autobiography in, 138–39, 143; existentialism in, 132–34; literary devices in, 132, 135–39, 141–42, 145–46, 150–52, 157; Soviet life in, 142–45, 153, 155; title of novel, 132
Suitcase, The, individual stories in: "The Army Belt," 145–49; "A Decent Double-Breasted Suit," 135, 143–45, 149–50, 151, 155, 219n97; "The Driving Gloves," 138, 153–56, 159–60, 193; "Fernand Léger's Jacket," 149–51, 238n43; "The Finnish Nylon Socks," 131, 138–39, 239n4; "The *Nomenklatura* Half Boots," 142–43, 149; "A Poplin Shirt," 131, 151–52; "The Winter Hat," 152–53
superfluity as theme, 160
"Superfluous" ("Lishnii"): existentialism in, 133; and "My First Cousin," 170; omitted in Russian publication of *Kompromiss,* 228n2; political sensitivity of, 52; as "Tenth Compromise," 93, 104–6, 232n54; translation of, 49

"Tales from a Suitcase" ("Rasskazy iz chemodana"), 131
"Tallin's Guests," 90, 107
tamizdat publication, 23, 25, 39, 219n90
theatrical code in Dovlatov, 157
theft and embezzlement as theme, 81, 142–43, 149, 158–59, 227n70. *See also* bribery and corruption
"They Met for a Chat" ("Vstretilis', pogovorili"), 133, 190
"Third Turn on the Left" ("Tretii povorot nalevo"), 175, 190
Third Wave of emigration, 37, 38–39
"Tomorrow Will Be an Ordinary Day" ("Zavtra budget obychnyi den"), 77
tone: in *A Branch Office,* 197
"Toy, The" ("Igrushka"), 189
translation and translators: of Dovlatov's works, 48–51, 207; and loss of control over works, 47; of love scenes, 174
"Trial by Freedom" ("Ispytanie svobodoi") (essay), 46
Tsvetaeva, Marina, 4
Tsvetkov, A., 41
Turonok, G. F. (editor of Soviet Estonia), 88–90, 97
Tvardovsky, Aleksandr, 13–14, 215n39

Ufa, Dovlatov honored by, 205
"Uncle Aron" ("Tetkin muzh—Aron"), 162, 165, 168
"Uncle Leopold" ("Diadia Leopol'd"), 162, 165, 166–67
"Uncle Roman," 165, 166, 240n13
urbanist movement, 13, 35
"USSR—One Big Camp, The" ("SSSR—Bol'shaia zona"), 64–65, 68

Vakhtin, Boris, 13, 15, 16, 18, 19
Vasil'ev, Georgy, 92
village prose (*derevenskaia proza*) movement, 13–14, 119–22, 129
"Vinograd" ("Grapes"), 158–60
violence in Soviet life, 153
Vladimov, Georgy, 6, 23, 85, 126, 211
"Voice, The" ("Golos"), 32, 68, 71
Voinovich, N. V., 191
Vol'f, Sergei, 16–17, 217n56
Volodin, Aleksandr, 11
Volokhonsky, Anri, 215n29
Vonnegut, Kurt, 42, 48, 71
Voznesensky, Andrei, 28, 87, 126

wanderings as literary phenomenon, 132
Western writers, publication of in Soviet Union, 4–5. *See also* American literature
"What's Your Complaint, Sergeant?" ("Na Chto zhaluetes' serzhant"), 32
"Winter Hat, The" ("Zimniaia shapka"), 152–53
writers in brotherhood of painters and poets, 135, 151
writing process: in *The Compromise,* 94–95, 229n30; poetry as therapy, 64, 225n22; use of constraints in, 52, 57–58, 97, 111. *See also* literary techniques

youth prose movement, 7–10, 227n72
Yurchak, A., 23–24, 219n91, 219n93

Zapisnye knizhki. See *Notebooks*
Zapovednik. See *Sanctuary, The*
Zibunova, Tamara (mother of daughter Aleksandra), 30, 33, 87, 111
Zone: A Prison Camp Guard's Story, The (*Zona*), 56–86; as autobiography, 29, 83–84, 210, 228n2; and *The Compromise,* 89, 97–98, 102–3, 106; influences on, 84–85; literary devices in, 56–66, 80–84, 238n35; on marriage, 175; and *Ours,* 166, 170; and posthumous reputation, 204; publication history, 85–86; and *Sanctuary,* 116, 117, 123; and *Suitcase,* 145, 146; translations of, 47, 226n43. *See also* "Captains on Land"; "Kuptsov and Others"; "Performance, The"; "Seance, The"; "Straight Ahead"; "Voice, The"
Zoshchenko, Mikhail, 3, 16–17, 126

About the Author

Jekaterina Young is an honorary senior research fellow at the University of Manchester and the editor of *Slavonica.*

green press INITIATIVE

Northwestern University Press is committed to preserving ancient forests and natural resources. We elected to print this title on 30% post consumer recycled paper, processed chlorine free. As a result, for this printing, we have saved:

1 Tree (40' tall and 6-8" diameter)
527 Gallons of Wastewater
1 Million BTUs of Total Energy
61 Pounds of Solid Waste
117 Pounds of Greenhouse Gases

Northwestern University Press made this paper choice because our printer, Thomson-Shore, Inc., is a member of Green Press Initiative, a nonprofit program dedicated to supporting authors, publishers, and suppliers in their efforts to reduce their use of fiber obtained from endangered forests.

For more information, visit www.greenpressinitiative.org

Environmental impact estimates were made using the Environmental Defense Paper Calculator. For more information visit: www.papercalculator.org.